Marx's *Capital* after 150 Years

Faced with a new crisis of capitalism, many scholars are now looking back to the author whose ideas were too hastily dismissed after the fall of the Berlin Wall. During the last decade, Marx's *Capital* has received renewed academic and popular attention. It has been reprinted in new editions throughout the world and the contemporary relevance of its pages is being discussed again. Today, Marx's analyses are arguably resonating even more strongly than they did in his own time and *Capital* continues to provide an effective framework to understand the nature of capitalism and its transformations.

This volume includes the proceedings of the biggest international conference held in the world to celebrate the 150th anniversary of *Capital*'s publication. The book is divided into three parts: I) 'Capitalism, Past and Present'; II) 'Extending the Critique of *Capital*'; III) 'The Politics of *Capital*'. It contains the contributions of globally renowned scholars from 13 countries and multiple academic disciplines who offer diverse perspectives, and critical insights into the principal contradictions of contemporary capitalism while pointing to alternative economic and social models. Together, they reconsider the most influential historical debates on *Capital* and provide new interpretations of Marx's *magnum opus* in light of themes rarely associated with *Capital*, such as gender, ecology, and non-European societies.

The book is an indispensable source for academic communities who are increasingly interested in rediscovering Marx beyond 20th century Marxism. Moreover, it will be of great appeal to students, as well as established scholars interested in critique of capitalism and socialist theory.

Marcello Musto is an Associate Professor of Sociological Theory at York University, Canada.

Routledge Frontiers of Political Economy

258 Political Pluralism, Disagreement and Justice
The Case for Polycentric Democracy
Julian F. Müller

259 Nonviolent Political Economy
Theory and Applications
Edited by Freddy Cante and Wanda Tatiana Torres

260 Cognitive Capitalism, Welfare and Labour
The Commonfare Hypothesis
Andrea Fumagalli, Alfonso Giuliani, Stefano Lucarelli and Carlo Vercellone

261 Political Economy for Human Rights
Manuel Couret Branco

262 Alternative Approaches to Economic Theory
Complexity, Post Keynesian and Ecological Economics
Edited by Victor A. Beker

263 The Dark Side of Nudges
Maria Alejandra Caporale Madi

264 Inequality and Governance
Andreas P. Kyriacou

265 A New Approach to the Economics of Public Goods
Thomas Laudal

266 Marx's *Capital* after 150 Years
Critique and Alternative to Capitalism
Edited by Marcello Musto

For more information about this series, please visit: www.routledge.com/books/series/SE0345.

Marx's *Capital* after 150 Years

Critique and Alternative to Capitalism

Edited by
Marcello Musto

Routledge
Taylor & Francis Group
LONDON AND NEW YORK

First published 2019
by Routledge
2 Park Square, Milton Park, Abingdon, Oxon OX14 4RN

and by Routledge
52 Vanderbilt Avenue, New York, NY 10017

Routledge is an imprint of the Taylor & Francis Group, an informa business

British Library Cataloguing-in-Publication Data
A catalogue record for this book is available from the British Library

Library of Congress Cataloging-in-Publication Data
A catalog record has been requested for this book

ISBN: 978-0-367-35008-6 (hbk)
ISBN: 978-0-429-32928-9 (ebk)

Typeset in Bembo
by Wearset Ltd, Boldon, Tyne and Wear

Contents

About the editor

Marcello Musto is Associate Professor of Sociological Theory at York University (Toronto – Canada). He is author of: *Ripensare Marx e i marxismi. Studi e saggi* (Carocci, 2011); *Another Marx: Early Manuscripts to the International* (Bloomsbury, 2018); *Karl Marx. Biografia intellettuale e politica 1857-1883* (Einaudi, 2018); *The Last Years of Karl Marx: An Intellectual Biography* (Stanford University Press, 2020); and *Travelling with Marx* (Europa Editions, 2020). Among his edited volumes there are: *Karl Marx's Grundrisse: Foundations of the Critique of Political Economy 150 Years Later* (Routledge, 2008); *Marx for Today* (Routledge, 2012); *Workers Unite! The International 150 Years Later* (Bloomsbury, 2014); *The International After 150 Years: Labour Versus Capital, Then and Now* (with George Comninel and Victor Wallis, Routledge, 2015); *Karl Marx's Life, Ideas, Influences: A Critical Examination on the Bicentenary* (with Shaibal Gupta and Babak Amini, Palgrave, 2019); *The Marx Revival: Key Concepts and New Critical Readings*, (Cambridge University Press, 2019); and *The Routledge Handbook of Marx's 'Capital': A Global History of Translation, Dissemination and Reception* (with Babak Amini, Routledge, 2021). His articles appeared in many journals, including the *International Review of Social History, Science & Society, Critique, Review of Radical Political Economics, Socialism and Democracy, Economic & Political Weekly*, and *Contemporary Sociology*. His writings – available at www.marcellomusto.org – have been published worldwide in more than twenty languages. He is also the editor (with Terrell Carver) of the Series *Marx, Engels, Marxisms* (Palgrave).

Contributors

Kevin B. Anderson is Professor of Sociology at University of California (Santa Barbara – USA). He is the author of *Lenin, Hegel, and Western Marxism: A Critical Study* (University of Illinois Press, 1995), *Foucault and the Iranian Revolution: Gender and the Seductions of Islamism* (with Janet Afary, University of Chicago Press, 2005), and *Marx at the Margins: On Nationalism, Ethnicity, and Non-Western Societies* (University of Chicago Press, 2010). Among his edited volumes are the *Rosa Luxemburg Reader* (with Peter Hudis, Monthly Review, 2004), and the *Dunayevskaya–Marcuse–Fromm Correspondence* (with Russell Rockwell, Lexington, 2012).

Étienne Balibar is Anniversary Chair of Contemporary European Philosophy at Kingston University (London – UK) and Visiting Professor at Columbia University (New York – USA). His books include *Race, Nation, Class. Ambiguous Identities* (with Immanuel Wallerstein, Verso, 1991), *Masses, Classes, Ideas* (Routledge, 1994), *The Philosophy of Marx* (Verso, 1995), *Spinoza and Politics* (Verso, 1998), *We, the People of Europe? Reflections on Transnational Citizenship* (Princeton, 2004), *Identity and Difference* (Verso, 2013), *Equaliberty. Political Essays* (Duke, 2014), *Violence and Civility* (Columbia, 2015), and *Citizen Subject: Foundations for Philosophical Anthropology* (Fordham, 2018).

Himani Bannerji is Emeritus Professor of Sociology at York University (Toronto – Canada). Her publications include *The Dark Side of the Nation: Essays on Multiculturalism, Nationalism and Racism* (Canadian Scholars Press, 2000), *Inventing Subjects: Studies in Hegemony, Patriarchy and Colonialism* (Tulika, 2001), *Of Property and Propriety: The Role of Gender and Class in Imperialism and Nationalism* (with Shahrzad Mojab and Judith Whitehead, University of Toronto Press, 2001), *Demography and Democracy: Essays on Nationalism, Gender and Ideology* (Canadian Scholars Press, 2011), and *Ideology and Resistance: Selected Essays on History, Race and Gender* (Brill, forthcoming 2019).

Pietro Basso is Associate Professor of Sociology at Ca' Foscari University (Venice – Italy). Among his authored volumes there are: *Modern Times, Ancient Hours. Working Lives in the Twenty-first Century* (Verso, 2003),

Le racisme européen. Critique de la rationalité institutionnelle de l'oppression (Syllepse, 2016), and *The Science and the Passion of Communism. Selected Writings of Amadeo Bordiga (1912–1965)* (Brill, forthcoming 2019). He is also the editor of *Razzismo di stato. Stati Uniti, Europa, Italia* (Franco Angeli, 2010).

John Bellamy Foster is Professor of Sociology at the University of Oregon (Eugene – USA). He is the author of *Marx's Ecology* (Monthly Review Press, 2000), *Naked Imperialism* (Monthly Review Press, 2006), *The Ecological Rift* (with Brett Clark and Richard York, Monthly Review Press, 2010), *What Every Environmentalist Needs to Know About Capitalism* (with Fred Magdoff, Monthly Review Press, 2011), *The Endless Crisis* (with Robert W. McChesney, Monthly Review Press, 2012), *Marx and the Earth* (with Paul Burkett, Brill, 2016), and *Trump in the White House* (Monthly Review Press, 2017).

Mauro Buccheri is Associate Professor of Literary Theory at York University (Toronto – Canada). He has co-edited *Italo Svevo, tra moderno e postmoderno* (with Elio Costa, Longo, 1995), *The Power of Words, Literature and Society in Late Modernity* (with Elio Costa and Donald Holoch, Longo, 2005), and *Towards a Democratic Cosmopolis: Recognition, Citizenship and Diaspora* (with Fahimul Quadir and Gabriele Scardellato, Soleil, 2017).

George C. Comninel is Associate Professor of Political Theory at York University (Toronto – Canada). He is the author of *Rethinking the French Revolution: Marxism and the Revisionist Challenge* (Verso, 1987) and *Alienation and Emancipation in the Work of Karl Marx* (Palgrave Macmillan, 2018). He has also edited *The International after 150 Years: Labor vs Capital, Then and Now* (with Marcello Musto and Victor Wallis, Routledge, 2015).

Silvia Federici is Emeritus Professor of Political Philosophy at Hofstra University (Hempstead – USA). Her published works include *Caliban and the Witch: Women, the Body and Primitive Accumulation* (Autonomedia, 2004), *Revolution at Point Zero: Housework, Reproduction and Feminist Struggle* (PM Press, 2012), and *The New York Wages for Housework Committee: Theory, History, Documents, 1972–1977* (with Arlen Austin, Autonomedia, 2017).

Alfonso Maurizio Iacono is Professor of History of Philosophy at the University of Pisa (Pisa – Italy). Among his works there are *Autonomia, potere, minorità* (Feltrinelli, 2000), *Storia, verità, finzione* (Manifestolibri, 2006), *L'illusione e il sostituto* (Bruno Mondadori, 2010), *Storie di mondi intermedi* (ETS, 2016), *Il sogno di una copia* (Guerini Scientifica, 2016), *History and Theory of Fetishism* (Palgrave Macmillan, 2016), and *The Bourgeois and the Savage* (Palgrave, forthcoming 2020).

Seongjin Jeong is Professor of Economics at Gyeongsang National University (Jinju – Republic of Korea). He has edited: *Marxist Perspectives on*

South Korea in the Global Economy (with Martin Hart-Landsberg and Richard Westra, Routledge, 2016), *Varieties of Alternative Economic Systems: Practical Utopias for an Age of Global Crisis and Austerity* (with Richard Westra and Robert Albritton, Routledge, 2017), and *Return of Marxian Macrodynamics in East Asia, Research in Political Economy* (with Masao Ishikura and Minqi Li, Emerald, 2017).

Bob Jessop is Distinguished Professor of Sociology at Lancaster University (Lancaster – UK). Among his authored books there are *State Theory: Putting the Capitalist State in Its Place* (Cambridge, 1990), *The Future of the Capitalist State* (Cambridge, 2002), *Beyond the Regulation Approach Putting Capitalist Economies in their Place* (with Ngai-Ling Sum, Edward Elgar, 2006), *State Power: A Strategic-Relational Approach* (Cambridge, 2007), and *The State: Past, Present, Future* (Polity Press, 2015). He has also edited: *Financial Cultures and Crisis Dynamics* (with Brigitte Young and Christoph Scherrer, Routledge, 2016), *Transnational Capital and Class Fractions: The Amsterdam School Perspective Reconsidered* (with Henk Overbeek, Routledge, 2019), and *The Pedagogy of Economic, Political and Social Crises: Dynamics, Construals and Lessons* (with Karim Knio, Routledge, 2019).

Michael R. Krätke is Professor of Sociology at Lancaster University (Lancaster – UK). Among his authored books there are *Kritik der Staatsfinanzen* (VSA Verlag, 1984), *Neun Fragen zum Kapitalismus* (with Georg Fülberth, Karl Dietz Verlag, 2007), *Kritik der Politischen Ökonomie heute* (VSA Verlag, 2017), and *Karl Marx' unvollendetes Projekt* (VSA Verlag, forthcoming 2019).

Marcello Musto is Associate Professor of Sociological Theory at York University (Toronto – Canada). He is the author of *Another Marx: Early Manuscripts to the International* (Bloomsbury, 2018), and *The Last Years of Karl Marx: An Intellectual Biography of the Late Marx* (Stanford University Press, forthcoming 2020).

Bertell Ollman is a Professor of Politics at New York University (New York – USA). Among his books there are *Dialectical Investigations* (Routledge, 1993), and *Dance of the Dialectic: Steps in Marx's Method* (University of Illinois Press, 2003). He has edited: *Market Socialism: The Debate among Socialists* (Routledge, 1998), *Dialectics for the New Century* (with Tony Smith, Palgrave Macmillan, 2008), and *Karl Marx* (with Kevin B. Anderson, Ashgate, 2012).

Leo Panitch is Emeritus Distinguished Research Professor of Political Science at York University (Toronto – Canada). Among his authored books there are *The End of Parliamentary Socialism* (Verso, 1997), *Renewing Socialism: Transforming Democracy, Strategy and Imagination* (Westview Press, 2001), *In and Out of Crisis: The Global Financial Meltdown and Left Alternatives* (with Greg Albo and Sam Gindin, PM Press, 2010), and *The Making* *of Global Capitalism: The Political Economy of American Empire* (with Sam Gindin, Verso, 2012).

Moishe Postone was Professor of Modern History at the University of Chicago (Chicago – USA). He has written *Time, Labor, and Social Domination: A Reinterpretation of Marx's Critical Theory* (Cambridge University Press, 1993), *Deutschland, die Linke und der Holocaust – Politische Interventionen* (Ça Ira Verlag, 2005), and *Critique du fétiche-capital: Le capitalisme, l'antisemitisme et la gauche* (PUF, 2013).

William Clare Roberts is Associate Professor of Political Science at McGill University (Montreal – Canada). He is the author of *Marx's Inferno: The Political Theory of* Capital (Princeton University Press, 2017).

Kohei Saito is Associate Professor of Political Economy at Osaka City University (Osaka – Japan). He is the author of *Karl Marx's Ecosocialism: Capital, Nature, and the Unfinished Critique of Political Economy* (Monthly Review Press, 2017) and the co-editor of *Marx-Engels-Gesamtausgabe*, vol. IV/18, *Exzerpte und Notizen: Februar 1864 bis Oktober 1868, November 1869, März, April, Juni 1870, Dezember 1872* (with Teinosuke Otani and Timm Graßmann, De Gruyter, 2019).

Gary Teeple is Professor of Sociology at Simon Fraser University (Vancouver – Canada). His authored books include *The Riddle of Human Rights* (Garamond Press, 2004), and *Relations of Global Power: Neo-liberal Order and Disorder* (with S. McBride, University of Toronto Press, 2011).

Richard D. Wolff is Professor of Economics at The New School University (New York – USA). His publications include *Re/Presenting Class: Essays in Postmodern Marxism* (with J. K. Gibson-Graham and Stephen Resnick, Duke University Press, 2001), *Theory and History: Capitalism and Communism in the USSR* (with Stephen Resnick, Routledge, 2002), *New Departures in Marxian Theory* (with Stephen Resnick, Routledge, 2006), *Capitalism Hits the Fan* (Olive Branch Press, 2009), *Contending Economic Theories: Neoclassical, Keynesian and Marxian* (with Stephen Resnick, MIT Press, 2012), and *Democracy at Work: A Cure for Capitalism* (Haymarket, 2016).

Acknowledgements

This volume contains the proceedings of the international conference *Marx's 'Capital' after 150 Years: Critique and Alternative to Capitalism*. This event, held at York University in Toronto, from 24–26 May 2017, was the largest international conference in the world convened to celebrate the 150th anniversary of the publication of *Capital*. It included the participation of over 30 scholars, from 13 countries, including some of the most prestigious scholars of Marx's thought.

The three days of the conference were organized into nine different sessions and this book contains a selection of 17 papers that were presented in eight sessions: 'The Politics of *Capital*', 'Beyond Labour and Capital', 'New Critical Stances', 'Extending the Critique of *Capital*', 'Elements of Future Society', 'Capitalism, Past and Present', 'New Grounds of Critique', and 'Which Marx for Today?' Five contributions presented at the session 'Dissemination and Reception of *Capital* in the World' were excluded from the proceedings and will be published in the volume Marcello Musto – Babak Amini (eds.), *The Routledge Handbook of Marx's 'Capital': A Global History of Translation, Dissemination and Reception*, London: Routledge, forthcoming 2020.

I would like to thank Enrico Campo for his valuable editorial work and Andy Humphries who, with his usual professionalism, helped me to publish this volume in the prestigious series Routledge Frontiers of Political Economy.

The editor and publisher would like to thank the Faculty of Liberal Arts & Professional Studies, York University, Toronto, Canada, for the financial support it provided to this work.

This research was supported by the Social Sciences and Humanities Research Council of Canada.

Social Sciences and Humanities Research Council of Canada
Conseil de recherches en sciences humaines du Canada
Canada

Marcello Musto
Toronto, 2019

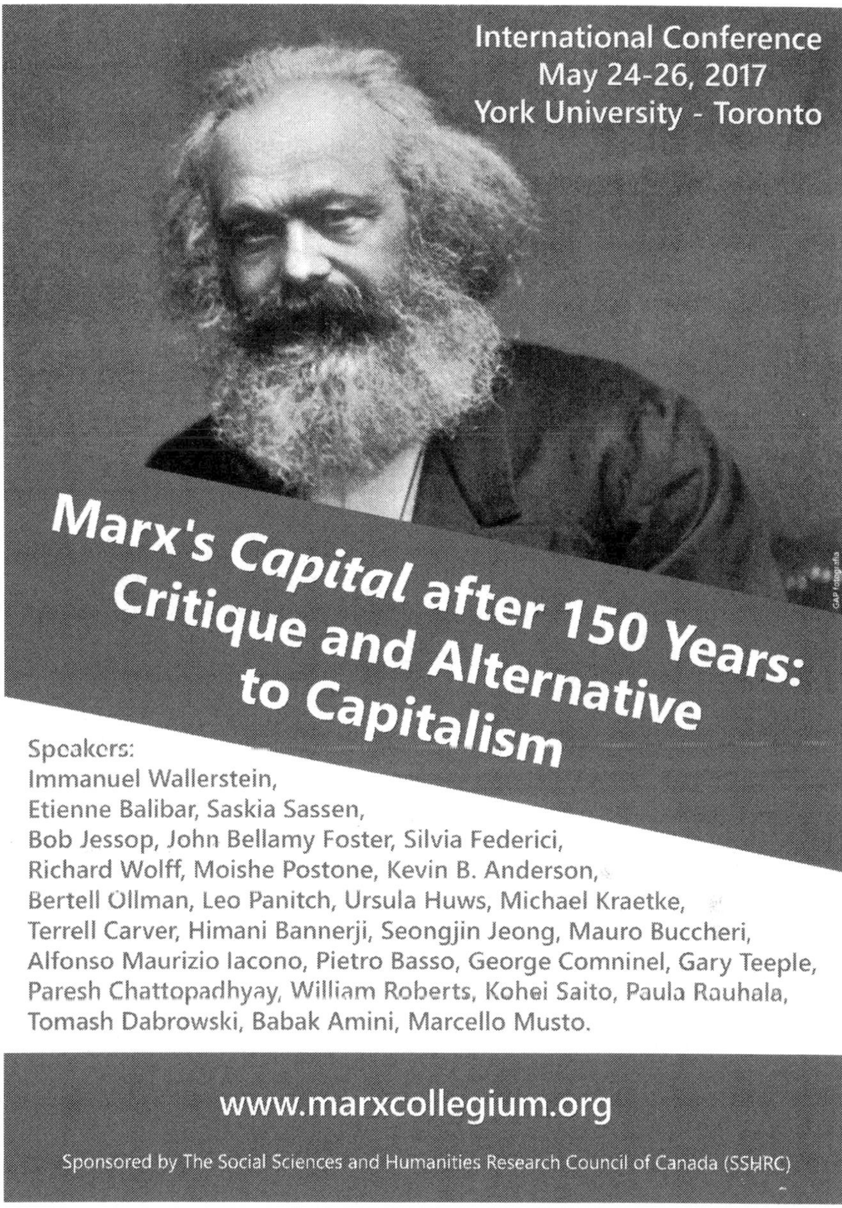
International Conference
May 24-26, 2017
York University - Toronto
Marx's Capital after 150 Years: Critique and Alternative to Capitalism
Speakers:
Immanuel Wallerstein,
Etienne Balibar, Saskia Sassen,
Bob Jessop, John Bellamy Foster, Silvia Federici,
Richard Wolff, Moishe Postone, Kevin B. Anderson,
Bertell Ollman, Leo Panitch, Ursula Huws, Michael Kraetke,
Terrell Carver, Himani Bannerji, Seongjin Jeong, Mauro Buccheri,
Alfonso Maurizio Iacono, Pietro Basso, George Comninel, Gary Teeple,
Paresh Chattopadhyay, William Roberts, Kohei Saito, Paula Rauhala,
Tomash Dabrowski, Babak Amini, Marcello Musto.
www.marxcollegium.org
Sponsored by The Social Sciences and Humanities Research Council of Canada (SSHRC)

1 Introduction

The unfinished critique of *Capital*

Marcello Musto

1 From the *Grundrisse* to the critical analysis of *Theories of Surplus Value*

Marx started to write *Capital* only many years after he had begun his rigorous studies of political economy. From 1843 onwards, he had already been working, with great intensity, towards what he would later define as his own 'Economics'.[1]

It was the eruption of the financial crisis of 1857 that forced Marx to start his work. Marx was convinced that the crisis developing at international level had created the conditions for a new revolutionary period throughout Europe. He had been waiting for this moment ever since the popular insurrections of 1848, and now that it finally seemed to have come, he did not want events to catch him unprepared. He therefore decided to resume his economic studies and to give them a finished form.

This period was one of the most prolific in his life: he managed to write more in a few months than in the preceding years. In December 1857, he wrote to Engels: 'I am working like mad all night and every night collating my economic studies, so that I might at least get the outlines *Grundrisse* clear before the deluge' (Marx to Engels, 8 December 1857, Marx and Engels 1983: 257).[2]

Marx's work was now remarkable and wide-ranging. From August 1857 to May 1858, he filled the eight notebooks known as the *Grundrisse*, while as correspondent of the *New-York Tribune* (the paper with the largest circulation in the United States of America, with whom he had collaborated since 1851), he wrote dozens of articles on, among other things, the development of the crisis in Europe. Lastly, from October 1857 to February 1858, he compiled three books of extracts, called the *Crisis Notebooks* (Marx 2017). Thanks to these, it is possible to change the conventional image of a Marx studying Hegel's *Science of Logic* to find inspiration for the manuscripts of 1857–1858. For at that time he was much more preoccupied with events linked to the long-predicted major crisis. Unlike the extracts he had made before, these were not compendia from the works of economists but consisted of a large quantity of notes, gleaned from various daily newspapers, about major developments in the crisis, stock market trends, trade exchange fluctuations and important bankruptcies in Europe, the United States of America, and other parts of the world. A letter he wrote to Engels in December indicates the intensity of his activity:

> I am working enormously, as a rule until 4 o'clock in the morning. I am engaged on a twofold task: 1. Elaborating the outlines of political economy (For the benefit of the public it is absolutely essential to go into the matter to the bottom, as it is for my own, individually, to get rid of this nightmare). 2. The present crisis. Apart from the articles for the [*New-York*] *Tribune*, all I do is keep records of it, which, however, takes up a considerable amount of time. I think that, somewhere about the spring, we ought to do a pamphlet together about the affair.
>
> (Marx to Engels, 18 December 1857, Marx and Engels 1983: 224)[3]

The *Grundrisse* were divided in three parts: a methodological 'Introduction', a 'Chapter on Money', in which Marx dealt with money and value, and a 'Chapter on Capital', that was centred on the process of production and circulation of capital, and addressed such key themes as the concept of surplus value, and the economic formations which preceded the capitalist mode of production. Marx immense effort did not, however, allow him to complete the work. In late February 1858 he wrote to Lassalle:

> I have in fact been at work on the final stages for some months. But the thing is proceeding very slowly because no sooner does one set about finally disposing of subjects to which one has devoted years of study than they start revealing new aspects and demand to be thought out further. [...] The work I am presently concerned with is a Critique of Economic Categories or, if you like, a critical exposé of the system of the bourgeois economy. It is at once an exposé and, by the same token, a critique of the system. I have very little idea how many sheets the whole thing will amount to. [...] Now that I am at last ready to set to work after 15 years of study, I have an uncomfortable feeling that turbulent movements from without will probably interfere after all.
>
> (Marx to Lassalle, 22 February 1858, Marx and Engels 1983: 270–1)

There was no sign of the much-anticipated revolutionary movement, which was supposed to be born in conjunction with the crisis and Marx abandoned the project to write a volume on the current crisis. Nevertheless, he could not finish the work, on which he had been struggling for many years, because he was aware that he was still far away from a definitive conceptualization of the themes addressed in the manuscript. Therefore, the *Grundrisse* remained only a draft, from which – after he had carefully worked up the 'Chapter on Money' –, in 1859, he published a short book with no public resonance: *A Contribution to the Critique of Political Economy*.

In August 1861, Marx again devoted himself to the critique of political economy, working with such intensity that by June 1863 he had filled 23 sizeable notebooks on the transformation of money into capital, on commercial capital, and above all on the various theories with which economists had tried to explain surplus value.[4] His aim was to complete *A Contribution to the Critique of Political Economy*, which was intended as the first instalment of his planned work. The book published in 1859 contained a brief first chapter, 'The Commodity', differentiated between use value and exchange value, and a longer second chapter, 'Money, or Simple Circulation', dealt with theories of money as unit of measure. In the preface, Marx stated: 'I examine the system of bourgeois economy in the following order: capital, landed property, wage-labour; the state, foreign trade, world market' (Marx 1987a: 261).

Two years later, Marx's plans had not changed: he was still intending to write six books, each devoted to one of the themes he had listed in 1859.[5] However, from Summer 1861 to March 1862, he worked on a new chapter, 'Capital in General', which he intended to become the third chapter in his publication plan. In the preparatory manuscript contained in the first five of the 23 notebooks he compiled by the end of 1863, he focused on the process of production of capital and, more particularly, on: (1) the transformation of money into capital; (2) absolute surplus value; and (3) relative surplus value.[6] Some of these themes, already addressed in the *Grundrisse*, were now set forth with greater analytic richness and precision.

A momentary alleviation of the huge economic problems that had beset him for years allowed Marx to spend more time on his studies and to make significant theoretical advances. In late October 1861 he wrote to Engels that 'circumstances ha[d] finally cleared to the extent that [he had] at least got firm ground under [his] feet again'. His work for the *New-York Tribune* assured him of 'two pounds a week' (Marx to Engels, 30 October 1861, Marx and Engels 1985: 323). He had also concluded an agreement with *Die Presse*. Over the past year, he had 'pawned everything that was not actually nailed down', and their plight had made his wife seriously depressed. But now the 'twofold engagement' promised to 'put an end to the harried existence led by [his] family' and to allow him to 'complete his book'. Nevertheless, by December, he told Engels that he had been forced to leave IOUs with the butcher and grocer, and that his debt to assorted creditors amounted to 100 pounds (Marx to Engels, 9 December 1861, Marx and Engels 1985: 332). Because of these worries, his research was proceeding slowly: 'Circumstances being what they were, there was, indeed, little possibility of bringing [the] theoretical matters to a rapid close'. But he gave notice to Engels that 'the thing is assuming a much more popular form, and method is much less in evidence than in Part I' (Marx to Engels, 9 December 1861, Marx and Engels 1985: 333). Against this dramatic background, Marx tried to borrow money from his mother, as well as from other relatives and the poet Carl Siebel (1836–1868). In a letter to Engels later in December, he explained that these were attempts to avoid constantly 'pestering' him. At any event, they were all unproductive. Nor was the agreement with *Die Presse* working out, as they were only printing (and paying for) half the articles he submitted to them. To his friend's best wishes for the new year, he confided that if it turned out to be 'anything like the old one' he would 'sooner consign it to the devil' (Marx to Engels, 27 December 1861, Marx and Engels 1985: 337–8). Things took a further turn for the worse when the *New-York Tribune*, faced with financial constraints associated with the American Civil War, had to cut down on the number of its foreign correspondents. Marx's last article for the paper appeared on 10 March 1862. From then on, he had to do without what had been his main source of income since the summer of 1851. That same month, the landlord of his house threatened to take action to recover rent arrears, in which case – as he put it to Engels – he would be 'sued by all and sundry' (Marx to Engels, 3 March 1862, Marx and Engels 1985: 344). And he added shortly after: 'I'm not getting on very well with my book, since work is often checked, i.e. suspended, for weeks on end by domestic disturbances' (Marx to Engels, 15 March 1862, Marx and Engels 1985: 352). During this period, Marx launched into a new area of research: *Theories of Surplus Value*.[7] This was planned to be the fifth[8] and final part of the long third chapter on 'Capital in General'. Over ten notebooks, Marx minutely dissected how the major economists had dealt with the question of surplus value; his basic idea was that 'all economists share the error of examining surplus-value not as such, in its pure form, but in the particular forms of profit and rent' (Marx 1988: 348).[9]

In Notebook VI, Marx began with a critique of the Physiocrats. First of all, he recognized them as the 'true fathers of modern political economy' (Marx 1988: 352), since it was they who 'laid the foundation for the analysis of capitalist production' (Marx 1988: 354) and sought the origin of surplus value not in 'the sphere of circulation' – in the productivity of money, as the mercantilists thought – but in 'the sphere of production'. They understood the 'fundamental principle that only that labour is productive which creates a surplus value' (Marx 1988: 354). On the other hand, being wrongly convinced that 'agricultural labour' was 'the only productive labour', they conceived of 'rent' as 'the only form of surplus value' (Marx 1988: 355). They limited their analysis to the idea that the productivity of the land enabled man to produce 'no more than sufficed to keep him alive'. According to this theory, then, surplus value appeared as 'a gift of nature' (Marx 1988: 357). In the second half of Notebook VI, and in most of Notebooks VII, VIII and IX, Marx concentrated on Adam Smith. He did not share the false idea of the Physiocrats that 'only one definite kind of concrete labour – agricultural labour – creates surplus value' (Marx 1988: 391). Indeed, in Marx's eyes one of Smith's greatest merits was to have understood that, in the distinctive labour process of bourgeois society, the capitalist 'appropriates for nothing, appropriates without paying for it, a part of the living labour' (Marx 1988: 388); or again, that 'more labour is exchanged for less labour (from the labourer's standpoint), less labour is exchanged for more labour (from the capitalist's standpoint)' (Marx 1988: 393). Smith's limitation, however, was his failure to differentiate 'surplus-value as such' from 'the specific forms it assumes in profit and rent' (Marx 1988: 389). He calculated surplus-value not in relation to the part of capital from which it arises, but as 'an overplus over the total value of the capital advanced' (Marx 1988: 396), including the part that the capitalist expends to purchase raw materials.

Marx put many of these thoughts in writing during a three-week stay with Engels in Manchester in April 1862. On his return, he reported to Lassalle:

> As for my book, it won't be finished for another two months. During the past year, to keep myself from starving, I have had to do the most despicable hackwork and have often gone for months without being able to add a line to the 'thing'. And there is also that quirk I have of finding fault with anything I have written and not looked at for a month, so that I have to revise it completely.
>
> (Marx to Lassalle, 28 April 1862, Marx and Engels 1985: 356)

Marx doggedly resumed work and until early June extended his research to other economists such as Germain Garnier (1754–1821) and Charles Ganilh (1758–1836). Then he went more deeply into the question of productive and unproductive labour, again focusing particularly on Smith, who, despite a lack of clarity in some respects, had drawn the distinction between the two concepts. From the capitalist's viewpoint, productive labour

> is wage labour which, exchanged against the [...] part of the capital that is spent on wages, reproduces not only this part of the capital (or the value of its own labour capacity), but in addition produces surplus value for the capitalist. It is only thereby that commodity or money is transformed into capital, is produced as capital. Only that wage labour is productive which produces capital.
>
> (Marx 1989a: 8)

Unproductive labour, on the other hand, is 'labour which is not exchanged with capital, but directly with revenue, that is, with wages or profit' (Marx 1989a: 12). According to Smith, the activity of sovereigns – and of the legal and military officers surrounding them – produced no value and in this respect was comparable to the duties of domestic servants. This, Marx pointed out, was the language of a 'still revolutionary bourgeoisie', which had not yet 'subjected to itself the whole of society, the state, etc.'

> illustrious and time-honoured occupations – sovereign, judge, officer, priest, etc. – with all the old ideological castes to which they give rise, their men of letters, their teachers and priests, are from an economic standpoint put on the same level as the swarm of their own lackeys and jesters maintained by the bourgeoisie and by idle wealth – the landed nobility and idle capitalists.
>
> (Marx 1989a: 197)

In Notebook X, Marx turned to a rigorous analysis of François Quesnay's (1694–1774) *Tableau économique* (Marx to Engels, 18 June 1862, Marx and Engels 1985: 381).[10] He praised it to the skies, describing it as 'an extremely brilliant conception, incontestably the most brilliant for which political economy had up to then been responsible' (Marx 1989a: 240).

Meanwhile, Marx's economic circumstances continued to be desperate. In mid-June, he wrote to Engels:

> Every day my wife says she wishes she and the children were safely in their graves, and I really cannot blame her, for the humiliations, torments and alarums that one has to go through in such a situation are indeed indescribable.
>
> (Marx to Engels, 18 June 1862, Marx and Engels 1985: 380)

Already in April, the family had had to re-pawn all the possessions it had only recently reclaimed from the loan office. The situation was so extreme that Jenny made up her mind to sell some books from her husband's personal library – although she could not find anyone who wanted to buy them.

Nevertheless, Marx managed to 'work hard' and in mid-June expressed a note of satisfaction to Engels: 'strange to say, my grey matter is functioning better in the midst of the surrounding poverty than it has done for years' (Marx to Engels, 18 June 1862, Marx and Engels 1985: 380). Continuing his research, he compiled Notebooks XI, XII and XIII in the course of the summer; they focused on the theory of rent, which he had decided to include as 'an extra chapter' (Marx to Engels, 2 August 1862, Marx and Engels 1985: 394) in the text he was preparing for publication. Marx critically examined the ideas of Johann Rodbertus (1805–1875), then moved on to an extensive analysis of the doctrines of David Ricardo (1772–1823).[11] Denying the existence of absolute rent, Ricardo had allowed a place only for differential rent related to the fertility and location of the land. In this theory, rent was an excess: it could not have been anything more, because that would have contradicted his 'concept of value being equal to a certain quantity of labour time' (Marx 1989a: 359); he would have had to admit that the agricultural product was constantly sold above its cost price, which he calculated as the sum of the capital advanced and the average profit (cf. Marx to Engels, 2 August 1862, Marx and Engels 1985: 396). Marx's conception of absolute rent, by contrast, stipulated that 'under certain historical circumstances [...] landed property does indeed put up the prices of raw materials' (Marx to Engels, 2 August 1862, Marx and Engels 1985: 398).

In the same letter to Engels, Marx wrote that it was 'a real miracle' that he 'had been able to get on with [his] theoretical writing to such an extent' (Marx to Engels, 2 August 1862, Marx and Engels 1985: 394). His landlord had again threatened to send in the bailiffs, while tradesmen to whom he was in debt spoke of withholding provisions and taking legal action against him. Once more he had to turn to Engels for help, confiding that had it not been for his wife and children he would 'far rather move into a model lodging house than be constantly squeezing [his] purse' (Marx to Engels, 7 August 1862, Marx and Engels 1985: 399).

In September, Marx wrote to Engels that he might get a job 'in a railroad office' in the new year (Marx to Engels, 10 September 1862, Marx and Engels 1985: 417). In December, he repeated to Ludwig Kugelmann (1828–1902) that things had become so desperate that he had 'decided to become a "practical man"'; nothing came of the idea, however. Marx reported with his typical sarcasm: 'Luckily – or perhaps I should say unluckily? – I did not get the post because of my bad handwriting' (Marx to Kugelmann, 28 December 1862, Marx and Engels 1985: 436). Meanwhile, in early November, he had confided to Ferdinand Lassalle (1825–1864) that he had been forced to suspend work 'for some six weeks' but that it was 'going ahead [...] with interruptions'. 'However,' he added, 'it will assuredly be brought to a conclusion by and by' (Marx to Lassalle, 7 November 1862, Marx and Engels 1985: 426).

During this span of time, Marx filled another two notebooks, XIV and XV, with extensive critical analysis of various economic theorists. He noted that Thomas Robert Malthus (1766–1834), for whom surplus value stemmed 'from the fact that the seller sells the commodity above its value', represented a return to the past in economic theory, since he derived profit from the exchange of commodities (Marx 1989b: 215). Marx accused James Mill (1773–1836) of misunderstanding the categories of surplus value and profit; highlighted the confusion produced by Samuel Bailey (1791–1870) in failing to distinguish between the immanent measure of value and the value of the commodity; and argued that John Stuart Mill (1806–1873) did not realize that 'the rate of surplus value and the rate of profit' were two different quantities (Marx 1989b: 373), the latter being determined not only by the level of wages but also by other causes not directly attributable to it.

Marx also paid special attention to various economists opposed to Ricardian theory, such as the socialist Thomas Hodgskin (1787–1869). Finally, he dealt with the anonymous text *Revenue and Its Sources* – in his view, a perfect example of 'vulgar economics', which translated into 'doctrinaire' but 'apologetic' language the 'standpoint of the ruling section, i.e. the capitalists' (Marx 1989b: 450). With the study of this book, Marx concluded his analysis of the theories of surplus value put forward by the leading economists of the past and began to examine commercial capital, or the capital that did not create but distributed surplus value.[12] Its polemic against 'interest-bearing capital' might 'parade as socialism', but Marx had no time for such 'reforming zeal' that did not 'touch upon real capitalist production' but 'merely attacked one of its consequences'. For Marx, on the contrary:

> The complete objectification, inversion and derangement of capital as interest-bearing capital – in which, however, the inner nature of capitalist production, [its] derangement, merely appears in its most palpable form – is capital which yields 'compound interest'. It appears as a Moloch

> demanding the whole world as a sacrifice belonging to it of right, whose legitimate demands, arising from its very nature, are however never met and are always frustrated by a mysterious fate.
>
> (Marx 1989b: 453)

Marx continued in the same vein:

> Thus it is interest, not profit, which appears to be the creation of value arising from capital as such [... and] consequently it is regarded as the specific revenue created by capital. This is also the form in which it is conceived by the vulgar economists. [...] All intermediate links are obliterated, and the fetishistic face of capital, as also the concept of the capital-fetish, is complete. This form arises necessarily, because the juridical aspect of property is separated from its economic aspect and one part of the profit under the name of interest accrues to capital in itself which is completely separated from the production process, or to the owner of this capital To the vulgar economist who desires to represent capital as an independent source of value, a source which creates value, this form is of course a godsend, a form in which the source of profit is no longer recognisable and the result of the capitalist process – separated from the process itself – acquires an independent existence. In M-C-M′ an intermediate link is still retained. In M-M′ we have the incomprehensible form of capital, the most extreme inversion and materialisation of production relations.
>
> (Marx 1989b: 458)

Following the studies of commercial capital, Marx moved on to what may be thought of as a third phase of the economic manuscripts of 1861–1863. This began in December 1862, with the section on 'capital and profit' in Notebook XVI that Marx identified as the 'third chapter' (Marx 1976a: 1598–675). Here Marx drew an outline of the distinction between surplus value and profit. In Notebook XVII, also compiled in December, he returned to the question of commercial capital (following the reflections in Notebook XV, Marx 1976a: 1682–773) and to the reflux of money in capitalist reproduction. At the end of the year, Marx gave a progress report to Kugelmann, informing him that 'the second part', or the 'continuation of the first instalment', a manuscript equivalent to 'about 30 sheets of print' was 'now at last finished'. Four years after the first schema, in the *Contribution to the Critique of Political Economy*, Marx now reviewed the structure of his projected work. He told Kugelmann that he had decided on a new title, using *Capital* for the first time, and that the name he had operated with in 1859 would be 'merely the subtitle' (Marx to Kugelmann, 28 December 1862, Marx and Engels 1985: 435). Otherwise he was continuing to work in accordance with the original plan. What he intended to write would be 'the third chapter of the first part, namely Capital in General'.[13] The volume in the last stages of preparation would contain 'what Englishmen call "the principles of political economy"'. Together with what he had already written in the 1859 instalment, it would comprise the 'quintessence' of his economic theory. On the basis of the elements he was preparing to make public, he told Kugelmann, a further 'sequel (with the exception, perhaps, of the relationship between the various forms of state and the various economic structures of society) could easily be pursued by others'.

Marx thought he would be able to produce a 'fair copy' (Marx to Kugelmann, 28 December 1862, Marx and Engels 1985: 435) of the manuscript in the new year, after which he planned to take it to Germany in person. Then he intended 'to conclude the presentation of capital, competition and credit'. In the same letter to Kugelmann, he compared the writing styles in the text published in 1859 and in the work he was then preparing: 'In the first part, the method of presentation was certainly far from popular. This was due partly to the abstract nature of the subject. [...] The present part is easier to understand because it deals with more concrete conditions'. To explain the difference, almost by way of justification, he added:

> Scientific attempts to revolutionize a science can never be really popular. But, once the scientific foundations are laid, popularization is easy. Again, should times become more turbulent, one might be able to select the colours and nuances demanded by a popular presentation of these particular subjects.
>
> (Marx to Kugelmann, 28 December 1862, Marx and Engels 1985: 436)

A few days later, at the start of the new year, Marx listed in greater detail the parts that would have comprised his work. In a schema in Notebook XVIII, he indicated that the 'first section (*Abschnitt*)', 'The Production Process of Capital', would be divided as follows:

> 1) Introduction. Commodity. Money. 2) Transformation of money into capital. 3) Absolute surplus value. [...] 4) Relative surplus value. [...] 5) Combination of absolute and relative surplus value. [...] 6) Reconversion of surplus value into capital. Primitive accumulation. Wakefield's theory of colonization. 7) Result of the production process. [...] 8) Theories of surplus value. 9) Theories of productive and unproductive labour.
>
> (Marx 1989b: 347)

Marx did not confine himself to the first volume but also drafted a schema of what was intended to be the 'third section' of his work: 'Capital and Profit'. This part, already indicating themes that were to comprise *Capital, Volume III*, was divided as follows:

> 1) Conversion of surplus value into profit. Rate of profit as distinguished from rate of surplus value. 2) Conversion of profit into average profit.

> […] 3) Adam Smith's and Ricardo's theories on profit and prices of production. 4) Rent. […] 5) History of the so-called Ricardian law of rent. 6) Law of the fall of the rate of profit. 7) Theories of profit. […] 8) Division of profit into industrial profit and interest. […] 9) Revenue and its sources. […] 10) Reflux movements of money in the process of capitalist production as a whole. 11) Vulgar economy. 12) Conclusion. Capital and wage labour.
>
> (Marx 1991: 346–7)[14]

In Notebook XVIII, which he composed in January 1863, Marx continued his analysis of mercantile capital. Surveying George Ramsay (1855–1935), Antoine-Elisée Cherbuliez (1797–1869) and Richard Jones (1790–1855), he inserted some additions to the study of how various economists had explained surplus value.

Marx's financial difficulties persisted during this period and actually grew worse in early 1863. He wrote to Engels that his 'attempts to raise money in France and Germany [had] come to nought', that no one would supply him with food on credit, and that 'the children [had] no clothes or shoes in which to go out' (Marx to Engels, 8 January 1863, Marx and Engels 1985: 442). Two weeks later, he was on the edge of the abyss. In another letter to Engels, he confided that he had proposed to his life's companion what now seemed an inevitability:

> My two elder children will obtain employment as governesses through the Cunningham family. Lenchen is to enter service elsewhere, and I, along with my wife and little Tussy, shall go and live in the same City Model Lodging-House in which Red Wolff once resided with his family.
>
> (Marx to Engels, 13 January 1863, Marx and Engels 1985: 445)

At the same time, new health problems had appeared. In the first two weeks of February, Marx was 'strictly forbidden [from] all reading, writing or smoking'. He suffered from 'some kind of inflammation of the eye, combined with a most obnoxious affection of the nerves of the head'. He could return to his books only in the middle of the month, when he confessed to Engels that during the long idle days he had been so alarmed that he 'indulged in all manner of psychological fantasies about what it would feel like to be blind or insane' (Marx to Engels, 13 February 1863, Marx and Engels 1985: 453). Just over a week later, having recovered from the eye problems, he developed a new liver disorder that was destined to plague him for a long time to come. Since Dr. Allen, his regular doctor, would have imposed a 'complete course of treatment' that would have meant breaking off all work, he asked Engels to get Dr. Eduard Gumpert [?] to recommend a simpler 'household remedy' (Marx to Engels, 21 February 1863, Marx and Engels 1985: 460).

During this period, apart from brief moments when he studied machinery, he began to 'attend a practical (purely experimental) course for working men given by Prof. Willis [...] (at the Institute of Geology, where [Thomas] Huxley also lectured)' (Marx to Engels, 28 January 1863, Marx and Engels 1985: 449). Apart from that, however, Marx had to suspend his in-depth economic studies. In March, however, he resolved 'to make up for lost time by some hard slogging' (Marx to Engels, 24 March 1863, Marx and Engels 1985: 461). He compiled two notebooks, XX and XXI, that dealt with accumulation, the real and formal subsumption of labour to capital, and the productivity of capital and labour. His arguments were correlated with the main theme of his research at the time: surplus value.

In late May, he wrote to Engels that in the previous weeks he had also been studying the Polish question[15] at the British Museum:

> What I did, on the one hand, was fill in the gaps in my knowledge (diplomatic, historical) of the Russian-Prussian-Polish affair and, on the other, read and make excerpts from all kinds of earlier literature relating to the part of the political economy I had elaborated.
>
> (Marx to Engels, 29 May 1863, Marx and Engels 1985: 474)

These working notes, written in May and June, were collected in eight additional notebooks A to H, which contained hundreds of more pages summarizing economic studies of the eighteenth and nineteenth centuries and covering more than 100 volumes.[16]

Marx also informed Engels that, feeling 'more or less able to work again', he was determined to 'cast the weight off his shoulders' and therefore intended to 'make a fair copy of the political economy for the printers (and give it a final polish)'. He still suffered from a 'badly swollen liver', however (Marx to Engels, 29 May 1863, Marx and Engels 1985: 474), and in mid-June, despite 'wolfing sulphur', he was still 'not quite fit' (Marx to Engels, 12 June 1863, Marx and Engels 1985: 479). In any case, he returned to the British Museum and in mid-July reported to Engels that he had again been spending 'ten hours a day working at economics'. These were precisely the days when, in analysing the reconversion of surplus value into capital, he prepared in Notebook XXII a recasting of Quesnay's *Tableau économique* (Marx to Engels, 6 July 1863, Marx and Engels 1985: 485). Then he compiled the last notebook in the series begun in 1861 – no. XXIII – which consisted mainly of notes and supplementary remarks.

At the end of these two years of hard work, and following a deeper critical re-examination of the main theorists of political economy, Marx was more determined than ever to complete the major work of his life. Although he had not yet definitively solved many of the conceptual and expository problems, his completion of the historical part now impelled him to return to theoretical questions.

2 The writing of the three volumes of *Capital*

Marx gritted his teeth and embarked on a new phase of his labours. From Summer 1863, he began the actual composition of what would become his *magnum opus*.[17] Until December 1865, he devoted himself to the most extensive versions of the various subdivisions, preparing drafts in turn of Volume I, the bulk of Volume III (his only account of the complete process of capitalist production) (Marx 2015), and the initial version of Volume II (the first general presentation of the circulation process of capital). In the manuscripts of 1863–1865, Marx grappled with new themes after his work of previous years. None of these, however, was tackled in an exhaustive manner.[18] As regards the six-volume plan indicated in 1859 in the preface to *A Contribution to the Critique of Political Economy*, Marx inserted a number of themes relating to rent and wages that were originally to have been treated in volumes II and III (See Rosdolsky 1977: 27).[19] In mid-August 1863, Marx updated Engels on his steps forward:

> In one respect, my work (preparing the manuscript for the press) is going well. In the final elaboration the stuff is, I think, assuming a tolerably popular form. [...] On the other hand, despite the fact that I write all day long, it's not getting on as fast as my own impatience, long subjected to a trial of patience, might demand. At all events, it will be 100% more comprehensible than No. 1.[20]
>
> (Marx to Engels, 15 August 1863, Marx and Engels 1985: 488)

Marx kept up the furious pace throughout the autumn, concentrating on the writing of Volume I. But his health rapidly worsened as a result, and November saw the appearance of what his wife called the 'terrible disease' against which he would fight for many years of his life. It was a case of carbuncles,[21] a nasty infection that manifested itself in abscesses and serious, debilitating boils on various parts of the body.

Because of one deep ulcer following a major carbuncle, Marx had to have an operation and 'for quite a time his life was in danger'. According to his wife's later account, the critical condition lasted for 'four weeks' and caused Marx severe and constant pains, together with 'tormenting worries and all kinds of mental suffering'. For the family's financial situation kept it 'on the brink of the abyss' (Jenny Marx in Enzensberger 1973: 288).

In early December, when he was on the road to recovery, Marx told Engels that he 'had had one foot in the grave' (Marx to Engels, 2 December 1863, Marx and Engels 1985: 495) – and two days later, that his physical condition struck him as 'a good theme for a short story'. From the front, he looked like someone who 'regale[d] his inner man with port, claret, stout and a truly massive mass of meat'. But 'behind on his back, the outer man, a damned carbuncle' (Marx to Engels, 4 December 1863, Marx and Engels 1985: 497). In this context, the death of Marx's mother obliged him to travel to Germany to sort out the legacy. His condition again deteriorated during the trip.

After he returned to London, all the infections and skin complaints continued to take their toll on Marx's health into the early spring, and he was able to resume his planned work only towards the middle of April, after an interruption of more than five months. In that time, he continued to concentrate on Volume I, and it seems likely that it was precisely then that he drafted the so-called 'Chapter Six. Results of the Immediate Process of Production'. In this text, Marx returned several times to a very important concept: 'commodities appear as the purchasers of persons'. In capitalism,

> means of production and [...] means of subsistence confront labour-power, stripped of all material wealth, as autonomous powers, personified in their owners. The objective conditions essential to the realization of labour are alienated from the worker and become manifest as fetishes endowed with a will and a soul of their own.
>
> (Marx 1976b: 1001)[22]

During this period, the early death of his friend Wilhelm Wolff, of whom both he and Engels were very fond, was a source of great pain for both. Wolff left a legacy of £800 to Marx, thanks to which he was able to move to a larger detached house at No. 1 Modena Villas.[23]

Despite this improvement in his finances, the arrival of summer did not change his precarious circumstances. Only after a family break in Ramsgate, in the last week of July and the first ten days of August, did it become possible to press on with his work. He began the new period of writing with Volume III: Part Two, 'The Conversion of Profit into Average Profit', then Part One, 'The Conversion of Surplus Value into Profit' (which was completed, most probably, between late October and early November 1864). During this period, he assiduously participated in meetings of the International Working Men's Association (cf. Musto 2014), for which he wrote the *Inaugural Address* and the *Statutes* in October. Also in that month, he wrote to Carl Klings (1828–?), a metallurgical worker in Solingen who had been a member of the League of Communists, and told him of his various mishaps and the reason for his unavoidable slowness:

> I have been sick throughout the past year (being afflicted with carbuncles and furuncles). Had it not been for that, my work on political economy, *Capital*, would already have come out. I hope I may now complete it finally in a couple of months and deal the bourgeoisie a theoretical blow from which it will never recover. [...] You may count on my remaining ever a loyal champion of the working class.
>
> (Marx to Klings, 4 October 1864, Marx and Engels 1987: 4)

Having resumed work after a pause for duties to the International, Marx wrote Part Three of Volume III, entitled 'The Law of the Tendency of the

Rate of Profit to Fall'. But his work on this was accompanied with another flare-up of his disease.

From January to May 1865, Marx devoted himself to Volume II. The manuscripts were divided into three chapters, which eventually became Parts in the version that Engels had printed in 1885: 1) The Metamorphoses of Capital; 2) The Turnover of Capital; and 3) Circulation and Reproduction. In these pages, Marx developed new concepts and connected up some of the theories in volumes I and III.

In the new year too, however, the carbuncle did not stop persecuting Marx, and around the middle of February, there was another flare-up of the disease. In addition to the 'foruncles', which persisted until the middle of the month, the International took up an 'enormous amount of time'. Still, he did not stop work on the book, even if it meant that sometimes he 'didn't get to bed until four in the morning' (Marx to Engels, 13 March 1865, Marx and Engels 1987: 129–30).

A final spur for him to complete the missing parts soon was the publisher's contract. Thanks to the intervention of Wilhelm Strohn [?], an old comrade from the days of the League of Communists, Otto Meisner (1819–1902) in Hamburg had sent him a letter on 21 March that included an agreement to publish 'the work *Capital: A Contribution to the Critique of Political Economy*'. It was to be 'approximately 50 signatures[24] in length [and to] appear in two volumes' (Marx 1985b: 361). By signing the agreement, Marx undertook 'to deliver the complete manuscript [...] on or before the last day of May of this year' (Marx 1985b: 362).

Between the last week of May and the end of June, Marx composed a short text *Wages, Price and Profit.*[25] In it, he contested John Weston's thesis that wage increases were not favourable to the working class, and that trade union demands for higher pay were actually harmful. Marx showed that, on the contrary, 'a general rise of wages would result in a fall in the general rate of profit, but not affect the average prices of commodities, or their values' (Marx 1985a: 144).

In the same period, Marx also wrote Part Four of Volume III, entitling it 'Conversion of Commodity-Capital and Money-Capital into Commercial Capital and Money-Dealing Capital (Merchant's Capital)'. At the end of July 1865, he gave Engels another progress report:

> There are 3 more chapters to be written to complete the theoretical part (the first 3 books). Then there is still the 4th book, the historical-literary one, to be written, which will, comparatively speaking, be the easiest part for me, since all the problems have been resolved in the first 3 books, so that this last one is more by way of repetition in historical form. But I cannot bring myself to send anything off until I have the whole thing in front of me. Whatever shortcomings they may have, the advantage of my writings is that they are an artistic whole, and this can only be achieved

> through my practice of never having things printed until I have them in front of me in their entirety.
>
> (Marx to Engels, 31 July 1865, Marx and Engels 1987: 173)

Two years later, Marx's fascination with art reasserted itself in *Capital*. He advised Engels to read *The Unknown Masterpiece* (1831) by Honoré de Balzac, which he described as a little 'masterpiece' in its own right, 'full of the most delightful irony' (Marx to Engels, 25 February 1867, Marx and Engels 1987: 348). The hero of the short story is Master Frenhofer, who, obsessed with the wish to make a painting of his as realistic as possible, delays completing it in the search for perfection. To those who ask what is still lacking, he answers: 'A trifle that's nothing at all, yet a nothing that's everything' (Balzac 2001: 16). To those who ask him to display the canvas, he stubbornly refuses: 'No, no, it must still be brought to perfection. Yesterday, toward evening, I thought I was done. Yet I'm still not satisfied – I have doubts' (Balzac 2001: 22). Eventually Balzac's masterly creation is driven to exclaim: 'It's ten years now … that I've been struggling with this problem. But what are ten short years when you're contending with nature?' (Balzac 2001: 24). And he adds: 'For a time I believed my painting was done; but now I'm sure several details are wrong, and I won't have a moment's peace till I've dispelled my doubts' (Balzac 2001: 32).

It is likely that Marx, with his usual sharpness of wit, identified with Frenhofer. Looking back, his son-in-law Paul Lafargue (1842–1911) said that a reading of Balzac's story had 'made a deep impression him because it partly described feelings that he had himself experienced'. Marx, too, was 'always extremely conscientious about his work', he 'was never satisfied with his work – he was always making some improvements and he always found his rendering inferior to the idea he wished to convey' (Lafargue in Enzensberger 1973: 307).

When unavoidable slowdowns and a series of negative events forced him to reconsider his working method, Marx asked himself whether it might be more useful first to produce a finished copy of Volume I, so that he could immediately publish it, or rather to finish writing all the volumes that would comprise the work. In another letter to Engels, he said that the 'point in question' was whether he should 'do a fair copy of part of the manuscript and send it to the publisher, or finish writing the whole thing first'. He preferred the latter solution, but reassured his friend that his work on the other volumes would not have been wasted:

> [Under the circumstances], progress with it has been as fast as anyone could have managed, even having no artistic considerations at all. Besides, as I have a maximum limit of 60 printed sheets,[26] it is absolutely essential for me to have the whole thing in front of me, to know how much has to be condensed and crossed out, so that the individual sections shall be evenly balanced and in proportion within the prescribed limits.
>
> (Marx to Engels, 5 August 1865, Marx and Engels 1987: 175)

Marx confirmed that he would 'spare no effort to complete as soon as possible'; the thing was a 'nightmarish burden' to him. It prevented him 'from doing anything else' and he was keen to get it out of the way before a new political upheaval: 'I know that time will not stand still for ever just as it is now' (Marx to Engels, 5 August 1865, Marx and Engels 1987: 175).

Although he had decided to bring forward the completion of Volume I, Marx did not want to leave what he had done on Volume III up in the air. Between July and December1865, he composed, albeit in fragmentary form, Part Five ('Division of Profit into Interest and Profit of Enterprise. Interest-Bearing Capital'), Part Six ('Transformation of Surplus-Profit into Ground-Rent') and Part Seven ('Revenues and Their Sources').[27] The structure that Marx gave to Volume III between Summer 1864 and the end of 1865 was therefore very similar to the 12-point schema of January 1863 contained in Notebook XVIII of the manuscripts on theories of surplus value.

In parallel with this work, in the second half of November 1865, Marx asked Engels to obtain from his acquaintance Alfred Knowles, a Manchester manufacturer, some information about the cotton industry, without which he would be unable 'to write out the second chapter' (Marx to Engels, 20 November 1865, Marx and Engels 1987: 199) of *Capital, Volume I.*[28]

The financial relief that allowed him to concentrate fruitfully on his work did not last long, and within a year the economic problems were back. In late July 1865, Marx confessed to Engels that he felt extremely uncomfortable about his plight and that he 'would rather have had [his] thumb cut off than' to be writing to him about it. The situation was indeed dramatic: 'For two months I have been living solely on the pawnshop, which means that a queue of creditors has been hammering on my door, becoming more and more unendurable every day'. Thinking back to what had led to this state, he recalled that he had 'been unable to earn a farthing and that 'merely paying off the debts and furnishing the house [had] cost [him] something like £500' (Marx to Engels, 31 July 1865, Marx and Engels 1987: 172).

On top of this, his duties for first conference of the International in London were particularly intense in September. To keep at least a modicum of time for the writing of *Capital*, Marx ending up telling a few white lies. To comrades in the International, he said he was about to leave on a trip, when in fact he was planning complete isolation so that he could work as much as possible without interruptions. However, he came down with a bad 'flu that only allowed him to write intermittently' (Marx to Engels, 19 August 1865, Marx and Engels 1987: 172). When the 'fellows and friends of the "International" discovered after all that [he was] not away', they sent 'a summons to attend a meeting of the Sub-committee' of the General Council to which he belonged. Marx complained to Engels that all this had prevented him from writing, and in addition the 'four weeks of [his]disappearance' had been 'spoiled by the doctor's prescriptions' (Marx to Engels, 22 August 1865, Marx and Engels 1987: 188).

3 The completion of *Capital* Volume I

At the beginning of 1866, Marx launched into the new draft of *Capital, Volume I*. In mid-January, he updated Wilhelm Liebknecht (1826–1900) on the situation: 'Indisposition, [...] all manner of unfortunate mischances, demands made on me by the International Association etc., have confiscated every free moment I have for writing out the fair copy of my manuscript'. Nevertheless, he thought he was near the end and that he would 'be able to take Volume 1 of it to the publisher for printing in March'. He added that its 'two volumes' would 'appear simultaneously' (Marx to Liebknecht, 15 January 1866, Marx and Engels 1987: 219). In another letter, sent the same day to Kugelmann, he spoke of being 'busy 12 hours a day writing out the fair copy' (Marx to Kugelmann, 15 January 1866, Marx and Engels 1987: 221), but hoped to take it to the publisher in Hamburg within two months. Marx was referring here only to Volume I, on the process of production of capital.

Contrary to his predictions, however, the whole year would pass in a struggle with the carbuncles and his worsening state of health. Despite everything, Marx's thoughts were still directed mainly at the task ahead of him:

> What was most loathsome to me was the interruption in my work, which had been going splendidly since January 1st, when I got over my liver complaint. There was no question of 'sitting', of course [...]. I was able to forge ahead even if only for short periods of the day. I could make no progress with the really theoretical part. My brain was not up to that. I therefore elaborated the section on the 'Working-Day' from the historical point of view, which was not part of my original plan.
>
> (Marx to Engels, 10 February 1866, Marx and Engels 1987: 223–4)

Marx concluded the letter with a phrase that well summed up this period of his life: 'My book requires all my writing time' (Marx to Engels, 10 February 1866, Marx and Engels 1987: 224). How much the more was this true in 1866.

The situation was now seriously alarming Engels. Fearing the worst, he intervened firmly to persuade Marx that he could no longer go on in the same way:

> You really must at last do something sensible now to shake off this carbuncle nonsense, even if the book is delayed by another 3 months. The thing is really becoming far too serious, and if, as you say yourself, your brain is not up to the mark for the theoretical part, then do give it a bit of a rest from the more elevated theory. Give over working at night for a while and lead a rather more regular life.
>
> (Engels to Marx, 10 February 1866, Marx and Engels 1987: 225–6)

Engels immediately consulted Dr. Gumpert, who advised another course of arsenic, but he also made some suggestions about the completion of his book. He wanted to be sure that Marx had given up the far from realistic idea of writing the whole of *Capital* before any part of it was published. 'Can you not so arrange things,' he asked, 'that the first volume at least is sent for printing first and the second one a few months later?' (Engels to Marx, 10 February 1866, Marx and Engels 1987: 226). Taking everything into account, he ended with a wise observation: 'What would be gained in these circumstances by having perhaps a few chapters at the end of your book completed, and not even the first volume can be printed, if events take us by surprise?' (Engels to Marx, 13 February 1866, Marx and Engels 1987: 227).

Marx replied to each of Engels's points, alternating between serious and facetious tones. With regard to arsenic, he wrote:

> Tell or write to Gumpert to send me the prescription with instructions for use. As I have confidence in him, he owes it to the best of "Political Economy" if nothing else to ignore professional etiquette and treat me from Manchester.
>
> (Marx to Engels, 13 February 1866, Marx and Engels 1987: 227)

As for his work plans, he wrote:

> As far as this 'damned' book is concerned, the position now is: it was ready at the end of December.[29] The treatise on ground rent alone, the penultimate chapter, is in its present form almost long enough to be a book in itself.[30] I have been going to the Museum in the day-time and writing at night. I had to plough through the new agricultural chemistry in Germany, in particular Liebig and Schönbein, which is more important for this matter than all the economists put together, as well as the enormous amount of material that the French have produced since I last dealt with this point. I concluded my theoretical investigation of ground rent 2 years ago. And a great deal had been achieved, especially in the period since then, fully confirming my theory incidentally. And the opening up of Japan (by and large I normally never read travel-books if I am not professionally obliged to). So here was the 'shifting system' as it was applied by those curs of English manufacturers to one and the same persons in 1848–50, being applied by me to myself.
>
> (Marx to Engels, 13 February 1866, Marx and Engels 1987: 227)

Daytime study at the library, to keep abreast of the latest discoveries, and night-time work on his manuscript: this was the punishing routine to which Marx subjected himself in an effort to use all his energies for the completion of the book. On the main task, he wrote to Engels: 'Although ready, the manuscript, which in its present form is gigantic, is not fit for publishing for anyone but myself, not even for you' (Marx to Engels, 13 February 1866, Marx and Engels 1987: 227).[31] He then gave some idea of the preceding weeks:

> I began the business of copying out and polishing the style on the dot of January first, and it all went ahead swimmingly, as I naturally enjoy licking the infant clean after long birth-pangs. But then the carbuncle intervened again, so that I have since been unable to make any more progress but only to fill out with more facts those sections which were, according to the plan, already finished.
>
> (Marx to Engels, 13 February 1866, Marx and Engels 1987: 227)

In the end, he accepted Engels's advice to spread out the publication schedule: 'I agree with you and shall get the first volume to Meissner as soon as it is ready'. 'But,' he added, 'in order to complete it, I must first be able to sit' (Marx to Engels, 13 February 1866, Marx and Engels 1987: 227).

In fact, Marx's health was continuing to deteriorate. Finally, Marx let himself be persuaded to take a break from work. On 15 March he travelled to Margate, a seaside resort in Kent, and on the tenth day sent back a report about himself: 'I am reading nothing, am writing nothing. The mere fact of having to take the arsenic three times a day obliges one to arrange one's time for meals and for strolling. [...] As regards company here, it does not exist, of course. I can sing with the Miller of the Dee:[32] "I care for nobody and nobody cares for me"' (Marx to Engels, 24 March 1866, Marx and Engels 1987: 249).

Early in April, Marx told his friend Kugelmann that he was 'much recovered'. But he complained that, because of the interruption, 'another two months and more' had been entirely lost, and the completion of his book 'put back once more' (Marx to Kugelmann, 6 April 1866, Marx and Engels 1987: 262). After his return to London, he remained at a standstill for another few weeks because of an attack of rheumatism and other troubles; his body was still exhausted and vulnerable. Although he reported to Engels in early June that 'there has fortunately been no recurrence of anything carbuncular' (Marx to Engels, 7 June 1866, Marx and Engels 1987: 281), he was unhappy that his work had 'been progressing poorly owing to purely physical factors' (Marx to Engels, 9 June 1866, Marx and Engels 1987: 282).

In July, Marx had to confront what had become his three habitual enemies: Livy's *periculum in mora* (danger in delay) in the shape of rent arrears; the carbuncles, with a new one ready to flare up; and an ailing liver. In August, he reassured Engels that, although his health 'fluctuate[d] from one day to the next', he felt generally better: after all, 'the feeling of being fit to work again does much for a man' (Marx to Engels, 7 August 1866, Marx and Engels 1987: 303). He was 'threatened with new carbuncles here and there', and although they 'kept disappearing' without the need for urgent intervention they had obliged him to keep his 'hours of work very much within limits' (Marx to Engels, 23 August 1866, Marx and Engels 1987: 311). On the same day, he wrote to Kugelmann:

> I do not think I shall be able to deliver the manuscript of the first volume (it has now grown to 3 volumes) to Hamburg before October. I can only

> work productively for a very few hours per day without immediately feeling the effects physically.
>
> (Marx to Kugelmann, 23 August 1866, Marx and Engels 1987: 312)

This time too, Marx was being excessively optimistic. The steady stream of negative phenomena to which he was daily exposed in the struggle to survive once more proved an obstacle to the completion of his text. Furthermore, he had to spend precious time looking for ways to extract small sums of money from the pawnshop and to escape the tortuous circle of promissory notes in which he had landed. He also said that 'for [his] family's sake' he 'must, however unwillingly, [...] observe the hygienic' limitations (linked to the prevention of new carbuncles) until he was 'fully recovered' (Marx to Kugelmann, 23 August 1866, Marx and Engels 1987: 312).

Marx's old friend and former member of the League of Communists, Friedrich Lessner, recalled that he 'often used to speak of the length of the working day'. At the end of the General Council meetings (which 'he never missed'), Marx more than once said: 'We are striving for an eight-hour day, but we ourselves often work twice as long in the space of twenty-four hours'. According to Lessner, Marx did 'much too much'; 'an outsider has no idea how much energy and time his work for the International cost him'. Besides 'Marx had to slave away to keep his family and to spend hours in the British Museum collecting material for his historical and economic studies' (Lessner in Enzensberger 1973: 293).

Very often, Marx's permanent intellectual curiosity led him to widen his range of studies. For example, despite the pressure to finish his book as well as his political responsibilities, he wrote to Engels in the summer of 1865 that he was 'studying Comte on the side just now, as the English and French are making such a fuss of the fellow'. He remained firm in what he thought of Comte's limitations: what attracted him was 'his encyclopaedic quality, la synthèse', although 'Hegel [was] infinitely superior as a whole'. 'And this shitty positivism came out in 1832!' he ended (Marx to Engels, 7 July 1866, Marx and Engels 1987: 292).

His prediction to Kugelmann that he might be able to take the manuscript to Hamburg in October also proved to be overoptimistic. In August, Marx wrote to Kugelmann that 'accumulated debts' had become 'a crushing mental burden' and that he had even been thinking of moving to the United States. He was soldiering on, though, convinced that he had 'a duty to [...] remain in Europe and complete the work on which [he had] been engaged for so many years' (Marx to Kugelmann, 23 August 1866, Marx and Engels 1987: 312). With regard to *Capital*, he assured his friend that, although he was spending much time writing documents in preparation for the Geneva congress of the International, he would not be attending it himself. 'For the working class,' he wrote, 'what [he was] doing through this work [was] far more important [...] than anything [he] might be able to do personally at any congress' (Marx to Kugelmann, 23 August 1866, Marx and Engels 1987: 312).

Writing to Kugelmann in mid-October, Marx expressed a fear that as a result of his long illness, and all the expenses it had entailed, he could no longer 'keep the creditors at bay' and the house was 'about to come crashing down about [his] ears' (Marx to Kugelmann, 13 October 1866, Marx and Engels 1987: 328). Not even in October, therefore, was it possible for him to put the finishing touches to the manuscript. In describing the state of things to his friend in Hannover, and explaining the reasons for the delay, Marx set out the plan he now had in mind:

> My circumstances (endless interruptions, both physical and social) oblige me to publish Volume I first, not both volumes together, as I had originally intended. And there will now probably be 3 volumes. The whole work is thus divided into the following parts:
>
> Book I. The Process of Production of Capital.
> Book II. The Process of Circulation of Capital.
> Book III. Structure of the Process as a Whole.
> Book IV. On the History of the Theory.
>
> The first volume will include the first 2 books. The 3rd book will, I believe, fill the second volume, the 4th the 3rd.
>
> (Marx to Kugelmann, 13 October 1866, Marx and Engels 1987: 328)

Reviewing the work, he had done since the *Contribution to the Critique of Political Economy*, which was published in 1859, Marx continued:

> It was, in my opinion, necessary to begin again from the beginning in the first book, i.e., to summarize the book of mine published by Duncker in one chapter on commodities and money. I judged this to be necessary, not merely for the sake of completeness, but because even intelligent people did not properly understand the question, in other words, there must have been defects in the first presentation, especially in the analysis of commodities.
>
> (Marx to Kugelmann, 13 October 1866, Marx and Engels 1987: 328–9)

Extreme poverty marked the month of November, too. But Marx was keen to point out that 'this summer and autumn it was really not the theory which caused the delay, but [his] physical and civil condition'. If he had been in good health, he would have been able to complete the work. He reminded Engels that it was three years since 'the first carbuncle had been lanced' – years in which he had had 'only short periods' of relief from it (Marx to Engels, 10 November 1866, Marx and Engels 1987: 332). Moreover, having been forced to expend so much time and energy on the daily struggle with poverty, he remarked in December: 'I only regret that private persons cannot file their bills for the bankruptcy court with the same propriety as men of business' (Marx to Engels, 8 December 1866, Marx and Engels 1987: 336).

At the end of February 1867, Marx was finally able to give Engels the long-awaited news that the book was finished. Now he had to take it to Germany, and once again he was forced to turn to his friend so that he could redeem his 'clothes and timepiece from their abode at the pawnbroker's' (Marx to Engels, 2 April 1867, Marx and Engels 1987: 351);[33] otherwise he would not have been able to leave.

Having arrived in Hamburg, Marx discussed with Engels the new plan proposed by Meissner:

> He now wants that the book should appear in 3 volumes. In particular he is opposed to my compressing the final book (the historico-literary part) as I had intended. He said that from the publishing point of view [...] this was the part by which he was setting most store. I told him that as far as that was concerned, I was his to command.
>
> (Marx to Engels, 13 April 1867, Marx and Engels 1987: 357)

Despite Marx's optimism, it should be noted that between 1862 and 1863 he had written only the history of the category of surplus value – and that he had done this before making significant theoretical progress. A few days later, he gave a similar report to Becker:

> The whole work will appear in 3 volumes. The title is *Capital. A Critique of Political Economy*. The first volume comprises the First Book: 'The Process of Production of Capital'. It is without question the most terrible missile that has yet been hurled at the heads of the bourgeoisie (land-owners included).
>
> (Marx to Becker, 17 April 1867, Marx and Engels 1987: 358)

After a few days in Hamburg, Marx travelled on to Hannover. He stayed there as the guest of Kugelmann, who finally got to know him after years of purely epistolary relations. Marx remained available there in case Meissner wanted him to help out with the proof-reading.

Marx stayed in Hanover until the middle of May. Happy with the results of the trip, he described his weeks with the Kugelmann family as 'an oasis in the desert of his life' (Kugelmann, in Enzensberger 1973: 323).[34] The most particularized accounts of Marx during this period have come down to us through the later recollections of Kugelmann's daughter, Franziska. She described her fears before the arrival of the unknown guest, of her mother's concern that he would be a man lost in 'his political ideas', with the manner of a 'gloomy revolutionary'. But both she and her mother had to think again as soon as they met Marx in person; he turned out to be a 'lively gentleman' and displayed a 'youthful freshness in his movements and conversation' (Kugelmann in Enzensberger 1973: 314). In fact, he was 'a thoroughly like-able and unpretentious presence, not only in get-togethers at home but also in the circle of my parents' acquaintances'. Franziska also recalled that Marx 'showed a lively interest in everything, and when someone pleased him in particular, or made an original remark, he would insert his monocle and look at the person with a cheerful and attentive expression'. The hospitality he received was returned with numerous anecdotes. On Hegel, he recounted how he had once said that 'none of his students had understood him, except [Karl] Rosenkranz – and that he had understood him badly' (Kugelmann in Enzensberger 1973: 315). Marx also often quoted Friedrich Schiller and once jokingly adapted a famous quotation of his from *Wallenstein's Camp*: 'He who has seen the best of his time has enough for all times!' (Kugelmann in Enzensberger 1973: 320).

In discussions on the struggle against capitalism, however, Marx spoke in authoritative tones and did not avoid polemic. To one man's question about who would polish boots in the future society, he replied: 'You should do it!' And someone who asked when communism would begin was told 'the time will come, but we'll have to be gone by then' (Kugelmann in Enzensberger 1973: 319).

From Hanover, Marx wrote to other comrades about the forthcoming publication of his work. To Sigfrid Meyer (1840–1872), a German socialist member of the International active in organizing the workers' movement in New York, he wrote: 'Volume I comprises the Process of Production of Capital. [...] Volume II contains the continuation and conclusion of the theory, Volume III the history of political economy from the middle of the 17th century' (Marx to Meyer, 30 April 1867, Marx and Engels 1987: 367). His schema was unchanged, however, and the idea was still that the second and third volumes would appear together.

Buoyed up with enthusiasm, Marx wrote to Engels in early May that the publisher Meissner was 'demanding the 2nd volume by the end of the autumn at the latest'. That should have included both Volume II and Volume III, so Marx thought he would have to 'get his nose to the grindstone' again, especially as – in the time since he had composed Volume III – 'a lot of new material relating to the chapters on credit and landed property ha[d] become available'. In the end, he expected to finish the third volume 'during the winter, so that [he would] have shaken off the whole *opus* by next spring'. Marx's overoptimistic predictions were based on the hope that 'the business of writing' would be 'quite different once the proofs for what ha[d] already been done' started to come in and he felt 'under pressure from the publisher' (Engels to Marx, 16 June 1867, Marx and Engels 1987: 382).

In mid-June, Engels became involved in the correction of the text for publication. He thought that, compared with the 1859 *A Contribution to the Critique of Political Economy*, 'the dialectic of the argument ha[d] been greatly sharpened' (Engels to Marx, 16 June 1867, Marx and Engels 1987: 381). Marx was heartened by this approval: 'That you have been satisfied with it so far is more important to me than anything the rest of the world may say of it' (Marx to Engels, 22 June 1867, Marx and Engels 1987: 383). However,

Engels noted that his exposition of the form of value was excessively abstract and insufficiently clear for the average reader; he also regretted that precisely this important section had 'the marks of the carbuncles rather firmly stamped upon it' (Engels to Marx, 16 June 1867, Marx and Engels 1987: 380). A further problem was Marx's rather dysfunctional subdivision of the volume. Its 800 pages were structured in just six long chapters, each with very few paragraph breaks. Engels therefore wrote:

> It was a serious mistake not to have made the development of these rather abstract arguments clearer by means of a larger number of short sections with their own headings. You ought to have treated this part in the manner of Hegel's Encyclopaedia, with short paragraphs, each dialectical transition emphasized by means of a special heading.

Then, 'a very large class of readers would have found it considerably easier to understand' (Engels to Marx, 16 June 1867, Marx and Engels 1987: 382). In reply, Marx fulminated against the cause of his physical torments – 'I hope the bourgeoisie will remember my carbuncles until their dying day' (Marx to Engels, 22 June 1867, Marx and Engels 1987: 383) – and convinced himself of the need for an appendix presenting his conception of the form of value in a more popular form. This 20-page addition was completed by the end of June.

The proof corrections were finished on 16 August 1867, at two in the morning. A few minutes later, he wrote to his friend in Manchester: 'Dear Fred: Have just finished correcting the last sheet. [...] So, this volume is finished. I owe it to you alone that it was possible! [...] I embrace you, full of thanks' (Marx to Engels, 24 August 1867, Marx and Engels 1987: 405). A few days later, in another letter to Engels, he summarized what he regarded as the two main pillars of the book:

> 1. (this is fundamental to all understanding of the facts) the twofold character of labour according to whether it is expressed in use value or exchange value, which is brought out in the very First Chapter; 2. the treatment of surplus value regardless of its particular forms as profit, interest, ground rent, etc.
>
> (Marx to Engels, 24 August 1867, Marx and Engels 1987: 407)

Capital was put on sale on 14 September 1867.[35] The high price of the book – three thalers – was equivalent to a worker's weekly wage. Jenny von Westphalen wrote to Kugelmann: 'There can be few books that have been written in more difficult circumstances, and I am sure I could write a secret history of it which would tell of many, extremely many unspoken troubles and anxieties and torments' (Jenny Marx to Kugelmann, 24 December 1867, Marx 1983: 578). Following the final modifications, the table of contents was as follows:

Preface
1. Commodity and money
2. The transformation of money into capital
3. The production of absolute surplus value
4. The production of relative surplus value
5. Further research on the production of absolute and relative surplus value
6. The process of accumulation of capital

Appendix to Part 1, 1: The form of value.

(Marx 1983: 9–10)

Despite the long correction process and the final addition, the structure of the work would be considerably expanded over the coming years, and various further modifications would be made to the text. *Capital, Volume I*, therefore continued to absorb significant energies on Marx's part even after its publication.

4 In search of the definitive version

In October 1867, Marx returned to *Capital, Volume II*. But this brought a recurrence of his medical complaints: liver pains, insomnia, and the blossoming of 'two small carbuncles near the *membrum*'. Nor did the 'incursions from without' or the 'aggravations of home life' leave off; there was a certain bitterness in his sage remark to Engels that 'my sickness always originates in the mind' (Marx to Engels, 19 October 1867, Marx and Engels 1987: 453). As always, his friend helped out and sent all the money he could, together with a hope that it 'drives away the carbuncles' (Engels to Marx, 22 October 1867, Marx and Engels 1987: 457). That is not what happened, though, and in late November Marx wrote to say: 'The state of my health has greatly worsened, and there has been virtually no question of working' (Marx to Engels, 27 November 1867, Marx and Engels 1987: 477).

The new year, 1868, began much as the old one had ended. During the first weeks of January, Marx was even unable to attend to his correspondence. His wife Jenny confided to Becker that her 'poor husband ha[d] once again been laid up and fettered hand and foot by his old, serious and painful complaint, which [was] becoming dangerous through its constant recurrence' (Jenny Marx to Becker, 'After 10 January 1868', Marx and Engels 1987: 580). A few days later, his daughter Jenny reported to Engels: 'Moor is once more being victimized by his old enemies, the carbuncles, and is, by the arrival of the latest, made to feel very ill at ease in a sitting posture' (Laura Marx to Engels, 13 January 1868, Marx and Engels 1987: 583). Marx began to write again only towards the end of the month, when he told Engels that 'for 2–3 weeks' he would 'do absolutely no work'; 'it would be dreadful,' he added, 'if a third monster were to erupt' (Marx to Engels, 25 January 1868, Marx and Engels 1987: 528).

As always, however, he returned as soon as he could to his research. During this period, he took a great interest in questions of history and agriculture, compiling notebooks of extracts from the works of various authors. Particularly important for him was the *Introduction to the Constitutive History of the German Mark, Farm, Village, Town and Public Authority* (1854) by the political theorist and legal historian Georg Ludwig von Maurer. Marx told Engels he had found Maurer's books 'extremely significant', since they approached in an entirely different way 'not only the primitive age but also the entire later development of the free imperial cities, of the estate owners possessing immunity, of public authority, and of the struggle between the free peasantry and serfdom' (Marx to Engels, 25 March 1868, Marx and Engels 1988: 557). Marx further approved of Maurer's demonstration 'at length that private property in land only arose later' (Marx to Engels, 14 March 1868, Marx and Engels 1988: 547). By contrast, he waxed sarcastic about those who were 'surprised to find what is newest in what is oldest, and even egalitarians to a degree that would have made Proudhon shudder' (Marx to Engels, 25 March 1868, Marx and Engels 1988: 557).

Also in this period, Marx studied in depth three German works by Karl Fraas: *Climate and the Vegetable World throughout the Ages, a History of Both* (1847), *A History of Agriculture* (1852) and *The Nature of Agriculture* (1857). Marx found the first of these 'very interesting', especially appreciating the part in which Kraas demonstrated that 'climate and flora change in historical times'. Writing to Engels, he described the author as 'a Darwinist before Darwin', who admitted 'even the species developing in historical times'. He was also struck by his ecological considerations and his related concern that 'cultivation – when it proceeds in natural growth and is not consciously controlled (as a bourgeois he naturally does not reach this point) – leaves deserts behind it'. Here too, Marx could detect what he called 'an unconscious socialist tendency' (Marx to Engels, 25 March 1868, Marx and Engels 1988: 559).

While affording Marx a little energy for these new scientific studies, the state of his health continued its ups and downs. In late March, he reported to Engels that it was such that he should 'really give up working and thinking entirely for some time'. But he added that would be 'hard' for him, even if he had 'the means to loaf around' (Marx to Engels, 25 March 1868, Marx and Engels 1987: 557). The new interruption came just as he was recommencing work on the second version of Volume II – after a gap of nearly three years since the first half of 1865. He completed the first two chapters in the course of the spring (Marx 2008), in addition to a group of preparatory manuscripts – on the relationship between surplus value and rate of profit, the law of the rate of profit, and the metamorphoses of capital – which occupied him until the end of 1868.[36]

At the end of April 1868, Marx sent Engels a new schema for his work, with particular reference to 'the method by which the rate of profit is developed' (Marx to Engels, 30 April 1868, Marx and Engels 1988: 21). This would be the last occasion when Marx referred in his correspondence to the law of the tendency of the rate of profit to decline. Despite the major economic crises that developed after 1873, Marx never again mentioned this concept to which the whole third section of Volume III (written in 1864–1865) is devoted – and which has received so much emphasis in later times; it was as if he thought it to have been superseded. In the same letter, he made it clear that Volume II would present the 'process of circulation of capital on the basis of the premises developed' in *Capital, Volume I.* He intended to set out, in as satisfactory a manner as possible, the 'formal determinations' of fixed capital, circulating capital and the turnover of capital – and hence to investigate 'the social intertwining of the different capitals, of parts of capital and of revenue (=*m*)'. Instead, Marx had decided to present 'the conversion of surplus value into its different forms and separate component parts' (Marx to Engels, 30 April 1868, Marx and Engels 1988: 21).

In May, however, the health problems were back. In the second week of August, he told Kugelmann of his hope to finish the entire work by 'the end of September' 1869 (Marx to Kugelmann, 10 August 1868, Marx and Engels 1988: 82). But the autumn brought an outbreak of carbuncles, and in Spring 1869, when Marx was still working on the third chapter – entitled in this version 'The Real Relations of the Circulation Process and the Reproduction Process' – of Volume II (Marx 2008). His plan to finish it by 1869 seemed realistic, since the second version of the text he had written since Spring 1868 represented an advance in both qualitative and quantitative terms. His liver took yet another turn for the worse. His misfortunes continued in the following years, with troublesome regularity, and prevented him from ever completing Volume II.

There were also theoretical reasons for the delay. From Autumn 1868 to Spring 1869, determined to get on top of the latest developments in capitalism, Marx compiled copious excerpts from texts on the finance and money markets that appeared in *The Money Market Review*, *The Economist* and similar publications.[37] His ever-growing interest in developments on the other side of the Atlantic drove him to seek out the most up-to-date information. He wrote to his friend Sigfrid Meyer that 'it would be of great value ... if [he] could dig up some anti-bourgeois material about landownership and agrarian relations in the United States'. He explained that, 'since [he would] be dealing with rent in [his] 2nd volume, material against H. Carey's "harmonies" would be especially welcome' (Marx to Meyer, 4 July 1868, Marx and Engels 1988: 61). Moreover, in Autumn 1869, having become aware of new (in reality, insignificant) literature about changes in Russia, he decided to learn Russian so that he could study it for himself. He pursued this new interest with his usual rigour, and in early 1870 Jenny told Engels that, 'instead of looking after himself, [he had begun] to study Russian hammer and tongs, went out seldom, ate infrequently, and only showed the carbuncle under his arm when it was already very swollen and had hardened' (Jenny Marx to Engels, 'About 17 January 1870', Marx and Engels 1988: 551).

Engels hastened to write to his friend, trying to persuade him that 'in the interests of the Volume II' he needed 'a change of life-style'; otherwise, if there was 'constant repetition of such suspensions', he would never finish the book (Engels to Marx, 19 January 1870, Marx and Engels 1988: 408).

The prediction was spot on. In early summer, summarizing what had happened in the previous months, Marx told Kugelmann that his work had been 'held up by illness throughout the winter', and that he had 'found it necessary to mug up on [his] Russian, because, in dealing with the land question, it ha[d] become essential to study Russian landowning relationships from primary sources' (Marx to Kugelmann, 27 June 1870, Marx and Engels 1988: 528).

After all the interruptions and a period of intense political activity for the International following the birth of the Paris Commune, Marx turned to work on a new edition of *Capital, Volume I.* Dissatisfied with the way in which he had expounded the theory of value, he spent December 1871 and January 1872 rewriting the 1867 appendix, and this led him to rewrite the first chapter itself. The result of this labour was the manuscript known as 'Additions and Changes to *Capital, Volume I*' (1871–1872) (Marx 1983: 1–55). During the revision of the 1867 edition, Marx inserted a number of additions and clarifications and also refined the structure of the entire book.[38] Some of these changes concerned surplus value, the difference between constant capital and variable capital, and the use of machinery and technology. He also expanded the new edition from six chapters to seven books containing 25 chapters, themselves subdivided into more detailed sections. The new edition came out in 1872, with a print run of 3,000 copies.

The year 1872 was a year of fundamental importance for the dissemination of *Capital,* since April saw the appearance of the Russian translation – the first in a long series (Musto and Amini forthcoming 2021). Begun by German Lopatin and completed by the economist Nikolai Danielson, it was regarded by Marx as 'masterly' (Marx to Davidson, 28 May 1872, Marx and Engels 1989: 385). Lessner related that 'the event, [which was considered] an important sign of the times, turned into a festive occasion for himself and for his family and friends' (Lessner 1907).

In a letter of May 1872 to Liebknecht, Jenny von Westphalen – who with her daughters had shared the joy of this success and other of Marx's achievements – described most effectively how gender differences also weighed in the common struggle for socialism. In all existing conflicts, she wrote,

> we women have the harder part to bear, because it is the lesser one. A man draws strength from his struggle with the world outside, and is invigorated by the sight of the enemy, be their number legion. We remain sitting at home, darning socks. That does nothing to dispel our fears and the gnawing day-to-day petty worries slowly but surely sap our spirit.
>
> (Jenny Marx to Liebknecht, 26 May 1872, Marx and Engels 1989: 580)

In this year, too, the publication of the French edition of *Capital* got under way. Entrusted to Joseph Roy, who had previously translated some of Ludwig Feuerbach's texts, it was scheduled to appear in batches with the French publisher Maurice Lachâtre, between 1872 and 1875. Marx agreed that it would be good to bring out a 'cheap popular edition' (Marx to Lafargue, 18 December 1871, Marx and Engels 1989: 283). 'I applaud your idea of publishing the translation ... in periodic instalments', he wrote. 'In this form the work will be more accessible to the working class and for me that consideration outweighs any other'. Aware, however, that there was a 'reverse side' of the coin, he anticipated that the 'method of analysis' he had used would 'make for somewhat arduous reading in the early chapters', and that readers might 'become discouraged when they were "unable to carry straight on"'. He did not feel he could do anything about this 'disadvantage',

> other than constantly caution and forewarn those readers concerned with the truth. There is no royal road to learning and the only people with any chance of scaling its sunlit peaks are those who have no fear of weariness when ascending the precipitous paths that lead up to them.
>
> (Marx to Lachâtre, 18 March 1872, Marx and Engels 1989: 344)

In the end, Marx had to spend much more time on the translation than he had planned for the proof correction. As he wrote to Danielson, Roy had 'often translated too literally' and forced him to 'rewrite whole passages in French, to make them more palatable to the French public' (Marx to Danielson, 28 May 1872, Marx and Engels 1989: 385).

Earlier that month, his daughter Jenny had told Kugelmann that her father was 'obliged to make numberless corrections', rewriting 'not only whole sentences but entire pages' (Jenny Marx to Kugelmann, 3 May 1872, Marx and Engels 1989: 578) – and a month later she added that the translation was so 'imperfect' that he had been 'obliged to rewrite the greater part of the first chapter' (Jenny Marx to Kugelmann, 27 June 1872, Marx and Engels 1989: 582). Subsequently, Engels wrote in similar vein to Kugelmann that the French translation had proved a 'real slog' for Marx and that he had 'more or less had to rewrite the whole thing from the beginning' (Engels to Kugelmann, 1 July 1873, Marx and Engels 1989: 515). At the end of his labours, Marx himself remarked that they had 'consumed so much of [his] time that [he would] not again collaborate in any way on a translation' (Marx to Sorge, 27 September 1877, Marx and Engels 1991: 276).

In revising the translation (Marx 1989c), moreover, Marx decided to introduce some additions and modifications. These mostly concerned the section on the process of capital accumulation, but also some specific points such as the distinction between 'concentration' and 'centralization' of capital. In the postscript to the French edition, he did not hesitate to attach to it 'a scientific value independent of the original' (Marx 1996: 24). It was no accident that in 1877, when an English edition already seemed a possibility, Marx wrote to Sorge that a translator 'must without fail … compare the 2nd German edition with the French edition, in which [he had] included a good deal of new matter and greatly improved [his] presentation of much else' (Marx to Sorge, 27 September 1877, Marx and Engels 1991: 276). In a letter of November 1878, in which he weighed the positive and negative sides of the French edition, he wrote to Danielson that it contained 'many important changes and additions', but that he had 'also sometimes been obliged – principally in the first chapter – to simplify [*aplatir*] the matter' (Marx to Danielson, 15 November 1878, Marx and Engels 1991: 343). For this reason, he felt it necessary to clarify later in the month that the chapters 'Commodities and Money' and 'The Transformation of Money into Capital' should be 'translated exclusively from the German text' (Marx to Danielson, 28 November 1878, Marx and Engels 1991: 346).[39]

The drafts of *Capital, Volume II,* which were left in anything but a definitive state, present a number of theoretical problems. The manuscripts of *Capital, Volume III,* have a highly fragmentary character, and Marx never managed to update them in a way that reflected the progress of his research.[40] It should also be borne in mind that he was unable to complete a revision of *Capital, Volume I,* that included the changes and additions he intended to improve his *magnum opus*.[41] In fact, neither the French edition of 1872–1875 nor the German edition of 1881 can be considered the definitive version that he would have liked it to be.

The critical spirit with which Marx composed his *magnum opus* reveals just how distant he was from the dogmatic author that many of his adversaries and self-styled disciples presented to the world. Unfinished though it remained, those who today want to use essential theoretical concepts for the critique of the capitalist mode of production still cannot dispense with reading Marx's *Capital*.

Translated from the Italian by Patrick Camiller

Notes

1 This expression has been often used by Maximilien Rubel (1981: 192ff.). Cf. also Musto (2018: 55–81).

2 The title later given to these manuscripts was inspired by this letter. On Marx's *Grundrisse* cf. Musto 2008.

3 A few days later, Marx communicated his plans to Lassalle: 'The present commercial crisis has impelled me to set to work seriously on my outlines of political economy, and also to prepare something on the present crisis' (Marx to Lassalle, 21 December 1857, Marx and Engels 1983: 226).

4 These notebooks total 1,472 quarto pages. See Engels (1996: 6).

5 Previously, in the *Grundrisse*, Marx had set forth a similar, though less precise, 'arrangement of the material' (Marx 1993: 108, 227–8, 264 and 27), at four separate points. He also anticipated the six-part schema planned for *A Contribution to the Critique of Political Economy* in two letters from the first half of 1858: one to Ferdinand Lassalle (Marx to Lassalle, 22 February 1858, Marx and Engels 1983: 268–71), and one to Friedrich Engels (Marx to Engels, 2 April 1858, Marx and Engels 1983: 296–304). Between February and March 1859, he also drafted a long

preparatory index for his work, which in the English edition of Marx (1993), became the 'Analytical Contents List', pp. 69–80. On the original plan and its variations, see the by now dated, but still fundamental work by Roman Rosdolsky (1977: 1–62). More limited, however, is Rubel (1974: 379, 389), which claims that Marx did not change the original plan he devised in 1857.

6 These notebooks were ignored for more than 100 years, before a Russian translation was finally published in 1973, in a supplementary Volume 47 of the Marx-Engels *Sochinenya*. An original German edition appeared only in 1976 in MEGA2, vol. II/3.1.

7 Between 1905 and 1910, Kautsky published the manuscripts in question in a form that deviated somewhat from the originals.

8 It was to have followed: 1) the transformation of money into capital; 2) absolute surplus value; 3) relative surplus value; and 4) a section – one he never actually wrote – on how these three should be considered in combination.

9 In the MECW these manuscripts are indicated with the title *Economic Manuscript of 1861–63*.

10 This notebook is the last of those comprising the so-called *Theories of Surplus-Value*, vol. I, in Marx (1989a).

11 These notebooks form part of the *Theories of Surplus Value*, vol. II, in Marx (1989a).

12 These are the final notebooks that form part of the *Theories of Surplus Value*, vol. III, in Marx (1989b).

13 See the index to the *Grundrisse*, written in June 1858 and contained in Notebook M (the same as that of the '1857 Introduction'), as well as the draft index for the third chapter, written in 1860: Marx (1987b: 511–17). Michael Heinrich (2016: 107) shows that, after the middle of 1863, Marx no longer used the concept of 'capital in general' in the subdivision of his work and never mentioned it again in either his manuscripts or his correspondence. It is therefore possible that he 'realised that the double requirement which he expected from the section of "Capital in General" – to present specific content [...] at a certain level of abstraction [...] – could not be fulfilled'.

14 The first chapter had already been outlined in Notebook XVI of the economic manuscripts of 1861–1863. Marx prepared a schema of the second in Notebook XVIII, see Marx (1991: 299).

15 See the more than 60 pages contained in IISH, Marx-Engels Papers, B 98. On the basis of this research, Marx began one of his many unfinished projects, see Marx (1961).

16 IISH, Marx-Engels Papers, B 93, B 100, B 101, B 102, B 103, B 104 contain some 535 pages of notes. Additionally, Marx also used material from three notebooks RGASPI f.1, d. 1397, d. 1691, d. 5583. In order to compile notebooks XXII and XXIII.

17 Heinrich (2011) argued that the manuscripts from this period should be regarded not as the third version of the work begun with the *Grundrisse*, but as the first draft of *Capital*. Krätke (2005) indicated that the overall outlook and scope of *Capital* remained unchanged, even though Marx changed his plans several times after 1857.

18 Heinrich (2016: 111) noted that, when he was writing the second and third volumes, Marx was 'far away from a situation in which these manuscripts could have served as a direct template for revision before going into print. In this respect one can say that *Capital* was still in a formation phase'.

19 In his view, Marx set aside the project of also writing books on the state, foreign trade and the world market.

20 With 'No. 1' Marx meant the 1859 *A Contribution to the Critique of Political Economy*.

21 In recent years, dermatologists have reviewed the discussion on the causes of Marx's disease. Sam Shuster (2008) suggested that he suffered from hidradenitis suppurativa, while Rudolf Happle and Arne Koenig (2008) claimed even less plausibly, that the culprit was his heavy smoking of cigars. For Shuster's reply to this suggestion, see Happle and Koenig (2008: 256).

22 The reasons why Marx did not insert this chapter into the published text of *Capital, Volume I,* remain unknown. For a commentary on it, see Napoleoni (1975).

23 This street was later renamed Maitland Park Road. Marx dedicated *Capital, Volume I,* to Wolff, his 'unforgettable friend. [...] Intrepid, faithful, noble protagonist of the proletariat'.

24 Fifty signatures were equivalent to 800 printed pages.

25 This was published in 1898 by Eleanor Marx, as *Value, Price and Profit.* This commonly used title was taken as the basis for the German translation that appeared the same year in *Die Neue Zeit* [The New Times].

26 The equivalent of 960 pages. Later, Meissner signaled his openness to modify his agreement with Marx: see Marx to Engels, 13 April 1867, Marx and Engels 1987: 357.

27 This division was followed by Engels when he published *Capital,* Volume III in 1894. See Vollgraf, Jungnickel and Naron (Spring 2002). See also the more recent: Vollgraf (2012/2013); Roth (2012/2013); and Krätke (2017), especially the final chapter 'Gibt es ein Marx-Engels-Problem?' For a critical assessment of Engels's editing, see Heinrich (1996–1997).

28 Marx used these data in the third chapter of Volume One. It should be noted, however, that in late 1865 Marx still envisaged the publication of Volume One of *Capital* as a continuation of his writings of 1859. Only from the letter Marx to Kugelmann, 13 October 1866 can we be certain that he had decided to rewrite the first part. See Marx and Engels (1987: 328).

29 Vollgraf (2018: 63–4) points out that, when Marx described *Capital* as being 'ready' since 1865, he was referring to the 'conceptual architecture', not the 'elaboration of the content chapter by chapter, and certainly not the complete exposition'. Marx continued to assess the work remaining to be done on the basis of size, not of 'the rational core of his arguments'.

30 Marx then inserted his analysis of ground rent into Part Six, 'The Transformation of Surplus Profit into Ground Rent', of Volume III.

31 This realistic assertion clashes with some previous over-confident descriptions of the state of his texts. Since, apart from a few additions, Marx had no further opportunity to work on Volume III after 1865, his statement testifies both to Engels's huge effort in preparing the book for publication and to its highly unfinished character. This should always be borne in mind by its readers and interpreters.

32 A traditional English folk song.

33 The most recent philological studies have shown that, contrary to what has always been believed, the original manuscript of *Capital, Volume I,* (of which the 'Chapter Six. Results of the Immediate Process of Production' was thought to be only surviving part) actually dates back to the 1863–64 period, and that Marx cut and pasted it into the copy he prepared for publication. See Vollgraf (2012).

34 For a full account of this period, see the recent Bönig (2017).

35 The distribution of the book began on 11 September 1867. See Institut für Marxismus-Leninismus, 'Entstehung und Überlieferung', in Marx (1983: 674).

36 These texts have recently been published in Marx (2012). The last part constitutes Manuscript IV of Volume II and contains new versions of Part One, 'The Circulation of Capital', and Part Two, 'The Metamorphoses of Capital'.

37 Still unpublished, these notes are included in the IISH notebooks, Marx-Engels Papers, B 108, B 109, B 113 and B 114.

38 In 1867 Marx had divided the book into chapters. In 1872 these became sections, each with much more detailed subdivisions.

39 For a list of the additions and modifications in the French translation that were not included in the third and fourth German editions, see Marx (1983: 732–83). For confirmation of the merits of this edition, see Anderson (1983) and D'Hondt (1985). On the research of the last period of Marx's life see Musto 2020 (forthcoming).

40 The editorial work that Engels undertook after his friend's death to prepare the unfinished parts of Capital for publication was extremely complex. The various manuscripts, drafts and fragments of Volumes II and III, written between 1864 and 1881, correspond to approximately 2,350 pages of the MEGA2. Engels successfully published Volume II in 1885 and Volume III in 1894. However, it must be borne in mind that these two volumes emerged from the reconstruction of incomplete texts, often consisting of heterogeneous material. They were written in more than one period in time and thus include different, and sometimes contradictory, versions of Marx's ideas.

41 See, for example, Marx to Danielson, 13 December 1881:

> In the first instance I must first be restored to health, and in the second I want to finish off the 2nd vol. [...] as soon as possible.... I will arrange with my editor that I shall make for the 3d edition only the fewest possible alterations and additions. [...] When these 1,000 copies forming the 3d edition are sold, then I may change the book in the way I should have done at present under different circumstances.
>
> (Marx and Engels 1993: 161)

References

Anderson, Kevin (1983) 'The "unknown" Marx's *Capital* Volume I: the French edition of 1872–75, 100 years later', in *Review of Radical Political Economics*, vol. 15, no. 4, pp. 71–80.

Balzac, Honoré de (2001) *The Unknown Masterpiece*, New York: Review of Books.

Bönig, Jürgen (2017) *Karl Marx in Hamburg. Der Produktionsprozess des Kapital*, Hamburg: VSA.

D'Hondt, Jacques (1985) 'La traduction tendancieuse du "Capital" par Joseph Roy', in Georges Labica (ed.), *1883–1983, l'œuvre de Marx un siècle après*, Paris: Presses Universitaires de France, pp. 131–7.

Engels, Frederick (1996) 'Preface to the First German Edition', in *Marx Engels Collected Works*, vol. 36: Karl Marx, *Capital, Volume II*, pp. 5–23.

Enzensberger, Hans Magnus (ed.) (1973) *Gespräche mit Marx und Engels*, Frankfurt: Suhrkamp.

Happle, Rudolf and Koenig, Arne (2008) 'A lesson to be learned from Karl Marx: smoking triggers hidradenitis suppurativa', in *British Journal of Dermatology*, vol. 159, no. 1, pp. 255–6.

Heinrich, Michael (1996–1997) 'Engels' edition of the third volume of capital and Marx's original manuscript', in *Science & Society*, vol. 60, no. 4, pp. 452–66.

Heinrich, Michael (2011) 'Entstehungs- und Auflösungsgeschichte des Marxschen Kapital', in Werner Bonefeld and Michael Heinrich (eds.), *Kapital & Kritik. Nach der 'neuen' Marx-Lektüre*, Hamburg: VSA, pp. 155–93.

Heinrich, Michael (2016) 'Capital after MEGA. Discontinuities, interruptions, and new beginnings', in *Crisis & Critique*, 3/2, pp. 92–138.

Krätke, Michael R. (2005) 'Le dernier Marx et le *Capital*', *Actuel Marx*, vol. 37, no. 1, pp. 145–60.

Krätke, Michael R. (2017) *Kritik der politischen Ökonomie Heute*, Hamburg: VSA.

Lessner, Frederick (1907) *Sixty years in the Social-Democratic movement, before 1848 and after: Recollections of an old Communist*, London: Twentieth Century Press.

Marx, Karl (1961 [1863–1864]) *Manuskripte über die polnische Frage*, S'-Gravenhage: Mouton.

Marx, Karl (1976a [1861–63]) 'Drittes Capitel. Capital und Profit', in Idem, *Zur Kritik der politischen Ökonomie (Manuskript 1861–1863)*, in MEGA^2, vol. II/3.5, pp. 1598–1675.

Marx, Karl (1976b [1864]) 'Appendix: results of the immediate process of production', in *Capital, Volume I*, London: Penguin/New Left Review, pp. 941–1084.

Marx, Karl (1983 [1867]) *Das Kapital. Kritik der Politischen Ökonomie. Erster Band, Hamburg 1867*, in MEGA^2, vol. II/5, Berlin: Dietz Verlag.

Marx, Karl (1985a [1865]) 'Value, prices and profit', in *Marx Engels Collected Works*, vol. 20: *Marx and Engels: Letters 1864–68*, Moscow: Progress Publishers, pp. 101–49.

Marx, Karl (1985b [1865]) 'Agreement between Mr. Karl Marx and Mr. Otto Meissner, publisher and bookseller', in *Marx Engels Collected Works*, vol. 20: *Marx and Engels: Letters 1864–68*, Moscow: Progress Publishers, pp. 361–2.

Marx, Karl (1987a [1859]) 'A contribution to the critique of political economy', in *Marx Engels Collected Works*, vol. 29: *Marx 1857–61*, Moscow: Progress Publishers, pp. 257–417.

Marx, Karl (1987b [1859]) 'Draft plan of the chapter on capital', in *Marx Engels Collected Works*, vol. 29: *Marx 1857–61*, Moscow: Progress Publishers, pp. 511–17.

Marx, Karl (1988 [1861–1863]) *Marx Engels Collected Works*, vol. 30: *Economic Manuscripts of 1861–63*, Moscow: Progress Publishers.

Marx, Karl (1989a [1861–1863]) *Marx Engels Collected Works*, vol. 31: *Economic Manuscripts of 1861–63*, Moscow: Progress Publishers.

Marx, Karl (1989b [1861–1863]) *Marx Engels Collected Works*, vol. 32: *Economic Manuscripts of 1861–63*, Moscow: Progress Publishers.

Marx, Karl (1989c [1872–1875]) *Le Capital, Paris 1872–1875*, in MEGA^2, vol. II/7, Berlin: Dietz Verlag.

Marx, Karl (1991 [1861–1863]) *Marx Engels Collected Works*, vol. 33, *Economic Manuscript of 1861–63*, Moscow: Progress Publishers.

Marx, Karl (1993 [1857–1858]) *Grundrisse*, Harmondsworth: Penguin Books.

Marx, Karl (1996 [1875]) 'Afterword to the French edition', in *Marx Engels Collected Works*, vol. 35: *Karl Marx, Capital, Volume I*, Moscow: Progress Publishers, p. 24.

Marx, Karl (1998 [1894]) *Capital, Volume III*, in *Marx Engels Collected Works*, vol. 37: *Karl Marx, Capital, Volume III*, Moscow: Progress Publishers.

Marx, Karl (2008 [1868–1870]) 'Das Kapital (Ökonomisches Manuskript 1868–1870). Zweites Buch. Der Zirkulationsprozess des Kapitals (Manuskript II)', in MEGA^2, vol. II/11, Berlin: Akademie Verlag, pp. 1–339.

Marx, Karl (2012 [1863–1868]) *Ökonomische Manuskripte 1863–1868*, in MEGA^2, vol. II/4.3, Berlin: Akademie Verlag.

Marx, Karl (2015 [1864–1865]) *Marx's Economic Manuscript of 1864–1865*, Leiden: Brill.

Marx, Karl (2017 [1857–1858]) *Exzerpte, Zeitungsausschnitte und Notizen zur Weltwirtschaftskrise (Krisenhefte). November 1857 bis Februar 1858*, in MEGA^2, IV/14, Berlin: De Gruyter.

Marx, Karl, IISH, Marx-Engels Papers, B 93, B 98, B 100, B 101, B 102, B 103, B 104, B 108, B 109, B 113 and B 114.

Marx, Karl, RGASPI f.1, d. 1397, d. 1691, d. 5583.
Marx, Karl and Engels, Friedrich (1983) *Marx Engels Collected Works*, vol. 40: *Letters, 1856–59*, Moscow: Progress Publishers.
Marx, Karl and Engels, Friedrich (1985) *Marx Engels Collected Works*, vol. 41: *Letters, 1860–64*, Moscow: Progress Publishers.
Marx, Karl and Engels, Friedrich (1987) *Marx Engels Collected Works*, vol. 42: *Letters, 1864–68*, Moscow: Progress Publishers.
Marx, Karl and Engels, Friedrich (1988) in *Marx Engels Collected Works*, vol. 43: *Letters 1868–70*, Moscow: Progress Publishers.
Marx, Karl and Engels, Friedrich (1989) in *Marx Engels Collected Works*, vol. 44: *Letters 1870–73*, Moscow: Progress Publishers.
Marx, Karl and Engels, Friedrich (1991) in *Marx Engels Collected Works*, vol. 45: *Letters 1874–79*, Moscow: Progress Publishers.
Marx, Karl and Engels, Friedrich (1993) in *Marx Engels Collected Works*, vol. 46: *Letters 1880–83*, Moscow: Progress Publishers.
Musto, Marcello (ed.) (2008), *Karl Marx's Grundrisse: Foundations of the Critique of Political Economy 150 Years Later*, London and New York: Routledge.
Musto, Marcello (ed.) (2014), *Workers Unite! The International 150 Years Later*, London and New York: Bloomsbury.
Musto, Marcello (2018), *Another Marx: Early Manuscripts to the International*, London–New York: Bloomsbury.
Musto, Marcello (Forthcoming 2020), *The Last Years of Karl Marx: An Intellectual Biography of the Late Marx*, Stanford, CA: Stanford University Press.
Musto, Marcello and Amini, Babak (eds.) (forthcoming 2021) *The Routledge Handbook of Marx's 'Capital': A Global History of Translation, Dissemination and Reception*, London and New York: Routledge.
Napoleoni, Claudio (1975) *Lezioni sul Capitolo sesto inedito di Marx*, Turin: Bollati Boringhieri.
Rosdolsky, Roman (1977) *The Making of Marx's Capital*, London: Pluto.
Roth, Regina (2012/2013) 'Die Herausgabe von Band 2 und 3 des Kapital durch Engels', in *Marx-Engels Jahrbuch*, vol. 2012/13, pp. 168–82.
Rubel, Maximilien (1974) *Marx Critique du marxisme*, Paris: Payot.
Rubel, Maximilien (1981) *Rubel on Karl Marx: Five Essays* in Joseph O' Malley and Keith Algozin (eds.), Cambridge: Cambridge University Press.
Shuster, Sam (2008) 'The nature and consequence of Karl Marx's skin disease', in *British Journal of Dermatology*, vol. 158, no. 1, pp. 1–3.
Vollgraf, Carl-Erich (2012) 'Einführung', in *MEGA*[2], vol. II/4.3, pp. 421–74.
Vollgraf, Carl-Erich (2012/13) 'Das Kapital – bis zuletzt ein "Werk im Werden"', in *Marx-Engels Jahrbuch*, vol. 2012/13, pp. 113–33.
Vollgraf, Carl-Erich (2018) 'Marx's further work on capital', in Marcel van der Linden and Gerald Hubmann (eds.), *Marx's Capital: An Unfinishable Project?*, Leiden: Brill, pp. 56–79.
Vollgraf, Carl-Erich, Jungnickel, Jürgen and Naron, Stephen (2002) 'Marx in Marx's words? On Engels' edition of the main Manuscript of Volume III of Capital', in *International Journal of Political Economy*, vol. 32, no. 1, pp. 35–78.

Part I

Capitalism, past and present

2 Revisiting the 'expropriation of expropriators' in Marx's '*Capital*'

Étienne Balibar

1 A displaced conclusion

'The Expropriators are expropriated' (Marx 1976a: 929) is one of Marx's most celebrated sentences, which is to be found towards the end of Chapter 24 of section 7 in *Capital, Volume I*. It is also one of the most enigmatic. I want to subject it to an exegesis at the same time literary, philological, philosophical, political and even theological: not for the sake of pure erudition (which would concern only 'Marxologists'), but to revisit some of the problems which, today, any idea of an *alternative to capitalism* is confronted with, when it may appear that historical capitalism (the category proposed by Immanuel Wallerstein (1983)) has entered a transition towards something like an 'absolute capitalism', with some apocalyptic features.[1] I am pursuing simultaneously two objectives: first, to clarify the sense of this formula, through an elucidation of where it comes from and what it does express at this specific place in Marx's text, written in a certain conjuncture; and second, to reflect on which problems that Marx addressed in his *magnum opus*, but left without a solution, it may indicate. And my underlying question will be: do we have, today, a clearer view of these problems? Or is it the case, on the contrary, that they have become even more enigmatic? Of course, it could be the case that all these questions belong, in fact, to a past that is foreclosed, only worth 'the gnawing criticism of the mice' (Marx 1987: 264); but even in that case, it would be worthwhile to undertake a rigorous scrutiny of a formulation and a thinker whose influence has been so great on our history and whose name remains a point of attraction for revolutionary expectations and the critique of dominant ideas.

Let me resume from the immediate context in which the formula is introduced, concluding a long syllogism. For lack of room, I only quote the final sentence in the indicated paragraph:

> The monopoly of capital becomes a fetter upon the mode of production, which has sprung up and flourished along with, and under it. Centralization of the means of production and socialization of labour at last reach a point where they become incompatible with their capitalist integument.

> This integument is burst asunder. The knell of capitalist private property sounds. The expropriators are expropriated.
>
> (Marx 1976a: 929)

The original 'German' has: 'Die Expropriateurs werden expropriiert', which any German reader will immediately identify as a 'Fremdwort', an *alien word*, among several others that pepper this eloquent development, in which dialectical form is combined with economic, historical and juridical content (a typically 'Marxist' combination). Several others are to be found: 'exploitieren', 'expropriiren', 'Usupatoren', etc., where Marx of course could have used more idiomatic German equivalents. This cannot be a loose stylistic improvisation, since Marx's writing in *Capital, Volume I*, is characterized by permanent accuracy in the use of the German language. We know that Marx wanted to be considered a writer as much as a scientist and a political essayist. This should be especially prevalent in a passage that formed the *political conclusion* of the whole book (and, to be sure, were continuously read as such in the Socialist tradition).

Here we face a first difficulty. I speak of a 'conclusion', but in which sense and to what extent is that the case? No doubt, the 'dialectical' idea of the expropriation of expropriators (also presented by Marx as a 'negation of the negation') names the 'end' of what Marx described in the book as violent process of transformation of the social relations, which is accomplished historically by capitalism and leads to a 'socialization' of the economy. Communism should be able to build on that result, provided it abolished private property and the corresponding power exercised upon labour. We are not surprised, therefore, that Marx immediately adds a *footnote* in which a passage from the *Manifesto of the Communist Party*, written (but hardly distributed) 20 years earlier, where the Communist revolution is announced, as the historical achievement of the proletariat:

> The advance of industry, whose involuntary but willing promoter is the bourgeoisie, replaces the isolation of the workers, due to competition, with their revolutionary combination, due to association. The development of large-scale industry, therefore. cuts from under its· feet the very foundation on which the bourgeoisie produces and appropriates products for itself. What the bourgeoisie, therefore, produces, above all, are its own gravediggers. Its fall and the victory of the proletariat are equally inevitable. (...) Of all the classes which confront the bourgeoisie today, the proletariat alone is a really revolutionary class. The other classes decay and disappear in the face of large-scale industry, the proletariat is its most characteristic product. The lower middle classes, the small manufacturers, the shopkeepers, the artisans, the peasants, all these fight against the bourgeoisie in order to save from extinction their existence as parts of the middle class (...) they are reactionary, for they try to roll back the wheel of history.
>
> (Marx 1976a: 930)[2]

In other terms, what Marx wants to indicate is the following: what could appear as a prophecy, to which the bloody suppression of the 1848 Revolutions had put an irreversible end, was in fact a very realistic anticipation. Through the analysis of the 'historical tendency of capitalist accumulation' proposed by *Capital* on the basis of its 'critique of political economy', it now receives an irrefutable scientific foundation. A knowledge of the 'laws' of development of capitalism and a forecast of the proletarian revolution meet precisely on this point. 'Marxism', often conceived as a 'fusion' of the revolutionary class struggle and the scientific theory of history, was built precisely on this certainty, for better or worse....

Yes indeed. But something is missing in this reading, calling for a 'symptomatic reading', which leads to one of the great puzzles in the history of modern socialism. It is simply the fact that the 'revolutionary conclusion' marking the 'achievement' of Marx's argument *is not at the end of the book*! It forms only the last paragraph in the penultimate chapter of the section on 'The so-called Primitive Accumulation' *die sogenannte ursprüngliche Akkumulation*, where Marx describes the origins of capitalism in the violent expropriation of small producers, which mainly took place in England (the '*locus classicus*' of modern capitalism), in the centuries before the industrial revolution. After this chapter comes still another one, on 'The Modern Theory of Colonization', which very few readers really take into account.[3] How can we explain this *decalage*, which prevents the 'end' to be located 'in the end place'? Given, once again, the careful composition of the book, we can't just see this as a mistake. We need an explanation matching the content.

One possibility would be simply that the end of Volume I is not the end of the attempted book. Marx's project evolved continuously, but in his 'last' plans, at the time of the publication of Volume I, he projected one or two more volumes, which remained as sketches after his death (later reconstructed and edited by Engels in his own way). Probably Marx believed that these would follow shortly, which would make it possible *then* to draw the practical lessons of the whole demonstration. But this suggestion can be reversed, leading to a reading that is more coherent with the text: after years of intense study of his material (economy, history, factory reports, etc.), Marx was convinced that he could *anticipate* the coming conclusions regarding the *overcoming of capitalism* and the consequences of its *internal contradictions*, at least in a general manner. This was even more necessary since the volume was published less than three years after the foundation (1864) of the International Working Men's Association (today known as 'First International'), whose General Council Marx coordinated (cf. Musto 2014). Through this organization, Marx wanted to interpellate the new generation of activists of the proletarian cause, which he saw as entering a new phase of development.

But if that is the case, why 'hide' the announcement of the 'expropriation' of capital, as it were, *inside* the text? Here another hypothesis comes to mind. I must admit that, for a long time, I thought it was the most convincing. Quite simply, it refers to *censorship*. As many other revolutionaries, or subversive writers, Marx had to struggle against this institution all his life. Occasionally he practised what Leo Strauss famously called the 'art of writing' in times of 'persecution' Strauss (1952). When *Capital, Volume I* was published in 1867 with a Hamburg publisher, it needed to pass through the censor's authorization in the first place. Perhaps Marx reflected that the not so intelligent police officials would look at the table of contents, plus the beginning and end of the book, would see there mere erudition, a 'scientific' treatise out of the grasp of the ordinary people, and wouldn't object. But, Marx, was hoping, real activists would have a closer look: they would find the 'expropriation of expropriators' in its place, and this would directly connect with their hopes and political objective. I am still including Marx's litigations with censorship in the understanding of his writing, but I am no longer certain that such an explanation is sufficient, because there is an *intrinsic difficulty* about the 'conclusions' of the argument in *Capital* that even the 'dialectics' of negation of the negation doesn't entirely resolve. Here, the *decalage* affecting the formulation of the revolutionary outcome of the 'historical tendencies' of capitalism must be considered a *symptom*. It had huge consequences in the subsequent history of uses and abuses of Marxism, which are still there with us, because *Capital* hasn't become a 'cold' text, but remains a 'hot' text: even today projects and plans of social transformation are made either 'with' *Capital* or, according to the famous Gramscian motto, 'against *Capital*' (Gramsci 2001), but never 'apart' from *Capital* with its analyses and prophecies.[4] Therefore we must go to the roots of the difficulties and enigmas harboured by the 'expropriation of expropriators' and, following Althusser's injunction, reveal its internal vacillation through a symptomatic reading.

2 Traces in the text

Capital is not only a book left unfinished by its author, essentially it *could not be finished*. Why was that? The thesis I want to defend now is: because its principal argument was leading to *several incompatible conclusions*. I will even submit that, becoming aware that there existed this logical uncertainty, did not content himself with a *passive* attitude, a 'victim' of his own writing as it were; but he decided *actively* to let some of the latent alternatives within his thought *become manifest* in the text, leaving it to us to draw the consequences – which leads me to suggesting that he 'unfinished' *Capital*, in the active sense. Let me show it by returning, first, to the complex references involved in the formula 'expropriation of expropriators', when we read it literally, trying to decrypt the multiple *traces* that overdetermine its meaning.

I just alluded to the strange accumulation of 'French' wording, more or less 'Germanized', in the surrounding paragraphs. Marx was born in Trier, a city of Rhineland full of French history and influences, where the memory of Revolution and Napoleonic Empire was very much alive. He was fluent in French and even wrote directly in this language one of his best-known early works: *The Poverty of Philosophy*, against Proudhon (Marx 1976b). Like some of his closest friends (Heinrich Hein, Moses Hess), he was convinced that France was 'the land of politics' (as England was the 'land of economy', and Germany 'the land of philosophy'). This accounts for a cultural tradition or a national myth, but there is more: in these passages from *Capital* we may read the insistence and continuity of egalitarian and 'proto-communist' movements during the French Revolution, particularly the 'Babouvistes' and 'Enragés' who thunder against 'expropriateurs', 'exploiteurs', 'usurpateurs' and 'accapareurs' (neighboring terms with which they defended the peasant uprisings and stigmatized the 'new class' of bourgeois owing their properties to the buying of Church estates, the military supplies and surrounding corruption, the privatization of 'commons'). Marx, who had wanted to write a history of the *Convention nationale* during the Jacobin period, had received this tradition through direct and indirect sources, the discourse of Utopian Socialism in the first half of the nineteenth century (Saint-Simonian, Fourierist, Blanquist), not least the pioneering book by Lorenz von Stein from which so many passages of the *Manifesto of the Communist Party* actually derive (von Stein 1841). The *quotation* from the *Manifesto* becomes clearer: even without using the word, it brings with it the idea of a 'revolutionary dictatorship', or a politics of *salut public* that counteracts a historical violence with another one of opposite intention. This marks at the same time a *continuity* from the 'radical' tendencies of the past 'bourgeois' revolution to the future 'proletarian' revolution, and a *progress* accomplished (rather: *to be accomplished*) by the latter over the former: in the meantime, the capitalist development will have transformed a utopian objective (equality among the producers) into historical necessity, reflecting the social form of the economy and the 'centralization' of the means of production imposed by capital.

I believe that this first layer of interpretation, that is suggested by the hybrid language invented by Marx, is rather indisputable. In a sense, this was not unexpected, because it concords with the use that Socialist parties, and particularly of course the Bolsheviks, made of the whole passage during the nineteenth and twentieth centuries, underpinning the great myth of the *new revolution to come* (the proletarian revolution, after the bourgeois revolution) (see Koselleck (1979). Interestingly, however, it doesn't exhaust the rhetorical dynamic involved in this figure: 'the expropriation of expropriators', or the *redress* of violence turned against itself. At this moment, we must invoke another register of meaning, which is not contained in 'pure' politics, but arises from the 'impolitical' element, in Roberto Esposito's sense[5]: a religious element that belongs to the treasure of eschatological hopes of liberation, periodically reactivated by apocalyptic and millenarist movements retrieving the tradition of Jewish and Christian Messianism. As I already indicated several times in the past (See Balibar 2015, 2014), the formula is a transposition of a key motto in the Book of Isaiah in the Bible: the great Book announcing the liberation of Israel from its enslavement in Babylon, from which then arise the great Christian theme of the 'remainder of Israel' – the ancestor of the 'Proletariat' – and the messianic name of the Redeemer, called

Emmanuel or 'God with us'. In Isaiah 14, 1–4, and again 27, 7–9 (King James Version), you can read the prophecy:

> And the people shall take them, and bring them to their place: and the house of Israel shall possess them in the land of the Lord for servants and handmaids: and they shall take them captives, whose captives they were; and they shall rule over their oppressors
>
> (Isaiah 14:2),

which is clearly a prototype of the formula in *Capital*.[6] Messianism of course is frequent in Marx, especially when it is a question of the revolutionary mission of the Proletariat, a radically disposed class whose rebellion will simultaneously put an end to capitalism and every historical form of a class domination.[7] However, the return of messianicism is especially remarkable in the 'conclusion' of *Capital*, because it comes at the end of the long development on the 'so-called primitive accumulation', where the expropriation of produces was described as an effet of the *State violence* that paved the way for the accumulation of capital. In this development, we find another messianic formula, which asserts that 'Violence [Gewalt] is the midwife of every old society which is pregnant with a new one. It is itself an economic power' (Marx 1976a: 916). In the Marxist tradition, this will be used to set up the comparison between the *violence of origins* and the *violence of end*. If you take the two formulas together, you can understand why the 'negation of the negation' doesn't simply have a *logical* meaning: it must evoke a decomposition of the institutional forms of law and politics followed by the 'birth' of a New Humanity in the midst of pain (what I called a moment ago the *impolitical*), it is the very symbol of radical historical transformations.[8]

3 Alternative tendency

The reading I just proposed pushes the idea of 'historical tendency' to the representation of an apocalyptic end. But it is not the only possible one, far from, since it has a reformist *double*, more precisely an *evolutionist double*, in which the forms of capitalist expropriation appear not only as *preparations* but virtual *instruments* of the collective appropriation called *association*, the very social form of future communism. We discover this possibility if we dig out from Volume III a development which, in a sense, is just a twin deduction of the 'expropriation of expropriators', but make a completely different use of the dialectical transformation of private property. As we know, *Capital, Volume III* is made up of texts written *before* the completion of Volume I, but published posthumously in a disposition chosen by Engels (much discussed today, but I leave this aside). The passage from chapter 27 on 'The Role of Credit in Capitalist Production' has acquired a special interest these days, because of its direct link to the analysis of 'financialization of capital', where Marx's category of 'fictitious capital' is at the same time referred to and criticized (see the discussion by Harvey 2013). There are three relevant passages. First of all, Marx wrote:

> This is the abolition of the capitalist mode of production within the capitalist mode of production itself, and hence a self-abolishing contradiction, which presents itself *prima facie* as a mere point of transition to a new form of production. It presents itself as such a contradiction even in appearance. It gives rise to monopoly in certain spheres and hence provokes state intervention. It reproduces a new financial aristocracy, a new kind of parasite in the guise of company promoters, speculators and merely nominal directors; an entire system of swindling and cheating with respect to the promotion of companies, issue of shares and share dealings. It is private production unchecked by private ownership.
>
> (Marx 1991: 569)

Moreover, Marx added:

> Expropriation now extends from the immediate producers to the small and medium capitalists themselves. Expropriation is the starting-point of the capitalist mode of production, whose goal is to carry it through to completion, and even in the last instance to expropriate all individuals from the means of production – which, with the development of social production, cease to be means and products of private production, and can only remain means of production in the hands of the associated producers, as their social property, just as they are their social product. But within the capitalist system itself, this expropriation takes the antithetical form of the appropriation of social property by a few; and credit gives these few ever more the character of simple adventurers.
>
> (Marx 1991: 571)

Finally, he stated:

> The cooperative factories run by workers themselves are, within the old form, the first examples of the emergence of a new form, even though they naturally reproduce in all cases, in their present organization, all the defects of the existing system, and must reproduce them. But the opposition between capital and labour is abolished here, even if at first only in the form that the workers in association become their own capitalist, i.e. they use the means of production to valorize their own labour (...). Capitalist joint-stock companies as much as cooperative factories should be viewed as transition forms from the capitalist mode of production to the associated one, simply that in the one case the opposition is abolished in a negative way, and in the other in a positive way (...). The credit system has a dual character immanent in it: on the one hand it develops the motive of capitalist production, enrichment by the exploitation of others'

> labour, into the purest and most colossal system of gambling and swindling, and restricts ever more the already small number of the exploiters of social wealth; on the other hand however it constitutes the form of transition towards a new mode of production. It is this dual character that gives the principal spokesmen for credit, from Law through to Isaac Pereire, their nicely mixed character of swindler and prophet.
>
> (Marx 1991: 571–3)

I gave these long quotations because this is less well-known than the passage in Volume I. It was never considered a 'conclusion', at most a side remark. But the formulas are very close, almost identical on crucial points. We find here the same hybrid French-German terminology of 'expropriation', to which is added 'association', one of the classical names of communism in Marx, and the same problematic of the 'dialectical reversal' which expresses the necessity of an overcoming of capitalism as consequence of its own internal contradictions. Above all we find the same idea that the essence of revolutionary change is a conversion of *expropriation* into *appropriation* [*Aneignung*] by the individuals of their own means of existence and their productive capacity, which had been 'estranged' from them [*entfremdet*]. Following another eschatological formula, capitalism thus becomes 'its own gravedigger'. However there are two essential differences with Volume I: first, by invoking the financial mechanisms of banking and credit, Marx goes much further in looking into the very institutions of capitalism for a 'prefiguration' of communism forms 'within the capitalist mode of production'; and second, the strategy of communism appears here as horizon of a combination or 'reconciliation' of two completely *heterogeneous* historical inventions, which however could be considered forms of 'socialization' or an overcoming of 'private property', albeit for opposite reasons: *socialization through money*, and *socialization through labour*, as it were. Summarizing all this, we see that the overcoming of capitalism depends on the emergence of a 'force' (whose exact identity remains to be found, or constructed) that can *join the opposites*: what is furthest from the classless society (the financial institutions), and what comes closest to making it alive in the present (the worker's cooperatives). Marx unfortunately says nothing about that force and the means it will have to make use of (including the State, excluding the State).

This is a variant of the 'expropriation of expropriators' that becomes today very relevant, not only because it forms an alternative to the messianic discourse, but because it finds echoes in some recent or current socialist projects. Still, we must concede that the 'opposite forms' that Marx wanted to unite remain, most of the time, separated terms. The idea of cooperatives (or, in the wake of Antonio Negri' s theories, the analogous idea of the 'new commons') is very much alive (See Hardt and Negri 2009). But, in a seeming paradox, the idea of using the financial structures of capitalism in a 'revolutionary' way is no less popular: not long ago, when big pension funds started to play a decisive role in financing shadow banking and the development of *hedge funds*, it was proposed by some European socialist theorists to 'redeem' capitalism through pension funds whose owners would be the workers themselves, or their unions (Aglietta 1998); more recently, we see Marxist (or Post-Marxist) analysts of 'liquidity' invent strategies for citizens to 'take power' within the financial speculative operations (Meissner 2016). This is a minor mode with respect to the great revolutionary tradition, but still a way of interpreting the dialectical scheme of transformation invented by Marx. I am convinced that we have to do here, not simply to a vacillation in the writing of the theory, but a genuine *alternative* rooted in the antithesis of 'private property' and 'collective property'. Before I draw some conclusions from this objective indetermination, however, I must make the picture even more complicated, invoking still another concept of the 'capitalist historical tendency' that can be read in *Capital*.

4 'Protracted civil war'

With much simplification, one could say that the central theme that is continuously redefined and complexified in *Capital*, as successive 'moments' of the dialectical relationship of capital and labour are succeeding one another, is an articulation of *contradiction(s)* and *antagonism* (or more generally *conflict*). A contradiction takes place between *tendencies* which are simultaneously unfolding, and periodically produce crises in the mechanism of the economy (e.g. the intensification of exploitation and the decreasing rate of profit, which Marx considers both consequences of the technological changes in a capitalist frame). Conflict essentially arises between 'classes' – in the first place the capitalist bourgeois class and the proletarianized working class – or also 'class fractions', which come to oppose each other because of their antagonistic interests in production, or the distribution of the product of labour, or in other correlative domains of social life. However, for a 'historical tendency' to exist that leads to transformations and mutations in the social relations, contradictions and crises must produce an intensification of conflict, and conflict must generate either a deepening or a displacement of the contradiction. This is the *object* of Marx's *political* theory of history (or theory of history from a *political viewpoint*), and there is no other. No doubt, in the passages that I commented, it is just this articulation, with conditions and effects, that was discussed. But alternative or even diverging possibilities emerge if we broaden our scope.

Take the long chapter on 'The Working Day': it is not only about illustrating the concept of 'absolute surplus-value' [*absoluter Mehrwert*], which had been defined as an *excess* of the value of the 'product' compared to the value of the 'labour power' (or 'labour force') consumed in the production, also 'measurable' as an excess of the amount of social labour time necessary to produce the commodities compared to the amount necessary to *reproduce* the labour power itself, or in 'equivalent' terms, to produce the means of consumption for the workers – what today would be called their 'real wages'.

It illustrates that there is permanent antagonism determining the *rate* of surplus-value (or rate of exploitation) that in turn leads to a contradiction, because it implies chronic underconsumption of the working class and a tendency towards the exhaustion of the labour power. In this conflict, the *interest of capital* is to continuously increase surplus-labour [*Mehrarbeit*], hence expanding daily (or weekly, or annual, in the end lifelong) labour time for the worker beyond any given limit. Whereas the interest of the working class is to *limit* labour time, which means a decreasing proportion of 'unpaid labour' (labour that is not compensated by worker's consumption) and a better protection of the living labour force (including individual organisms, the family, etc.) against exhaustion. This conflict is called by Marx 'a protracted and more or less concealed civil war between the capitalist class and the working class' (Marx 1976a: 412–3). Throughout the first half of the nineteenth century in England; following the worker's demand of a 'normal labour day', the relationship of forces was evolving, with the intervention of numerous factors: the degree of organization of the workers themselves (who first had to impose, against violent repression, their right to form unions), the counter-effects of the political revolutions on the continent, the attitude of the public opinion influenced by the 'factory reports' and the nascent 'sociology of labour', the *common interests* of the capitalist class, which are not the same as the interests of individual entrepreneurs in this or that branch, and above all the position of the *State* which seeks to 'regulate' the class struggle and keep the contradictions of capitalism within sustainable limits. What is fascinating, of course, is the fact that such description, provided some historical data are updated, remains completely relevant today, in particular because the 'wild' forms of exploitation of the labour power, which have been more or less completely, more or less provisionally eliminated from the 'central' region of capitalism through labour legislation, trade unionism, and the more general democratic evolution of society, have been massively transplanted into the 'periphery' (before partially returning to the centre as global competition and the 'neo-liberal turn' of the State eliminates the social rights and weakens the unions).

Which concept of 'historical tendency' can we associate with such a pattern? Here again we could be tempted to speak of reformism, but it seems more adequate, if we consider the long-term fluctuations in the relationship of forces, to use the same category as Marx himself: it is a *civil war*, or a *social war*, more or less 'declared' and 'regulated', which sometimes rises to the extremes, sometimes remains within the limits of a 'social contract' (that, in Europe, was the aim of the Social-democracy, largely inspired by Keynes). Contrary to the representation of the 'expropriation of expropriators', in either of its interpretations, this civil war doesn't have a predetermined *end*. We observe here in Marx's thought what could be called a 'Machiavellian' concept of the class struggle and its result, where the social reforms and the labour legislation in modern capitalist societies play a role analogous to that of the 'tribune of the plebs' in Ancient Rome.[9]

5 Total subsumption

Strikingly, Marx also developed an antithetic view on this point. Once again, we must look for it in the unpublished material, although very well-known today: the 'Unpublished Chapter Sixth of *Capital, Volume I*', also known as 'Results of the immediate production process' (Marx 1991: 1027–1047), a fragment from the 1863–1864 manuscript that, eventually, Marx decided not to rework it and not to include it in the final version of Volume I. Readers of this chapter are not at one to decide why Marx did not include it (or a revised version) in the final version of 1867, which was responsible for the reception and understanding of Marxism for more than one century.[10] Not discarding other elements, I tend to believe that a decisive reason lies in the potentially *nihilistic picture* (therefore also politically disheartening) of the 'historical tendency' of capitalism that can be derived from this chapter, for what concerns the articulation of 'contradiction' and 'conflict', the transformations of capitalism and the possibilities of class struggle. Why? Because the chapter develops and pushes to the extreme an indication only quickly sketched in Volume I, this time regarding the mechanism of '*relative surplus-value*': capitalism evolves from a mere 'formal subsumption' (*formale Subsumption*) of labour forces under capital (in which, individually, workers maintain a relative autonomy and capacity of resistance, based on their professional skills, which also fosters their collective projects of emancipation) to a 'real subsumption' (*reale Subsumption*), in which the labour powers are completely incorporated into the technological system and subjected to its norms, which makes them useless, unless they are subjected to the capitalist relationship of production, through machinery and 'scientific' organization of labour.[11] At the edge of the description, there is even the idea that capitalism not only *organizes the production process*, but also organizes the *process of reproduction* of life and everyday life, subjecting it entirely to the law of profit and the commodity form and making it the object of a new industry: an idea that was retrieved by theorists of the 'mass consumption' and the 'alienation of social needs' that it generates. At this point, admittedly extrapolating Marx, we could speak not only of 'real' but of something like a 'total subsumption', which produces a new form of 'voluntary servitude', an absolute control exercised by capital on the life of citizens (workers and non-workers alike). We may hypothesize that Marx – with despair – perceived that his analysis of capitalism's development lead to the possibility of a 'totalitarian' system, where class struggle is *neutralized*, reduced to impotency, because it is anticipated, instrumentalized or controlled by capitalism, if necessary through violence, but above all through the complete incorporation of the labour power in its own reproduction process. This is the absolute opposite of the 'Machiavellian' civil war that could be read in the chapter on 'The Working Day', and *a fortiori* of the revolutionary outcome for the contradictions of capitalism: a quasi-totalitarian biopolitics of capital becoming the social norm.

If this possibility did exist, it becomes understandable (or it can be imagined) that Marx decided rather to 'repress' the argument, or postpone its examination. This may have also led to substituting, at the last minute, the conclusion in which the tendency of evolution of property relations *validates* the 'optimistic' scenario of a 'political revolution' that expresses (or 'accelerates') the economic tendency itself, in a more 'secular' or a more 'messianic' formulation. At the end, however, if we consider *all the alternative scenarios*, which no doubt were not granted in Marx's writing the same validation, but really existed in his thought, we are faced with a *bundle of strategic possibilities*, where – on either side of the 'standard' idea of the 'expropriation of expropriators' (itself presented in two opposite manners) – we also have the political scenario of 'indefinite social war', and the nihilistic scenario of 'total subjection'.[12] And *for us, today*, Marx the *theorist*, the author of the theory of *Capital*, must be identified with this bundle of possibilities itself, less determined, but also more productive than in the 'Marxist' tradition.

6 Open work

Now I am aware that the reader/listener, who was hoping for a resolution of the dilemmas, leading to a definition of the *good interpretation* of Marx's 'conclusions' in *Capital*, is very unsatisfied (probably also bored by pedantic philological considerations). If not, what can we conclude? In my opinion this all means that *Capital*, as history revealed its structure, is unfinished in a *positive way*: it is, to borrow the category from Umberto Eco, an 'open work', therefore a work that *problematizes* different theoretical and practical issues (Eco 1989). What we observe is that Marx, analysing capitalism, as he was *progressing* in the analysis, also never ceased to *bifurcate* in the interpretation of the 'tendencies' and the political outcomes that they anticipated. These bifurcations are more or less completely explored, but in any case, they don't have a purely *subjective* meaning. They correspond to *real tendencies* in the development of capitalism, which are more or less actualized, depending on conditions, counter-tendencies, and the historical transformations themselves.

Today's capitalism is more than ever subjected to the 'logic' of endless accumulation and the maximization of profit, whose concept was derived by Marx from the critique of political economy. The sarcastic motto: 'Accumulate, accumulate! That is Moses and the prophets!' (Marx 1976a: 742) has lost nothing of its validity. But capitalism's institutions and social forms have considerably changed, particularly because it has been *globalized* (something Marx, despite his views on colonization as alternative to revolution, did not perfectly reflect, the reason why it should be invoked *against him* by some continuators),[13] and at the end of the globalization process it has been *financialized*, thus radically modifying the mechanism of crises, although not suppressing them, and even has proved able to draw a benefit from *socialist experiences* for its own modernization.[14] This capitalism that is 'post-historical' because it is post-colonial and post-socialist, may appear as unsurpassable and invincible, because it has dissolved the forms and classical representations of the class struggle around which such themes as 'expropriation of expropriators' were build and which served to imagine a revolutionary social transformation. This doesn't mean that it is stable or peaceful. Rather, it is ultra-violent, involving organically endemic wars, brutal segregations of humans divided into educated and non-educated, sedentary and migrant, efficient and non-adapted, useful and disposable humans, etc., in other terms a generalized 'Hobbesian' competition among individuals and peoples. For us, 'post-Marxists', the great question is how to define and construct the possible bifurcations, the immanent alternatives in this capitalism. This is a political and intellectual labour, for which a meditation on the various ways that Marx had tried to explore doesn't suffice, but remain indispensable. We must *rethink* entirely his theory, but embarking on this journey we find him continuously walking on our side, as a good companion.

Notes

1 I prefer to speak hypothetically of 'absolute capitalism', rather than simply 'neoliberalism', because I don't want to just address the dominant ideology, but the social structure itself.

2 This «quotation» is in reality a *collage* in *inverted order* of two passages at the end of Chapter One of the *Manifesto of the Communist Party* (Marx and Engels 1976: 494).

3 This is probably a mistake, since this chapter also deserves a «symptomatic reading», e.g. in the following manner: by including this chapter at the end, Marx would suggest that *colonization* is an alternative to *revolution*, or at least is a way to *postpone the revolution*, perhaps indefinitely, perhaps only to prepare a revolution on a *broader* (i.e. a world) scale.

4 In his *magnum opus*, Bloch (1986) contrasted the 'hot stream' of Marxism involved in the social struggles and the 'cold stream' of institutionalized Marxism. Gramsci (2001), a young theorist and leader of Italian socialism, strongly influenced by the 'voluntarism' of Georges Sorel, would greet the October 1917 Revolution in Russia in a piece with the title: 'Revolution against Capital', an extraordinary pun.

5 Esposito (1999) himself borrowed the notion of the *impolitical* (*l'impolitico*) from a long tradition, carried over by Thomas Mann (1918).

6 Marx, the son of a Jewish lawyer who converted to Protestantism when he was still a child, did not know Hebrew (although coming from a rabbinic family). He was indeed familiar as any German with the Luther version of the Bible.

7 See my essay 'The Messianic Moment in Marx' in Balibar (2016). I am greatly indebted to the various studies by Michael Löwy on the intersections of Marxism and Jewish Messianicism.

8 The potential of extra-institutional violence is involved in the idea of a revolution marking the absolute end of exploitation, and the beginning of an era of perfect freedom (entering the 'Kingdom of Liberty') – what the theological tradition called the 'Glory' – as indicated in *Capital*, Volume III (Marx 1991: 953ff., ch. 'The Trinity Formula Marx'). This was commented by various authors who, from opposite points of view, saw it as the key to the political uses of the dialectical idea: on one side Engels (1990), followed by Lenin (1894); on the other side Arendt (2000).

9 The reference is of course not *The Prince* of Machiavelli (which inspired Marxist theories of the revolutionary party, especially in Gramsci and after him), but to the *Discourses on Livy* (Book 1, chapters 1–5), a main source of the 'republican'

tradition in political philosophy. To my knowledge, it was French political theorist Lavau (1981), who first proposed this analogy. On the transformations of Marx's concept of 'civil war', see the appendix in the revised edition of my book (Balibar 2017).

10 According to some «plans», it should have become the *final section* of Volume I. For the same reasons as mentioned above, this development was therefore written *before* the development on the 'expropriation of expropriators' commented above, it is in fact *intermediary* between the *Grundrisse* and the 1859 *Contribution to the Critique of Political Economy* on the one hand, and *Capital,* Volume I on the other.

11 This means that, just as the scheme of the 'civil war', which invokes the labour movement, was based on the analysis of 'absolute surplus-value', the scheme of 'real/total subsumption', which makes its traditional forms inefficient, is based on the analysis of 'relative surplus value'. This is a crucial symmetry for the understanding of Marx's articulation of the critique of political economy and the political in *Capital.*

12 I must admit that the idea of organizing in this manner the *alternative possibilities* that are present in Marx, as explained here, owes much to the description of Stanley Moore (1963), in his remarkable little book: almost (but unjustly) forgotten today.

13 We think of theorists of imperialism, above all Rosa Luxemburg (1951), and later such theorists of the capitalist 'world-economy' such as Immanuel Wallerstein and Giovanni Arrighi.

14 I am increasingly inclined towards this hypothesis of a *post-socialist 'absolute' capitalism,* which seems to me necessary to understand the discourse and the aims of so-called 'neo-liberalism'.

References

Aglietta, Michel (1998) *Le capitalisme de demain*, Paris: Fondation Saint-Simon.

Arendt, Hannah (2000) *On Violence*, New York: Harcourt Harvest Book.

Balibar, Étienne (2014) *Equaliberty*, Durham, NC: Duke University Press.

Balibar, Étienne (2015) *Violence and Civility: On the Limits of Political Philosophy*, New York: Columbia University Press.

Balibar, Étienne (2016) *Citizen Subject. Foundations for Philosophical Anthropology*, New York: Fordham University Press.

Balibar, Étienne (2017) *The Philosophy of Marx*, London: Verso.

Bloch, Ernst (1986) *The Principle of Hope*, Oxford: Basil Blackwell.

Eco, Umberto (1989) *The Open Work*, Cambridge, MA: Harvard University Press.

Engels, Frederick (1990) 'The role of force in history', in *Marx Engels Collected Works*, vol. 26: *Engels: 1882–1889*, New York: International Publishers, pp. 453–510.

Esposito, Roberto (1999) *Categorie dell'Impolitico*, Bologna: Il Mulino.

Gramsci, Antonio (2001) *Selection from Political Writings 1910–1920*, London: Electric Book Co.

Hardt, Michael and Negri, Antonio (2009) *Commonwealth*, Cambridge, MA: Harvard University Press.

Harvey, David (2013) *A Companion to Capital*, Volume II, London: Verso.

Isaiah, *The Bible King James Version*, www.biblegateway.com/passage/?search=Isaiah+14%3A2&version=KJV.

Koselleck, Reinhard (1979) *Vergangene Zukunft Zur Semantik geschichtlicher Zeiten*, Frankfurt am Main: Suhrkamp.

Lavau, Georges E. (1981) *A quoi sert le parti communiste français?*, Paris: Fayard.

Lenin, Vladimir (1894) *What are the Friends of the People, and How They Fight the Social-democrats*, Moscow: Progress Publishes.

Luxemburg, Rosa (1951) *The Accumulation of Capital*, London: Routledge.

Mann, Thomas (1918) *Betrachtungen eines Unpolitischen*, Berlin: Fischer.

Marx, Karl (1976a) *Capital*. Vol. I, London: Penguin.

Marx, Karl (1976b) *The Poverty of Philosophy*, in *Marx Engels Collected Works*, vol. 6: *Marx and Engels 1845–48*, Moscow: Progress Publishers.

Marx, Karl (1987) 'A contribution to the Critique of Political Economy', in *Marx Engels Collected Works*, vol. 29: *Marx 1857–61*, Moscow: Progress Publishers, pp. 257–417.

Marx, Karl (1991) *Capital*. Vol. III, London: Penguin.

Marx, Karl and Engels, Fredrich (1976) *Manifesto of the Communist Party*, in *Marx Engels Collected Works*, vol. 6: *Marx and Engels Works, Autumn 1845–March 1848*, Moscow: Progress Publishers, pp. 477–517.

Meissner, Robert (2016) 'Liquidity', in Benjamin Lee and Randy Martin (ed.), *Derivatives and the Wealth of Society*, Chicago: The University of Chicago Press, pp. 143–73.

Moore, Stanley (1963) *Three Tactics. The Background in Marx*, New York: Monthly Review Press.

Musto, Marcello (ed.) (2014) *Workers Unite! The International 150 Years Later*, New York: Bloomsbury.

Strauss, Leo (1952) *Persecution and the Art of Writing*, Chicago: The University of Chicago Press.

von Stein, Lorenz (1841) *Sozialismus und Kommunismus im heutigen Frankreich*, Leipzig: O. Wigand.

Wallerstein, Immanuel (1983) *Historical Capitalism*, London: Verso.

3 'Every beginning is difficult, holds in all sciences'

Marx on the economic cell form of *Capital* and the analysis of capitalist social formations

Bob Jessop

1 Introduction

In the manuscript on Ludwig Feuerbach that forms part of the text known as *The German Ideology*, Marx and Engels write:

> we know only a single science, the science of history. One can look at history from two sides and divide it into the history of nature and the history of men. The two sides are, however, inseparable; the history of nature and the history of men are dependent on each other so long as men exist.
>
> (Marx and Engels 1975: 28n)[1]

When Marx and Engels broke with their 'former philosophical consciousness' (Marx 1987c: 264) after critiquing fellow young Hegelians and Max Stirner, they continued to follow advances in the natural sciences and to study human history. Marx's interest in nature and the natural sciences had profound implications for his developing critique of political economy and, indeed, in political ecology (on the latter, see Saito 2017). Later, writing on nineteenth-century scientific developments, Engels noted that Feuerbach (*1804-†1872) 'had lived to see all three of the decisive discoveries - that of the cell, the transformation of energy, and the theory of evolution named after Darwin' (Engels 1990: 372). The same holds, of course, for Karl Marx (*1818-†1883). Engels had already referred to the first two discoveries in a letter to Marx on 14 July 1858 (Engels to Marx, 14 July 1858, Marx and Engels 1983: 326),[2] when he referred to cell theory and thermodynamics; and Marx in turn had written excitedly to Engels about Darwin's new book, *On the Origin of the Species*, on 13 December 1859 (Marx to Engels, 13 December 1859, Marx and Engels 1983: 551).

2 The three decisive scientific discoveries

The most discussed of these three discoveries over many decades in commentaries on Marx is probably Darwin's theory of evolution (for a good review of the topic, see Pancaldi 1994). Indeed, his comments on Darwin while preparing *Capital* focused later attention on this discovery, which he and Engels praised as undermining teleological arguments in natural history just like they sought to subvert them in human history. In addition, Marx once suggested, half seriously in a letter to Ferdinand Lassalle on 16 January 1861, that Darwin had introduced the class struggle into nature with his account of natural selection as 'a struggle for life' (Marx to Lassalle, 16 January 1861, Marx and Engels 1986: 246–7); another letter strongly criticized Friedrich Lange's lazy, simplistic, bombastic, ahistorical, mock-scientific readings of Darwin's analysis (Marx to Ludwig Kugelmann, 27 June 1870, Marx and Engels 1988: 527). However, these epistolary remarks are less significant than Marx's use of the English natural historian's ideas in *Capital.* Thus, in the Preface to the first German edition of *Capital,* Volume I, Marx wrote that, for him, 'the evolution of the economic formation of society is viewed as a process of natural history' (Marx 1996: 10; cf. the afterword to the second German edition, 1996: 18). He proceeded to identify analogies between natural selection and the evolution of tools and technology in the division of labour (Marx 1996: 346; cf. 489–91; also, Marx 1989a: 387–8). He also presented competition as a crucial mechanism of natural selection in relations among those 'hostile brothers', individual capitalists, whereby 'one capitalist kills many' (Marx 1998: 252, 1996: 750; cf. Moseley 2002).[3] He also commented, perhaps semi-seriously, on 'natural selection' in the labour force (Marx 1996: 274–5); and he probably drew his contrast between a bee's *instinctive* hive-building capacities and the *pre-imagined* achievements of the worst architect from Darwin's discussion of hive-bees' 'inimitable architectural powers' (Darwin 1859: 227–8; Marx 1996: 188).

The laws concerning the conservation and transformation of energy imply that the whole motion of nature is reduced to its incessant transformation from one form into another (Engels 1990: 385). Their impact on Marx has generally been recognized far more recently than Darwin's influence, thanks to examination of Marx's *Exzerpthefte* (excerpt notebooks) from the 1850s onwards as well as the published and preparatory works for *Capital.* As Foster and Burkett note, 'Marx's political economy was unique in the 19th century in incorporating thermodynamics into the core of its analysis, thus providing the foundations for an ecological economics' (Foster and Burkett 2008: 3). An emphasis on the *correlation of physical forces* and their mutual transformation was a key theme in William Grove's book of that title (Grove 1846), much-admired by Marx, as well as the work of Hermann von Helmholtz. His interest was further demonstrated in his analysis of the transformative power of the steam engine in industrial production (Wendling 2009). For some commentators,[4] thermodynamics and energetics even facilitated Marx's turn from the classical political economists' concern with *labour* to his own interest in *labour-power* (*Arbeitskraft*) as the universal substratum of production and the key to its special status as a commodity. According to Anson Rabinbach, it was von Helmholtz, whose work was known to Marx, who introduced this concept. The German physicist extended the scope of the term '*Kraft*' (power) beyond its original context, where it denoted the forces unleashed by machines that converted chemical or heat energy into mechanical energy, to describe all of nature, including animal and human labour power, in terms of this sort of conversion and thereby included nutrition into his discussion (e.g. von Helmholtz 1853, 1995). Thus, 'labour, reconceived as a part of the continuous fabric of energy ... became *Arbeitskraft*, or labour-power' (Rabinbach 1990: 46).[5] Marx adopted this broad interpretation of *Kraft*. This influenced his analysis of labour-power as well as machinery, especially of human labour and machines as alternative forms of motive power (Marx 1996: 378ff).[6] Temporality and (ir)reversibility were also key emerging themes in thermodynamics (expressed in the idea of entropy) and crucial to Marx's exploration of the political economy of time. These ideas informed his analysis of the results of the direct production process, the division of labour, machinery, the substitutability of machines and labour-power, and so on. Moreover, writing to Engels on 24 August 1867, he reported that one of the two best points in *Capital*, Volume I was the two-fold character of labour according to whether it is expressed in use-value or exchange-value, the other being the treatment of surplus-value regardless of its particular forms as profit, interest, ground rent, etc. (Marx to Engels, 24 August 1867, Marx and Engels 1987: 407).

Nineteenth-century thermodynamics and cell biology shared an interest in metabolism (*Stoffwechsel*). This concept was developed in the 1830s by cellular biologists and physiologists and then applied in physics and chemistry (including Justus Liebig, another key influence in Marx's analyses). Marx applied it in his accounts of the metabolic relation between humanity and nature in the labour process,[7] emphasizing that it always takes socially mediated and historically specific forms (Pawelzig 1997; cf. Burkett and Foster 2006; Foster 2013; Angus 2018). He also applied the concept metaphorically in the discussion of the *conversion* and *reconversion* of different moments of the capital relation (commodity, money, etc.) in the expanded reproduction of capital (see also below). Indeed, it is the abstract possibility of ruptures in the conversion process that informs Marx's analysis of crisis. Thus, writing in *Theories of Surplus Value* (part of the 1861–1863 Manuscripts), he noted:

> The *possibility* of crisis, which became apparent in the *simple metamorphosis* of the commodity, is once more demonstrated, and further developed, by the disjunction between the process of production (direct) and the process of circulation.... The *general possibility* of crisis is the formal *metamorphosis* of capital itself, the separation, in time and space, of purchase and sale. But this is never the *cause* of the crisis. For it is nothing but the *most general form of crisis*, i.e., the crisis itself in *its most generalised expression*. But it cannot be said that the *abstract form of crisis* is the *cause of crisis*. If one asks what its cause is, one wants to know why *its abstract form*, the form of its possibility, turns from possibility into *actuality*.
>
> (Marx 1989a: 138, 145, italics in original)

The third major scientific discovery was 'the cell as the unit from whose multiplication and differentiation the whole plant and animal body develops' (Engels 1990: 385). Although cell biology evolved differently in different scientific communities in the early nineteenth century (notably France, Germany, and Britain), Marx's ideas on cell biology came initially from two German scientists, Matthias Schleiden and Theodor Schwann, who studied plant and animal cells respectively.[8] They discovered that both kinds of cell shared the same properties and they thereby established the unity of organic nature. They presented their joint discovery in *Mikroskopische Untersuchungen über die Übereinstimmung in der Struktur und dem Wachstum der Thiere und Pflanzen* (1839). Marx owned a copy of the 1847 English translation (cited here as Schwann 1910 and Schleiden 1910), underlining passages from the section on 'a general retrospect of the previous researches – the formative process of cells – the cell theory' (Schwann 1910: 161–201).[9] Marx also read other work on comparative physiology that discussed phylogenesis, ontogenesis, embryology, organogenesis, and how elementary cells could produce diverse tissues (e.g. nerves, muscles, ligament, cartilage, bone, blood, capillary vessels, epidermis, alveolar tissue, and teeth). These processes are crucial to cell formation, reproduction, transformation, metabolism, and so on.

Cell biology is the least often discussed of the three discoveries in relation to Marx's critique of political economy. Yet, I will argue in the next two sections, it had a crucial, if often overlooked, heuristic role in the development of Marx's method. The neglect of this role may have arisen both because the volume of excerpts and marginalia is smaller than for mechanics, chemistry, agriculture, etc., and because the relevant materials have not yet been published in the *Marx-Engels Gesamtausgabe*.[10] The theme is also less evident in published work. For example, Marx mentions economic cell form (*Zellenform*) or germ form (*Keimform*) only once each and elementary form (*Elementarform*) just twice in the three published volumes of *Capital* compared with 13 times for the more generic notion of simplest form (*einfachste Form*), which also has Hegelian connotations.[11] Conversely, he employs many other analogies, metaphors or references drawn from the natural sciences in relevant preparatory and published texts. One example, noted above, is *Stoffwechsel*, which figures in cell theory, physiology, physics, chemistry, and agronomy and was also applied to industrial production. This term occurs 28 times. More significant still, *Verwandlung* (conversion) and *Rückverwandlung* (reconversion) are mentioned over 1,300 times in the three volumes (my calculation). In addition, cell biology is easily subsumed into Marx's more general interest in physiology and its relevance to anthropology[12] and land economy.[13] Yet its significance for Marx's method is hidden in plain sight in his Preface to the first German edition of *Capital,* Volume I.

3 Method in political economy

The Preface remarks that 'every beginning is difficult, holds in all sciences' (Marx 1996: 7). This could be an indirect reference to Hegel's concern in the

Science of Logic with 'the difficulty of finding a beginning in philosophy', especially as, for Hegel, this was also a science, indeed, a pure science (*reines Wissen*) (Hegel 1998: 67; cf. Hegel 2010: 28).[14] More directly, it refers to the difficulties that Marx felt his readers might have with *Capital*'s opening chapters (Marx 1996: 7), which he reworked several times both in draft and across successive editions. In addition, it could refer, again indirectly, to the difficulties that the Physiocrats and their opponents found in finding establishing the starting point of political economy. For, as he wrote in *Contribution to the Critique of Political Economy*:

> The crucial issue was not what kind of labour creates *value* but what kind of labour creates *surplus value.* They were thus discussing the problem in a complex form before having solved it in its elementary form; just as the historical progress of all sciences leads only through a multitude of contradictory moves to the real point of departure.
>
> (Marx 1987a: 297)

Marx's quest for an entry-point also involved many contradictory moves. Thus, his comment could also refer to his own difficulties in finding the right starting point for his critique of the categories, practices, and dynamic of political economy.

These challenges pervaded not only the method of research but also the method of presentation that was appropriate for reproducing the real-concrete as a concrete-in-thought (see below). A fortiori, this also concerned the interweaving of phases of research, drafting, and final editing. Indeed, his intellectual development reveals that he tried several possibilities before eventually identifying the commodity both as the elementary or simplest form of capitalist wealth and, hence, as the starting point for his critique. These options are obviously conditioned by the ontological assumptions that Marx makes about his changing object of inquiry – the real-concrete both as it appears to the senses and as it is transformed into an object of scientific analysis. Thus, initially, his work in political economy began with the separation between state and civil society (Marx 1974a) and with money as a central component of bourgeois social relations (Marx 1974b); he then turned, with Engels, to the changing social relations of production and reproduction (Marx and Engels 1975), followed by use- and exchange-value, the division of labour, and the nature of money (Marx 1976), before returning to civil society (the bourgeois form of 'individuals producing in a society') in the unfinished Introduction (Marx 1986a) to *Contribution to the Critique of Political Economy*.[15] The account of method in political economy that he offered in the 1857 introduction is confusing because it juxtaposes two approaches that seem hard to reconcile with the approach that he eventually adopted in *Capital*.

The first approach involves the decomposition of a real and concrete precondition of production that remains an empty phrase, amounting to a chaotic conception of the whole, until it has been decomposed into its simplest determinations and then recomposed, this time as 'a rich totality of many determinations and relations' (Marx 1986a: 37). This approach corresponds to the 'descending' method of political economy in the seventeenth century and is illustrated by William Petty's *Political Arithmetyk* (1690) (Marx 1986a: 37). Adopting an analytical method, its 'comprehensive' starting point in the real world – here population – is, at the same time, 'the starting point of perception and conception'. In other words, population is the most visible form in which the object of national economics appears. Early political economy then aims to reproduce this 'real starting point' in thought 'as a synthesis of many determinations' (Marx 1986a: 38). While focusing on political economy, Marx also took the opportunity to criticize Hegel's phenomenology. Specifically, he attacks its idealist premises that take the real starting point as the product of the thinking mind rather than as having an existence 'outside the mind and independent of it' (Marx 1986a: 38–9).

The second approach takes the simplest (or most abstract) element of a specific mode of production as its point of departure. It then explores the historical presuppositions of the simple or abstract existence of this element (its 'concrete substratum'), how this elementary form develops historically into its most abstract expression and becomes articulated with other elements to form more complex moments of production, and/or how more complex moments can be derived logically, with due recognition of historical contingencies, from the simple, elementary form that is chosen as the starting point. This 'ascending' approach is characteristic of classical political economy, as exemplified in Adam Smith's synthetic method in *The Wealth of Nations*. Marx's praised Smith's theoretical breakthroughs but also emphasized the limits of his bourgeois standpoint. Nonetheless, with important corrections, reflecting his historicization of Smith's categories and, relatedly, Marx's emphasis on the formal rather than material aspects of capitalist production, the German also adopted the ascending approach in his emerging critique of political economy. He aimed to identify the historical *differentia specifica* of the capitalist mode of production (CMP) vis-à-vis elements common to 'production in general' (which he presented as a rational abstraction). Marx briefly illustrated this approach from Hegel's analysis of possession as the simplest legal relation of the subject as the starting point a philosophy of law. Then, referring to Smith, he considered *labour* (not, be it noted, labour-power) as the simplest element identified in classical political economy and comments on the historical conditions in which 'labour as such' (rather than specific kinds of labour) can become an abstract starting point for the analysis of modern political economy as labour becomes 'a means to create wealth in general' (Marx 1986a: 39–42).

In discussing the scientific basis for choosing a departure point, Marx stressed that it should be the social form that dominates all others in a given social formation. Where the CMP is this dominant form, the arrangement of categories (or order of presentation) must differ from the historical succession of different forms and reflect 'their mutual relation in modern bourgeois society' (Marx 1986a: 44). Thus, after presenting the general abstract determinations that characterize all forms of society, attention must turn to 'the categories which constitute the internal structure of bourgeois society and on which the principal classes are based' (Marx 1986a: 45). Next comes a progressive movement from more abstract-simple to more concrete-complex categories, culminating in the world market, which Marx describes in the *Grundrisse* as

> the conclusion, the world market, in which production is posited as a totality and all its moments also, but in which simultaneously all contradictions are set in motion. Hence the world market is likewise both the presupposition of the totality and its bearer.
>
> (Marx 1986b: 160)

The dialectical relation between external or historical presuppositions of the real emergence of a real-concrete totality and the subsequent positing of these conditions as internal presuppositions resulting from the consolidation and self-realization of the totality is a recurrent theme in Marx's analysis of capitalist social formations in this and other texts. As such, it indicates a debt to Hegel's *Logic* (cf. Uchida 1988), especially the concept of Notion, more than to his *Phenomenology*. It is also clear, as Marx noted in his afterword to the second German edition of *Capital,* Volume I, that he had coquetted with Hegelian modes of expression in writing it (Marx 1996: 19). But it does not follow that he followed to the letter the second method of inquiry outlined in the Introduction. This can be seen in Table 3.1, which indicates that Marx adopts a third method in the first edition (and subsequent versions) of *Capital* as compared to the various preparatory manuscripts. This owes far more to cell biology as a metaphor or analogy.

This comparison suggests that Marx took seriously Engels's comment, in a letter sent to him on 14 July 1858, that the discovery of the cell as an elementary form of organic life is reminiscent of Hegel's 'being in itself' (Marx to Engels, 14 July 1858, Marx and Engels 1983: 326, for further discussion, see the next section). This comment could have served both as a guide in the process of discovery and as a presentational device. There is a hermeneutic dilemma here. On the one hand, if too much attention is paid to the Hegelian form of presentation, one could miss the role of cell biology in pointing Marx towards the commodity as 'being in itself', as the simplest element of the CMP. On the other hand, had Marx paid overemphasized the role of cell biology in presenting his analysis of the commodity as 'being in itself', he would soon have run out of analogies and fallen into a 'mock-scientific', 'abstract materialism' (on the limits of the analogy with cell biology, see below). The key point here is that we must focus on the *substance* of the argument as well as its *form* of presentation and the substance is, of course, an unfolding of the *value form* of the commodity as the presupposition and posit of the unfolding dynamic, contradictory character, and inherent crisis-tendencies of the capital relation.

Table 3.1 From the 1857 Introduction to *Capital, Vol. 1* (1867)

	1857 Introduction		*Capital I <1867>*
	Method 1	*Method 2*	*Marx's method*
Example	Early Political Economy	Classical Political Economy	Critique of Political Economy
Starting point	Chaotic conception of the whole as it appears at first sight to a naïve observer	Decomposition of the whole by an informed theorist into analytically distinct but connected parts	Identify the ultimate morphological element that is also nucleus of all further development
Initial object	The real-concrete	Several abstract-simple elements	The simplest element
Method	Descending analysis into constituent elements to better grasp the whole	Ascending synthesis to create a rich totality that reproduces real-concrete as a concrete-in-thought	Logical-historical analysis of dialectical relations between the simplest element as both presupposition and posit of the whole

Source: original elaboration.

Thus, as Roberto Fineschi noted, the commodity provides the ideal starting point because it is not abstract content but a unity of form and content. Specifically:

> 1) … the economic cell must at the same time express *the universal character of the content and the formal determinacy it assumes in the capitalist mode of production.* The commodity seems to respond to this need: this is the criterion for choosing it [as the starting point]. 2) Its ability to represent at the most abstract level possible the unity of material content and social form is not, however, enough to characterize [the commodity as] the economic cell: *it must contain, potentially, in itself, the exposition of the whole theory of capital.*
>
> (Fineschi 2001: 44, my translation; italics in original)[16]

This excludes both the one-sided descending method of Early Political Economy and the one-sided ascending method of classical political economy. It requires a unique combination of (1) logical analysis based on 'the force of abstraction' (Marx 1996: 8) to identify the simplest social relation of the CMP that can be linked *in potentia*, by virtue of its inherent contradictions, to other bourgeois social relations such that what is initially an immediate presupposition is revealed, as the presentation reaches its conclusion, to be the product of the capital relation as an organic whole; (2) historical analysis of the genesis of specific economic and social forms and their changing significance in different contexts; and (3) attention to the empirical details of relevant contemporary examples of the CMP to identify emergent tendencies and/or demonstrate the plausibility of logical arguments. This can be described, controversially perhaps because of its negative connotations in other theoretical contexts, as a 'logical-historical method'.[17]

Marx develops these reflections on method elsewhere but nowhere in the detail that he once promised. On this promise, on 16 January 1858, he wrote to Engels that he intended to write a short book on method once he had finished *Capital.* This would comprise two or three printers' sheets, i.e. between 32 and 48 printed pages, and present 'the *rational* aspect of the method in Hegel's *Logic*' (Marx to Engels, 16 January 1858, Marx and Engels 1983: 249). Ten years later, after the publication of the first edition of *Capital,* Volume I, he wrote that, 'when I have shaken off this economic burden, I shall write a 'Dialectic'. The correct laws of the dialectic are already contained in Hegel, although in a mystified form. They must be stripped of this form' (Marx to Joseph Dietzgen, 9 May 1868, Marx and Engels 1988: 31). One way to understand these remarks is to recall that Hegel's *Logic* begins with the immediate, simplest, most concrete notion and then reconstructs it so that, 'although it is something thought, even abstract, the rational is at the same time something *concrete*, because it is not a *simple, formal* unity, but a *unity of distinct determinations*' (Hegel 2010: 132).

Igor Hanzel develops this argument persuasively in a recent analysis. He suggests that the commodity as a germ form is the equivalent of Hegel's elementary form:

> Why did Marx take this method from Hegel? The answer is, at least in my view, that Marx saw the strength of Hegel's method as proved by the fact that the latter employed it successfully in the construction of network integrating over two hundred philosophical categories. So, at least in my view, Marx could have viewed this method as suitable also for the construction of his network of categories of political economy. This network, according to my first tentative count, integrates at least 30 such categories.... Since Marx applied the cyclical feature of the method of ascent from the abstract to the concrete in Capital, it may seem that he made an attempt, like Hegel, at the creation of a network of categories as a purely self-justifying system. However, as shown above, Marx's network is, due to the methods employed in its construction, open to the theoretical treatment of new economic facts.
>
> (Hanzel 2015: 436)

In the absence of Marx's promised text on dialectic, we have four main sources for explaining Marx's method and his choice of the commodity as a starting point for his dialectic. These comprise Marx's *Preface* to the first German edition (1867); different editions of Volume I (1867–1883); the initially unpublished 'Chapter 6: Results of the Direct Process of Production' (Marx 1994), which was intended as a bridge at the end of Volume I to Volume II, and Marx's 'Marginal Notes on Adolph Wagner's *Lehrbuch der politischen Oekonomie*' (Marx 1989b). In the following two sections, I link these to the overall argument in the preparatory texts and published volumes of *Capital*.

4 The commodity as starting point

So, what exactly happened between 1857 and 1867 to prompt Marx to begin *Capital* with the commodity rather than one of the economic categories that get far more attention in the 1857 Introduction, namely, money, price, labour and wage-labour? Commodities are mentioned only once in the 1857 introduction and in relation to commodity prices rather than the commodity form. In contrast, money is referenced 11 times, capital in different forms appears 28 times, and labour and wage-labour together figure around 50 times. In turn, the *Grundrisse* (Marx 1987b) manuscripts begin effectively with Chapter 2, on money, which ends rather than starts with some remarks on the commodity (which largely rehearsed earlier arguments in the *Poverty of Philosophy*, 1847/1976), and then move to Chapter 3, on capital, which is ten times as long as the chapter on money. In contrast, by 1859, the first topic of Chapter 1 in *Contribution to the Critique of Political Economy* is the commodity as the 'elementary existence' (*elementarisches Dasein*) of the capitalist form of wealth, followed by a chapter on money, but without the promised chapter on capital.

The obvious theoretical and methodological answer is that the commodity is logically prior to the other forms of the capital relation mentioned in the 1857 Introduction. It must therefore be presented before the discussion of labour-power, money as money, and money as capital, which are the key categories for analysing the capitalist mode of production. Further, given that wealth in capitalist social formations presents itself (appears) as an immense accumulation of commodities, this starting point corresponds to Hegel's remark in the *Science of Logic* that one should begin with the immediate (Hegel 1998: 67–72, 77–8; cf. Hegel 2010: 27, 40, 134).[18] Likewise, the opening pages of *Contribution* and *Capital* both describe the singular commodity as the 'elementary existence' or 'elementary form' (*Elementarform*) of wealth in social formations in which the CMP is dominant.

In contrast to the 1857 Introduction with its focus on *method in political economy*, the 1867 Preface highlights *method in the natural sciences*. This analogy concerns their capacity to drill down to the micro-foundations of macro-level phenomena. This would hold for cell biology, thermodynamics, and Darwin's theory of evolution among other scientific discoveries. Indeed, Marx specifically cites microscopy and chemical reagents (staining agents for disclosing tissue structures), in an allusion to the newly burgeoning field of histology and its accompanying cell theory or cell doctrine.

> The value-form, whose fully developed shape is the money-form, is very elementary and simple. The human mind has for more than 2,000 years

> sought in vain to get to the bottom of it all, whilst on the other hand, to the successful analysis of much more composite and complex forms, there has been at least an approximation. Why? *Because the body, as an organic whole, is more easy of study than are the cells of that body.*[19] In the analysis of economic forms, moreover, neither microscopes nor chemical reagents are of use. The force of abstraction must replace both. But in bourgeois society, the commodity-form of the product of labour - or value-form of the commodity - is the *economic cell-form*. To the superficial observer, the analysis of these forms seems to turn upon minutiae. It does in fact deal with minutiae, but they are of the same order as those dealt with in microscopic anatomy.
>
> (Preface to First German edition of *Capital*, 1996: 7–8, italics added)

Marx then presents 'mikrologische Anatomie' (where micrological refers to the analysis of phenomena at a microscopic scale and is translated as 'microscopic anatomy') as the model for his point of departure, with a view to moving from the commodity as the economic cell-form of the CMP through the process of cell formation, differentiation, repetition (simple reproduction), and growth (expanded reproduction or accumulation) to provide a complete account of the whole organism formed by a social formation dominated by the CMP. Since microscopy cannot be applied in the analysis of social forms, it must be replaced by the power of abstraction. Abstraction is not a purely logical procedure. Instead, Marx focused on the English case as the closest parallel to physicists' observation of natural processes where they exist in their most typical (*prägnateste*) form with the least external disturbance and/or to their use of experiments in conditions that isolate the normal case (in German, *rein* or pure) (Marx 1996: 8). Later, Marx showed growing interest in the USA as a site of even more advanced forms of the capital relation regarding the enterprise form and finance.

So far, so good. But if the commodity is the simplest, most elementary, most immediate and self-evident form of the capital relation, why describe it as the economic cell form? A first answer seems to lie in Engels' and Marx's readings in physiology (cf. Han 1997: 115). Specifically, on 14 July 1858, Engels wrote to Marx

> One has no idea, by the way, of the progress made in the natural sciences during the past, 30 years. Two things have been crucial where physiology is concerned: 1. the tremendous development of organic chemistry, 2. the microscope, which has been properly used only during the past 20 years. This last has produced even more important results than chemistry; what has been chiefly responsible for revolutionising the whole of physiology and has alone made comparative physiology possible is the discovery of the cell – in plants by Schleiden and in animals by Schwann (about 1836). *Everything consists of cells. The cell is Hegelian 'being in itself'*

> *and its development follows the Hegelian process step by step right up to the final emergence of the 'idea' – i.e. each completed organism.*
>
> (Engels to Marx, 14 July 1858, Marx and Engels 1983: 326)

This observation could have been a trigger, especially as Marx acknowledges in a letter written on 4 July 1864, that, in the natural sciences, Engels is always ahead of him and 'I always follow in your footsteps' (Marx to Engels, 4 July 1864, Marx and Engels 1986: 546). He continued:

> During this time, being utterly incapable of work, have read Carpenter, *Physiology*, Lord, ditto, Kölliker, *Gewebelehre* [Histology],[20] Spurzheim, *The Anatomy of the Brain and the Nervous System*, and Schwann and Schleiden, on the cells business.[21]
>
> (Marx to Engels, 4 July 1864, Marx and Engels 1986: 546)

Around this time,[22] Marx also read Virchow's *Cellular Pathology* (Virchow 1857), which begins with a general introduction to cell theory. These texts all emphasize that the most elementary or simplest form of organic life is the cell and that, in different ways, reflecting disciplines such as histology, embryology, organology, and physiology, it is the point of departure for studying cell formation, the differentiation of tissues, and the arrangement of simple and more developed cells to produce a functioning organism.

Of special interest is that, in his personal copy of Schwann's *Microscopic Investigations*, Marx underlined these passages, among others, on cell-theory:

> The elementary parts of all tissues are formed of cells in an analogous, though very diversified manner, so that it may be asserted, *that there is one universal principle of development for the elementary parts of organisms, however different, and that this principle is the formation of cells.*
>
> (Schwann 1910: 165, italics in original)

> The existence of a common principle of development for all the elementary parts of organic bodies lays the foundation of a new section of general anatomy … having for its object – firstly, to prove the general laws by which the elementary parts of organisms are developed; and, secondly, to point out the different elementary parts in accordance with the general principle of development, and to compare them with one another.
>
> (Schwann 1910: 168)

> We have seen that all organized bodies are composed of essentially similar parts, namely, of cells; that these cells are formed and grow in accordance with essentially similar laws and, therefore, that these processes must, in every instance, be produced by the same powers.
>
> (Schwann 1910: 189–90)

Moreover, in an appendix to this text, Matthias Schleiden wrote:

> Each cell leads a double life: an independent one, pertaining to its own development alone; and another incidental one, in so far as it has become an integral part of a plant. It is, however, easy to perceive that the vital process of the individual cells must form the very first, absolutely indispensable fundamental basis, both as regards vegetable physiology and comparative physiology in general.
>
> (Schleiden 1910: 231–2)

We do not (yet) have the benefit of knowing what attracted Marx's attention in the other texts that he cited or might have learnt about through Engels or other friends and acquaintances who were practising natural scientists or interested in natural science might have cited. Among these, we can mention Roland Daniels, Ernst Haeckel, Thomas Huxley, Edwin Lankester and E. Ray Lankester, Carl Schorlemmer, and Rudolf Virchow. We also know that Marx attended popular lectures in London on the natural sciences and wanted to observe anatomy lessons (Marx and Engels 1986: 546).

Six principles of (economic) cell theory

Based on the above-mentioned texts and other pioneering work published between 1857 and 1867 that Marx was likely to have known directly or indirectly, we can distil six key propositions in cell theory:

1 All living organisms – plants and animals alike – are composed of one or more cells (Schwann 1847). Or, as Virchow expressed it: 'the cell is really the ultimate morphological element in which there is any manifestation of life, and … we must not transfer the seat of real action to any point beyond the cell' (Virchow 1858: 3, 1860: 3).
2 Following from this, the cell is the most basic unit (*Elementarteil*) of life (Schwann 1847).
3 Cells lead independent lives that, at least in animals, are shaped by the life of a larger organism of which they are part (Schwann 1847).
4 *Omnis cellula e cellula*, i.e. 'all cell arises from other cells' (Virchow 1855: 23, 1860: 27).
5 Cellular reproduction depends on metabolic exchanges with the environment (including other cells) that convert food/fuel into energy to run cellular processes, create the building blocks for cell formation, and eliminate waste.
6 Embryonic cells can – but need not – differentiate into other kinds of cell, generating the higher order forms (specialized tissues, organs) that comprise a functioning organism.[23]

These points find parallels, conscious or unconscious, in Marx's analysis of the commodity, the circuits of capital, and the differentiation of different moments of the value-form and other categories of the capital relation. Thus:

1 The living organism or *Gesellschaftskörper* (social body) of the CMP consists in the dynamic arrangement of the value-form and its cognate forms into concrete-complex relations (Marx 1986a, 1987a, 1996).
2 The elementary unit (*Elementarteil*) of the value-form is the commodity, which is also the economic cell-form (*Zellenform*) of the CMP (Marx 1996: 45, 8).
3 Commodities lead independent lives that are shaped by the life of the CMP of which they are a part – they are both the presupposition and the posit of simple and expanded reproduction alike.
4 *Omnis merx e mercibus*, i.e. all commodities from commodities. This can take the form of simple commodity circulation, i.e. C-M-C, or of the circuit of capital, with the potential for expanded reproduction, i.e. M-C-M′). As Marx wrote, '[i]n capitalist production of products as commodities, on the one hand, and the form of labour as *wage-labour*, on the other, becomes absolute' (Marx 1989a: 445, italics in original; cf. Marx 1989a: 375).
5 Production, distribution, and exchange are analysed as metabolic processes, examining how different elements are converted into each other and how a 'metabolic rift' can produce pathological effects in the overall production process as it unfolds in time-space (see especially Foster 2000; Saito 2017).
6 Embryonic contradictions in the commodity as cell-form (or germ form) of the value relation generate further developments in the capital relation. Thus Marx soon moves from the commodity to two of its special forms: first, labour-power (which also has a dual character as use-value and exchange-value and is also explored in terms of its dual character as concrete labour and abstract labour) (cf. Marx 1989b: 546); and, second, money as the universal commodity or universal equivalent, which is later analysed in terms of its metamorphosis into capital. It also provides the starting point for unfolding dialectically from the commodity form all the remaining forms of the capital relation can be unfolded dialectically from the value-form of the commodity.

All six principles merit extended treatment in a longer chapter. Here, however, I ignore the first principle to focus on the remaining five, which subsume and illustrate the first.

Ad 2:
The simple commodity (*not*, be it noted, simple commodity production as an actually existing historical precursor to a consolidated CMP, which was no part of Marx's analysis) is the presupposition of distinctive capitalist forms. As

Marx records in his marginal notes of Wagner's textbook of political economy, it was therefore appropriate to start from 'the simplest social form in which the product of labour presents itself in contemporary society, and this is the "*commodity*"' (Marx 1989b: 544). It was important to investigate the commodity initially in its purest form, 'the *form in which it appears*':

> Here I find that on the one hand in its natural form it is a *thing for use*, alias a *use-value*; on the other hand, a *bearer of exchange-value*, and from this point of view it is itself an 'exchange-value.' Further analysis of the latter shows me that exchange-value is merely a '*form* of appearance,' an independent way of presenting the *value* contained in the commodity, and then I start on the analysis of the latter.... Thus I do not divide *value* into use-value and exchange-value as opposites into which the abstraction 'value' splits up, but the *concrete social form* of the product of labour, the '*commodity*,' is on the one hand, use-value and on the other, 'value,' not exchange value, since the mere *form* of appearance is not its own *content*.
>
> (Marx 1989b: 544)

This argument directly affects Marx's chosen method of presentation. Hence:

> before turning to these [more developed] forms, the analysis of 'the 'commodity' – the simplest concrete element of economics ... must exclude all relations which have nothing to do with the particular object of the analysis'.
>
> (Marx 1989b: 545)

> ... when analysing the commodity, I do not immediately drag in definitions of 'capital', not even when dealing with the 'use-value' of the commodity. Such definitions are bound to be sheer nonsense as long as we have advanced no further than the analysis of the elements of the commodity.
>
> (Marx 1989b: 546–7)

Ad 3:
On this basis, Marx could then explore the 'double life' of the commodity: as a single commodity (which nonetheless presupposes that other commodities exist) and as an integral part of the overall logic of the capitalist mode of production. This is typically expressed in Hegelian terms as a relation between presupposition and posit. Thus, in the *Grundrisse*, he writes:

> Circulation therefore presupposes both the production of commodities by labour as well as their production as exchange values. This is its point of departure and by its own movement it returns into the production which creates exchange values as its result. Once again, therefore, we have arrived back at the point of departure: *production* which creates, which posits,

> exchange values. But now it *presupposes circulation as a developed moment* and appears as a constant process positing circulation and continually returning from circulation back into itself, in order to posit it anew.
>
> (Marx 1986b: 186)

Later in the same text he writes:

> If in the fully developed bourgeois system each economic relationship presupposes the other in a bourgeois-economic form, and everything posited is thus also a premise, *that is the case with every organic system*. This organic system itself has its premises as a totality, and its development into a totality consists precisely in subordinating all elements of society to itself, or in creating out of it the organs it still lacks. This is historically how it becomes a totality. Its becoming this totality constitutes a moment of its process, of its development.
>
> (Marx 1986b: 208)

This is further explained in the original draft of the chapter on money for *Contribution to the Critique of Political Economy*:

> Money and commodity, like their relation to each other in circulation, now equally appear as mere premises of capital, as, on the one hand, the form of its being; equally as mere existing elementary premises for capital, as, on the other hand, forms of its being and its results.
>
> (Marx 1987c: 497)

Likewise, in the *1861–63 Manuscript*, Marx comments on the commodity as follows:

> … the *prerequisite*, the *starting-point*, of the formation of capital and of capitalist production is the development of the product into a commodity, commodity circulation and consequently money circulation within certain limits, and consequently trade developed to a certain degree. It is as such a prerequisite that we treat the commodity, since we proceed from it as *the simplest element in capitalist production*. On the other hand, the product, the result of capitalist production, is the commodity. *What appears as its element is later revealed to be its own product. Only on the basis of capitalist production does the commodity become the general form of the product and the more this production develops, the more do the products in the form of commodities enter into the process as ingredients*. The commodity, as it emerges in capitalist production, is different from the commodity taken as the element, the starting-point of capitalist production. We are no longer faced with the individual commodity, the individual product.… [It is] a *part* both really and conceptually of production *as a whole*.
>
> (Marx 1989a: 301, italicization BJ; see also Marx 1989a: 356)

Similarly, Chapter 6 begins with the statement:

> The *commodity*, as the elementary form of bourgeois wealth, was our starting point, the presupposition for the emergence of capital. On the other hand, *commodities* now appear as the *product of capital.*
>
> (Marx 1994: 355, italics in original)

And, once more, in *Capital Volume I*, Marx declares:

> The *individual commodity - as the product of capital, in fact as the elementary constituent of reproduced and valorised capital* - displays the difference between it and the individual commodity from which we started out as the presupposition of capital formation, the commodity considered in its *independence.*
>
> (Marx 1996: 376, first and final italicization in original)

Ad 4:
In the unpublished Chapter 6 (written in 1864), Marx argued:

> The commodity is a direct unity of use value and exchange value; in the same way, the production process, which is a *process of the production of commodities*, is a direct unity of the labour and valorisation processes. *Commodities*, i.e. use value and exchange value directly united, emerge from the process as *result*, as product; similarly, they enter into it as constituent elements. But *nothing at all can ever emerge from a production process without first entering into it in the form of the conditions of production.*
>
> (Marx 1994: 387–8, final italics mine)

Ad 5:
I have already shown that Stoffwechsel (metabolism) is a recurrent theme in *Capital* and the preparatory works and that the processes of conversion (*Verwandlung*) and reconversion (*Rückverwandlung*) are the most frequent metaphor from the natural sciences. All three concepts are common to cell biology, physiology, and thermodynamics, making it hard to disentangle their respective influences. An interesting example from thousands occurs in the *1861–63 Manuscripts*:

> The *conversion* of money, which is itself only a *converted* form of the commodity, into capital only takes place when once labour-power [*Arbeitsvermögen*] has been *converted* into a commodity for the worker himself.... Only when the working population has ceased either to form part of the *objective* conditions of labour, or to enter the market as a production of commodities, selling its labour itself – or more precisely its labour capacity – instead of the product of its labour, does production become *the production of commodities* over the whole of its length and breadth. Only

> then are all products converted into commodities, and only then do the objective conditions of each individual sphere of production enter into production as commodities themselves. Only on the basis of capitalist production does the commodity in fact become *the universal elementary form of wealth.*
>
> (Marx 1989a: 359, italicization of conver* stem words by BJ, other italics in original)

To give just one further example, from the unpublished chapter 6 of 1864:

> The *conversion* of money, which is itself only a *converted* form of the commodity, into capital only takes place once labour-power [*Arbeitsvermögen*] has been *converted* into a commodity for the worker himself.... Only then are all products converted into commodities, and only then do the objective conditions of each individual sphere of production enter into production as commodities themselves.
>
> (Marx 1994: 359, my italics)

Ad 6:
Marx considered the commodity as the unity of exchange-value and use-value, as a unity of [historical] form and [universal] content (cf. Fineschi 2001). In this sense, the value-form of the commodity contains the embryonic contradiction that becomes the germ form (*Keimform*) of other contradictions. For example, the commodity form of value 'is a mere germ form (*Keimform*), which must undergo a series of metamorphoses before it can ripen into the price form' (Marx 1996: 72). In brief, the commodity form is the common principle of development for other forms of bourgeois society and therefore provides its most elementary form. It is the simple concretum from which all other forms can be derived through a combination of logical reflection and historical analysis (a logical-historical approach) in order, eventually, to reproduce the real-concrete as a concrete-in-thought, as 'a rich totality of many determinations and relations' (Marx 1986a: 37). This enables Marx to reveal the specificity of the CMP vis-à-vis the features of production in general (a rational abstraction) as he then moves on from the simple commodity to its two particular forms: the generalization of the commodity form to labour-power (which also has a dual character as use-value and exchange-value, reflected in the dual character of labour as concrete labour and abstract labour) (cf. Marx 1989b: 546); and the development of money as the universal commodity (and its subsequent metamorphosis into capital). Later, in *Capital,* Volume III, Marx discusses land as another special commodity (Marx 1998). More generally, contradiction is the mechanism that drives the metamorphosis of the value-form and capitalist societalization (*Vergesellschaftung*) and, as such, also creates the abstract possibility of crisis due to breaks in this metamorphosis or (re)conversion process.

Excursus on stem cells and DNA

As someone who kept up-to-date with recent developments in the natural sciences, Marx would have encountered the modern notion of 'stem cell' in the 1870s, in a period when he was once again busy excerpting works in this field. Given the cumulative knowledge about cells and stem cells since then, it is tempting to speculate that Marx might well have described the commodity today as the stem-cell form of capitalist social formations. But this notion was already implicit in the argument that cells could replicate themselves and differentiate into different kinds of tissue with specialized functions. Stem cell (*Stammzelle*) already appeared in the German scientific literature in the work of Haeckel (1868, 1877) to describe the ancestor unicellular organism from which he assumed all multicellular organisms evolved. By 1877, in the revised third edition of his book, *Anthropogenie* (translated in 1880 by E. Ray Lankester, a friend of Marx and Engels), he had extended the concept from evolution (phylogeny) to embryology (ontogeny) and suggested that the fertilized egg can also be described as a stem cell. That is, *Haeckel used the term stem cell in two senses: as the unicellular ancestor of all multicellular organisms and as the fertilized egg that gives rise to all cells of the organism* (Ramalho-Santos and Willenbring 2007, italics in original). Later, influenced by Haeckel, Theodor Boveri demonstrated that these cells were carriers of germ plasm and were the starting points for embryological development of differentiated body cells as well as germ cells. Boveri's concept of a stem cell included both a capacity for self-renewal and a capacity for differentiation (Maehle 2011: 11). Scientific confirmation of the role of stem cells came in the 1880s and 1890s from German cell biologists. A further discovery, which came in the 1960s, is, of course, DNA (Deoxyribonucleic acid). Several commentators have suggested that, had Marx been aware of the late nineteenth-century experimental confirmation of the nature and functions of stem cell or, indeed, of the discovery of DNA he would have described the commodity as the economic *stem-cell* form of the capitalist mode of production or, indeed, the *DNA* of capitalism (for example, Altvater 2012: 20–2; Rotta and Teixiera 2016: 1190; and, on DNA, Marsden 1998: 308, and 1999: 106–7; and, for a provocative but misconceived analogy with nineteenth-century embryology, see Wouters 1993).

Stem cells are vital to bodily renewal and embryonic stem cells differentiate into many kinds of specialized cell. This was already implicit in the idea that every cell develops from other cells and that the simple cell can generate different kinds of tissue (see above). Today, it is recognized that stem cells reproduce themselves through simple repetition but are also pluripotent, having the capacity to form very different kinds of cell with different properties and functions. Building on the remarks in earlier sections and employing the metaphor of the 'economic stem-cell form', I suggest that the value-form of the commodity can be seen from two perspectives: as the elementary unit of the capital relation that reproduces itself through the circuit of capital *and* as a pluripotent stem cell that can differentiate [logically and/or historically] into many other special forms of the capital relation that are often essential to its expanded reproduction – as well as further abstract possibilities for crises to erupt. The first dimension concerns the commodity as the elementary unit of the capital relation that reproduces itself through the metamorphosis in the circuit of capital in the form of M-C-M′ (or, in an earlier stage of the argument, as simple commodity circulation, in the form C-M-C). The second dimension – the pluripotency of the commodity form – can be elaborated conceptually by showing how the contradiction within the value-form of the commodity leads to differentiation, for example, with the development of wage-labour and money as special forms of the commodity and, subsequently, further forms of the capital relation. These are not simple expressions of the value-form of the commodity. They have their own specific properties, contradictions, and impact on the expanded reproduction of capital and the nature of capitalist social formations. While the stem-cell metaphor might enable these arguments to be presented more clearly, they are already implicit in the cell theory with which Marx and Engels were familiar in the years between 1857 and 1867, when Marx was drafting *Capital.* The heuristic power of these suggestions depends not on their capacity to restate what Marx already said but on whether they can generate new insights. That is a topic for another paper.

5 The limits of analogy and metaphor

As noted in the introduction, Marx and Engels believed in the unity of the natural and human sciences. However, while their critique of capitalist social formations and advocacy of socialism was influenced by their reading of the natural sciences, these were not the immediate grounds of their theoretical work and political commitments.

> The scientific basis of Marxism is not demonstrated by the number of natural scientific references, or analogies its founders insert into their works. Rather their approach to history, by basing it on a science (political economy), and by treating it in a scientific (that is, dialectical and theoretical) manner, rendered their socialism 'scientific'.
>
> (Mitchell 1978: 399–400)

Indeed, Marx and Engels were opposed to making categorical political arguments based on analogies with biology and other natural sciences (Darwinism, a cooperative republic of individual citizens akin to the cooperation of cells in plants or a monarchical cell state akin to their hierarchical arrangement in animals, a federation of cells, social colonies of cells, the state as an organism, the body politic, and so on (e.g. Weindling 1981; Reynolds 2008; Nyhart 2009; Sander 2012). This kind of argument was already criticized in the first German edition of *Capital,* Volume I, when Marx noted:

> The weak points in the abstract materialism of natural science [*abstrakt naturwissenschaftlichen Materialismus*], a materialism that excludes history and its process, are at once evident from the abstract and ideological conceptions of its spokesmen, whenever they venture beyond the bounds of their own speciality.
>
> (Marx 1996: 375–6n; MEGA^2 II-5: 303n)

A particular example, relevant to cell theory, was that contemporary German 'scientific materialists', such as Ludwig Büchner, Karl Vogt and Jacob Moleschott, invoked science, including cell biology and Darwinism, in their attacks on scientific socialism (see Mitchell 1978).

In another example of false or misleading analogies, Ludwig Kugelmann tried to use the publication of Marx's *Capital* in 1867 to convert the cell pathologist, Rudolf Virchow, a vocal and influential German liberal, to scientific socialism. In a letter written in early 1868, he informed Marx that he had sent Virchow a copy:

> P.S. In making him aware of your work, I told him how you regard commodities as cells, [how you] analyse bourgeois society, etc., that you follow the same method in political economy as he does in medicine: that your *Capital* could therefore be dubbed the social pathology of bourgeois society, etc.
>
> (cited in de Rosa 1964: 595)

Marx replied to Kugelmann on 17 April 1868

> You have done me a great service with your lines to Virchow, though I doubt whether he will have the patience and time to immerse himself in a subject out of his line. I know it cost me a great effort to read his *Cellularpathologie* [1858] in Manchester [see above, BJ], particularly because of the way it was written.
>
> (Marx to Kugelmann, 17 April 1868, Marx and Engels 1988: 13)

Another theme that emerges from stem cell science is, of course, the failure of cell replication and differentiation, leading to harmful or morbid developments in the organism. But the mechanisms of cellular pathology have nothing in common with the crisis-tendencies of the CMP, which must be grounded in its own immanent logic as this is grounded in the metabolism of the circuits of capital.

The principal limits to the analogy as developed above are presented in Table 3.2. In essence, whereas cells are the universal basis of organic life and operate through known universal chemical, physiological, and metabolic processes, the value form of the commodity as the economic cell-form of the capital relation is historically specific and its laws and tendencies are doubly tendential, in the sense that, they exist only to the extent that the

Table 3.2 Some limits of the cell analogy

Cell theory	*Economic cell theory*	*Limits of analogy*
All living organisms are composed of cells	Social body of the CMP is composed of value forms	Not a universal truth but historically specific
Cell is most basic element of life (single cells can exist)	Commodity is the elementary unit of CMP	A single commodity without other commodities is irrational, commodities are always plural
Cells lead independent lives but are shaped by larger organism	Commodities circulate as commodities but are shaped by the overall logic of the CMP	Cell theory's ontological claim vs Marx's methodological use of presupposition and posit
Omnis cellula e cellula	Omnis merx e mercibus	Not automatic for CMP: it requires generalization of commodity or price form to all inputs into M-C-M′
Cellular reproduction involves fallible metabolism (hence cellular pathology)	Production, distribution, exchange involve fallible metabolism (hence crises)	Metabolism of CMP is internally contradictory, conflictual, crisis-prone
Embryonic cells may differentiate into other kinds of cell	Contradictions in basic cell form generate more developed social forms	Ontological statement vs logical-historical analysis of successive forms

Source: original elaboration.

contradiction-rife and crisis-prone capital relation is reproduced in and through social practices that are historically contingent and contested.

A remark by Alan Freeman on the contrast between classical political economy and the critique of political economy is apposite here: whereas classical political economy regards capitalism as eternal and crises as external, critical political economy regards capitalism as historical and crises as internal to the logic of capital (Freeman 2010: 89). Mutatis mutandis, this could also be applied to the contrast between cell biology and critical political economy. For cellular processes are also eternal and, in general, less prone to systematic crisis (as opposed to contingent variation) than the circuits of capital.

6 Conclusions

This chapter explored three paradigm-shifting scientific discoveries that influenced Marx as he developed his critique of political economy. It focused on the least discussed of these in a Marxological context: cell biology. In contrast to the other two, it was cell biology that eventually guided Marx to his solution to the challenge that 'every beginning is difficult, holds in all sciences'. There are several good reasons why this influence has been neglected, which were explored above; but this is a pity because there are also good reasons for taking it seriously. In particular, I suggest that there are at least six key foundational principles of cell theory that could have inspired Marx's profound shift in the choice of starting point for his critique of political economy between the 1857 Introduction and the 1867 first edition of *Capital*. My argument is based only on the texts in cell theory with which Marx was acquainted, directly or indirectly, and on clues in Marx's relevant methodological texts, the economic manuscripts, and correspondence. Crucial here is the identification of the nucleus (cytoplasts) in cell formation, differentiation, and reproduction. The analogy in the commodity is the nucleus (*Keimform*) of the contradiction between use- and exchange-values as two necessary moments of the value form of the commodity.

Marx's idea that the commodity is the 'economic cell-form' of the CMP also provides a possible mediating link between the scientific presentation of Marx's critique of the CMP and his use of Hegel's *Logic* as a rhetorical – or coquettish – device in presenting this argument. Marx was well aware of the limitations of taking arguments from the natural sciences beyond their appropriate field of application and criticized the German 'scientific materialists' for doing so, especially where they invoked natural science to critique the scientific socialism that he and Engels were developing in the 1870s–1980s.

This explains why Marx's interest in cell theory belongs more to the *discovery* phases (the role of analogies and metaphors as positive heuristic devices as sources of inspiration and self-clarification, cf. Bertell Ollman in this volume) than to the more systematic *research* or logical-historical *presentation* phases[24] of his critique of political economy. In contrast, say, to thermodynamics, chemistry, or agronomy, it is not a crucial part of the research process in political economy, which focuses on the historically specific features of the capitalist mode of production. Thus, his focused more on material directly relevant to the critique of political economy (hence the stronger focus on other natural sciences) and his analysis of the commodity as economic cell-form did not seek exact parallels with plant and animal life. This is understandable in terms of the limits of the analogy between cell formation in plants and animals (a universal phenomenon) and the development of the commodity as the economic cell form of the capitalist mode of production (a historically specific, transitory development). Nor, given the limits of the analogy, could or should cell biology have played a major role in the presentation of Marx's scientific results in *Capital*. Its influence is more subterranean but no less important for that. For, in the logic of discovery, cell biology seems to have suggested ways to link the commodity as its simplest morphological element to the logic of the CMP and capitalist social formations considered as organic totalities. Recognizing the limits of reducing investigation of the social world to the logic of the natural sciences (whilst noting the unity of the natural and social worlds), it would make little sense to derive and develop the analysis of the CMP through strict analogical unfolding. Here the method of presentation relies on a logical-historical method that owes more to Hegel than to the pioneers of cell biology but also goes beyond Hegel because of its emphasis on the contingently necessary development and dynamic of the capital relation and their mediation in and through social action.

Notes

1 This contribution was inspired by re-reading Engels's comment on cell biology. Its final version has benefitted from e-mail communication with Pradip Baksi, reading Seungwan Han's book, *Marx in epistemischen Kontexten* (1995), comments by Riccardo Bellofiore, and discussion at the 2017 York conference with Moishe Postone. I dedicate this paper to Moishe's memory. All defects and errors are my responsibility.

2 In the text and references, MECW refers to the 50-volume *Marx-Engels Collected Works*, published in London by Lawrence & Wishart between 1975 and 2004.

3 Marx to Engels: 'It is remarkable how Darwin rediscovers, among the beasts and plants, the society of England with its division of labour, *competition, opening up of new markets, "inventions"* and the Malthusian "struggle for existence"' (18 June 1862, Marx and Engels 1986: 381).

4 In contrast, Biernacki (1996: 42–43) suggests that labour power was an everyday term in nineteenth-century Germany and Marx would have easily learnt it there. But Marx referred to *Arbeitsvermögen* (labouring capacity) in earlier work, employing it and *Arbeitskraft* in the *Grundrisse* and, increasingly thereafter, *Arbeitskraft* alone (my calculations).

5 The issue is perhaps less clear-cut than Rabinbach suggests: von Helmholtz mentioned *bewegende Kraft, mechanische Arbeit*, and *Arbeit* as well as *Arbeitskraft*, (Kuhn 1977: 88n) and, later, living power (*lebendige Kraft*) (my reading).

6

> As soon as man, instead of working with an implement on the subject of his labour, becomes merely the motive power of an implement-machine, it is a mere accident that motive power takes the disguise of human muscle; and it may equally well take the form of wind, water or steam.
>
> (Marx 1996: 378)

7 Interestingly, von Helmholtz discusses nutrition in these terms in relation to the reproduction of labour power in animals and humans (von Helmholtz 1995: 36–8).

8 He later read French cellular theorists.

9 On the passages underlined or marked as important, see *MEGA*^{2} IV-32: 593.

10 Namely, *MEGA*^{2} *IV-10, IV-18*, and *IV-22/23*.

11 Hegel's *Science of Logic* (shorter version) recommends starting with the simplest form and then moving stepwise to the totality considered as a concrete-in-thought.

12 For example, Marx and Engels both posted detailed comments in 1851 to their close friend, Roland Daniels, on his manuscript, *Mikrokosmos: Entwurf einer physiologische Anthropologie*, which was first published in 1988.

13 For example, Schleiden and Schmid (1850), annotated by Marx, consider, inter alia, the relevance of plant and animal physiology to land economy.

14 Anneliese Griese records that, beween April 1860 and May 1863, Marx copied extracts from Hegel's *Enzyklopedie der philosophischen Wissenschaften im Grundrisse* (the shorter logic), especially Paragraphs 83–111, concerned with the doctrine of being, the importance of *Denkformen*, such as quantity-quality-measure, and the relation between existence and essence (Griese 1997: 32).

15 For an excellent critical commentary on the 1857 introduction, including its theoretical context and references, see Jánoska,Bondeli, Kindle and Hofer (1994).

16 Cf. McCarthy on the commodity as the 'simplest category', the '*Keimform*' (or germ form), that 'contains within itself the totality of all forms of capitalist social structure and their contradictions of the capital relation' (McCarthy 1988: 115–16).

17 'Logical-historical' is used here idiosyncratically to capture the essence of the three elements combined in Marx's method. This usage differs from four other accounts: (1) economic categories should be introduced in the sequence in which they were historically decisive, an approach explicitly rejected by Marx in the 1857 Introduction in favour of presenting them in terms of their organic relations in modern bourgeois society (Marx 1986a: 44); (2) a claim that Marx opted for a logical method of presentation over an historical narrative but this is 'nothing but the historical method, stripped of interfering contingencies' (Engels 1980: 475), a view dismissed by Albritton for assuming that 'a hyphen would allow us to slide easily from the theoretical to the historical and back' (Albritton 1986, 15) and by Arthur for conflating the historical dialectic and systematic dialectic (Arthur 1998, 447); (3) the *Ableitung* approach, which seeks to unfold all concepts through logical derivation, and the systematic dialectic (e.g. Arthur 1998), which explores the links among economic categories, showing how each step reveals further aspects of the organic totality that is the CMP; and (4) the philosophy of internal relations, which lacks the sophisticated presupposition-posit approach of systematic dialectics, and focuses on the internal connections of all categories within an organic totality. *Ableitung* ignores the fact that, as the analysis moves from abstract-simple derivation towards concrete-complex articulation, the real relations among categories and their actual links become more contingent – they could have been otherwise – with forms shaping, without determining, development in a dynamic that has no telos that is shaped by class and other forms of agency. The fourth approach mistakes a contingent and potentially reversible process of totalization for an already achieved and stable organic totality. In contrast, for me, while 'logical' is close to Arthur's systematic dialectic and Fineschi's interpretation of Marx's search for the right beginning (Fineschi 2001), 'historical' does not refer to a historical dialectic. Instead it indicates the roles of historical inquiry in research *and* of historical and contemporary evidence in illustrating arguments and/or proving that abstract possibilities can occur in specific, overdetermined situations.

18 'The definition with which any science makes an absolute beginning cannot contain anything other than the precise and correct expression of what is *imagined* to be the *accepted* and *familiar* subject matter and aim of the science' (Hegel 1998: 49). The commodity is just such a phenomenon. Hegel continued:

> because that which forms the beginning is still undeveloped, devoid of content, it is not truly known in the beginning; it is the science of logic in its whole compass which first constitutes the completed knowledge of it with its developed content and first truly grounds that knowledge.
>
> (Hegel 1998: 72)

This also holds for Marx's method of presentation in *Capital*.

19 Kölliker's *Gewebelehre* (*Histology*) opens with two remarks: microscopic anatomy (*mikroskopische Anatomie*) has reached the point where it is just as much one of the foundations of medicine as is the anatomy of the organs and systems; and a basic study of physiology and pathological anatomy is impossible without exact knowledge also of the most minute, fine-grained [*feinsten*] form relations (Kölliker 1852: iii, my translation). His book first reviews the body's elementary parts (*Elementartheile*) and then the finer construction (*Bau*) of organs (Kölliker 1852: iii).

20 Histology studies the anatomy of cells and tissues of plants and animals using microscopy.
21 He first read Schwann and Schleiden in 1864 but the known excerpts and marginal comments only date from 1876 (on these see MEGA IV-31).
22 See Marx to Ludwig Kugelmann, 17 April 1868 (Marx and Engels 1988: 13), quoted later.
23 Schwann, for example, identified five types of human tissue that could emerge from an embryonic cell.
24 These phases are not sequential and linear but overlap and interact.

References

Albritton, Robert (1986) *A Japanese reconstruction of Marxist theory*, New York: St Martin's Press.

Altvater, Elmar (2012) 'Marx neu entdecken. Das hellblaue Bändchen zur Einführung', in *die Kritik der Politischen Ökonomie*. Hamburg: VSA.

Angus, Ian (2018) 'Marx and metabolism: Lost in translation?', in *Climate and Capitalism*, 1 May. Online at: climateandcapitalism.com/2018/05/01/marx-and-metabolism-lost-in-translation.

Arthur, Christopher J. (1998) 'Systematic dialectic',in Science & Society, vol. 62, no. 3: 447–459.

Biernacki, Richard (1996) *The fabrication of labour. Germany and Britain, 1640–1914*. Berkeley: University of California Press.

Burkett, Paul, and Foster, John Bellamy (2006) 'Metabolism, energy, and entropy in Marx's critique of political economy: Beyond the Podolinsky myth', in *Theory & Society*, vol. 35: 109–56.

Daniels, Roland (1988) *Mikrokosmos: Entwurf einer physiologische Anthropologie. Erstveröffentlichung des Manuskripts von 1851*, Berlin: Peter Lang.

Darwin, Charles (1859) *On the origin of species by means of natural selection*, London: John Murray.

de Rosa, Renato (1964) 'Rudolf Virchow und Karl Marx: Zu einem unveröffentlichten Brief von Kugelmann an Marx über Virchow (1868)', in *Virchows Archiv*, vol. 337: 593–95.

Engels, Friedrich (1980) 'Karl Marx, A contribution to the critique of political economy', in *Marx Engels Collected Works*, vol. 16: *Marx and Engels 1858–60*, London: Lawrence & Wishart, pp. 465–77.

Engels, Friedrich (1990 [1886]) 'Ludwig Feuerbach and the end of classical German philosophy', in *Marx Engels Collected Works*, vol. 26: *Engels 1882–89*, New York: International Publishers, pp. 353–98.

Fineschi, Roberto (2001) *Ripartire da Marx: processo storico ed economia politica nella teoria del 'capitale'*, Rome: La Città del Sole.

Foster, John Bellamy (2000) *Marx's ecology*, New York: Monthly Review Press.

Foster, John Bellamy (2013) 'Marx and the rift in the universal metabolism of nature', in *Monthly Review*, vol. 65, no. 7: 1–19.

Foster, John Bellamy and Burkett, Paul (2008) 'Classical Marxism and the second law of thermodynamics: Marx/Engels, the heat death of the universe hypothesis, and the origins of ecological economics', in *Organization & Environment*, vol. 21, no. 1: 3–37.

Freeman, Alan (2010) 'Marxism without Marx: a note towards a critique', in *Capital & Class*, vol. 34, no. 1: 84–97.

Griese, Anneliese (1997) 'Die Naturwissenschaftlichen Studien von Karl Marx. Zwischen philosophischer Tradition und modernen Wissenschaftsverständnis', in Griese, Anneliese and Sandkühler, Hanz Jörg (eds), *Karl Marx – Zwischen Philosophie und Naturwissenschaften*, Berlin: Peter Lang, pp. 15–44.

Grove, William Robert (1846) *On the correlation of physical forces. Being the substance of a course of lectures delivered in The London Institution, in the Year 1843*, London: London Institution.

Haeckel, Ernst (1868) *Natürliche Schöpfungsgeschichte*, Berlin: Georg Reimer.

Haeckel, Ernst (1877) *Anthropogenie*, 3rd edn, Leipzig: Wilhelm Engelmann.

Haeckel, Ernst (1880) *The history of creation*, translator E. Ray Lankester. New York: D. Appleton and Co.

Han, Seungwan (1995) *Marx in epistemischen Kontexten: Eine Dialektik der Philosophie und der 'positiven Wissenschaften'*, Berlin: Peter Lang.

Han, Seungwan (1997) 'Die Metapher der Zelle. Zur Rekonstruktion Marxscher epistemischer Kontexte', in Griese, Anneliese and Sandkühler, Hanz Jörg (eds), *Karl Marx – Zwischen Philosophie und Naturwissenschaften*, Berlin: Peter Lang, pp. 105–27.

Hanzel, Igor (2015) 'Marx's methods of theory construction: Categories, magnitudes, and variations of sizes of magnitudes under certain idealizations', in *International Critical Thought*, vol. 5, no. 4: 413–38.

Hegel, Georg Wilhelm Friedrich (1998 [1831]) *Hegel's science of logic*, trans. Miller, Arnold V., Amherst: Humanity Press.

Hegel, Georg Wilhelm Friedrich (2010 [1816]) *Encyclopedia of the philosophical sciences in basic outline. Part I: Science of logic*, trans. Brinkmann, Klaus and Dahlstrom, Daniel O., Cambridge: Cambridge University Press.

von Helmholtz, Hermann (1853[1847]) 'On the conservation of force' [trans. John Tyndall], *Taylor's Scientific Memoirs* 2: 114–62.

von Helmholtz, Hermann (1995 [1853]) 'On the interaction of natural forces', in von Helmholtz, Hermann, *Science and culture: Popular and philosophical essays*, Chicago: University of Chicago Press, pp. 18–45.

Jánoska, Judith, Bondeli, Martin, Kindle, Konrad, and Hofer, Marc (1994) *Das »Methodenkapitel« von Karl Marx. Ein historischer und systematischer Kommentar*, Basel: Schwabe & Co.

Kölliker, Albert (1852) *Gewebelehre des Menschen für Aerzte und Studierende*, Leipzig: Wilhelm Engelmann.

Kuhn, Thomas Samuel (1977) *The essential tension: Selected studies in scientific tradition and change*, Chicago: University of Chicago Press.

Maehle, Andreas-Holger (2011) 'Ambiguous cells: The emergence of the stem cell concept in the nineteenth and twentieth centuries', in *Notes and Records of the Royal Society of London*, vol. 65, no. 4: 359–78.

Marsden, Richard (1998) 'The unknown masterpiece: Marx's model of capital', in *Cambridge Journal of Economics*, vol. 22, pp. 297–324.

Marsden, Richard (1999) *The nature of capital: Marx after Foucault*, London: Routledge.

Marx, Karl (1974a [1843]) 'Contribution to the Critique of Hegel's Philosophy of Law', in *Marx Engels Collected Works*, vol. 3, pp. 3–129.

Marx, K. (1974b [1844]) 'Economic and philosophical manuscripts of 1844', in *Marx Engels Collected Works*, vol. 3, pp. 229–346.

Marx, Karl (1976 [1847]) *The poverty of philosophy. Answer to the Philosophy of poverty by M. Proudhon*, in *Marx Engels Collected Works*, vol. 6, pp. 105–212.

Marx, Karl (1986a [1857]) 'Introduction', in *Marx Engels Collected Works*, vol. 28, pp. 17–48.

Marx, Karl (1986b) 'Economic Works, 1857–1861', in *Marx Engels Collected Works*, vol. 28.

Marx, Karl (1987a [1859]) 'Contribution to the critique of political economy', in *Marx Engels Collected Works*, vol. 29, pp. 266–417.

Marx, Karl (1987b) 'Outlines of the critique of political economy (Rough draft of 1857–58)' [Second Instalment], in *Marx Engels Collected Works*, vol. 29, pp. 1–255 <*Grundrisse*>.

Marx, Karl (1987c) 'From the preparatory materials', in *Marx Engels Collected Works*, vol. 29, pp. 420–532.

Marx, Karl (1989a) Economic manuscript of 1861–63 (Continuation) A contribution to the critique of political economy, *in Marx Engels Collected Works*, vol. 32, pp. 3–541.

Marx, Karl (1989b) 'Marginal notes on Adolf Wagner's Lehrbuch der politischen Oekonomie', in *Marx Engels Collected Works*, vol. 24, pp. 531–59.

Marx, Karl (1994) 'Chapter 6. Results of the direct production process', in *Marx Engels Collected Works*, vol. 34, pp. 354–466.

Marx Karl (1996[1883]) '*Capital*, Vol. I', in *Marx Engels Collected Works*, vol. 35: *Capital,* Vol. 1, New York: International Publishers.

Marx Karl (1998[1895]) '*Capital*, Vol. III', in *Marx Engels Collected Works*, vol. 37: *Capital,* Vol. 3, New York: International Publishers.

Marx, Karl and Engels, Friedrich (1975) 'The German ideology', in *Marx Engels Collected Works*, vol. 4: *Marx and Engels 1844–1845*, pp. 19–539.

Marx, Karl and Engels, Friedrich (1983) *Marx and Engels Collected Works*, vol. 40: *Letters 1856–59*, Moscow: Progress Publishers.

Marx, Karl and Engels, Friedrich (1986) *Marx and Engels Collected Works*, vol. 41: *Letters 1860–64.*

Marx, Karl and Engels, Friedrich (1987) *Marx and Engels Collected Works*, vol. 42: *Letters 1864–68.*

Marx, K. and Engels, F. (1988) *Marx and Engels Collected Works*, vol. 43: *Letters 1868–70.*

McCarthy, George E. (1988) *Marx's critique of science and positivism: The methodological foundations of political economy*, Dordrecht: Kluwer Academic.

Mitchell, Ian (1978) 'Marxism and German scientific materialism', in *Annals of Science*, vol. 36: 379–400.

Moseley, Fred (2002) 'Hostile brothers: Marx's theory of the distribution of surplus-value in Volume 3 of *Capital*', in Reuten, Geert and Williams, Michael (eds), *The culmination of capital*, Basingstoke: Palgrave-Macmillan, pp. 65–101.

Nyhart, Lynn K. (2009) *Modern nature: the rise of the biological perspective in Germany*, Chicago: University of Chicago Press.

Pancaldi, Giuliano (1994) 'The technology of nature: Marx's thoughts on Darwin', in Cohen, Ierome Bernard (ed.), *The natural sciences and the social sciences: Some critical and historical perspectives*, Dordrecht: Kluwer Academic, pp. 257–74.

Pawelzig, Gerd (1997) 'Zur Stellung des Stoffwechselsbegriffs im Denken von Karl Marx', in Griese, Anneliese and Sandkühler, Hanz Jörg (eds), *Karl Marx – Zwischen Philosophie und Naturwissenschaften*, Berlin: Peter Lang, pp. 129–50.

Rabinbach, Anson Gilbert (1990) *The human motor: energy, fatigue, and the rise of modernity*, New York: Basic Books.

Ramalho-Santos, Miguel, and Willenbring, Holger (2007) 'On the origin of the term "stem cell"', in *Cell Stem Cell*, 1 July: 35–38.

Reynolds, Andrew (2008) 'Ernst Haeckel and the theory of the cell-state: Remarks on the history of a bio-political metaphor', in *History of Science*, vol. 46: 123–53.

Rotta, Tomas Nielsen and Teixiera, Rodrigo Alves (2016) 'The autonomisation of abstract wealth: new insights on the labour theory of value', in *Cambridge Journal of Economics*, vol. 40: 1185–1201.

Saito, Kohei (2017) *Marx's Ecosocialism: capitalism, nature and the unfinished critique of political economy*, New York: Monthly Review Press.

Sander, Kathrin (2012) *Organismus als Zellenstaat. Rudolf Virchows Körper-Staat-Metapher zwischen Medizin und Politik*, Freiburg: Centaurus Verlag.

Schleiden, Matthias Jakob (1910 [1847]) 'Contributions to phytogenesis', in Schwann, Theodor, *Microscopical researches into the accordance in the structure and growth of animals and plants*, London: Sydenham Society, pp. 229–63.

Schleiden, Matthias Jakob and Schmid, Ernst Erhard (1850) *Encyclopädie der gesammten theoretischen Naturwissenschaften in ihrer Anwendung auf die Landwirthschaft*, Bd. 1–3. Braunschweig: Vieweg.

Schwann, Theodor (1910 [1847]) *Microscopical researches into the accordance in the structure and growth of animals and plants*, London: Sydenham Society.

Uchida, Hiroshi (1988) *Marx's Grundrisse and Hegel's Logic*, London: Routledge.

Virchow, Rudolf (1855) 'Cellular pathologie', in *Archiv für pathologische Anatomie und Physiologie und für klinische Medicin*, vol. 1: 1–39.

Virchow, Rudolf (1858) *Die Cellularpathologie in ihrer Begründung auf physiologische und pathologische Gewebenlehre*, Berlin: Georg Reimer.

Virchow, Rudolf (1860) *Cellular pathology as based upon physiological and pathological histology* (English translation of second German edition), New York: Robert M. De Witt.

Weindling, Paul (1981) 'Theories of the cell state in Imperial Germany', in Webster, Charles (ed.), *Biology, medicine and society, 1840–1940*, Cambridge: Cambridge University Press, pp. 99–105.

Wendling, Amy E. (2009) *Karl Marx on technology and alienation*, Basingstoke: Palgrave-Macmillan.

Wouters, Arno (1993) 'Marx's embryology of society', in *Philosophy of the Social Sciences*, vol. 23, no. 2:149–79.

4 The challenge of transcending *Capital*

Leo Panitch

1 A passing stage?

In addressing why some of the terminology Marx deployed in *Capital* was entirely new to political economy, Engels' Preface to the first English edition of Volume One published in 1887, explained this in terms of it being self-evident that

> a theory which views modern capitalist production as a mere passing stage in the economic history of mankind, must make use of terms different from those habitual to writers who look upon that form of production as imperishable and final.
>
> (Engels 1938: xii)[1]

This distinction is indeed fundamental – and not only for theory. It is also fundamental for orienting socialist strategy and working class ambitions and capacities in transformative directions.

Yet as we look back today, we cannot but wonder about the implications, both theoretically and strategically, of already regarding capitalism in the second half of the nineteenth century as a *mere passing stage*? Indeed, if that had turned out to be correct, Marx's *Capital* would have long passed its 'best before' date far in advance of the 150th anniversary of publication. However great its contribution would still be for understanding the nature of capitalism as the previous mode of production, it would be of little contemporary relevance for understanding the world of the twenty-first century. It is by virtue of capitalism's longevity rather than brevity that Marx's great book has remained so very relevant, And this is all the more manifestly so amidst the spread and deepening of capitalist social relations in the contemporary era as the dynamics and contradictions of commodification and accumulation have permeated almost all facets of life around the globe.

The theoretical problems raised by treating capitalism as a mere passing stage go very deep. A foundational claim of historical materialism is that the capitalist mode of production is fundamentally different from those that came before it, not least in terms of its unparalleled transformation of nature as well as societies. It was this, moreover, that provided the basis for a materialist rather than an idealist vision of socialist possibilities, based on the notion of humanity being able to draw on capitalism's material legacy to finally overcome scarcity, conflict and the despoliation of nature. It is precisely because capitalism has not turned out to be a mere passing stage that we find even so many ecological Marxists speaking more about the end of world than any socialist future. Indeed, even without going so far as this, we cannot but recognize that the ecological conditions that capitalism has created will pose an awesome challenge for a post-capitalist socialist order.

The implications of having regarded capitalism as a mere passing stage must also be addressed in terms of the impact this has had on socialist strategy, and the ways in which working people as well as intellectuals were mobilized to support it. As Engels boasted in his Preface to the 1887 English edition:

> 'Das Kapital' is often called, on the Continent, 'the Bible of the working class'. That the conclusions arrived at in this work are daily more and more becoming the fundamental principles of the great working class movement, not only in Germany and Switzerland, but in France, in Holland and Belgium, in America, and even in Italy and Spain; that everywhere the working class more and more recognises, in these conclusions, the most adequate expression of its condition, and of its aspirations, nobody acquainted with that movement will deny. And in England, too, the theories of Marx, even at this moment, exercise a powerful influence upon the socialist movement which is spreading in the ranks of 'cultured' people no less than in those of the working class.
>
> (Engels 1938: xiii)

But what were they supposed to be learning from this new socialist bible? If it was primarily that capitalism was a mere passing stage, workers might well have been mobilized, organized and educated on the premise that it would be easier to get to socialism than it has proved to be. Most problematic was the notion that capitalism was bound to succumb to the economic crises it spawned. This is what underpinned Engels' claim that capitalism was a mere passing stage in his 1887 Preface. Over the two decades since *Capital* was first published 'capitalism's previous cycles of stagnation, prosperity, overproduction and crises' had been replaced by a 'permanent and chronic depression', as part of which the 'the industrial system of this country [England], impossible without a constant and rapid extension of production, and therefore of markets, is coming to a dead stop' (Engels 1938: xiv). It was on this basis that Engels urged the unemployed English workers whose number 'keeps swelling from year to year' to take heed of Marx's 'voice' as expressed through the 'life-long study' that had yielded *Capital*.

Marx actually sounded a rather different note in *Capital*, in fact, reinforcing in many ways the *Communist Manifesto*'s claims on revolutionary nature of the bourgeoisie's capacity to transform the world. The central remit of

Chapter XV on 'Machinery and Modern Industry' (at 140 pages the longest by far) was to unveil the process, whereby modern industry changed itself 'to take hand of the machine, its characteristic instrument of production, and to construct machines by machines.' While it traced the origins of this back to the first decades of the nineteenth century, what was especially significant was that 'it was only during the decade preceding 1866, that the construction of railways and ocean steamers on a stupendous scale called into existence the cyclopean machines now employed in the construction of the prime movers'. In other words, the capitalist 'revolution in the modes of production of industry and agriculture [which] made necessary a revolution in the general conditions of the social process of production, i.e. in the means of communication and transport' (Marx 1938a: 380) was really just exploding during the decade that Marx was writing *Capital*.

Although in his own 1867 Preface, Marx claimed that 'the progress of social disintegration is palpable' in England, the question of whether the 'birth pangs' of capitalist development which countries on the Continent were just going through would 'take a form more brutal or more humane' would depend on 'the degree of development of the working-classes itself' (Marx 1938b: xviii-xix).[2] In this respect, much could be learned from the 'history, the details and the results of the English factory legislation' to which he had 'given so large a space in this volume'. Notably Marx stressed 'the removal of legal hindrances' to struggles over wages, hours and conditions of the employed working class rather than the frustrations of the unemployed, as Engels would do in his Preface two decades later. But especially notable was the extent to which Marx looked to what was happening in the USA as more determining than events in Europe.[3] Indeed, the concluding pages of *Capital*, far from pointing to capitalism's demise, emphasized how capitalist production in the USA 'advances with great strides, even though the lowering of wages and the dependence of the wage-worker are yet far from being brought down to the normal European level' (Marx 1938a: 799). It was not capitalism's demise on its own accord which the final words of Marx's great book emphasized but rather

> the secret discovered in the new world by the political economy of the old world, and proclaimed from the house-tops: that the capitalist mode of production and accumulation, and therefore capitalist private property, have for their fundamental condition the annihilation of self-earned private property; in other words, the expropriation of the labourer.
>
> (Marx 1938a: 800)

2 *Capital*'s changing conjunctures

The conjuncture in which Engels wrote the 1887 Preface was very different than when *Capital* was published in 1867. The difference needs mainly to be understood in terms of the long capitalist world crisis that began 1873, and stretched on and off over the following two decades. What came to be called 'Marxism' would to a considerable extent define itself, as Dona Torr pointed out in her appendix to the 1938 facsimile edition of the English edition, in terms of the stress it laid on that crisis as the 'chief turning point … which marked the transition between two eras: the epoch defined by England as 'the workshop of the world' was passing to the epoch of imperialism and proletarian revolution' (Torr 1938: 847). Even before writing the 1887 Preface, Engels in particular had begun to speak, as he did in 1884 shortly after Marx's death, in terms of the 'inevitable collapse of the capitalist mode of production which is daily taking place before our eyes' (Hansen 1985: 36–7). This type of language was never far from earshot in Marxist debates from this time forward, including during 'the gilded age' before World War One. Indeed, the very prescience with which Marxism in this period theorized interimperial rivalry was rooted in an expectation that continuing limits to domestic accumulation would carry to new levels the export of capital and drive for colonies that defined the fragmented and competitive globalization process among national bourgeoisies and their states in the last decades of the nineteenth century.

Marxists theorists were especially influenced in this respect by J.A Hobson's classic study, *Imperialism* (1902). And Hobson was himself influenced by US business economists who in the wake of the deep US recession of the 1890s drew on Frederick Jackson Turner's 'closing of the American frontier' thesis to argue that the domestic market was no longer able to sustain the enormous productive capacity of the newly-emerged corporate form or provide sufficient outlets for the capital accumulated through it (see Cain 2002: 111–15). Their claims were, of course, soon to prove wildly wrong. By 1898 the recession had ended, and home markets continued to dwarf exports. The frontier may have been filled territorially but accumulation within it was only in its very early stages when Turner identified its 'closing'.[4] Ironically, these misleading American business notions of surplus capital also went on to influence the development in Europe of the theory of 'finance capital' – the institutional combination of industry and banking under the dominance of the latter to limit competition at home while aggressively advancing it abroad.

Marxist crisis theorists at the time not only seriously misinterpreted the kind of capitalism developing in the United States, they more generally underestimated the potential for domestic consumption and accumulation within the leading capitalist states. This was partly due to their failure to appreciate the extent to which the working class industrial and political organizations emerging at the time would undermine the 'immiseration of the proletariat' thesis that underlay Marxism underconsumption theories. But it was also due to their undeveloped theory of the state, which reduced it to an instrument of capital and underestimated its relative autonomy in relation to both imperial and domestic interventions. This shortcoming was also much in evidence among those Marxist theorists who rather than focusing on underconsumptionist crisis tendencies instead saw interimperial rivalry as based on the concentration and centralization of capital leading to the fusion of industry and finance. It was ironic that Hilferding's *Finance Capital* (1910), so highly influential despite mistakenly generalizing from German developments at the time, actually recognized that it was 'impossible to derive general laws about the changing character of crises from the history of crises in a single country … [or from] specific phenomena peculiar to a particular phase of capitalism which may perhaps be purely accidental' (Hilferding 1981: 288).

Many of these limitations in classical Marxist crisis theories have lingered to this day (see Panitch and Gindin 2010). This especially applies to the great concern on the part of Marxist economists with the empirical confirmation of a tendency towards a falling rate of profit, as posited in the later volumes of *Capital*, as edited and published by Engels *after* Marx's death. However, there was always a basic problem with this concept; the many 'counter-tendencies' that Marx himself adduced to explain why the tendency does not always manifest itself were, as often as not, the very substance of capitalism's dynamics: i.e. the development of new technologies and commodities, the emergence of new markets, international expansion, innovations in credit provision, not to mention state interventions of various kinds.

What the falling rate of profit thesis offered in terms of theoretical certainty it lost as an expression of historical materialism. Too often its presentation as an economic law tended to be ahistorical and its materialism tended to be mechanical. This was reflected in Marxism's undeveloped theory of the state, which reduced it to an instrument of capital and underestimated its relative autonomy in regards to openness to democratic pressures and shifts in the balance of class forces as well as in relation to imperial interventions. It was also due to the failure to appreciate the extent to which working class industrial and political organizations then emerging would undermine the thesis of the 'immiseration of the proletariat'. Whether the extraction of greater surplus value from labour could be counted on to offset falling profits would depend on capacity of labour to resist this. Indeed working class unions and parties not only expanded capacity to secure a portion of the surplus value yielded by increased productivity but also transformed was conceived as subsistence, reinforcing the crucial point on the first pages of *Capital*, where a commodity is defined as 'in the first place … a thing that by its properties satisfies human wants of some sort or another. The nature of such wants, whether, for instance, the spring from the stomach or from fancy, makes no difference' (Marx 1938a: 1–2).[5]

3 Going beyond *Capital*

None of this is to deny that the great value (if I may appropriate that term in this manner) of reading *Capital* today remains how much it helps to understand so much about the twin capitalist fundamentals of exploitation and competition that underpins capital accumulation in the twenty-first. But its value to us must also lie in the extent to which it can also help us understand how – in good part precisely through it being a system 'capable of changing' and in fact 'constantly changing' – capitalism persisted, deepened and expanded into the twenty-first century. This is not only a matter of what it helps us understand about the significance of new technological developments and changing patterns of commodity production and accumulation, but also appreciating the salience of both of these not only in terms of their spatial scales but also in their impact on local labour and consumption processes. It is also a matter of how far reading *Capital* today helps us understand why capitalism has *not* succumbed to the four great world economic crises it produced, including the present one.

Marx's Preface to the 1873 German edition noted that classical political economy's characteristic tendency to look upon 'the capitalist regime … as the absolutely final form of social production, instead of a passing historical phase of its evolution' could retain its scientific garb only so long as 'the class-struggle is latent or manifests itself only in isolated and sporadic phenomena' (Marx 1938c: xxii). In light of the highly successful continuing practice of the discipline of economics to present capitalism in ahistorical modular terms with no sense whatever of a past before it and of any possible future beyond it – which is itself reflected very extensively in popular perception – we need to ask how much this has to do with why and how and where class struggle has either remained or lapsed backed being manifest as 'only isolated or sporadic phenomena'.

In other words, we need to think about how Marx's *Capital* needs to be transcended in order to help figure out how to eventually transcend capital itself.[6] However valuable a window on Victorian working conditions is Marx's brilliant deployment of the factory inspectors reports, the presentation of such immiseration as an immutable law of capitalist development is obviously much less so. Yet even so, it does encourage us to ask where and when what might be called re-immiseration might occur. After the vast growth in wealth inequality, the defeat of trade unionism, the stagnation of wages, the growing precarity of work over the past four decades, there is much that sounds very contemporary in *Capital's* account of exploitation. 'Accumulation of wealth: at one pole is, therefore; at the same time accumulation of misery, agony of toil; slavery, ignorance, brutality, mental degradation, at the opposite pole' (Marx 1938a: 661).

Marx's comparison of the exploitation of wage labour to the exploitation of soil by capitalist agriculture at the end of Chapter XV together with his account in Chapter X of capitalists' resistance to state regulation of the working day and of factory standards, is especially relevant to what may well be termed mental degradation today across the whole class spectrum. The current undoing of environmental regulations under the Trump regime brings to mind Marx's footnote in that chapter which cites – 'contrary to what some employers were fond of asserting' – a senior hospital physicians report on the effects of night work on children's health: 'That such a question should furnish the material of serious controversy shows plainly how capitalist production acts on the brains of capitalists and their retainers' (Marx 1938a: 242). This applies to workers too. Just as in *Capital* Marx quotes evidence of the support capitalists were able to secure from their workers, whether 'through, bribery or threats', in their petitions against their own 'oppression' by state regulations of employment of their children or even regarding the length of the working day, so do we find the same thing happening in the case of environmental regulation today. A *New York Times* investigation on the rolling back of regulations to the immediate benefit of an energy company in Wyoming with which Trump's head of the Environmental Protection Agency, Scott Pruitt, had 'close ties', cites the support this got from Frenchie Warren, a member of the Arapaho tribe who, even though he had already lost his $23 an hour job as a workers in the energy sector after his hand was mangled in a chain, expressed his hostility to the EPA: '"They aren't helping us," Mr. Warren said. "If I had a gun, I'd shoot them"' (quoted in Tabuchi and Lipton 2017: 19).

This brings me finally to what has always seemed to me most needed in terms of transcending Marx's *Capital*, which is the further development of historical materialist theory of the capitalist state. Not that there isn't plenty of insight in *Capital* in this respect, beginning early in the volume with the observation in Chapter 3 that underpinning market exchange from the beginning is a 'juridical relation which expresses itself as a contact' (Marx 1938a: 56).[7] Marx's notion of the state acting 'as the trade union of the capitalists against the labourers' may be seen as no less insightful. Yet the actual passage where Marx coins the latter term also reveals its weaknesses. Marx claimed in this passage that it was only under the pressure of the masses that the English Parliament give up the laws against strikes and trade unions, after it had itself, for 500 years, held with shameless egoism the position of a permanent 'Trade's Union of the capitalists against the labourers' (Marx 1938a: 765). What this occludes is the long historical process of the state becoming capitalist through a logic of its own pertaining to securing revenue and legitimacy. Passages like this, which demand so much historical explanation and elaboration, especially in comparison with the minute but overwhelming attention paid to the intricacies of the categories of value, are precisely what led E.P. Thompson to lament that Marx had himself for a period been 'caught in the trap' of classical political economy's search for fixed and eternal laws independent of historical specificity' (Thompson 1978: 251–3).

In fact, the changes that state institutions undergo over time, including the shifting hierarchies among them, are the outcome of both incremental and contested processes inside the state itself. These are related to shifts in the balance of class forces but not reducible to them. Often confronting the very problems which capitalists could not solve for themselves, actors in the state, unlike capitalists, cannot avoid dealing with 'the law of unintended consequences'. Indeed, they are usually trained to anticipate other problems that will arise from taking certain steps, including upsetting relations and generating contestations among states institutions themselves. This is true not only for career civil servants, but even for those who have entered the state from the business world, but who, once embedded in state institutions, take on responsibilities specifically framed by those institutions. Understanding what states have actually done that capitalist classes themselves could not do in promoting and sustaining capital accumulation and social relations is in fact crucial to answering the question of why capitalism has survived into the twenty-first century (see Panitch and Gindin 2015).

But no less crucial is our responsibility as Marxist intellectuals is to contribute to understanding how states would need to undergo fundamental transformation in the process of transcending capitalism (see Panitch and Gindin 2016). To stress the importance of a socialist strategy for entering the state to the end of transforming the state is today less than ever – amidst the deep political and social as well as economic contradictions of the neoliberal era – a matter of discovering a smooth gradual road to socialism. Ruptures, or extended series of ruptures of various intensities, are inescapable. This is so because of the contradictions inherent in reaching beyond capitalism while still being of it, and the virtual inevitability of conditions being premature as the project is attempted in circumstances not of our own choosing. The contradictions for any radical government that would be engaged in this process will include responsibilities for managing a capitalist economy that is likely in crisis while simultaneously trying to satisfy popular expectations for the promised relief, and yet also embarking on the longer-term commitment to transform the state, i.e. not pushing the latter off to an indefinite future.

This is why strategic preparations undertaken well before entering the state on how to avoid replicating the non-transformative experience with social democracy are so very important. But even with this, the process of transforming the state cannot help but be complex, uncertain, crisis-ridden, with repeated interruptions and possibly even reversals. Beginning with local or regional levels of the state might allow for developing capacities of state transformation before coming to national power. Developing alternative means of producing and distributing food, health care and other necessities depends on autonomous movements moving in these directions through takeovers of land, idle buildings, threatened factories and transportation networks. All this in turn would have to be supported and furthered through more radical changes in the state that would range over time from codifying new collective property rights to developing and coordinating agencies of democratic planning. At some points in this process more or less dramatic initiatives of nationalization and socialization of industry and finance would have to take place.

For state apparatuses to be transformed so as to play these roles, their institutional modalities would need to undergo fundamental transformations, given how they are now structured so as to reproduce capitalist social relations. State employees would need to become explicit agents of transformation, aided and sustained in this respect by their unions and the broader labour movement. Rather than expressing defensive particularism, unions themselves would need to be changed fundamentally so as to actively be engaged in developing state workers' transformational capacities, including by establishing councils that link them to the recipients of state services.

Such reflections on the state must be part of envisioning a socialist order of a kind which Marx, far from ignoring, neatly outlined quite near the beginning of *Capital.*

> Let us now picture to ourselves, by way of change, a community of free individuals, carrying on their work with the means of production in common, in which the labour power of all the different individuals is consciously applied as the combined labour-power of the community.... The total-product of our community is a social product. One portion serves as fresh means of production and remains social.... But another portion is consumed by the members as means of subsistence. A distribution of this portion amongst them is consequently necessary. The mode of this distribution will vary; with the productive organization of the community, and the degree of historical development attained by the producers. We will assume, but merely for the sake of a parallel with the production of commodities, that the share of each individual in the means of subsistence is determined by his labour-time. Labour-time would, in that case, play a double part. Its apportionment in accordance with a definite social plan maintains the proper proportion between the different kinds of work to be done and the various wants of the community.
>
> (Marx 1938a: 50)

Notes

1 This 'reprint entirely re-set page for page from the stereotyped edition of 1889' includes a supplement with prefaces, changes and notes on the fourth German edition and on the French and English editions by Dona Torr.

2 At the end of his Preface to the second German edition published in 1873, Marx notes 'the preliminary stage' to a 'universal crisis ... once again approaching' (Marx 1938c: xxxi).

3 The American civil war, he argued in the 1867 Preface, had 'sounding the tocsin' for the European working classes just as the American war of independence had for the European middle classes at the end of the eighteenth century (Marx 1938b: xvii). This reinforced the argument advanced in Chapter X on *The Working Day*:

> In the United States of North America, every independent movement of the workers was paralysed so long as slavery disfigured a part of the Republic. Labour cannot emancipate itself in the white skin where in the black it is branded. But out of death of slavery a new life at once arose. The first fruit of the Civil War was the eight hours' agitation that ran with the seven leagued boots of the locomotive from the Atlantic to the Pacific, from New England to California.
>
> (Marx 1938a: 287)

4
> The transcontinental railway symbolized the completion of the national territory – by the 1860s America was a linked continental empire. But distant connections to isolated Western towns and farms, Pony Express mail service, and peripheral mudflats like Los Angeles, do not a national market make. Instead for fifty years (roughly from 1890 to 1940) Americans peopled and filled in the national territory. At the same time that the US became the leading industrial power in the world … the dominant tendency was expansion to the coast and exploitation of a vast and relatively new market.
>
> (Cumings 1999: 282)

5 To which Marx added a note, quoting from Nicolas Barbon: 'Desire implies want; it is the appetite of the mind, and as natural as hunger to the body.… The greatest number (of things) have their value from supplying the wants of the mind.'

6 One cannot help being struck by how arcane some of what is in Volume I appears today The extensive discussion on gold, let alone silver, might not have appeared to be of mainly historical interest as late as 1971 before the crumbling of the Bretton Woods agreement's attempt to keep the Gold Standard on limited life support as a façade for the American dollar as capitalism's works currency. But today almost a half century on, Capital's pages on gold seem very arcane indeed.

7 In recognizing that 'Coinage, like the establishment of a standard of prices, is the business of the state', Marx was also insightful regarding the contradictions to which the creation of money as 'the business of the state' (p. 100) this gives rise to, going all the way back to the

> lawyers [who] started long before economists the idea that money is a mere symbol, and that the value of the precious metals is purely imaginary. This they did in the sycophantic service of the crowned heads, supporting the right of the latter to debase the coinage.
>
> (Marx 1938a: 63)

References

Cain, Peter (2002) *Hobson and Imperialism: Radicalism, New Liberalism and Finance 1887–1938*, Oxford: Oxford University Press.

Cumings, Bruce (1999) 'Still the American Century', *Review of International Studies*, vol. 25, no. 5: 271–99.

Engels, Frederick (1938 [1886]) 'Editor's Preface', in Karl Marx, *Capital: A Critical Analysis of Capitalist Production, Volume I*, London: George Allen & Unwin, pp. ix–xiv.

Hansen, Fay R. (1985) *The Breakdown of Capitalism: A History of the Idea in Western Marxism, 1883–1983*, London: Routledge and Kegan Paul.

Hilferding, Rudolf (1981 [1910]) *Finance Capital: a Study of the Latest Phase of Capitalist Development*, Brighton: Harvester Press.

Marx, Karl (1938a [1867]) *Capital: A Critical Analysis of Capitalist Production, Volume I*, London: George Allen & Unwin.

Marx, Karl (1938b [1867]) 'Author's Preface to the First Edition', in *Capital: A Critical Analysis of Capitalist Production, Volume I*, London: George Allen & Unwin, pp. xv–xx.

Marx, Karl (1938c [1873]) 'Author's Preface to the Second German Edition', in *Capital: A Critical Analysis of Capitalist Production, Volume I*, London: George Allen & Unwin.

Panitch, Leo and Gindin, Sam (2010) 'Capitalist Crises and the Crisis This Time', in Leo Panitch, Greg Albo, Vivek Chibber (eds.), *Socialist Register 2011*, London: Merlin: pp. 1–20.

Panitch, Leo and Sam Gindin (2015) 'Marxist Theory and Strategy: Getting Somewhere Better', *Historical Materialism* vol. 23, no. 2: 3–22.

Panitch, Leo and Sam Gindin (2016), 'Class, Party and the Challenge of State Transformation', in *Socialist Register 2017*, London: Merlin: pp. 35–58.

Tabuchi Hiroko and Eric Lipton (2017) 'Pruitt's E.P.A. is Boon to Oil and Gas', *New York Times*, 21 May 2017.

Thompson, Edward P. (1978) *The Poverty of Theory and Other Essays*, London: Merlin.

Torr, Dona (1938) 'The English Edition of "Capital," 1887', Appendix V, in Karl Marx, *Capital: A Critical Analysis of Capitalist Production, Volume I*, London: George Allen & Unwin, pp. 848–62.

5 The current crisis and the anachronism of value

Moishe Postone

1 Marx and theorizing the current crisis

The election of Donald Trump, like the Brexit vote and the wave of right-wing populism sweeping much of Europe are expressions of a deep crisis of the political legitimacy of liberal democracies, as far-reaching and potentially dangerous as that in the interwar period in Europe.

This political crisis, one expression of which is the unhappy opposition of global neoliberalism and authoritarian nationalism, has its roots, arguably, in the overarching structural transformations of recent decades, which became manifest with the crash of 2008 and its aftermath. In addition to eliciting the rise of movements such as Occupy and a wave of populisms in a number of countries, the crisis and the Great Recession have given new impetus to attempts to understand contemporary historical developments critically and in an encompassing manner. Relatedly, the term "capitalism" has been reintroduced to broader academic as well as general intellectual discussions as a conception that now appears more analytically adequate than that of "modernity," which had been more dominant in the postwar decades.

Nevertheless, it has not always been evident how "capitalism" has been understood. I suggest that a critical theory of capitalism, should grasp it not only as a determinate form of inequality, or, relatedly, as a system of exploitation based on class, a category that in recent years has been frequently joined with those of gender and race as categories of identity and oppression.

Rather, especially as viewed from the vantage of the present, I suggest that capitalism should first and foremost be understood as a historically specific form of social life that is characterized by a historically unique abstract form of domination that finds expression in a global historical dynamic. This form of life arose contingently in Western Europe, which it fundamentally transformed even as it also proceeded to transform and constitute the globe. That is, contrary to some widespread assumptions, this form of life is not intrinsically or ontologically Western, but has itself reshaped the West. It cannot, therefore, be adequately grasped in culturalist terms. Rather, I would suggest, a theory that could adequately grasp the dynamic character of this form of social life can most rigorously be developed on the basis of a renewed encounter with Marx's mature works.

It is the case, of course, that for many, the collapse of the Soviet Union and China's transformation marked the final end of socialism and of the theoretical relevance of Marx. This demise was also expressed, on another level, by the emergence of other kinds of theoretical approaches, such as post-structuralism and deconstruction, which sought to provide critiques of domination that avoided what they regarded as the pitfalls of grand programs of human emancipation.

The current global crisis, however, has dramatically revealed the fundamental limitations of such newer approaches—including those associated with thinkers as disparate as Habermas, Foucault, and Derrida—as attempts to grasp the contemporary world. It also has exposed the one-sidedness of what had been termed the "cultural turn" in the humanities and the social sciences. The continued existence of severe economic crises as a feature of capitalist modernity, as well as the structural transformations of industrial societies (which recently have generated massive right-wing populist reactions), the existence of "premature de-industrialization" in other parts of the world (where the statist road to national capital accumulation no longer appears as a viable option), the growing financialization of social life, coupled with the prevalence of mass poverty, structural exploitation on a global scale, the dramatic growth of inequality, and – above all – the dual crisis of environmental degradation and the hollowing out of working society, call into question the triumphalism both of neoliberalism and much of post-Marxism. It seems that the downfall of what was called "actually existing socialism" and the efflorescence of post-Marxist thought have not obviated the need for a critical theory of capitalism.

Nevertheless, it would be a mistake to think that one can simply return to Marx, as he generally was understood during much of the twentieth century. Both the demise of traditional Marxism and the increasingly manifest inadequacies of much post-Marxism are rooted in historical developments that suggest the need to rethink, as well as reappropriate, Marx.

2 Capitalism and historical development

My focus on the historically dynamic character of capitalist society attempts to respond to the pattern of overarching global transformations of the past century. As is well known, researchers such as Piketty, focusing on issues of inequality, have recently established the existence of an overarching, supranational historical pattern of changes in inequality that has characterized the past century from a period of great inequality in the late nineteenth and early twentieth centuries, to a period around the middle of the twentieth century during which inequality was sharply reduced. This was followed after the early 1970s by a sharp resurgence of increased inequality.

This pattern not only reveals the extreme skewing of wealth and political power in the contemporary world, but also calls into question understandings of modern historical developments in linear terms—as is arguably the case of modernization theory, for example.

Significantly, this pattern of changes in inequality parallels other overarching patterns. For example, the average rate of *economic growth* for advanced capitalist countries was relatively low during the first half of the century, then more than doubled in the mid-twentieth-century period—which was the period of lowest inequality. Economic growth then declined after the 1970s as inequality grew. Changes in rates of GDP per capita follow a similar pattern.

These patterns—and many others—seem to be interrelated. All of them can be seen with reference to a still larger pattern—the supersession of nineteenth-century liberal capitalism by state-centric, Fordist capitalism from its beginnings in World War I and the Russian Revolution, through its high point in the decades following World War II, and its decline after the early 1970s, and its supersession, in turn by neoliberal global capitalism (which might, in turn, be undermined by the emergence of huge competing economic blocks).

What is significant about this trajectory is its global character. It encompassed Western capitalist countries and communist countries, as well as colonized lands and decolonized countries. Although important differences in historical development occurred, of course, from the vantage point of the twenty-first century they appear more as different inflections of a common pattern than as fundamentally different developments. This does not mean that this pattern is homogeneous or modular. How unevenness is understood, however, depends on how the overarching historical developments of modernity are understood.

The existence of such general developments cannot convincingly be explained in contingent terms. They strongly suggest the existence of general structural constraints on political, social, and economic decisions, as well as of dynamic forces not fully subject to political control.

These general patterns also suggest that the theoretical focus on agency and contingency in recent decades was as one-sided as the structural-functionalism it superseded. If the latter achieved widespread currency during the high tide of state-centric capitalism, the former has done so during the neoliberal epoch. Neither approach, however, thematized their own relation to their historical context. This suggests that, unlike such approaches, a critical theory should be able to problematize its own historical situatedness. That is, it should be reflexive.

These overarching patterns suggest the importance of a renewed engagement with Marx's critique of political economy, for the problematic of historical dynamics and global structural change is at the very heart of that critique. Nevertheless, as mentioned above, the history of the last century also suggests that an adequate critical theory must differ fundamentally from traditional Marxist critiques of capitalism—by which I mean a general interpretive framework in which capitalism is analyzed essentially in terms of class relations that are rooted in private property and mediated by the market, and social domination is understood primarily in terms of class domination and exploitation.

Within this basic framework, there has been a broad range of approaches that have generated powerful economic, political, social, historical, and cultural analyses. Nevertheless, the limitations of the overarching framework itself have become increasingly evident in light of twentieth-century historical developments. These developments include the non-emancipatory character of "actually existing socialism," the historical trajectory of its rise and decline, paralleling that of state-interventionist capitalism (suggesting they were similarly situated historically), the growing importance of scientific knowledge and advanced technology in production (which seemed to call into question the labor theory of value), growing criticisms of technological progress and growth (which opposed the productivism of much traditional Marxism), and the increased importance of non-class based social identities. Together, they suggest that the traditional framework no longer can serve as a point of departure for an adequate critical theory.

And, indeed, I would suggest that a sense of the inadequacy of the traditional Marxist framework has—at least tacitly—informed critical politics for decades. The notion of postcapitalism, of socialism, as a society based on industrial labor, public ownership of the means of production and central planning, began to lose its hold on the imaginaries of many progressive intellectuals, students and workers during the crisis of Fordist capitalism in the late 1960s and early 1970s. This inadequacy was frequently sensed rather than explicitly theorized. But, I suggest, it was expressed implicitly in widespread critiques of labor and industrial growth, weakening of support for social democratic and communist parties, the growing loss of orientation of those parties, as well as attempts to locate new revolutionary subjects—for example in anti-colonial movements.

What remained elusive was a new imaginary of socialism, of postcapitalism, that not only would entail reevaluating the relations of distribution (including property relations), but the relations of production themselves—and hence the nature of social labor. And the absence of such an imaginary has hobbled progressive movements.

Putting aside such considerations for a moment, I am suggesting that consideration of the general historical patterns that have characterized the past century, calls into question both traditional Marxism, with its affirmation of labor and history, as well as poststructuralist understandings of history as essentially contingent. Nevertheless, such consideration does not necessarily negate the critical insight informing attempts to deal with history contingently—namely, that history, understood as the unfolding of an immanent necessity, delineates a form of unfreedom.

This form of unfreedom, as I will elaborate, is the central object of Marx's critique of political economy, which grounds the historically dynamic character and structural changes of the modern world in imperatives and constraints that are historically specific to capitalist society. Far from viewing history affirmatively, Marx grounds this directional dynamic in the category of capital, thereby grasping it as a form of domination, of heteronomy.

Within this framework, Marx's critique, then, is not undertaken from the *standpoint* of history and of labor, as in traditional Marxism. On the contrary, the historical dynamic of capitalism and the seemingly ontological centrality of labor, have become the *objects* of Marx's critique. By the same token, Marx's mature theory no longer purports to be a transhistorically valid theory of history and social life, but is self-consciously historically specific and calls into question any approach that claims for itself universal, transhistorical validity. These central dimensions of Marx's analysis render his critical theory more adequate to our historical context than either traditional Marxism or poststructuralism.

It should be evident that the critical thrust of Marx's analysis, according to this reading, is similar in some respects to poststructuralist approaches inasmuch as it entails a critique of totality and of a dialectical logic of history. However, whereas Marx treats such conceptions as expressing the reality of capitalist society, poststructuralist approaches deny their validity by insisting on the ontological primacy of contingency. From the point of view of Marx's critique of heteronomous history, any attempt to recover historical agency by insisting on contingency in ways that deny or obscure the dynamic form of domination characteristic of capital, is, ironically, profoundly disempowering.

3 Historically specific history: the dynamic of capitalist social relations

These contentions are based on a reading that reconsiders the most fundamental categories of Marx's mature critique with reference to the heteronomous dynamic that characterizes capitalism. Within the traditional framework, his categories—such as value, commodity, surplus value, and capital—have generally been taken as economic categories that affirm labor as the source of all social wealth and demonstrate the centrality of class-based exploitation in capitalism (Cohen 1984: 209–8; Dobb 1981: 70–8; Elster 1985: 127; Meek 1973; Roemer 1981: 158–9; Sweezy 1968: 52–3).

Such interpretations attribute to Marx the same transhistorical understanding of labor as the source of wealth in all societies as that of Smith and Ricardo. According to this traditional approach, labor in capitalism is exploited because the surplus is appropriated by the capitalist class. Hence, labor is hindered by property relations from becoming fully realized. Emancipation, then, is realized in a society where transhistorical labor has openly emerged as the regulating principle of society. This notion, of course, is bound to that of socialism as the 'self-realization' of the proletariat. Labor here provides the standpoint of the critique of capitalism.

A close reading of Marx's mature critique of political economy, however, calls into question the transhistorical presuppositions of the traditional interpretation. Marx explicitly states in the *Grundrisse* that his fundamental categories are historically specific (Marx 1973: 106). Even categories such as money and labor that *appear* transhistorical because of their abstract and general character, are valid in their abstract generality only for capitalist society, according to Marx (cf. Postone 2008).

This calls into question many understandings of Marx's categories. I shall briefly refer to Volume I of *Capital* to outline a non-traditional understanding. That work begins with the category of commodity, which does not refer to commodities, as they might exist in many different kinds of societies (Marx 1973: 881, 1996: 46). Rather, Marx takes the term and uses it to refer to the most basic social relation of capitalist society, its fundamental form of social mediation and structuring principle. This form, according to Marx, is characterized by a historically specific dual character (use value and value) (Marx 1973: 100–8, 1996: 45–93). He then seeks to unfold the nature and underlying dynamic of capitalist modernity from the dual character of this basic structuring form. At the heart of his analysis is the idea that labor in capitalism has a unique socially-mediating function that is not intrinsic to laboring activity transhistorically.

In a society in which the commodity is the basic structuring category of the whole, labor and its products are not socially distributed by traditional norms, or overt relations of power and domination, as is the case in other societies. Instead, labor itself constitutes a new form of interdependence (Marx 1996: 179–81), where people do not consume what they produce, but where, nevertheless, their own labor or labor products function as a quasi-objective means of obtaining the products of others. In serving as such a means, labor and its products in effect preempt that function on the part of manifest social relations; they mediate a new form of social interrelatedness.

In Marx's mature works, then, the notion of the unique centrality of labor to social life is not a transhistorical proposition. Rather, it refers to the historically specific constitution by labor in capitalism of a form of social mediation that fundamentally characterizes that society. By unfolding this mediation, Marx tries to socially ground and elucidate basic features of modernity, such as its overarching historical dynamic.

Labor in capitalism, then, is both labor as we transhistorically and commonsensically understand it, according to Marx, and a historically specific socially-mediating activity. Hence, what labor produces, its objectifications—and here I am referring to the commodity and to capital—are both concrete labor products and objectified forms of social mediation. According to this analysis, then, the social relations that most basically characterize capitalist society are very different from the qualitatively specific, variegated, and overt social relations—such as kinship relations or relations of personal or direct domination—that characterize non-capitalist societies. Because constituted by labor, those relations have a peculiar quasi-objective, formal character and are dualistic—they are characterized by the opposition of an abstract, general, homogeneous dimension and a concrete, particular, material dimension, both of which appear to be "natural," rather than social (and condition social conceptions of natural reality).

The form of wealth associated with such relations, according to Marx, is value—which also is historically specific. Most accounts still treat Marx's category of value as if it were the same as that of Smith or Ricardo—that is, as a transhistorical category of the constitution of wealth at all times and in all places. Marx, then, purportedly refined and radicalized political economy and, using its categories, proved the existence of exploitation. This very common account, however, is based on a fundamental misunderstanding. Marx did not simply refine or radicalize political economy. He did not write a critical political economy but a critique of political economy. That is, he transformed the object and nature of the analysis. It no longer is primarily concerned with exchange or even with unequal exchange and exploitation. Instead, with his categories, Marx sought to reveal and analyze the specificity of capitalist society, its dynamic development and its possible overcoming.

In his mature works, Marx explicitly distinguishes value—as the historically specific, structuring form of wealth in capitalism—from what he calls material wealth, which is measured by the amount produced and is a function of knowledge, social organization, and natural conditions, in addition to labor (Marx 1973: 702–5). Value, according to Marx, is essentially temporal. It is constituted solely by the expenditure of socially necessary labor time (Marx 1996: 49).

Within the framework of Marx's analysis, the duality of the commodity form as value and use value generates a dialectical interaction that gives rise to a complex temporal dynamic that both drives value forward and eventually renders it increasingly anachronistic. To claim, as Marx does, that value is historically specific to capitalism is to claim not only that non-capitalist societies were not structured by value, but also that a post-capitalist society would also not be based on value (Marx 1973: 704–6). This, in turn, entails showing that value becomes increasingly anachronistic in the course of capitalist development.

Let me begin to elaborate by considering Marx's determination of the magnitude of value in terms of socially necessary labor time. This term is not simply descriptive, but delineates a socially-general compelling norm. Production *must* conform to this temporal norm if it is to generate the full value of its products. In the process, the time frame (e.g., an hour) becomes constituted as an independent variable. The amount of value produced per unit time is a function of the time unit alone; it remains the same regardless of individual variations or the level of productivity. It follows—as a peculiarity of value as a temporal form of wealth—that, although increased productivity increases the amount of use-values produced per unit time, it results only in short term increases in the magnitude of value created per unit time. Once the increases in productivity become general, the magnitude of value generated per unit time falls back to its base level (Marx 1996: 49). The result is a sort of a treadmill. Higher levels of productivity result in great increases in material wealth, but not in proportional long-term increases in value per unit time. This, in turn, leads to still further increases in productivity.

This treadmill dynamic expresses and constitutes a new form of social domination. The norm of socially necessary labor time is the first determination in *Capital* of the historically specific abstract form of social domination intrinsic to capitalism: it is *the domination of people by time*, by a historically specific form of temporality—abstract Newtonian time—which is constituted historically with the commodity form (Postone 1993: 200–16).

It would, however, be one-sided to view temporality in capitalism only in terms of Newtonian time, that is, as empty homogenous time (as Benjamin would have it) (Benjamin 1977: 257, 260–2). Once capitalism is fully developed, its temporal forms generate ongoing increases in productivity. Those increases, as we have seen, do not change the amount of value produced per unit time. However, they do change the determination of what counts as a given unit of time. The unit of (abstract) time remains constant; the same unit of time generates the same amount of value. Yet changes in productivity redetermine that unit; they push it forward, as it were. This movement is one *of* time. Hence it cannot be apprehended within the frame of Newtonian time, but requires a superordinate frame of reference within which the frame of Newtonian time moves. This movement of time can be termed *historical time*. The redetermination of the abstract, constant time unit redetermines the compulsion associated with that unit. In this way, the movement of time acquires a necessary dimension. Historical time here does *not*, then, represent the negation of abstract time (as Lukács would have it) (Postone 1993: 287–98). Rather, abstract time and historical time are dialectically interrelated. Note that, within this framework, neither form of temporality is a purely cultural construct; instead, both are moments of a historically constituted process. Both, within the framework of Marx's analysis, emerge historically with the development of the social forms of capitalism—whereby they are constituted as structures of domination.

Rather than considering temporality as a pre-given, unmoving frame within which all forms of social life move, then, such a theory grasps capitalism as a very peculiar organization of social life that constitutes its own, historically specific temporality; It is structured by historically unique forms of social mediation that are intrinsically temporal. These forms underlie a peculiar historical dynamic that is both historically specific and global. The temporalities of capitalism, then, are not extrinsic to it, but are intrinsic to its structuring social forms.

This historically new form of social domination is one that subjects people to impersonal, increasingly rationalized, structural imperatives and constraints that cannot fully be grasped in terms of class domination, or, more generally, in terms of the concrete domination of social groupings or of institutional agencies of the state and/or the economy. It has no determinate locus and, although constituted by determinate forms of social practice, appears not to be social at all. I am suggesting that Marx's analysis of abstract domination is a more rigorous and determinate analysis of what Foucault attempted to grasp with his notion of power in the modern world. Moreover, the form of domination Marx analyzes is not only cellular and spatial, as in Foucault, but also processual and temporal—it generates a historical dynamic (Foucault 1995). Rather than presupposing history, Marx now seeks to ground an ongoing dynamic of history as a historically unique characteristic of capitalism. That is, he historicizes history.

At the heart of this analysis is the peculiar treadmill dynamic I've outlined, which underlies a very complex, non-linear, historical dynamic that is at the heart of capitalist modernity. On the one hand, it is characterized by ongoing, even accelerating, transformations of more and more spheres of life—production, technology, patterns of habitation, transportation, communication, education, and forms of interpersonal relations. At the same time, however, it reconstitutes its own basis: that value remains the essential form of wealth and that therefore, value-creating labor remains at the heart of the system regardless of the level of productivity. The historical dynamic of capitalism ceaselessly generates what is "new," while regenerating what is the "same." As I will elaborate, it both generates the possibility of another organization of labor and of social life and, yet, at the same time, hinders that possibility from being realized.

The dynamic generated by the dialectic of abstract time and historical time is at the heart of the category of capital, which, for Marx, does *not* refer to means of production that are owned privately. Rather, it is a category of movement, what Marx calls self-valorizing value (Marx 1996: 164–6); it is value in motion. It has no fixed material embodiment, but unfolds as the dialectic of transformation and reconstitution briefly outlined above.

Within this framework, the "essential relations" of capitalism are the forms of social mediation expressed by the categories such as commodity, value, capital, and surplus value. These are not categories of wealth that are the objects of struggle between the social classes—whereby the latter are understood as the basic social relations of capitalism. Rather, they *are* the essential social relations of capitalism themselves—temporally dynamic, contradictory forms of social mediation that underlie a complex dynamic.

It is significant that, when Marx first introduces the category of capital he describes it with the same language Hegel used in the *Phenomenology* with reference to *Geist*—the self-moving substance that is subject (Marx 1996: 164–6). In so doing, Marx suggests that Hegel's notion of history as having a logic, as the dialectical unfolding of a Subject, is indeed valid—but only for capitalist modernity. Moreover, Marx does not identify that Subject with the proletariat or even with humanity. Instead he identifies it with capital, a dynamic structure of abstract domination that, although constituted by humans, becomes independent of their wills, and is generative of a historical dynamic.

Marx's mature critique of Hegel, then, does not entail an anthropological inversion of the latter's idealist dialectic. Rather, Marx now implicitly argues that the "rational core" of Hegel's dialectic is precisely its idealist character. It expresses a mode of domination constituted by relations that acquire a quasi-independent existence vis-à-vis the individuals, exert a form of compulsion on them, and that, because of their dualistic character, are dialectical in character.

Within this framework, history, as presented by Hegel—is historically specific. It is not a universal feature of human social life, but is constituted by historically specific forms of practices that it, in turn, molds and constrains. This implies that human history as a whole cannot be characterized transhistorically—either in terms of an overarching logic, as in Hegel, or as transhistorically contingent, as in Nietzsche. Rather, an immanently driven, directional dynamic, is one of the characterizing features of capitalism. Note that, here, the historical Subject, totality and the labor constituting it have now become the *objects* of critique in Marx's mature theory, not its *standpoint*.

The understanding of capitalism's complex dynamic I have outlined could help illuminate the looming contemporary dual crisis—that of environmental degradation and the demise of laboring society. Marx's categories of surplus value and capital allow for a critical social (rather than technological) analysis of the trajectory of growth in modern society. The temporal dimension of value, especially in the form of what Marx calls relative surplus value, underlies a determinate pattern of "growth," driven by pressures for ongoing, even accelerating increases in productivity (Marx 1996: 521–2). This generates increases in material wealth far greater than those in surplus value (which remains the relevant form of the surplus in capitalism), and hence, an accelerating demand for raw materials and energy, which contributes centrally to the accelerating destruction of the natural environment. Within this framework, then, the problem with economic growth in capitalism is not only that it is crisis-ridden. Rather, the *form* of growth itself is problematic. This suggests that the trajectory of growth would be different if the ultimate goal of production were increased quantities of goods, rather than surplus value.

At the root of this problem, within this theoretical framework, is that value, as a temporal form of wealth, transforms production into a peculiar process, whereby matter is transformed into units of abstract time. As a temporal form of wealth, capital strives toward boundlessness, ignoring, as it were, the necessary boundedness of its natural environment, the planet.

This approach also provides the basis for a social analysis of the structure of social labor and production in capitalism with reference to its basic contradiction. Within the framework of Marx's analysis, the drive for ongoing increases in productivity leads to the increasing importance of science and technology in production. What is entailed here is the rapid accumulation of socially general knowledge, which is promoted by the dynamic of capital. The tendency of this historical development is to render production based on labor time—that is, on value and, hence, on proletarian labor—increasingly anachronistic. On the one hand, this opens the possibility of large-scale socially general reductions in labor time, and fundamental changes in the nature and social organization of labor, which suggests that, for Marx, the abolition of capitalism would *not* entail the *self-realization* of the proletariat, but its *self-abolition*.

And yet, on the other hand, because the dialectic of transformation and reconstitution not only drives productivity forward, but also reconstitutes value, it thereby also structurally reconstitutes the necessity of value-creating labor, that is, proletarian labor.

The historical dynamic of capitalism, then, increasingly points beyond the necessity of proletarian labor while reconstituting that very necessity. It both generates the possibility of another organization of social life and yet hinders that possibility from being realized.

This tension skews the form in which that historical possibility emerges. As a result, ultimately, of the ongoing reconstitution of capital's fundamental forms, the possibility of the abolition of proletarian labor emerges historically in an inverted form, in the form of increases in superfluous labor, in the superfluity of an increasingly large portion of working populations, in the growth of the underemployed, the permanently unemployed and the precariat. The possibility of the abolition of proletarian labor and hence the emergence of the *emancipatory* possibility of a society in which surplus production no longer must be based on the labor of a subaltern class, is at the same time, the emergence of a *disastrous* development in which the growing superfluity of labor is expressed as the growing superfluity of people, with the fraught political possibilities this entails.

The approach I've outlined, then, suggests considering the current configuration of capital as one in which value-creating labor becomes increasingly anachronistic and, yet, remains structurally necessary for capital. This might also shed light on the current centrality of financialization. One could, perhaps, suggest that some dimensions of that financialization also point beyond capitalism (as paradoxical as that might sound)—for example, in the development of truly global ways of coordinating production and distribution, of creating the nervous system and sinews, as it were, of what could be a nexus of global coordination that is not international, but supranational.

Nevertheless, most basic aspects of neoliberal financialization do not point beyond capitalism but, on the contrary, can be viewed as forms that seek to maintain capital even when it has run up against what, arguably, are its limits.

I would like to suggest—and all of this is no more than a suggestion—that it is possible to regard the crisis-ridden end of the enormously productive, postwar Keynesian-Fordist configuration of capitalism as the expression of a secular crisis of valorization. Responding to this development, capital sought not only to reverse labor's previous gains under Fordism, but also to develop new forms of generating wealth. Within this framework, however, financialization now would not be exactly the same as financialization in the past, for now the expansion of a debt economy would be occurring against the background of stagnating surplus value production.

One well-known set of responses to that stagnation includes weakening of unions, shifting production to low wage areas, and substituting technology for labor. Financial capital was, of course, important in helping effect those changes. But one could also see the expansion of the debt economy as attempting to develop new sources of revenue. This in itself is not necessarily new. Marx's analysis of the tendency for value to become anachronistic, however, could cast a different light on the current configuration of financial capital. Debt, speaking very broadly, entails an explicit or tacit promissory note. It implicitly presupposes that, at some point in the future, there will be enough wealth to cover the debt. If, however, the current economy of debt is considered against the background of stagnating surplus value production, financial capital could become seen as attempting, as it were, to constitute its own realm of wealth production. The wide variety of promissory notes and meta-promissory "instruments" developed are oriented toward the horizon of the future. That horizon, within the framework of value theory, however, recedes as surplus value production stagnates; there is not enough wealth production in the underlying form of value to eventually cover those debts.

A consequence is an increasingly frenzied attempt to transform everything possible into sources of future wealth. What had been fairly simple and straightforward forms of debt—for example mortgages—become "financialized"—that is, are treated as the raw materials, as it were, of wealth that supposedly could be tapped in the future. More and more dimensions of life—from mortgages to infrastructure—become transformed into the content of new forms of purported wealth.

Within this interpretative framework, then, the crisis of value production is masked by the financially mediated attempt to transform more and more dimensions of life into the "raw materials" of price and profit—into forms of purported wealth that supposedly will guarantee ever more complex so-called financial instruments, as if such "wealth" were independent of value in capitalism. What David Harvey called "accumulation by dispossession" is one manifestation of this development (Harvey 2004). However, it does *not*, I suggest, entail the accumulation of *value*, but modes of the extraction of purported *wealth* to compensate for the *absence* of such accumulation. It can be understood as an unintentional effort to abolish value within a framework that remains structured by value. As the accumulation of value slows down, the search for wealth becomes perversely reflexive, like an autoimmune disease—it begins to feed on the substance of society and nature.

4 Transforming capitalist society

What I have outlined is a fundamental systemic crisis that occurs as the underlying social forms of capitalism become anachronistic while remaining necessary. This gives rise to enormous shearing pressures with potentially disastrous consequences. It also suggests that categories such as class (or gender or race) are not stable historically, but are in flux, constituted and reconstituted by the dynamic flow of capital.

As an aside, it should be noted that within this framework, the idea of another possible form of social life, beyond capitalism, is immanent to capitalist modernity itself. It is not derived from cultural contact or the ethnographic study of fundamentally different forms of social life; nor is it based on the experience of a previous social order with its own moral economy that is being destroyed by capitalism—although that experience certainly has been generative of opposition. Opposition to capitalism, however, does not necessarily point beyond it. It can be—and often has been—subsumed by capital itself or swept aside as inadequate to the exigencies of the larger historical context. Marx's analysis is directed less toward the emergence of "*resistance*," (which is politically and historically indeterminate) than toward the possibility of *transformation*. It seeks to delineate the emergence of a form of life that, as a result of capitalism's dynamic, is constituted as a historical possibility, and yet is constrained by that very dynamic from being realized. This gap between what is and what could be, allows for a future possibility that, increasingly, has become real historically. It is this gap that constitutes the basis for a historical critique of what is. It reveals the historically specific character of the fundamental social forms of capitalism—not only with reference to the past, or another society, but also with reference to a possible future.

It is capital, itself, as objectified human capacities, which generates the possibility of a future society. Yet it does so in a form that, at the same time, is increasingly destructive of the environment and the working population. Within the framework of the approach outlined here, the growing anachronistic character of value in the absence of a widespread imaginary of a future beyond value—that is, a post-proletarian future—is having enormously destructive economic, social, political, and environmental consequences. It is capital itself that is confronting us with the increasingly stark choice of socialism or barbarism.

References

Benjamin, Walter (1977) 'On the Concept of History', in *Illuminations*. New York: Schocken Books.

Cohen, Paul A. (1984) *Discovering History in Chica: American Historical Writings on the Recent Chinese Historical Past*, New York: Columbia University Press.

Dobb, Maurice (1981) *Political Economy and Capitalism: Some Essays in Economic Tradition*, London: Routledge & Kegan Paul.

Elster, Jon (1985) *Making Sense of Marx*, New York: Cambridge University Press.

Foucault, Michel (1995) *Discipline and Punished: The Birth of the Prison*, New York: Vintage Books.

Harvey, David (2004) 'The "New" Imperialism: Accumulation by Dispossession', *Socialist Register*, 40: 63–87.

Marx, Karl (1973) *Grundrisse: Foundations of the Critique of Political Economy (Rough Draft)*, Harmondsworth: Penguin.

Marx, Karl (1996) '*Capital*, vol. 1', in *Marx and Engels Collected Works*, vol. 35: *Capital, vol. 1*, New York: International Publishers.

Meek, Ronald L. (1973) *Studies in the Labour Theory of Value*, London: Lawrence and Wishart.

Postone, Moishe (1993) *Time, Labor, and Social Domination: A Reinterpretation of Marx's Critical Theory*, Cambridge; New York: Cambridge University Press.

Postone, (2008) *Rethinking Capital in light of the* Grundrisse', in Marcello Musto (ed.), *Karl Marx's Grundrisse Foundations of the Critique of Political Economy 150 years later*, New York: Routledge.

Roemer John (1981) *Analytical Foundations of Marxian Economic Theory*, Cambridge: Cambridge University Press.

Sweezy, Paul (1968) *The Theory of Capitalist Development*, New York: Oxford University Press.

6 Marx's new concept of class

Richard D. Wolff

1 Concepts of class

The complex changes in socialism around the world since the 1970s and especially after 1989 exposed a profound, if not new, problem. The concept of class had faded (was repressed) from much social analysis during and because of the Cold War. Discussions of social issues were routinely reduced to crudely politicized polarizations. Many dismissed class analysis altogether as "tainted by a lack of objectivity" (a quality they located in those concepts they used instead of class). Rare usages of class occurred as epithets when each side in the Cold War insisted that it had erased class differences while excoriating the other side's class differences. Only quite recently, after the 2008 global capitalist crash as disillusionment with capitalism deepened, have concepts of class resurfaced in public discussion. Then it became clear that "the" concept of class was in fact a collection of different definitions rarely acknowledged as such. Proliferating references to class – academic, journalistic, and political – raised the problem of its multiple, different meanings.

The return of the repressed discourse of class is problematic because of the significantly different meanings among those who think and communicate using it. Only a small minority of users explicitly identifies and justifies which meaning it prefers. Most users think, speak, and write as if the particular concept of class they use is the universally agreed concept. Because that is not the case, discourses using class categories are often confused and misunderstood. When the relation between class and social change arises as a practical matter, the problematic of multiple class concepts becomes historically urgent.

For thousands of years people analyzed societies by dividing (or "classifying") their populations into subgroups according to their wealth and/or incomes. Classes were the nouns applied to those subgroups. Classifications generated two polar classes, the rich and the poor. Some subdivided populations further into more classes located between the rich and the poor. Such middle classes held more wealth and/or received more income than the poor but less than the rich. Wealth and income classifications presupposed notions and measures of private property (much as age classifications presupposed notions and measures of age).

Concepts of class *defined in terms of wealth and/or income* served people to think, speak or write about social problems and to act to solve them. For example, concerned citizens might explain their society's tensions and conflicts as consequences of particular configurations of rich, poor, and middle classes. Their solutions might then entail changed distributions of wealth and/or income. Class-qua-property concepts thus proved central to their struggles for social change.

Another, equally ancient but quite different concept of class – likewise still widely used – defines it *in terms of power wielded over others*. It classifies populations into those who give orders and those who follow them. A powerful class confronts a powerless class: rulers and the ruled. Power definitions of class also extend to intersperse middle classes, members of society who both take orders from some while giving orders to others. Class qua power thinkers explain social problems in terms of the distributions of power and act to solve them usually by changing the distribution of power, for example, from monarchy to democracy.

The two different concepts of class usually yield different understandings when applied to actual societies. The social distribution of property is not identical to the social distribution of power. Individuals and subgroups who own the most property may or may not wield the most power, and so on. Using the same term, "class analysis," while defining it differently risks communicative confusion. People unaware of definitional differences do not acknowledge, identify or justify which definition they use. That makes confusion all but certain.

Periodically in human history, social revolutions took "class" seriously. Revolutionaries then undertook to change a society's class structure as a key, necessary component of the social transformation they sought. Revolutionaries committed to class-qua-property concepts focused on changing distributions of wealth and/or income. Their goal was often a more egalitarian distribution. In contrast, revolutionaries who conceived of class in terms of power focused on redistributing power: often targeting a more egalitarian or democratic distribution.

Not infrequently, class analyses mixed both property and power concepts although rarely with much self-consciousness about the definitional problems. Some property theorists of class simply assumed that altering its distribution would likewise and in some necessary way alter the social distribution of power. Similarly, power theorists of class sometimes run the same determinist argument in reverse: from changing power distributions to necessary, particular redistributions of property.

Across history's revolutions, the importance of class analyses within people's consciousness varied. The two basic definitions of class, if significantly present, alternated in terms of which prevailed or how they were combined. Yet a certain insufficiency and failure dogged revolutions even when they "succeeded." Despite the progress they achieved, they so far never reached and sustained fully egalitarian distributions of wealth and/or income or fully egalitarian (democratic) distributions of power. For some, those failures provoke a fatalism that holds the goals themselves as beyond human reach. Others have questioned the thinking that guided past revolutions. They asked whether revolutionary theory had been inadequate to the revolutionary project. A few undertook to rectify perceived inadequacies.

2 Marx adds a new concept of class

Marx was one such questioner and rectifier. His work generated and applied a new and different concept of class alongside his use of the old property and power concepts of class that he inherited from previous revolutionaries.[1] Marx believed they had not achieved equality and democracy because their social analyses and revolutionary projects had missed a basic process in all societies. What they had overlooked analytically and thus left untransformed practically undermined past revolutions even when they achieved progressive changes in property and power distributions. They fell short of the levels of equality and democracy to which they had aspired. Or those levels, if occasionally approached, could not be sustained. For Marx, the most important example was the French Revolution. It overthrew feudalism, radically altered distributions of property and power, but never reached its goals of *liberté, égalité, fraternité*.

Marx's *Capital* identifies and analyzes the social process missed by his revolutionary forbears. The production and distribution of the surplus are in fact two closely intertwined processes that occur in all societies but take crucially different forms in capitalism as compared to feudalism, slavery, communism and so on. The two processes of producing and distributing surpluses together amount to a new concept of class: something Marx added to – that was also different from – concepts of class-qua-property or power.

Of course, class in terms of the social organization of the surplus interacts with the social distributions of property and power, but that neither requires nor warrants ignoring their basic differences. The old, pre-Marxian concepts of class refer to groups of people. Marx's new concept of class refers to social processes connecting people in particular ways. Marx's new concept is his contribution to rectify the inadequacies of previous revolutions. Where they often understood property and power distributions, they failed to attend to or transform the organization of the surplus. Marx's class analysis – his identification and explanations of how the capitalist system produces and distributes the surplus – provides the insights revolutionaries will need to reach their goals. To achieve and sustain equality and democracy requires more than changed distributions of property and power; it requires a transformation of the organization of surplus beyond its capitalist form and limits.

Early in *Capital,* Volume I, Marx identifies his new notion of class as a particular social process that occurs together with the physical labor process within the activity known as production. In production, men and women use brains and muscle to transform naturally occurring (or partly worked-up) objects into useful products. They labor on and with their means of production: *on* raw material inputs *with* tools and equipment inside buildings, etc. But the labor process is not the same thing as the class process. The class process refers to a specific connection among the people engaged in production that is different from the labor process that connects them in a different way. Class, for Marx, refers to how, in production, alongside the labor process of making of a product (a good or a service), a surplus gets produced. By surplus Marx means the residue of output left after a portion of output is given to the laborers (wages) and another portion is given to replace the means of production used up to produce that output.

All human societies produce such surpluses and then distribute them among their members. However, societies differ in how they organize the production and distribution of their surpluses. In Marx's view, all human communities (from families through villages to whole nations) assign subsets of their populations to perform labor that produces goods and services. Those subsets taken together always produce more output than they themselves consume: the "surplus" output or simply the surplus. Specific people receive that surplus and then distribute it to themselves and/or others.

Any society's class structure is then its distinct organization of the production and distribution of surplus. A specific subgroup of individuals is assigned, consciously or unconsciously, by custom or deliberation, to produce the surpluses. Either those same individuals or other individuals receive the surplus. The surplus recipients then distribute some or all of it to still others: recipients of distributed shares of the surplus. Each community or society designates which individuals can receive distributed shares of the surplus, consume them, and thereby live without themselves producing surpluses. Likewise, every society designates a subgroup to do work that does not itself produce a surplus but rather provides conditions for the labor of others who do produce the surplus. Such *enablers* of surplus production by others need to receive a distribution of the surplus produced by those others: that distribution provides the enablers with their own consumption and with the means for performing their enabling functions. For example, a person who keeps the necessary records of what surplus-producing laborers do is such an enabler; so too is a supervising person who makes sure the surplus-producers keep to their tasks, etc. Marx differentiated between "productive" workers (those who directly produced surpluses) and "unproductive" workers (the enablers who provided needed conditions for surplus production). Both productive and unproductive workers were needed for any class structure to exist and persist, but their relationship to surplus production is crucially different. One kind of worker produces the surplus while the other, the enabler, lives off distributions of that surplus.

Pre-Marxian concepts of class (qua property or power distributions) ignored or marginalized such a surplus concept of class. When pre-Marxian concepts were applied to understand and/or transform societies, the results reflected the fact that the people involved did not recognize, know, or use the surplus concept. They did not take into account how the societies they scrutinized organized the production and distribution of surpluses. They were, in effect, blind to the changes in the organization of the surplus needed to achieve and sustain their revolutionary goals.

Marx's contributed the concept of class-qua-surplus to revolutionary theory and practice. Revolutionary projects had henceforth to address and change how society organized the production and distribution of its surpluses. If a society's class-qua-surplus structure were not transformed, then reforms in the distributions of property and power, if won by revolutionary struggles, would be insecure. The relatively unchanged class-qua-surplus structure would likely undo the reforms. For example, the 1917 revolution's transformations of property and power distributions in Russia were eventually undone by the insufficiently changed organization of the surplus across the USSR's production sites.[2]

In *Capital*, Marx spelled out the change he sought in societies' class-qua-surplus structures required to surpass the limitations of past revolutions. That change was from *exploitative to non-exploitative* class-qua-surplus structures. By exploitative, Marx explained, he meant a class structure in which the people who produced the surplus were different from the people who received and then distributed that surplus. In slave economic systems, slaves produced while masters received and distributed surpluses. In feudal economic systems, serfs produced the surpluses received and distributed by lords.

Marx's *Capital* explained that in capitalism, workers' labor added value to the values embodied in the means of production used up to make the output. The value of the capitalist output or product is the addition of two components. The first is the value carried over to – embodied in – the finished product from the used-up means of production. The second component is the value added by living labor as it works, transforming raw materials by means of tools and equipment. Exploitation exists in capitalism, Marx showed, because the value added by direct laborers in their labor activity during production generally exceeds the value paid to the direct laborers for performing that labor activity.

In other words, a portion of the value added by labor in production is a surplus. The surplus is the excess of the value added by their labor over the value of the wage they receive. In capitalism, the employer receives (Marx uses "appropriates") that surplus and then distributes it. The capitalist employer, who is usually a different person from the employee, exploits that employee by receiving the latter's surplus product. He literally, as Marx so painstakingly shows, takes the entire product, sells it, and then divides the revenue into wage payments, outlays to replace used-up means of production, and a residue – a surplus – that accrues to the employer. The capitalist/employer then also distributes that surplus.

Capitalism therefore did NOT liberate slaves and serfs *from exploitation*. Capitalism's revolutionary arrival altered the distributions of property and power of prior slave and feudal societies; it overthrew their class structures;

but it did not end exploitative class structures. Establishing capitalism merely changed the form, the particular social organization, of continuing exploitation: from slave/master and serf/lord to employee/employer. That unchanged *exploitative* class structure is why the French Revolution's promises of liberty, equality and brotherhood could not be realized.

3 Equality and democracy

Capitalist exploitation imposes on its workplaces conflict-ridden tensions between employees and employers. One side seeks higher wages in exchange for providing labor power. Employers seek to pay lower wages and/or reduce the number of employees while also striving to extract more surplus from the production process. Resource disparities brought to their conflicts favors employers over employees. Surpluses appropriated by employers tend to rise faster than real wages. That inequality ramifies throughout capitalist societies countering any egalitarian tendencies within their politics and culture.

Capitalism's inequality tendencies can interact with its other dimensions (e.g., capitalist cycles) to provoke social backlashes that reverse capitalism's inequalities. The reversals prove temporary because they are undone (reversal of the reversal) by capitalism's underlying tendencies toward inequality (see Piketty 2014). For example, the US left in the 1930s (CIO unionization drives, large socialist and communist parties) forced a reversal of the extreme inequality built up in US capitalism before 1929. That reversal lasted to the 1970s, only to be then undone by capitalism's resurgent underlying inequality tendencies (veneered by the term "neo-lilberalism"). The latter reasserted themselves precisely because of the underlying, exploitative class-qua-surplus structure of US capitalism. The US left's struggles in the 1930s and the reforms it achieved had not transformed that structure.

Similarly, capitalism's organization of the surplus both directly contradicts economic democracy and also undermines democracy elsewhere in society when it occurs. The direct contradiction lies in the organization of typical capitalist enterprises, large, medium and small. A tiny subset of the persons involved with the enterprise usually owns and directs the enterprise: in corporations, for example, this subset comprises major shareholders and the boards of directors their votes select. They exclude the mass of employees from genuine participation in ownership or direction of the enterprise. The democratic logic – that persons affected by decisions have the right to participate in making them – is denied entry into the capitalist enterprise. The democracy celebrated at least formally in politics is banished from the economic sphere of modern society.

This absence of democracy from the workplace – where adults spend most of their waking lives – undermines the capacity and often the desire of workers for real democracy in politics. The inequalities generated by capitalism provide employers with financial resources to shape politics and culture to their liking. The results are *formal* but little *real* political democracy.

Periodic upsurges of democratic demands and even achieved democratic reforms fail to last because the unchanged class-qua-surplus structure of capitalism undermines them.

In *Capital,* Volume I, Marx shows how and where capitalism's surplus is produced and received/appropriated. In *Capital,* Volumes II and III, Marx explores how capitalists distribute the surpluses they appropriate from workers. Surplus distributions aim to secure certain conditions for the continuation of class exploitation. For example, they provide wages and means of production for enablers of capitalist exploitation, Marx's *unproductive workers.* These include supervisors who make sure direct laborers do their work, security guards who protect the enterprise, and an army of other enablers such as the secretaries, clerks, various managers, sales and purchasing personnel. This argument is spelled out in detail for the capitalist class process elsewhere (see Resnick and Wolff 1987, chapter 3; Wolff and Resnick 2012, chapter 4). Marx's basic point is that the production of the surplus enables its distribution and vice versa: a class structure is that interdependent, intertwined organization of the surplus.

No class structure's reproduction is assured or self-contained; it depends on its environment. Surplus distributions merely try to secure the class structure's conditions of existence and reproduction by shaping its environment. The surplus distributions may or may not succeed. Capitalists may not appropriate enough surplus to distributed the requisite portions to each recipient. There may be enough surplus, but the appropriators may divert too much to their own consumption or too little to secure one or another particular condition of existence of the class structure. How the surplus is distributed will shape the evolution of the class structure, the amount of surplus it generates, and social evolution generally. A class structure's continual changes include the open-ended possibility of its transformation into another, different class structure.

4 A communist class structure

For Marx, communist class structures are defined by the absence of exploitation. Producers and appropriators of the surplus in a communist class structure are exactly the same people. In the capitalist class structure, they are different people. In an enterprise whose class structure is communist, the productive laborers collectively appropriate and then distribute the surpluses they produce. Productive laborers displace capitalists within the communist organization of the surplus (see Mulder 2015).

The distribution of communist surpluses defines two positions at its poles: the "productive workers" who also appropriate and distribute the surplus, at one pole, and the recipients of distributed shares of the surplus (including "unproductive" workers) at the other pole. As in all class structures, the process of distributing the surplus is an object of struggle between distributors and recipients. However, the key difference separating the communist from all exploitative class structures is this: in the latter, the exploiting classes (slave masters, feudal lords, and capitalist employers) interpose themselves between the productive and unproductive laborers. In the communist class structured enterprise, the productive and unproductive laborers have no interposers. They negotiate and determine together both the size and the distribution of the surplus.

The significance of this difference is huge. First, capitalists are in the position of distributing portions of the surplus to themselves (as owners, shareholders and/or as top corporate executives). These portions are often – and for obvious reasons – large. The deep tendency toward inequality exhibited in and by capitalism is closely linked to who distributes its surpluses. The small minority that decides the distribution in capitalism serves itself and thereby worsens inequalities over time. Were surplus distributions decided democratically by productive and unproductive workers, there would likely be far less economic and social inequality than in capitalism.

Second, consider the example of a technical change in production methods that enhances an enterprise's profitability but is also ecologically toxic. The capitalist enterprise will likely choose to implement the change because the extra profit means more to distribute. The capitalists making the decision are few, profit is their goal, and they can afford individual escapes from the toxic consequences. The communist enterprise will likely choose otherwise, since its collective decision-makers (productive and unproductive workers deciding democratically) will weigh the health risks and costs that they, their families and neighbors cannot afford to escape if the toxic technology is used. One cause of ecological damage would be reduced by a class change from capitalist to communist class structures in enterprises.

Third, consider the example of moving production from a relatively high-wage to a relatively low-wage location. Capitalists have been doing that in large numbers for nearly half a century, leaving north America, western Europe and Japan for China, India, Brazil and so on. Capitalists made those choices for their enterprises because relocation enabled them to extract more surpluses. They used those additional surpluses to better secure their conditions of existence but also to pay themselves higher salaries, dividends, etc. Had their enterprises been instead organized as communist class structured enterprises, their decision-makers (their productive and unproductive workers together democratically) would have evaluated relocation differently in terms of its impacts on them and their communities. The alternative class structures with their different sets of decision-makers would have identified, counted, and weighed costs and benefits differently. They would thereby have reached different conclusions and made different decisions. The massive relocation of enterprises since the 1960s would have occurred far less often had communist class structures of enterprise played larger roles in our economies.

On a more general level, inside a capitalist enterprise, its governance – the process of defining and choosing among alternative courses of action in and by the enterprise – is undemocratic. In the corporate form of capitalist enterprise – the major form in our time – the board of directors makes the basic decisions of what, how and where to produce and what to do with the surplus. Boards of directors typically include 12–20 individuals elected by shareholders, or more accurately, by the few major shareholders (since elections assign one vote per share and share ownership is highly concentrated). The hundreds or thousands of corporate employees – the vast majority of persons working in those enterprises – are excluded from participating in the decisions made by the board of directors. Those employees depend on and live with the consequences of board decisions but have no role in making them.

The opposite is the case in a communist enterprise. There, the combined productive and unproductive workers collectively and democratically make the decisions that, in capitalist enterprises, are reserved for corporate boards of directors and owners. The democracy of enterprise governance intrinsic to the communist class structure supports and reinforces democracy in the politics of the larger society. Democratizing the enterprise – in class terms, converting it from a capitalist into a communist class structure – is a way of converting formal into real political democracy.

5 The varieties of class analyses

The logic of class-qua-surplus analysis entails posing a basic question of any site of production in a society chosen for scrutiny. Production here means a place where human beings are using brains and muscles to transform less into more useful objects where "useful" is socially determined. The question to be posed: is a surplus being produced at that site? If the answer is yes, class analysis follows. That is, the specifics of the production and distribution of the surplus are investigated to determine how they participate in shaping the economic, political and cultural aspects of the society in which the production occurs.

The answer could have been no. Production can occur without any surplus being involved. When someone walks through the woods and carves a piece of wood into a figurine for a nearby child, no surplus – hence no class process – is involved. If, however, a wage-receiving carver works with a knife and raw wood provided by an employer who sells the resulting figurines, a surplus is involved. Class analysis does then apply.

Enterprises are not the only social site where production and class processes occur. Those processes can happen elsewhere, for example in households and in the state as an institution. In households over the last two centuries, as capitalist class structures have spread across enterprises, capitalist class structures have NOT similarly prevailed within households. Households certainly are sites of production. Labor uses tools and equipment to transform raw foods into finished meals, unclean rooms and clothing into neat and clean residences and outfits, and so on. Moreover, the direct performers of the labors of cooking, cleaning, etc. typically produce more output than they themselves consume, a household surplus. It is possible to identify the appropriator and distributor of that surplus and hence to pinpoint the class structure of the household. We have produced a systematic class analysis of the modern household elsewhere.[3]

It follows that modern "capitalist societies" have more and variegated class structures than the adjective "capitalist" accommodates (Gibson-Graham 1996). Their households have often been the sites of very different, non-capitalist class structures. That means that individuals in those societies were engaged with, participated in and were shaped in part by multiple, different class structures. Class-qua-surplus analysis generates a much more complex, nuanced analysis of individuals and groups than merely locating them in relation to property and power distributions or merely locating them in relation to the particular surplus organization of only enterprises.[4]

The state may also be a social site of production and class (see Resnick and Wolff 2002, 2006, part V). This occurs, for example, if and when state officials establish – as their official function – organizations in which surpluses are produced, appropriated and distributed. Popular language has often depicted these organizations as "state enterprises" precisely because they do what enterprises outside the state do. In the US, for example, state governments own and operate state institutions of higher learning that produce and sell credits to students; the federal government sells postal services and train services to the public; local governments sell transport services; and so on. In such state institutions, surpluses get produced, appropriated, and distributed. Such institutions include productive and unproductive workers. Unlike households, class structures in the state – state enterprises – do largely replicate the capitalist structures found in private enterprises.

Class-qua-surplus analyses of the state have some provocative implications. For example, increasing the size and productive role of state enterprises – say at the expense of private enterprises – has nothing to do with any change in the society's class structure from capitalist to something non-capitalist, say "socialist." Such an argument misunderstands what class means or defines it in terms other than the organization of the surplus. Government enterprises in modern times usually are capitalist in their class structures just as private enterprises have been. More government and less private production merely changes the site of capitalist class structures; it has not been a displacement of capitalism for an alternative system – at least so far as class–qua-surplus is concerned.

Only if the state enterprises were organized to produce and distribute surpluses in a different, non-capitalist way would the shift from private to state production also entail a shift from capitalist to non-capitalist class structures of production. If state enterprises were required to operate as communist class structures, for example, such that their productive workers would also function, collectively and democratically, as appropriators and distributors of the surpluses they produced, then the shift from private to state would coincide with a shift from capitalist to communist class structures of production.

6 Class and income

The class-qua-surplus analysis of income is simple and straightforward. Most individuals obtain income by being performers of surplus labor (and therefore paid a wage or salary for that performance) and/or by being recipients of distributions of the surplus. Capitalist employers are merely middle-persons who appropriate the surplus from some and then distribute it. They can and often do keep some of the appropriated surplus for themselves, but that reduces what they can distribute to secure the reproduction of their enterprises. Typically, capitalists distribute portions of the surpluses they appropriate to themselves as managers or other unproductive enablers of their enterprise's success.

Productive workers who produce surpluses get wages – the non-surplus portion of the value added by their labor. Unproductive laborers also get wages, but those are portions of the surplus appropriated by capitalists from productive laborers. Capitalists then distribute such portions to unproductive laborers for securing certain conditions of existence of capitalist production. Class-qua-surplus analysis thus differentiates productive from unproductive labor, laborers, and wages. From this standpoint notions such as "the wage-earning class" or "the working class" are problematic. All wage-earners or workers are not occupants of the same class position. They divide into two different class positions that often generate different perspectives on how the economy and society function, different notions of what is to be done to improve and change the economy, and different social change strategies.

Of course, if the goal is to unify productive and unproductive workers into a combined social force, then class-qua-surplus analysis would entail the need to recognize and accommodate their class differences to construct and sustain that unity. Assuming the unity because they are all wage-earners, working class, etc. would not be strategically appropriate or likely very effective. Indeed, to head off such unity, capitalists and their ideological supporters have long sought to stress other differences among wage-earners (age, gender, race, skills, education, ethnicity, white versus blue collar, etc.) as means to block unity among them, especially unity around a critical attitude towards capitalism itself. Advocates of such unity had to learn to accommodate the reality of those differences within a unifying project. Marx's new concept of class requires doing likewise for wage-earners' class-qua-surplus differences. Otherwise, efforts to build unity risk failure.

Relatively few individuals become rich from the wage or salary payments they earn as producers of surplus. Wealth accrues chiefly to those in a position to secure large portions of distributed surpluses from the surplus appropriators. Major shareholders thus secure wealth by receiving dividend payments. Top managers secure huge salaries and pay packages that are surplus distributions. Lenders and landlords obtain interest and rentals from appropriators of the surplus who thereby secure access to money and land – conditions of their surplus appropriation. Private property is what allows the owners of means of production (land, money, etc.) to withhold it from production. Those owners enable access to their means of production – so production can occur – only if they get interest and rental payments from the surpluses appropriated and distributed in capitalist enterprises.

Capitalists have always used their position within the class structure – qua appropriators and distributors of the surplus – to enrich themselves by keeping (or distributing to themselves) major portions of the surplus. This has been and continues to be the key cause or support for the capitalism's tendency to deepen inequalities.

7 Struggles over class

Marx's new class-qua-surplus concept yields a correspondingly new approach to the notion of class struggles. Class processes are objects of struggle, rather than classes being the subjects struggling. Class-qua-surplus as the object of social struggles has both quantitative and qualitative dimensions. The quantitative dimensions concern (1) the size of the surplus produced and appropriated, and (2) the sizes of the portions of the surplus distributed to its various recipients. Social groups struggle over those quantitative dimensions. For example, productive workers struggle with capitalists over the size of the wages paid to them, the length of the working day, and thus the size of the surplus to be appropriated. Capitalists struggle with governments over the size of that portion of the capitalist surplus paid to governments as taxes on profits. Class struggles over the quantitative dimensions of surplus production and distribution are more or less constant features of class structures.

Sometimes, politics, cultural, and economics combine to provoke struggles over the qualitative dimensions of class-qua-surplus. For example, the object of struggle becomes a capitalist versus a non-capitalist class structure for enterprises. In the United States today, an emerging social movement supports worker cooperatives as a preferred alternative to capitalist corporations. It represents an early stage in a qualitative class struggle.

8 Property, power, and surplus conceptualizations of class today

Marx's class analysis defined in terms of organizations of the surplus still contests with formulations – inside and outside of Marxism – that stress the alternative property and power definitions of class. Capitalism continues widely to be conceptualized chiefly as "private enterprise plus free markets" and differentiated from "socialism" or "communism" defined as "state-regulated or state-operated enterprises plus state-regulated or state-planned distributions of resources and products." The key dimensions of class are thus property (who owns enterprises) and power (who/what distributes inputs and outputs). Enterprises' internal organization of the surplus then drops out of the prevailing public discussions altogether.

However, contemporary rethinking of traditional Marxian conceptualizations of class is moving closer to Marx's surplus definition and the analytics it yields. That has been stimulated by two social changes. First was the demise of so many socialist economies built upon property and power definitions of class. Perceptions that they lacked genuine democratic participation eventually deepened into recognitions of basic things lacking in prevailing definitions of capitalism and socialism. Rethinking those definitions returned many to Marx's writings and to the discovery there of class-qua-surplus arguments of the sort discussed above.

The second social change has been the 2008 global capitalist crisis and its aftermath. Perceptions have grown that the old centers of capitalism in western Europe, north America and Japan are increasingly dysfunctional for all but their richest residents, economically divided, and decreasingly democratic. Criticisms of the neoliberal versions of private and market capitalism proliferated. Such criticisms too rediscovered and worked their way back to the Marxist tradition.

Worker cooperatives and theories and theorists associated with them returned as important inspirations for critics of capitalism (Azzellini 2015). The latter saw them as components of a systemic alternative to capitalism that yet also differed crucially from twentieth century socialism. Worker coops had been marginalized in popular and academic discourses during the Cold War. They and their supporters, fearing association with a demonized anti-capitalism, socialism, etc., kept very low profiles. Now they are resurfacing. Cooperative worker ownership of enterprise, cooperative worker self-management, workers self-directed enterprises and still other pointedly non-capitalist firm organizations have become major organizing principles of critiques of contemporary capitalism and the construction of non-capitalist enterprises. Writers such as Gar Alperovitz and David Schweikart, while making little direct reference to Marx's class-qua-surplus theory, have focused their critiques of capitalism on the undemocratic internal workings of capitalist firms far more than traditional socialists did (see Alperovitz 2011; Schweickart 2011). Michael A. Lebowitz's work on Cuba's turn of its economic development strategy to focus far more than ever before on worker cooperatives reflects a rethinking of socialism that is also wending its way toward class-qua-surplus theory and practice (see Lebowitz 2014). Cliff DuRand makes explicit his and his colleagues commitment to "moving beyond capitalism" (DuRand 2016).

The groups gathered around the website *democracyatwork.info* and the journal *Rethinking Marxism* have been producing a growing body of work that uses and explicitly extends Marx's class-qua-surplus theory. It combines systemic critique of global capitalism with advocating the transformation of capitalist enterprises into workers self-directed enterprises as the economic base of a new system, perhaps defining a new socialism for the twenty-first century. Its goal is to return worker cooperative enterprises – understood in Marx's surplus-focused way – to center stage in strategies of social change (see Wolff 2012; Mulder 2015). Marx's new and different concept of class, like so much else in Marx's work, is returning to the forefront of critical thinking as yet again capitalism hits the fan.

Notes

1 An excellent recent collection of articles explores the originality, uniqueness and implications of Marx's new concept of class: Burczak, Garnett and McIntyre (2018, see especially the essays in Parts II, III, VII, and IX).

2 See this argument made in detail for the entirety of Soviet history: Resnick and Wolff (2002).

3 See the detailed class analyses of households gathered in Graham Cassano (2009). Note that if households were reduced to sites where no production was undertaken, where only consumption occurred, class-qua-surplus analysis would not apply.

4 See numerous illustrations of such analyses in David M. Brennan, et al. (2017).

References

Alperovitz, Gar (2011) *America Beyond Capitalism: Reclaiming Our Wealth, Our Liberty, and Our Democracy*, Takoma Park, MD and Boston, MA: Democracy Collaborative Press and Dollars and Sense.

Azzellini, Dario (ed.) (2015) *An Alternative Labour History: Worker Control and Workplace Democracy*, London: ZED Books.

Brennan, David M., Kristjanson-Gural, David, Mulder, Catherine P., and Olsen, Erik K. (eds.) (2017) *Routledge Handbook of Marxian Economics*, London and New York: Routledge.

Burczak, Theodore, Garnett, Robert and McIntyre, Richard (eds) (2018) *Knowledge, Class, and Economics*, London and New York: Routledge.

Cassano, Graham (ed.) (2009) *Class Struggle on the Home Front: Work, Conflict, and Exploitation in the Household*, New York: Palgrave Macmillan.

DuRand, Cliff (ed.) (2016) *Moving Beyond Capitalism*, London and New York: Routledge.

Gibson-Graham, Julie-Katherine (1996) *The End of Capitalism as we Knew It*, Cambridge, MA: Blackwell.

Lebowitz, Michael A. (2014) *The Contradictions of Real Socialism*, New York: Monthly Review Press.

Mulder, Catherine P. (2015) *Transcending Capitalism Through Cooperative Practices*, New York: Palgrave Macmillan.

Piketty, Thomas (2014) *Capital in the Twenty-first Century*, Cambridge: Harvard, MA University Press.

Resnick, Stephen and Wolff, Richard (1987) *Knowledge and Class: A Marxian Critique of Political Economy*, Chicago and London: University of Chicago Press.

Resnick, Stephen and Wolff, Richard (2002) *Class Theory and History: Capitalism, Communism and the USSR*, New York and London: Routledge.

Resnick, Stephen and Wolff, Richard (2006) *New Departures in Marxian Theory*, London and New York: Routledge.

Schweickart, David (2011) *After Capitalism*, Lanham, MD: Rowman and Littlefield.

Wolff, Richard and Resnick, Stephen (2012) *Contending Economic Theories: Neoclassical, Keynesian and Marxian*, Cambridge, MA: MIT Press.

Wolff, Richard D. (2012) *Democracy at Work: A Cure for Capitalism*, Chicago: Haymarket Books.

Part II

Extending the critique of *Capital*

7 Revolution begins at home

Rethinking Marx, reproduction and the class struggle

Silvia Federici

1 Introduction

One reason for the enduring power of Marx's political theory has been undoubtedly his capacity to read the future and anticipate forms of capitalist development that are now unfolding under our eyes, in ways that still make his work, 150 years later, a guide for the present. With great intuitional power, Marx anticipated the globalization process that is capital's relentless drive to conquer every corner of the world and submit every form of production to the logic of profit and the market. Most important, he anticipated that the internationalization of capital would lead to the formation of not only a global market but a global accumulation cycle, such that "the division of the world in nation states would lose its economic significance" (Ferrari Bravo 1975: 20–1). Similarly, the *Grundrisse*, especially in the "Fragment on Machines" (Marx 1973: 690–710) has been credited with predicting the growing dominance of knowledge and science in the capitalist organization of work, which (quite problematically, I believe) has led some to postulate a new phase of accumulation designated as "cognitive capitalism."[1]

In one respect, however, Marx was not ahead of his time. Surprisingly, he did not foresee a development that, in the space of a few decades, would change the composition of the working class and the landscape of class struggle in Europe and the United States. This was the formation of a new proletarian family, a process that took place (roughly) between 1860 and World War I, with the gradual exclusion of women and children from factory work, the introduction of the "family wage," and the creation of the proletarian housewife and housework itself as a specific branch of capitalist production, entrusted with the reproduction of the workforce (Seccombe 1993).

With these developments, that inaugurated a new patriarchal regime built on the power of the male wage, a transformation occurred in class relations that escaped Marx's analysis, although in *Capital,* Volume I, we find many references to the reports of the government-appointed factory inspectors that in England paved the way to this change. That the capitalist class was in the process of revolutionizing the proletarian family and gender relations and creating new hierarchies between men and women, and with them new divisions in the proletariat, cannot be deduced from a reading of the book, which is the only place in *Capital* where references to the working-class household are found. Like Engels, Marx remained anchored to the belief that capitalism destroys the proletarian family and creates the material conditions for more egalitarian gender relations. As he put it in the *Manifesto of the Communist Party:*

> The more modern industry becomes developed, the more is the labor of men superseded by that of women. Differences of age and sex have no longer any distinctive social validity for the working class. All are instruments of labor....
>
> (Marx and Engels 1967: 88)

Why would Marx – otherwise so futuristic in his analysis of capitalist development – fail to acknowledge that a reorganization of social relations was underway that would restructure in a more hierarchical way male-female relations and generate new divisions among workers affecting the relation between capital and labor?

I ask these questions not to rehearse a critique of Marx's theory that has already been articulated by feminists of my generation, especially in the Wages For Housework movement (see Dalla Costa 1971; Federici and Cox 1975; Fortunati 1981), but because this "oversight" in Marx's work denotes problematic aspects of his political and theoretical perspective that we must acknowledge, not only for a proper appraisal of his work, but because they shed light on the limits of the socialist movement of his time, and they reveal gender biases that are still affecting the politics of the left worldwide. I refer to the tendency to exclude from the sphere of capitalist relations and working class organizing some of the activities that are most important for the reproduction of human life, such as domestic work, sex work, child raising and procreation. I also refer to Marx's underestimation of the function of unequal gender relations as instruments of cooptation of sectors of the working class, and to his undue optimism concerning the role of industrial work, and in particular automation, as levelers of gender and skill-based labor hierarchies.

It is the thesis shaping this chapter that Marx did not anticipate or commented upon the restructuring of the proletarian family and the construction of new patriarchal relations within the proletariat because, according to his political theory, familial relations have no specific function in capital accumulation or the constitution of workers' subjectivity and class formation (Meyer 2014: 274–6). This is why he did not give the (re)production of labor-power the "importance that could be expected from a theory of labour," (Meillassoux 1975: xi) and did not grasp the significance of the family reform that was underway. One consequence of this strategic error has been the rift, to which (as we shall see) Marx contributed as head of the First International, between the socialist movement and the feminist movement that was growing in the later part of the nineteenth century, a rift that has continued almost to our days. Thus, revisiting Marx's perspective on the family, women's work, and the activities by which our life is reproduced is a way of dialoguing with the present, and rethinking the patriarchalism of capital and the left, as well as the conditions of a cooperation between Marxism and Feminism.

My argument is divided into four parts. In part 1, I examine the evidence and reasons for Marx's "under-theorization" of reproduction, focusing on his reductive concept of work and production, and his implicit assumption that only waged industrial workers have the power and knowledge to subvert capitalism and create the material conditions for communist society. In part 2, I examine Marx's response, as head of the First International, to workers' demands for a policy change with regard to women's labor and family life, confirming his silence with regard to the manifest patriarchalism of sectors of the English male working class. In part 3, I contrast Marx's seemingly neutral stand on the contemporary reorganization of family life with the consequences of this reorganization on social life and class relations, arguing that it was a significant instrument of cooptation of at least important sectors of the industrial workforce. Last, in section 4, I reflect on the long term political consequences of the marginalization of women and reproductive work in the program of both the socialist movement and the Marxist tradition, arguing it is time we ask to what extent this theoretical and political "mistake" affected their organizational capacity and their vision of the society to be built from the ruins of capitalism.

2 Marx on social reproduction and the reproduction of labor-power

A key to understanding the reasons for Marx's failure to acknowledge the momentous changes that were in the make in England, in the nineteenth century, with regard to family-life and male-female relations, is his treatment, in both *Capital* and the *Grundrisse*, of the reproduction of labor-power. This should have been a central issue in Marx' work, considering the strategic function that labor and labor-power play in his analysis of capitalist society and the capitalist organization of work. Labor for Marx is the activity by which human beings not only reproduce themselves and perpetuate their existence, but constantly create and recreate "human nature" – what we are, feel, think, are capable of doing. As a consciously chosen activity, labor differentiates us from animals, it is the essence of our "species being" and, throughout history, the source of social wealth. The expenditure of labor-power, our capacity to work – is the engine of capital accumulation. It is the principle of value creation and the terrain on which the struggle for human liberation is decided. Thus, the activities that (re)produce this precious capacity should have had a central place in Marx theoretical and political framework. But, as is well known, they are scarcely discussed by Marx and, when they are, it is in ways that fail to recognize their nature of and extent.

Marx acknowledges – for instance – that being daily consumed in the process of production, our capacity to work, must be continuously regenerated, and he argues that this incessant reproduction "remains a necessary condition of the reproduction of capital." (Marx 1976: 718) He, however, places the realization of this process totally within the circuit of commodity production. Workers – in his account – buy the necessities of life and by consuming them reproduce themselves. No other work is needed. No mention is made of the contribution of domestic work to this production. In Volume I, the only one of the three volumes in which women have a presence, we only have two references to domestic work, relegated to footnotes, essentially arguing that female factory workers had no time for it being employed from sun up to sundown on the factory floors.[2] At no point, does Marx recognize that the reproduction of labor-power requires some domestic work – to prepare food, wash clothes, raise children, make love – and that this work was mostly done by women. Also, when considering the needs that workers must satisfy, he remains in the realm of commodities, projecting the image of a machine-like, sexless, waged worker with only such needs as the purchase of commodities can satisfy. Among these, in Volume I, he cites food, fuel, housing, clothing, furniture, but he strangely omits sex, assuming an immaculate worker's life, presumably male, since throughout *Capital,* Volume I proletarian women are described as prone to sell their sexual services in prostitution.[3]

Even when discussing how the workforce is generationally reproduced (Marx 1976: 711–24), Marx is silent on women's contribution to it, nor does he envisage the possibility of a conflict of interests between women and men, and between women and the state, with regard to procreation, although for women a pregnancy was often a death sentence, especially when out of wedlock, and by the mid-nineteenth century many were receptive to the campaign that advocates of contraception were making within the workers' movement.[4] Apparently oblivious to the high cost of pregnancy and procreation for women, to the anguish that they would experience with every unwanted pregnancy, and the often deadly efforts they would make to abort, Marx speaks of the "natural increase of the population," argues that, "the capitalist may safely leave this [procreation] to the workers' drives for self-preservation and propagation" (Marx 1976: 718) and, in his otherwise trenchant critique of Malthus' population theory, suggests that capitalism does not depend on women's procreative capacity for the expansion of the workforce, since it can presumably satisfy its labor-needs by means of constant technological revolutions periodically creating a "surplus population." (Marx 1976: 784–5).[5] In reality, as a system that makes of labor the substance of value, capitalism has been extremely interested in demographic movements and has strictly regulated women's reproductive capacity, imposing heavy penalties on their tampering with procreation,[6] penalties that were in force in most of Europe in Marx's time.[7] Indeed, the capitalist class has never relied exclusively on changes in the organization of production for the creation of a surplus population and the determination of an optimally sized workforce. Marx himself acknowledged that the rate at which industrial capital was consuming workers' lives was such that always new recruits were always needed, to be drawn mostly from the rural areas and the employment of women and children; and he was certainly aware of the concern that the high rates of infant mortality in the industrial districts were generating among the elite. Even in the twentieth century, despite continuous technological revolutions, capitalism has relied on migratory movements, as well as the regulation of women's reproductive capacity, to satisfy its need for the quantity and quality of labor-power that the development of the productive forces and the breakdown of workers' resistance to exploitation required.

In sum, we do not find in Marx a discussion of a field of activities and forces – affective relations, sexual desires, practices concerning housework and procreation – that previous socialists and bourgeois thinkers (like Fourier and Malthus) had recognized as having a political potential.

In Marx, by contrast, love, sexual passion, procreation, appear to be natural givens, outside the world of capital's economic relations and workers' decision-making and struggle. Mothering is only mentioned with reference to the female workers' neglect of their children. The prostitute too is invisible as a worker and as a subject. In Sheila Rowbotham's words, "She appears as an indication of the state of society, not as [a member of] a social group in movement, developing consciousness in history." (Rowbotham 1974: 63). Pictured as a victim of poverty and moral degradation, she is described part of that *lumpenproletariat* that in *The 18th of Brumaire of Louis Bonaparte* Marx described as "the "refuse of all classes." (Marx 1963: 75) Marx's view of female factory workers is also reductive. We see their suffering bodies, the inequities to which they were subjected, but we are not told how women's entrance into the factories transformed their subjectivity, changed their relations with men, whether it enhanced or diminished their capacity for struggle, and in what ways their demands and forms of struggles differed from men's. Exception made for occasional comments on the degrading impact of industrial and agricultural work on women's and girls' "moral character" – due to overwork and exposure to promiscuous work conditions – Marx does not discuss the conduct of female workers. In *Capital*, they remain shadow figures, only represented as victims of abuse, an image in stark contrast with that projected by contemporary political reformers who pictured them – especially when single and not burdened with children – as enjoying a new sense of freedom, thanks to having a wage, leaving home at an early age "to be their own mistresses," (Pinchbeck 1930: 311–13) and behaving like men.[8]

3 From the manifold of work to wage labor and "production"

Accounting for these silences, questioning why Marx did not extend his critique of political economy to "a detailed examination of social reproduction in the household," John Bellamy Foster has argued that in *Capital* Marx was concerned with providing a critique of capitalism articulated "from the standpoint of its own ideal conception," i.e., "in terms of its inner logic" and, from this viewpoint, reproductive work fell outside the boundaries of value creation (Foster 2013: 11). Marx – Bellamy Foster writes, "moved more and more towards embracing the contradictions of the inner and outer determination of capital as a system." That is, he embraced the capitalist obliteration of unpaid reproductive labor and here – it seems to me – lies the problem. For in so doing, Marx failed to unmask the very presuppositions of classic political economy. Instead of revealing unpaid reproductive work as the source, indeed, the "secret," of the reproduction of labor-power, he codified the separation, typical of the logic and history of capitalist development from its start, between production and reproduction, and the naturalization of the latter as "women's labor." Significantly, he relegated the only references to domestic work to be found in the three volumes of *Capital* to footnotes (Marx 1976: 517–18, n.38; 1976: 518, n.39). Arguing – in defense of Marx – that there is a difference between the *exploitation* of labor-power and the *expropriation* of the conditions of its production – such as women's work and nature – will not do (Foster 2018: 12–13),[9] given Marx's contention that *all activity* that produces labor-power is an essential part of capitalist production. Furthermore, even if reduced to a minimum, "usurped" by capital as it may have been, domestic work, in the industrial districts, continued: in the night, on Sundays,[10] performed by youngster or elderly women that female factory workers hired to care for their children. And not all women worked in the mills. Many retired after their first child; in some factories, moreover, by the mid-nineteenth century, female operatives had won a free Saturday afternoon.

More is needed to explain why, writing in the midst of a governmental program aiming to reorganize factory and family life, accompanied by choruses of complaints denouncing the collapse of the proletarian family and women's reproductive work, Marx could so easily ignore it in his analysis of capitalist exploitation. It helps to know that Marx was not alone in his dismissal of the "feminine side of the dialectic" and reductive interpretation of work and the class struggle. As Federico Tomasello has shown in *L'Inizio del Lavoro* (The Beginning of Work, 2018) since 1830, especially in France, a complex social process had developed, whereby both the state and the incipient workers' movement redefined work and the figure of the worker in ways excluding the wageless and privileging those engaged in industrial work (Tomasello 2018, especially pp. 96–8, 105–6). The historic insurrection of the Parisian proletarian in 1830, that Victor Hugo immortalized in *Les Misérables*, followed one year later by the take-over of the city of Lyon by revolting weavers, triggered a process of "integration" of selected sectors of the rebel workers, whose result (Tomasello points out) was the emergence of the laborious, honest wage worker as a juridical figure, recognized by the state as the carrier of social rights, such as the right to work, soon to become the foundation of the modern state and all modern constitutions. The election of waged work as a privileged status with regard to social rights – i.e., the beginning of a unitary representation of the world of work and the corresponding separation of the waged from the rest of the "dangerous classes" – also marked, in the same years, the beginning of the workers' and socialist movements. Thus, Marx's exclusionary account was not the fruit of contingent decisions concerning his book project, but expressed an existing state of affairs, that however his analysis contributed to consolidate, the more so as presented as the result of a scientific study of social reality.

Contextualizing Marx's reductive conception of work and production and tracing its roots in the politics of the contemporary socialist movement[11] is especially important in view of the confusion generated by the academic debates on the question of productive and unproductive labor. What such debates have hidden is that the construction of "productive work" has been the result of a political operation whereby the interest of a particular sector of workers have been prioritized, both in institutional and radical politics and a general image of the worker has been constructed that canonized the figure of the *ouvrier*, "l" *operaio as the generally male, white, waged industrial worker, to the exclusion of the broader world of unwaged subjects capitalism has exploited – houseworkers, campesin@s, enslaved African and other colonial subjects.* I will not, therefore, in this chapter, try to "prove," once more, that reproductive work is "productive." My main interest, instead, is to comment on two consequences of the reductive concept of work and the worker in capitalism that Marx embraced.

First is Marx's assertion of the historical necessity of capitalist development as an instrument of historical and social progress, a thesis that was to become the flag of the third-worldist bourgeoisie in the 1960s and 1970s and the justification for the assimilation between "capitalist development" and "revolution." By erasing, in fact, the debt capitalism has historically owed to the exploitation of the unwaged, in the colonies as in the metropoles, "modernizers" of all sorts have been able to hide that, from its earliest phase, *capitalist development has been* (in André Gunder Frank's famous formulation) "*the development of underdevelopment*" (Frank 1969: 55). More specifically, it has been the development of impoverished populations and hierarchies, unequal relations among those it has exploited, based on a multiplicity of factors but above all gender, race and age. And these hierarchies and inequalities have had an essential economic and political dimension as sources of "super-exploitation" and divisions among the global workforce.

Had Marx acknowledged that (a) from its start capitalism has been a gendered and racialized system, that is a system structurally requiring the existence of unequal hierarchical relations among workers, enabling it to extract immense quantities of unpaid labor, far beyond the unpaid labor extracted from the waged working day, and (b) that these unequal/hierarchical divisions have been the main obstacle to the unification of the working class on which, in his view, the overthrow of capitalism is predicated, he would have been less optimistic, less sanguine about the "revolutionary" role of capitalism as the creator of the material conditions of communist society.

He would be forced to acknowledge that the extraordinary development of the "productive forces," which he so admired in capitalism, was obtained at such a social, ecological and human cost as to jeopardize the very possibility of "human liberation."

As it is, all throughout *Capital* every articulation of capitalist society, money, credit, rent, machinery, is subjected to the most minute analysis, constantly re-elaborated trough hundreds of pages, and yet we do not find in it any analysis of either the function or political consequences of unequal power relations within the world proletariat in capitalism, except for scattered observations such as that the employment of women and children served to lower the cost of labor. Differences in the conditions of work of women and men are acknowledged but only with respect to their impact on women's physical constitution and "moral character." Nothing, instead, is said in this work on the sexual division of labor – the only division of labor Marx recognizes being that between intellectual and manual work. Nor are women and children mentioned in the chapter on wages. On two occasions only does Marx acknowledges the existence of unequal relations between proletarian women and men, and male workers' patriarchal attitudes. Both are in the chapter on "Modern Industry and Machinery." Here Marx anticipates the liberation of women and children, through their employment in factory work, from the patriarchal dominance of the father typical of the organization of work in the cottage industry, and, at the same time, deplores that with the rise of industrial work, the male adult worker, the father, becomes "a slave dealer,"[12] selling the work of his wife and children to his employers and clearly collecting their wages. But in both cases these abuses appear destined to be superseded by the expansion of automation, and here too a serious discussion of these phenomena is missing. We are not told, for instance, that male workers could become slave dealers, selling their wives' labor to the factories, because until the last decades of the nineteenth century, married women were not considered legal subjects, capable of confronting capital as free possessors of their labor-power and stipulating contractual relations. Only with the passing of the Marriage Property Act, in 1870, the medieval *coverture* system, that erased married women's existence before the law, was terminated.[13] So entrenched was the subordination of women to men in England that the popular custom, among laborers, of ending a marriage by selling one's wife at the local market continued into the late nineteenth century, with cases reported as late as 1901 and 1913.[14] This explains why the patriarchal relations that had prevailed in the so-called "put-out-system," did not vanish when cottage-work was displaced by industrialization, but were reconstituted in the factories, so that, in a first phase at least, production was again structured according to a gender hierarchy, with the father subcontracting the labor of his wife and children or selling their labor together with his own and making a claim to their wages.

Again, had Marx analyzed the social roots and implications of this patriarchal policy, he would have recognized the existence of a fundamental anomaly in capitalist relations. He would have seen that the condition that he stipulated for the development of wage labor – i.e. "freedom" intended as "ownership of one's body" and capacity to work – was never extended to women. He would have further realized that the women's rights which feminists in his time were fighting for, especially with regard to women's position in marriage and the family, *were also labor issues*, as "being covered" by their husbands affected their ability to hold a job, keep their wages, and participate in the workers' movement, for the power that men had to restrict their wives' actions certainly limited women's ability to struggle.

The question of patriarchal relations within the working class was of special importance in Marx's time as in the very years in which Marx was starting to work on *Capital* the opposition of male workers to women's presence in the factories intensified, after an individual system of wages was introduced that gave women control over their earnings. As Judy Lown reports, in *Women and Industrialization*, such a move was met with hostility by workers, resulting in attempts to define female labor as unskilled and confine women to the worst tasks. (Lown 1990: 107) Trade Unions too upheld "the principles of patriarchy," mobilizing for the passing of "protective legislation" and supporting the male workers' demand for a "family wage," enabling them to support a presumably non-working wife' (Lown 1990: 213). By the mid-nineteenth century, the "male-breadwinner norm" was a rallying point for working class organizations. (Seccombe 1993: 111–24) Again, Marx's *Capital* makes no mention of this gendered struggle, though plausibly it undermined workers' unity and threatened women's source of livelihood. All we find in the three volumes is again a footnote, stating that "the shortening of the hours of labor for women and children was exacted from capital by the adult male workers" (Marx 1976: 519, n. 40).

4 Gender, labor and the family wage in the first Working Men International Association

Were Marx's silences on such crucial matters the product of political expedience? This is a legitimate question as we know, from his correspondence with Engels, that Marx always saw his work in *Capital* as directly connected to the politics and debates within the International Working Men's Association of which he was a leader and founder (see on this Pelz 2017: 36–7ff.). We also know that women's rights were a subject of much debate within the organization, and that it was so split on this question that it took it seven months, after its foundation, to vote on the eligibility of women as its members and two years before a well-known woman, Harriet Law, was placed in a leadership position as a member of the General Council. Yet, Marx made no mention of women's special situation in his inaugural speech. According to the record, he "did not made any specific place for working women, whose oppression was apparently considered to be simply part of that of workers." (Fauré 2003: 345–6). He also campaigned, in the early 1870s, to expel Section 12 of the IWA, its most feminist wing,[15] supporting women's suffrage, "free love" and what its leader, Victoria Woodhull, called "social freedom": i.e. women's independence from the male wage and the domestic slavery inscribed in marriage.[16] It is worth noting that the wage was used in the expulsion process, for the General Council of the IWA (largely under the influence of Marx) "inaugurated a 'two-thirds' rule, holding that two-thirds of the members of any IWA section had to be wage laborers, a decision that favored participation by workers in trades and crafts but largely excluded reform-minded women" (Frisken 2004: 44). This expulsion had a profound impact on the development of the working-class revolutionary movement, possibly as important as the anarchist-communist split that pit Marx against Bakunin, for it put the questions concerning sexuality and women's power into the realm of the future or, even worse, into the no-go land of bourgeois rights.

As one of International's main spokesmen, Marx undoubtedly knew that the majority of its male members supported a strong limitation of women's factory employment and the institution of a "family wage," and he was likely reluctant to take positions that might have exacerbated divisions.

He was also ambivalent on the matter, possibly in the same way as he was with regard to the destruction of the family of the time of manufacture, which he deplored but also considered instrumental to the liberation of women and children from patriarchal rule (see Marx 1976: 620). For his ambivalence on the "family wage" we have the testimony of Harriet Law the only woman member of the General Council of the International. According to Law's protest against his intervention in a debate on this issue [as reported in the minutes of the First International's General Council], Marx had been in favor of women's industrial work, but he had stated that the way in which [women and children] worked under existing conditions was abominable (Fauré 2003: 346), thus strengthening the position of the advocates of the family wage.[17] Law believed that Marx had betrayed the interest of working class women and registered her protest. It is possible, however, that Marx considered the institution of the "family wage" and the reduction of women's factory work a temporary phenomenon, for the progress of industrialization would require women's participation in it, and (as he wrote in Volume I) "create a new economic foundation for a higher form of the family and of relations between the sexes" (Marx 1976: 620–1).

If this was Marx's assumption in his support for the "family wage," it was a miscalculation. By the 1870s an epochal reform program was underway that by the turn of the century transformed class relations, and diffused class conflict, sending many former female factory workers back to the home, and inaugurating a new type of patriarchal regime that can be labeled the "patriarchy of the wage" (Federici 2004).

5 The reconstruction of the proletarian family, domestic work and the patriarchy of the wage

While Marx dismissed the question of the generational reproduction of the work-force arguing that capital could rely on the workers' "instinct for self-preservation," by the 1860s the fear that the proletariat was "was in danger of extinction," (Fortunati 1995: 170; Seccombe 1993: 77). because of overwork, undernourishment and exposure to continuous epidemics, was confronting the capitalist class with a major crisis. Indeed, years of overwork and under-payment were severely undermining workers' capacity to reproduce themselves, the average life expectancy in the industrial areas being for men less than 30 years of age. A major concern among reformers was also the growing evidence of working-class women's disaffection with family and reproduction. Employed in the factories all day, earning a wage of their own, used to living in a public space with other women and men for most of their waking hours, English working class women and especially factory "girls" "had no interest producing the next generation of workers;" refused to take up a housewife role, and challenged bourgeois morality with their boisterous manners and male-like habits, like smoking and drinking (Fortunati, 1995: 170–1; Lown 1990: 43–5, 116).

Complaints about the female workers' lack of domestic skills and wastefulness – their tendency to buy everything they needed, their inability to cook, sew, and keep a clean home forcing their husbands to retreat to the "gin shop," their lack of maternal affection – were a staple of reformers' reports from the 1840s to the turn of the century. Typically, a Children Employment Commission complained in 1867 that:

> Being employed from eight in the morning till five in the evening they [i.e. the married women workers] return home tired and wearied, and unwilling to make any further exertion to render the cottage comfortable, thus "when the husband returns, he finds everything uncomfortable, the cottage dirty, no meal prepared, the children tiresome and quarrelsome, the wife slatternly and cross, and his home so unpleasant to him that he not rarely betakes himself to the public house and becomes a drunkard."
>
> (Hewitt 1958: 70)

Added to the concern for the crisis of domesticity that women's employment produced was the fear of women's usurpation of male prerogatives, which was believed to undermine the stability of the family and trigger social unrest. A broken family, it was assumed, would make for an unstable country. Neglected husbands would leave the home, spend their free time in public houses, beer/shops or gin/shops, make dangerous encounters encouraging a riotous disposition (see Hewitt 1958: 70).[18] The rise of the Chartist and Trade union movements, and the threat of another 1848 were certainly on the mind of proponents of family reform.

The obvious inability of the working class to provide a steady, sufficient flow of workers was particularly problematic as the period between 1850 and the turn of the century saw, both in Britain and the U.S., a major transformation in the system of production, calling for a stronger and more productive type of worker. Generally referred to as the "Second Industrial Revolution" (see Seccombe 1993: vi) this was the change from light to heavy industry, that is, from textile to coal and iron as the leading industrial sectors and the leading sources of capital accumulation, which was made possible by the creation of an extensive railroad network and the introduction of steam-power (see Hobsbawm 1968: 94–101 on this topic).

It was among the architects of this new industrial revolution that, already by the 1840s, a new doctrine began to take hold, associating higher productivity and a more intensive rate of exploitation with higher male wages, shorter hours and, more importantly, better living conditions among the working class to be provided by laborious and thrifty wives. It is no surprise, then, that in this same period the reports of factory inspectors began to recommend that the number of hours that women, especially married ones, worked in the factories should be reduced, to enable them to perform their domestic duties and that employers abstain from hiring pregnant women. Behind the creation of the working class housewife and the extension to the working class of the kind of family life once reserved to the middle class there was the need for a new type of worker, healthier, more robust, more productive and, above all more disciplined and domesticated.

In England this process began with the passing of the Mine Act of 1842, that forbid all women and boys under ten from working in the mines, and then the Ten Hours Act of 1847 which workers, especially in Lancashire, had been agitating for since 1833. In addition to the passing of this legislation, other reforms were introduced that contributed to the construction of the working-class family and women's role as unpaid domestic laborers in the home. Wages for male workers were substantially increased, by 40 percent between 1862 and 1875, rising rapidly after that date, so that by 1900 they were one-third above what they had been in 1875 (Hobsbawm 1968: 133). Then in 1870 the Marriage Property Act was legislated, which (as we have seen) put an end to the system of *coverture* that had shaped married women's lives since the Middle Ages,[19] so that women could be recognized as legal subjects and marriage itself could be placed on a contractual basis.[20] In the same year, a national system of education was introduced that became compulsory in 1891. In its wake, "domestic science courses and practical lessons in domestic subjects were introduced in public elementary schools." Sanitary reforms such as "drainage, water supply [and] street cleaning," were introduced in English cities putting a brake to recurrent epidemics. A consumer market for workers also appeared, with the rise of the neighbor-hood shop, providing for groceries but also for clothing and footwear.

Not last, the creation of the working class family and of a healthier, more productive workforce brought about the institution of a clear separation between the housewife and the prostitute, as reformers recognized that it would not be easy to convince women to remain at home and work for free, when their own friends and sisters would have more money and less work selling their bodies in the streets (Acton 1969: 232, note 1).[21]

With these changes the fear of a working-class revolution that had haunted the capitalist class since 1848 was largely dispelled. By the 1880s in England, as across the Atlantic, a new predominantly male waged workforce emerged that might not have regarded the laws of the capitalist organization of work "as natural laws" – as Marx predicted it would in the course of capitalist development – but was socially and politically domesticated, clearly having new reasons for "feeling at home when not working."[22]

6 Conclusion

I have argued in this chapter that the limited attention that Marx gave in his major works to such issues as the family, reproductive activities and gender hierarchies – those that existed in the first phase of industrialization and those that were being constructed in response to the reproductive crisis of the mid-nineteenth century – cannot be attributed solely to the conditions in which working class families lived during the first phase of the Industrial Revolution or to a masculinist oversight. Rather, like the contemporary socialist movement, Marx embraced a narrow concept of work and the worker in capitalism, mostly because of his overestimation of the role of capitalist development in the construction of communist society. He also overestimated the power of industrialization to create the material basis for a more egalitarian society and was so convinced that the waged industrial workers were the revolutionary subjects that he was ready to sacrifice to their cause issues and interests in his view not directly related to the confrontation between capital and labor, such as women's desire for liberation from social and economic dependence on men. Thus, while he may have recognized that the demand for a "family wage" and for restrictions on women's factory work inevitably implied a consolidation of patriarchal relations within the working class, he accepted it in the name of a narrowly defined conception of the unity of the class and the class struggle, confident that the revolutionary process capitalist development would inevitably spark off would redress the situation.

Making this critique of Marx does not detract from recognizing the powerful contribution he has made to our understanding of capitalist society and (indirectly) to feminist theory. As the recent celebrations of the anniversary of the publication of *Capital* have demonstrated, 150 years later even critics must take Marx's analysis as a point of reference for deciphering the movements of capital and the prospects for its future development. Whether or not the labor theory of value still describes the process of capital accumulation, and whether we can explain today's political economy through the falling the rate of profit remain as important questions today as they were at the end of Marx's life, and it is hardly imaginable to presently discuss social and political relations that will not rely on such concept as commodification, alienation, and exploitation. Feminist theory as well has been strengthened by Marx's methodology, which stresses the historically constructed character of social reality and thereby rejects naturalized/eternalizing identitarian concepts. Most important, Marx has given us tools to detect capital's reach into the most intimate spheres of our domestic and affective life. But the same tools also demonstrate the limits of his own theory. In particular, they demonstrate that his silence on the role of reproductive activities in capitalism was not a minor omission, as it led him to both fail to anticipate the consequences of the hierarchies built on the sexual division of labor structured through the production and reproduction relation, and confide in capitalist development as the development of a revolutionary working class.

Highlighting these limits in Marx's work is especially important today, as in front of the seemingly unlimited destructive powers of capitalist development we must ask why the inevitable revolution that Marx predicted has not taken place. It helps us in fact, to reflect, in seeking for an answer to this question, that the Marxist account of capitalist exploitation has until recently ignored the largest sector of work and workers on earth, and has excluded from the class struggle a host of issues that are crucial to the lives of workers and their relation to capital and the state. There is no denying in fact that women, domestic work, sex work and child raising have been absent from Marxist/communist theory and organization and with rare exception, for in the Marxist tradition the worker was white and male. Exemplary is also the way in which socialist/communist movements have for a long time dismissed, if not ostracized, concerns of the utmost importance for proletarian women and men, such as e.g., birth control. As Seccombe reports, even in the 1910s and 1920s socialist parties opposed the use of contraceptives and family limitation, picturing it as a Malthusian plot "to blame poverty on the poor." Clara Zetkin – for instance – denounced birth control, calling it an "individualistic indulgence," and arguing that "the proletarians must consider the need to have as many fighters as possible" (Seccombe 1993: 164–6, and especially 165). It must be noted, in this context, that only in 1891 had the SPD "officially accepted women's equal rights, and then only in a very limited legal sense" (Rowbotham 1974: 80). Generations of Marxists have also viewed the fulltime houseworker as a backward subject incapable of organization. Typically, when in the 1940s Mary Inman, a Los Angeles factory worker, in her *In Woman's Defense* (1945) stressed the productivity of housework, the U.S. Communist Party forbade her from teaching in its school for workers' education (see Weigand 2001 on this topic). Along similar lines, consider also the Marxists' inability in the 1960s and 1970s to recognize the importance of the feminist movement and even more specifically the feminist struggle against unpaid domestic labor as a determinant in the definition of the value of labor-power. Much has changed today with respect to the 1970s, when feminists were routinely accused of dividing the working class. The development of the student, feminist and ecological movements, as well as the crisis of waged work, have forced Marxists to look beyond the factory into the school, the environment and more recently "social reproduction" as key terrains for the reproduction of the workforce and working class struggle. But, with some exceptions, the Marxist Left's inability to see the reproduction of human life and labor-power and the gender hierarchies built upon it as key elements in the process of accumulation continues. Witness the autonomist Marxists' theorization of the dominance, in the present phase of capitalist development, of "immaterial labor", and the associated argument (expanding Marx's vision in the "Fragment on Machines" in the *Grundrisse*) (Marx 1973: 690–710) that capitalism is working towards the elimination of living labor from the "production process," which ignores that reproductive work, especially in the form of child-care, is irreducible to industrialization, and is a paradigmatic example of the interpenetration of emotional and material elements in most forms of work. Witness also the continuing reluctance among many Marxists to criticize Marx's theory that the revolutionary process is premised on the globalization of capitalist production even though it is now patently clear that this can only occur at the cost of the destruction of the means of reproduction of many populations across the planet. Indeed, if we accept Marx's thesis, about capitalism's progressive character, we would have to dismiss some of the most powerful struggles presently taking place across the world as ineffective if not outright reactionary. For they are clearly struggles *against* capitalist development which, in the eyes of indigenous peoples' communities fighting, for instance, against the destruction of their lands and cultures by mining, petroleum drilling companies, or companies building hydro-electric plants and other "mega projects" – is nothing short of another name for violence (Klein 2014).

In conclusion, if the "revolutionary kernel" of Marx's theory is to be is to be rescued from the mountain of developmentalists interpretations and applications under which it has been buried, and that Marx undoubtedly inspired, we have to rethink Marxism and capitalism from the viewpoint of the process of reproduction, as some of us have been doing now for four decades, recognizing that this is the most strategic ground both in the struggle against capitalism and the construction of a non-exploitative society.

Notes

1 For advocates see Hardt and Negri (2004), Vercellone (2007). For a critique of the concept of "cognitive capitalism" see Caffentzis (2013).

2 In one note, citing a doctor sent by the British government to report on the health of female workers in the industrial districts during the Civil War in the United States, which had cut the import of cotton and shut down the textile factories in England, Marx ironically commented that "An American revolution and a universal crisis were needed in order for working girls, who spin for the whole

world, to learn to sew," and that "The women now had sufficient leisure to give their infants the breast, instead of poisoning them with 'Godfrey's Cordial'" (an opiate) (Marx 1976: 518). In another note, Marx points out that:

> Since certain family functions, such as nursing and suckling children, cannot be entirely suppressed, the mothers who have been confiscated by capital must try substitutes of some sort. Domestic work, such as sowing and mending, must be replaced by the purchase of ready-made articles. Hence the diminished expenditure of labour in the house is accompanied by an increased expenditure of money outside.
>
> (Marx 1976: 518, n.39)

3 Marx also fails to inform us that some of the commodities most important for the reproduction of labor-power in Europe – those that fueled the Industrial Revolution – sugar, tea, tobacco, rum, cotton – were not produced by waged workers but by slave labor in the American plantations, through an international division of work further cutting the cost of reproducing the "metropolitan" proletariat, while keeping slave and wage workers geographically and socially divided.

4 Notable here was the organizational work of Francis Place, who already in 1822 advocated the use of contraceptive techniques in order for workers to escape a Malthusian fate, and begin to control their birthrate. A worker himself, father of 15 children, Place launched a campaign to advertise his ideas on the matter, circulating handbills addressed to married couples, later continuing his advocacy after becoming a founder of the Chartist movement. Very popular among workers, especially in the northern districts, Place is considered one of the fathers of the birth control movement. See Himes (1970) on this issue.

5 For a critique of Marx's "surplus population" theory see Henninger (2014: 301–2). He writes: "Much like the reproduction-schemes in *Capital Vol. II*, Marx's theory of relative-surplus population effaces the possibility of autonomous underclass-behaviour and recognizes no other logic but that of capital-valorisation."

6 On the relations between the capitalist conception of labor as the essence of value creation and the regulation of women's reproductive capacity, see Federici (2004), Chapter 3, and in particular her discussion of the European witch-hunt.

7 An act of 1803 by the British government made abortion a statutory crime punishable with whipping, transportation and even death if the woman was proven quick with child. The statute was re-enacted in 1828. Then the Offences Against Persons Act of 1861 established that any person attempting to abort, if convicted would be punished to penal servitude for life. In every country of Europe, in Marx's time, interfering with procreation was a felony, punishable with many years of imprisonment.

8 See, e.g., Lord Ashley's intervention during the Parliamentary debates surrounding the Ten Hours Bill of 1847. He complained that the "females not only perform the labor, but occupy the places of men; they are forming various clubs and associations, and are gradually acquiring those privileges that are held to be the proper portion of the male sex." (Lown 1990: 181 and 44–5).

9 As evidence Foster Bellamy quotes a text by Eleanor Marx, in which she speaks of the "expropriation" of women and workers from their rights.

10 Factory workers won Saturday afternoon off.

11 Tomasello stresses the important role of the Sansimonians in the centralization of the figure of the industrial worker, and the disappearance from the program of the socialist/working class movements of a series of issues that had been crucial for earlier anti-capitalist struggles, such as "the critique of work and technology, of family and the criminal system" (Tomasello 2018: 132, n.38).

12 As he wrote in *Capital,* Volume I:

> Previously the worker sold his own labour-power which he disposed of as a free agent, formally speaking. Now he sells his wife and child. He has become a slave dealer. Notices of demands for children's labour often resemble in form the inquiries for Negro slaves that were formerly read among the advertisements in American journals.
>
> (Marx 1976: 519)

13 According to William Blackstone, whose *Commentaries on the laws of England*, systematized English bourgeois legal and judicial practice:

> By marriage the very being or legal existence of a woman is suspended, or at least is incorporated or consolidated into that of the husband, under whose wing, protection and cover she performs everything and she is therefore called in our law "*femme covert.*"
>
> (in Holcombe 1983: 25–6)

14 On the sale of wives see E.P. Thompson (1991). According to Thompson, who has assembled a documentation on this practice, the sale or exchange of a wife for sexual or domestic services took place on occasion in most places and at most times, in most parts of England, above all among laborers, such as miners, bakers, chimney-sweepers, ironworker, bricklayers, brick-makers, cloth workers, stone cutters and many other lower class occupations (Thompson 1991: 408–9 and 413–14). Tolerated by the law, the custom was so entrenched that sales of wives are recorded even in the first quarter of the twentieth century. Workhouses in some cases forced husbands to sell their wives so that they dind not have to support them. It was the quickest way, among the lower classes, to end a marriage. Customarily, after parading his wife with a halter around her neck, arm or waist, a husband would publicly auction her to the highest bidder. (Wikipedia. https://en.wikipedia.org/wiki/Wife_selling_(English_custom)).

15 Whereas most of sections of the IWA were identified by the part of the production process their largely immigrant German membership belonged to , Section 12 which was dominated by US-born radicals (often called "Yankee Internationalists"). As the two factions began sparring, Marx himself recommended the expulsion of the faction that gave "predominance to the women's question over the question of labor" (Folbre 2009:103). Echoing Marx, a member of Section 1 defended the expulsion: "This nonsense which they talk of, female suffrage and free love, may do to consider in the future, but the question that interests us as working-men is that of labor and wages" (Frisken 2004: 44).

16 As she wrote, I have heard women reply when this difficulty was pressed upon them, "We cannot ostracize men as we are compelled to [ostracize] women, since we are dependent on them for support" (quoted in Frisken 2004: 39).

17 It is interesting, in this context, that one of the few references in Marx's work to a women's struggle is to a wives' mobilization in support of their husbands' demand for a "family wage." As Heather A. Brown reports, in an article written in 1853, Marx, without any comment, described the "efforts by women to ensure that men would be paid a 'family wage'," citing an organizers' argument that every man should have a fair wage, so that "he could support himself and his family in comfort" (Brown 2012: 103).

18 And in the same work the entire Chapter VI, "The Factory Operative as a Homemaker."

19 It was reasserted, however, by William Blackstone Commentaries on English Law, in the eighteenth century.

20 By the same act, women became entitled to hold the wages they earned and other forms of property, and were declared not responsible for their husbands' debts.

21 At the same time new regulations were introduced intended to make sex work more controlled and degrading, such as the registration of the lodging houses where prostitution was practiced, compulsory medical visits, enforced through the Contagious Diseases Acts of 1864, 1866 and 1869, and detention in hospitals, up to a period of six months, of those found to be diseased.

22 The reference here is to Marx's comment, in the section of *The Economic and Philosophical Manuscripts of 1844* in which he discusses "estranged labor," that since work in capitalism is for the worker an alienating activity

> The worker therefore only feels himself outside his work, and in his work he feel outside himself, and when he is working he is not at home. He is at home when he is not working. His labour is therefore not voluntary but forced labour.
>
> (Marx 1976: 72)

This comment has often been criticized by feminists as a further example of his devaluation of reproductive activities.

References

Acton, William (1969 [1857]) *Prostitution*, New York: Frederick A. Praeger Publishers.

Brown, Heather A. (2012) *Marx on Gender and the Family. A Critical Study. Historical Materialism* 39, London, Boston: Brill.

Caffentzis, George (2013) "A Critique of "Cognitive Capitalism," in *Letters of Blood and Fire: Work, Machines, and the Crisis of Capitalism*, Oakland, CA: PM Press and Common Notions, pp. 95–123.

Chevalier, Louis (1958) *Classes laborieuses et classes dangereuses à Paris au XIX siècle* Paris: Plon.

Cockburn, Cynthia (2015) "The Standpoint Theory," in Shahrzad Mojab (ed.), *Marxism and Feminism*, London: Zed Books, pp. 331–46.

Dalla Costa, Mariarosa (2015) [1971]) *Family Welfare*, New York: Common Notions.

Fauré, Christine (2003) *Political and Historical Encyclopedia of Women*, New York: Routledge.

Federici, Silvia (2004) *Caliban and the Witch. Women, the Body and Primitive Accumulation*, Brooklyn: Autonomedia.

Federici, Silvia and Cox, Nicole (1975) *Counter Planning from the Kitchen*, Bristol: Falling Wall Press.

Ferrari Bravo, Luciano (1975) "Vecchie e nuove questioni nella teoria dell'imperialismo," Introduction to Luciano Ferrari Bravo (ed.), *Imperialismo e classe operaia multinazionale*, Milano: Feltrinelli, pp. 7–67.

Folbre, Nancy (2009) "Socialism, Feminist and Scientific," in Marianne A. Ferber and Julie A. Nelson (eds.), *Beyond Economic Man: Feminist Theory and Economics*, Chicago: University of Chicago Press, pp. 94–110.

Fortunati, Leopoldina (1995 [1981]) *The Arcane of Reproduction: Housework, Prostitution, Labor and Capital*, New York: Autonomedia.

Frank, André Gunder (1969 [1967]) *Capitalism ad Underdevelopment in Latin America*, New York: Monthly Review Press.

Frisken, Amanda (2004) *Victoria Woodhull's Sexual Revolution: Political Theater and Popular Press in Nineteenth-Century America*, Philadelphia: University of Pennsylvania Press.

Foster, John Bellamy (2018) "Women, Nature and Capital in the Industrial Revolution," *Monthly Review*, vol. 69, No. 8: 1–25.

Foster, John Bellamy (2013) "Marx and the Rift in the Universal Metabolism of Nature," *Monthly Review*, vol. 65, No. 7: 1–19.

Henninger, Max (2014) "Poverty, Labor, Development: Towards a Critique of Marx's Conceptualizations," in Marcel van der Linden and Karl Heinz Roth (eds.), *Beyond Marx: Theorising the Global Labour Relations of the Twenty-First Century*, Boston: Brill, pp. 281–304.

Hardt, Michael and Negri, Antonio (2004) *Multitude: War and Democracy in the Age of Empire*, Minneapolis: University of Minnesota Press.

Hayden, Dolores (1985) *The Grand Domestic Revolution: A History of Feminist Designs for American Homes, Neighborhoods, and Cities*, Cambridge, MA: The MIT Press.

Hewitt, Margaret (1958) *Wives and Mothers in Victorian Industry. A Study of the Effects of the Employment of Married Women in Victorian Industry*, London: Rockliff.

Himes, Norman Edwin (1970 [1936]) *Medical History of Contraception*, New York: Schocken Books.

Hobsbawm, Eric (1968) *Industry and Empire. The Making of Modern English Society, Vol. II, 1759 to the Present Day*, New York: Pantheon Books.

Holcombe, Lee (1983) *Wives and Property. Reform of the Married Women's Property Law In Ninenteenth century England*, Toronto and Buffalo: University of Toronto Press.

Inman, Mary (1945 [1940]) *In Woman's Defense*, Los Angeles: Committee to Organize the Advancement of Women.

Klein, Naomi (2014) *This Changes Everything: Capitalism vs. Climate*, New York: Simon and Schuster.

Lown, Judy (1990) *Women and Industrialization: Gender at Work in Nineteenth-Century England*, Minneapolis: University of Minnesota Press.

Marshall, Alfred (1890 [1938]) *Principles of Economics. An Introductory Volume*, London: Macmillan and Co., Limited.

Marx, Karl (1963) *The 18th of Brumaire of Louis Bonaparte*, New York: International Publishers.

Marx, Karl (1969) *Theories of Surplus Value, Part 1*, Moscow: Progress Publishers.

Marx, Karl (1973) *Grundrisse: Foundations of the Critique of Political Economy*, London: Pelican Books.

Marx, Karl (1976) *Capital Vol. I*, London: Penguin

Marx, Karl (1981) *Capital Vol. III*, London: Penguin.

Marx, Karl and Friedrich Engels (1959) *The First Indian War of Independence. 1857–1859*, Moscow: Progress Publishers.

Marx, Karl and Friedrich Engels (1967) *The Communist Manifesto*, Harmondsworth, UK: Penguin Books.

Marx, Karl and Friedrich Engels (1970) *The German Ideology*, London: International Publishers.

Meillassoux, Claude (1975) *Maidens, Meal and Money. Capitalism and the domestic community*, Cambridge: Cambridge University Press.

Meyer, Ahlrich (2014) "A Theory of Defeat. Marx and the Evidence of the Nineteenth Century", in Marcel van der Linden and Karl Heinz Roth (eds.), *Beyond Marx: Theorising the Global Labour Relations of the Twenty-First Century*, Boston: Brill, pp. 258–79.

Mies, Maria (2014 [1985]) *Patriarchy and Accumulation on a World Scale: Women in the International Division of Labor*, London: Zed Books.

Mojab, Shahrzad (ed.) (2015) *Marxism and Feminism*, London: Zed Books.

Negri, Antonio (1991 [1979]) *Marx Beyond Marx. Lesson on the Grundrisse*, Brooklyn: Autonomedia and Pluto.

Pelz, William A. (2017) "Capital and the First International," in Ingo Schmidt and Carlo Fanelli (eds.), *Reading "Capital" Today*, London: Pluto Press, pp. 36–47.

Pinchbeck, Ivy (1930) *Women's Workers and The Industrial Revolution, 1750–1850*, New York: F. S. Crofts & Co.

Rowbotham, Sheila (1974) *Women, Resistance, and Revolution*, New York: Vintage Books.

Seccombe, Wally (1993) *Weathering the Storm. Working-Class Families from the Industrial Revolution to the Fertility Decline*, London: Verso.

Thompson, E.P. (1991) *Customs in Common. Studies in Traditional Popular Culture*, New York: The New Press.

Tomasello, Federico (2018) *L'Inizio del lavoro. Teoria politica e questione sociale nella Francia di prima metà Ottocento*, Roma: Carrocci Editore.

Van de Linden, Marcel and Roth, Karl Heinz (eds.) in collaboration with Max Henninger (2014) *Beyond Marx. Theorising the Global Labor Relations of the Twentieth-First Century*, Leiden-Boston: Brill.

Vercellone, Carlo (2007) "From Formal Subsumption to General Intellect: Elements for a Marxist Reading of the Thesis of Cognitive Capitalism," in *Historical Materialism*, vol. 15: 13–36.

Wallach Scott, Joan (1988) *Gender and the Politics of History*, New York: Columbia University Press.

Weigand, Kate (2001) *Red Feminism. American Communism and the Making of Women's Liberation*, Baltimore, MD: The Johns Hopkins University Press.

8 Towards a communist revolution

Gender and class in *Capital*, Volume I

Himani Bannerji

1 Introduction

Capital, Volume I, first published in 1867, has not dated. Any fresh reading always yields new insights to our social analysis and critique.[1] *Capital* will remain relevant for as long as capitalism lasts, and even after. Both its content and its method of inquiry, namely, historical materialism rooted in the critique of ideology, will remain indispensable for the production of knowledge for changing the world. *Capital* will continue to provide an invaluable resource for a conscious making of history, for any project of socialist/communist[2] revolution.

Capital, Volume I is used here to explore an uneasy relation between feminism and Marxism,[3] especially Marxism of organized communist politics. Most feminists and Marxists have attributed separate ontologies to gender and class, and attempts to integrate them have been stymied by theoretical and organizational difficulties. Thus, class is disassociated from gender, and struggle against gender/patriarchy from class struggle.[4] Historically, communist parties and associated labour organizations put gender equality into to their political agendas, but these early efforts were not pursued in a sustained manner and could not articulate gender and class constitutively.[5] The result was an abstract or partial understanding of the social organization of capitalism, producing either a metatheory or a particularist, for example an economistic, understanding of the mode of production. Thus, gender came to be considered as a cultural superstructure reflecting or corresponding to the economic base (for these terms see Williams 1976, 1977). Such theoretical exercises fractured the concrete unity of the social (for a comprehensive understanding of this term see Smith 2005), producing conceptual binaries such as social production and reproduction, gender and class, the public and the private, and so on. I read *Capital*, Volume I using Marx's method of enquiry, namely historical materialism, whose salient aspect is the critique of ideology (see Marx and Engels 1976, 1975; see also Smith 1990).

As the concept of ideology has been understood in different ways (see Williams 1977), it is necessary to clarify my understanding of it. This is derived from Marx's own definition in *The German Ideology*, where the notion is treated as not only 'ruling ideas' of the ruling classes, but as an epistemological device – as an 'epistemological grammar' which is perfected at an advanced state of division between mental and manual labour. He presents us with the 'secret' of its production process, explaining the 'three tricks' used. The first step is to separate ideas from their social and individual origins and contexts and in using this decontextualization for the purpose of extrapolation. These extrapolated notions are evacuated of their socio-historical content and of concrete materiality. The process involves dislocation, displacement and abstraction. The second 'trick' is to provide a 'mystical' or secondary level of theoretical connection between these extrapolated and abstracted notions or expressions, conferring upon them a metaphysical/universal status. Thus enabled, these ideas or ahistorical abstractions assume a fabricated autonomy and human-like agency, distracting attention from actual social relations, and are themselves presented as causes or actors in history and thus serve as ideology. The notion of 'the proletariat' as critiqued here is an apt example of an ideological category (see Bannerji 2015; see also Smith 1990).

It is immaterial that Marx did not directly use the word 'ideology' in Volume I or engage in an explicit critique of it. But the way he demystified the notion of primitive accumulation articulated by Adam Smith and others or resolved the phenomenon of commodity fetishism into social relational components, are brilliant demonstrations of critique of ideology. It should be noted that the subtitle of *Capital,* Volume I is 'a *critique* of political economy' (my emphasis). Through Marx's critical method it becomes possible to conceptualize class and gender in non-binary terms, thereby avoiding either an abstract or an over-particularized dualist reading of the social. This Marxist feminist critique, conducted from the standpoint of historical materialism, exposes formative relations between multiple social determinations which provide a concrete character to the mode of production as a whole (see Bannerji 2011).[6] To do so is important because otherwise the particularities of complimentary and contradictory social relations which texture the mode of production are liable to be treated as separate formations which are theoretically aggregated. This has been the case with class and gender. It does not help matters to refine this aggregation with the idea of intersectionality,[7] since an essential sense of qualitative difference between what we call class and gender still remains. This theoretical problem cannot be solved by merely valorizing each category separately and then making them intersect. If class and social production are to be mainly seen economically and gender in terms of biology and social reproduction, conferring on them equal value fails to show that they are constitutively inseparable. Pursuing this conceptually separatist path posed problems as well, creating barriers for communists/Marxists and feminists in their organizing practices. Communist parties tried to cope with this problem by creating separate mass organizations for women to deal with gender oppression, but to limited effect. Feminist movements, on the other hand, have struggled against gender oppression and women's poverty to equally small effect because they cannot incorporate class within their framework, which leaves the capitalist context of gender unaddressed. It is my contention that tacit or explicit acceptance of a class-gender binary separating production and reproduction leaves us with an incomplete revolution. Though there is no guarantee that formulating the right theory will be followed by successful revolutionary organization, because the reality of politics on the ground, impinged as it is with so many political and social forces, is too fluid for that, it is very important to get the conceptual groundwork of the critique right. Otherwise the organizations we put in place might not only be ineffectual, but counterproductive. Giving gender a separate but equal status, or according it a secondary position to class, or subsuming gender within class, will produce counterrevolutionary consequences. The present chapter is an attempt to explore how class and gender might be seen as informing each other. This is only possible if we use Marx's method of inquiry rooted in historical materialism.

Before going further, I need to specify my particular understanding of historical materialism that I apply to Volume I. In this I make a distinction between the *content* that Marx presents based on his historical and social research and the *form* or *method of inquiry* he uses to produce a reliable and actionable knowledge of society. The historical empirical content he does not always subject to his critical method. Thus, we find that while his content, based upon available contemporary records and research, may be erroneous and in need of factual and critical correction, his form of inquiry, however, is reflexive and therefore capable of critique of even his own facts and ideas. Thus, while I can use one aspect of historical materialism, namely the critique of ideology, to identify Marx's writings on India, influenced by Hegel, James Mill and others, to be tainted with elements of Orientalism or racism, so can I deploy the same method of historical materialism to critique some aspects of his own content. This would demonstrate how gender and class are categorical summations of social relations which exist constitutively as practical, material historical processes and their forms of consciousness. This critical exercise should be undertaken to present the specific aspect of social formations while retaining an overview of the mode of production as a whole, which the particularity of the social relations specifies. This avoids discretely particularistic, fragmentary and reificatory reading of the organization of the social and allows more careful thinking about issues of difference/specificity and identity.

Considering gender and class according to this framework leads us to realize that not all differences are irreconcilable, though initially they may appear to be so, and in fact may hold a constitutive relation to each other. In this I rely on Marx's statement in *Grundrisse* that there are necessary differences among social determinations, and these very differences allow them to enter into internal formative relations with each other vital to the formation of the overall social (Marx 1973: 90–94; see also Bannerji 2011). This point is best understood by considering the difference pointed out in *Grundrisse* between production and consumption both in specific and constitutive terms. Marx states that though production and consumption involve specifically different activities, through this very difference they provide the motive force or the ground for each other's activation and formation. Nodding to internal relations of identity embedded in their difference, he shows how production itself is a type of consumption, namely the consumption of labour power, and consumption is the motive force of production. This dynamic obtaining between specific difference and necessary formative relations between them ensures the reproduction of the overall social organization. I hope to show that such a formative relationship also exists between gender and class, along with their specificities. The various relations of bourgeois society thus prove to be an ensemble which simultaneously through formative contradictions preserve specific differences while producing the social concrete (see Bannerji 2011). The difficulty arises when certain constellations of social relations are named as 'gender' or 'class' and take on a categorical substantiveness and thus function ideologically. It is then that pre-scribed interpreted understandings of these appellations not only become a point of departure for theorization but distract from an exploration of historical and social reality. *Capital*, Volume I, provides us with a method of inquiry for challenging such ideological categories describing the historical social relations as the ground for the creation of codes for naming them. It takes apart the composition of the capitalist mode of production by not beginning from the categories of class and gender, but rather from the constitutive social relations, practices and ideas.[8] Marx reveals the concreteness through pointing out the spatializations of the social in terms of the actual existence whose activities bring the space of capital into being. Thus, class and gender, instead of being substantive categories, signal to social and sexual division of labour. As such, in integrating the natural and the constructed social through the mediation of human labour he spares us a dualist perception of class and gender as developed from discrete premises. Though this dualist ideological form of thinking has achieved a commonsensical status, it can still be challenged through Marx's critical method – even when, as we shall see, Marx himself sometimes did not.

Thinking about gender and class in dualist terms has had extensive implications for revolutionary politics. Given that communism insists on a clear social analysis, even a 'scientific' one, to ground its organizational practices, we need to clarify the prevailing understanding of gender and class, social production and social reproduction, men's and women's revolutionary subjectivities and agencies. As a communist project depends on human subjectivities and political agencies, they should include those of women as well. But in existing and past communist practices they have not been accorded a central role. I will treat the concept of the proletariat, meant as a code for working class historical agency, as an heuristic device for exploring this problem, showing how by excluding women it serves as an ideological category. In the *Manifesto of the Communist Party* the working class has been singularized as the proletariat, the collective protagonist in the historical drama for changing the world. From the nineteenth century to now this Promethean icon has been engraved on the plinth of all communist revolutionary projects.[9] But this collective configuration of the working class is commonsensically masculine.[10] Reminiscent of the figure of the sovereign in the frontispiece of Hobbes's *Leviathan*, the proletariat is also a collage consisting of working men. Excluding women by omission, this construction of the revolutionary agent expresses a gendered perception. This is in keeping with Marx's characterization of men as creative, productive and transformative social beings (Marx 1974: 173),[11] but not so women. Not signified as producers who transform nature and thereby themselves, women are by default or directly posited as biological and social reproducers. From the era of the *Manifesto of the Communist Party* to the modern times of communist parties and labour unions the masculine character of the proletariat has not changed in substance. While women were overwhelmingly engaged in the communist cause as their own (for example, in the events leading up to the Bolshevik Revolution of 1917), political subjectivities and agencies for class struggle were associated with men. Class and productive labour continue to be male identified, while gender and reproductive labour are commonsensically feminized. Women are placed within the discourse of oppression primarily as passive objects of societal powers, calling for aid and rescue. Similar to the peasants described by Marx in *The Eighteenth Brumaire of Louis Bonaparte*, '[t]hey cannot represent themselves, they must be represented' (Marx 1979: 187). But men, placed within the political language of class, are projected as active subjects with capacities for resistance and revolution.

2 Gender and labour in transition from feudalism to industrial capitalism

To understand how such gendered class relations with active and passive subjectivities developed, we need to examine the transition from feudalism to capitalism. This is where *Capital*, Volume 1 is of great importance, because it provides an extensive account of this transition, showing that the process was neither linear nor without contradictions regarding gender roles in class formation. The changes in gender-class relations occurred over a period of time during which, and even after, aspects of feudal social relations or their modifications continued to co-exist or blend with capitalism. The chapters of *Capital*, Volume 1 most useful for us are on the labour process (Chapter 7), the working day (Chapter 10), machinery and modern industry (Chapter 15, the largest chapter in Volume I), as well as those on the so-called primitive accumulation (Part Eight). Chapters 10 and 15, especially, provide a wealth of detail regarding women's labour in the transition, which occurred from the mid-seventeenth century to the end of the nineteenth century. Here women are central to the productive processes that usher in large scale industrial capitalism. From mining to manufacture, as adjuncts to machines in the partially mechanized factories and in the interstices of the emerging technology, women work in vast numbers in commodity production and comprise a substantial portion of the working class. From eyewitness accounts, reports of factory inspectors, doctors and others we see the unceasing labour and the horrific conditions in workplaces and the mental and physical degradations of the workers. These chapters etch the picture of an intense proletarianization, of a dispossessed and subsistence-denied population whose labour is both cheap and expendable. Our current understanding of gender and class derives largely from the type of material that *Capital,* Volume I depicts.[12]

In the chapters on the so-called primitive accumulation Marx shows the origin of this desperate labour force, which arose from the dissolution of feudal agricultural and property relations.[13] This dissolution also involved profound changes in men and women's participation in production and reproduction. Under feudalism productive labour was not unknown to women and young persons. They participated in various forms of agricultural and small commodity production. Women also provisioned the kin-based, worker-inclusive households they lived in, as well as participated in some market production.[14] As they were neither unused to hard work nor subscribed to strict sexual division of labour, it was not out of their mental and physical capacity to join the capitalist labour force. But the violence they experienced lay in the speed of dispossession and the ruthlessness of rising capitalism in the types and hours of work demanded from them. Men also faced the predations of 'primitive accumulation', but there was differential participation on their part. Landless and land-poor male peasants and sharecroppers entered the labour force early, while landed farming classes and artisans entered at a slower pace (Hill 1961). The male urban artisans, with their strong production bases and market networks and guilds controlling technological secrets and recruitment of apprentices, resisted longer. But the largest supply of labourers were women and children from the countryside, as capitalism first developed there in agriculture, then in manufactories. For the dispossessed population the only recourse was wage labour, since the market was now the main source of acquiring subsistence. The working class in the earlier stages of the transition consisted largely of cheap manual labour or women and children. Moving ultimately towards mechanization, capitalists relied for a long time on this type of labour in some combination with machinery. About this Marx remarks:

> Before the labour of women and children under 10 years was forbidden in the mines, the capitalists considered the employment of naked women and girls, often in company with men, so far sanctioned by their moral code, and especially by their ledgers, that it was only after the passing of the [Factory Acts] that they had recourse to machinery.
>
> (Marx 1974: 516)

And even then, these laws were more honoured in the breach. Thus, arose the first working class of England, consisting of a large female labour force.

Marx denounced the unconscionable and grotesque labour exploitation of women, young people and children. As noted in *Capital,* Volume 1,

> [i]n England women are still occasionally used instead of horses for hauling barges, because the labour required to produce horses and machines is an accurately known quantity, while that required to maintain the women of the surplus population is beneath all calculation.
>
> (Marx 1974: 517)

He described the physical and mental deterioration of the labour force and the terminal illnesses visited upon them (Marx 1974: 520–21). The greed, inhumanity and sordid sadism of capitalist exploitation of women, children and the poor at large have been exhaustively documented by social historians and historians of British criminal law (see Linebaugh and Rediker 2000).

3 A Reproductive catastrophe: the birth of capitalist patriarchy and the nuclear family

What Marx depicts in *Capital,* Volume I is a catastrophic crisis in biological and social reproduction, though Marx did not describe the situation in these terms. In the course of transition from feudalism to capitalism, for the majority all social ties and sources for survival were falling apart. Peasant and small artisanal households were destroyed or mutated into living arrangements hitherto unknown. Any stable space for bio social reproduction ceased to exist for them, and there was no blueprint for working through this life crisis. But as the process unfolded new social forms and existential modes, including the bourgeois nuclear family, emerged.[15] In a world 'turned upside down' by the Puritan Revolution (Hill 1972)[16] and the cascade of enclosures, encroachments and privatization of commons, all forms of reproduction carried on under feudalism were now left to the victims themselves (see Perelman 2000). Since in feudalism the separation of work and life was not rigidly demarcated and people lived in extended households rather than in small families, the nuclear family was neither necessary nor conceivable. But in capitalism, as production and reproduction came to be spatially separated because the labour process left no room for reproductive activities in the same space where production took place, life had to be separated from labour, and thus emerged the two spaces of the private and the public. This took a long time, and the gender arrangements were not clearly formed, as women, at least, traversed both spaces. As the market came to control the supply of food and other basic needs people thronged to the mills and factories, which could not absorb the supply of available labour. Thus hunger spread, and children were plunged into the same vortex with their resourceless parents. Sometimes they drifted or were put away into the workhouses, or roamed like feral animals.[17]

The crisis of reproduction, with its miserable condition of children and a fear of the possible extinction of expendable sources of labour, gave rise to much consternation among the English middle classes. This resulted in periodic legislation against child labour, which was routinely ignored by both capitalists and parents. Marx spoke of the sordid trafficking needs of parents and referred to a Children's Employment Commission report which stated that in England women 'have taken children from the workhouse and let anyone have them out for 2s and 6d a week' (Marx 1974: 520). Parents were claimed to be selling infant labour 'to work for their own daily bread' (Marx 1974: 520, n.20). It was well known, writes Marx, that '[i]n the notorious London district of Bethnal Green a public market is held every Monday and Tuesday morning, at which children of both sexes, from nine years of age upwards, hire themselves out to the silk manufacturers' (Marx 1974: 520). Infanticide and abandonment of children were noted in the district medical and factory inspector records that Marx consulted, but the actual numbers were much higher (see Sauer March 1978, also Linebaugh 1991).

This crisis of developing capitalism, in conjunction with the rising bourgeois classes and the state, produced notions of gender, class and family as we now understand them. This includes our present-day conventional mores of parenthood. The so-called woman question emerged as a part of the so-called child question. Practically speaking, the new family form was at the service of general reproduction, but ideologically it was touted as a remedy for the horrific life-labour crisis of society as a whole. The management of the crisis resulted in the removal of women from production to domesticity and projected the family as their proper domain. Thus, production and reproduction parted company and two gendered social sites, the family and the factory, organized a divided social space. Unable to offer any real solution to the crisis, the state, social reformers and the church all supported easing women out of production. They knew that this panacea of the family for the working classes was solely ideological. Its actualization under the circumstances was impossible. They disregarded the reality not only of extreme economic hardship, but also the realities of desertion, violence, accidental conception, rape, risky abortions and other components of domestic life.

The gender typification of production and reproduction arose from such exclusion of women. Men of their own families and male co-workers also demanded this, because they saw working women as competitors, as hindrances to rising wages and to their opportunities for becoming skilled workers in large scale industries. They resented the availability of manual labour of women, children and male destitutes. Male authority and pride were compromised by working spouses and daughters threatening men's status as head of the family. This situation contributed to working men's demand for a family wage that would permit them to have a family at their disposal. The supposition of adequate support for their wives and children conferred a legitimation on the idea of family wage.[18]

The new bourgeois family, which restricted women's right to productive work and coerced them into the role of biological and social reproducers, generally lowered their social status. This family, lasting until today, is a unit of social reproduction which is simultaneously gynocentric and under a patriarchal authority in various guises. Conversely, the world of production is typically androcentric. While ideology kept these spaces under the moral regulation of gender, the practicalities of existence were less morally defined under the imperative of earning a living. The ideological and moral dimension of the family largely derived from a Protestant bourgeois worldview (on this see Weber 1958). This bourgeois institution of the family, which made women responsible for management of the reproduction crisis, was bound to fail. But women were scapegoated for this failure. Expected to be stay-at-home mothers, wives and homemakers, they clearly could not do so. In actuality they mostly remained workers as before. Also, as before, they were manual workers in the lowest factory positions, or worked as domestic servants, cleaners of public spaces, nannies, or sellers of breastmilk to bourgeois families.[19] Prostitution was also common, ranging from young girls to unmarried and married adults (see Walkowitz 1980: 246–56). Women's paid work was deemed informal or as supplementary to their husband's wages, if such husbands actually existed or did not desert them along with their children. Thus, women continued to work, but they lost their identity as workers and their labour was de-valued. This meant that they were beneath the attention of labour organizers and denied their role as class subjects and their place in class struggle.[20] In this way gender was rendered distinct from class.

4 Marx's ambiguity regarding industrial capitalism and the gender of labour

The historical materialist narrative of labour in *Capital,* Volume I shows us how gender and class arise in the same site through the same labour and life processes, such that perceiving them as two discrete realities would be erroneous. Intersectionality is not an adequate term for describing their originary and formative relations, which in their twists and turns concretize the whole mode of production in and through their constitutiveness. Their differences are necessary and specific determinations for the making of the capitalist mode of production. In the face of such overwhelming evidence of women as producers, it is puzzling that they do not feature as members of the proletariat in communist discourse. At least a part of the puzzle lies in the fact that Marx does not pull together his description of women's labour and life to the theoretical project he undertakes in the rest of *Capital.* Failing this, his historical narration of labour is held suspended in mid-air, thus acquiring a kind of incidental character. Therefore, we need to explore Marx's own attitude towards sexual division of labour, coded as gender, which provides the basis for his representation of women in the labour force and the value of their labour. Here we find an ambiguity on Marx's part both about capitalism itself and sexual division of labour specific to it. Marx of course condemns capitalism in the strongest terms. Written in 'the annals of mankind in letters of blood and fire', '[i]n actual history, it is a notorious fact that conquest, enslavement, robbery, murder, in short, force, play the great part.' The new waged workers emerged 'only after they had been robbed of all their means of production, and all the guarantees of existence afforded by the old feudal arrangements' (Marx 1974: 874–75). Legitimized by notions of freedom and ownership, capitalism is exposed as an intrinsically violent mode of production (see Marx 1974, ch.27). Yet in the *Manifesto of the Communist Party* he also displays an admiration for the ingenuity, energy and the productive forces that capital unleashes, transforming every space that it enters (Marx and Engels 1976b: 488; see also Berman 1988). The same admiration and a horrified fascination are found in *Capital* Volume 1 as Marx watches cyclopean machines dominating human workers. The large-scale industries and their unending production of profit resonate with Faust's bargain with Mephistopheles. Similarly, the *Economic and Philosophical Manuscripts of 1844* is a discourse on alienation and the necessity of overcoming it, but the same admiring attitude to the development of productive forces, which he considers as an expression of human capacity, is also present. Marx does not consider these productive forces as destructive in and of themselves, except under capitalism (see Benjamin 1968), and instead sees them as resources for a better life under communism which are to be ultimately controlled by the victorious proletariat. If capitalism would be the motive force for the birth of such productive forces, of civilization in short, then in spite of all its problems, Marx could not gainsay it as a necessary step towards a communist society. In the meanwhile, all the human suffering that he registered so keenly leaves him trapped between outrage and admiration, horror and wonder.

It is in this context of ambiguity that we must situate Marx's vision of gender and of women as essentially reproducers rather than producers. Though he depicts women as workers, he is silent regarding their revolutionary or socially transformative potential. For man the *homo faber*, the maker, he offers a different place in his schema. Men transform themselves and nature, develop productive forces and revolutionize society. Women, on the other hand, are essentially biological and social reproducers, and as such, to be protected and sympathized with. In these attitudes Marx shares with Victorian gentlemen a romantic/sentimental form of patriarchy, which is accompanied by a paternal reproach when women allegedly neglect their homes and are derelict in maternal duties.

An ambiguity is also to be found in Marx's approach to the family and women's sole reproductive role within it. In *The German Ideology* he characterizes tribal society as an extension of the patriarchal family and associates it with slavery. This is close to the Roman definition of the family as a unit of ownership by a patrician of women, children and slaves. The situation does not improve for women with time, except that the patriarchal family form itself takes on a subordinate role because of growth of population and new consumption needs. But even in this context Marx still makes an extraordinary statement by saying that 'men … daily re-create their own life, begin to make other men, to propagate their kind: the relation between man and woman, parents and children, *the family*' (Marx and Engels 1976: 42–43, original emphasis). This statement is extraordinary because even in the context of engendering progeny and reproducing their daily life and originating the family, Marx privileges men as their own begetters in a biblical tradition in which every patriarch begot his next generation. It would appear that even in the case of the family and reproduction women are subordinated, and the family, as we heard before, becomes *his* family, with *his* wife and *his* children. This puts us in a curious situation, in which Man becomes the originator, and Woman the executor of the patriarchal story of generations. Marx is simultaneously critical and yet sees the family, implying sexual division of labour, as the foundational social institution. He offers no resolution to this conundrum.

Marx is scathing about the bourgeois family. In the *Manifesto of the Communist Party* he advocates the abolition of this family, which rests on capital and private gain. But he is not consistent. He is simultaneously critical about the bourgeois family and yet laments its absence among the proletariat when he says that '… this state of things finds its complement in the practical absence of the family among the proletarians, and in public prostitution' (Marx and Engels 1976b: 501). And further:

> The bourgeois clap-trap about the family and education, about the hallowed co-relation of parent and children, becomes all the more disgusting, the more by the action of Modern Industry, all family ties among the proletarians are torn asunder, and their children transformed into single articles of commerce and instruments of labour.
>
> (Marx and Engels 1976b: 502)

The themes of subordination and possession of women and children continue in Marx's (and Engels') work, and family is shown to be the device through which patriarchal designs were accomplished since antiquity. Therefore, we are constrained to ask how much of the critical edge of Marx's view of the family can be maintained, when we find no presentation of an alternative vision to the bourgeois family. In keeping with this vision, if women cannot be considered as legitimate workers, they must be mothers and social reproducers. What does this acquiescence to gender indicate about the possibility of women's participation in communism?

5 Between actuality and ideology: Marx's ideological retreat into the bourgeois/nuclear family

From the above we can deduce that Marx extended a tacit acceptance of the nuclear family, even for the working class. He glosses over the public and private segmentation of society and leaves unexamined the practical division of labour between reproduction and production necessary for bourgeois social organization. This lack of critical reflection on Marx's part confers on bourgeois social organization a different status from that of the economic organization and its spatial existence. Thus, relegated to a zone outside of critique, bourgeois social reproduction acquires a natural, and therefore, ideological character. As an answer to the violence of capitalism's consumption of labour, especially in its earlier phase when women and children were the primary workers, Marx offered a male-headed family and the withdrawal of female labour for the working class. Intentionally or not, Marx thus concurs with women's marginalization from the labour force proper. This makes him adopt family wage as his cause. He fails to draw the right conclusion from the wretched life situation he presents so well. It escaped his attention that women did equally demanding and demeaning physical work both inside and outside of the home, leading to an ever-escalating cycle of devaluation of their labour. Marx needed to develop an adequate account and critique of constitutive relations between social production and reproduction, which would entail going beyond the rigidity of sexual division of labour. The critique of ideology, which is the centre piece of his analytical method, was inconsistently applied to gender and the bourgeois family form. How did Marx himself become susceptible to an ideological form of thinking (by his own definition) in the context of women's labour and social reproduction?

This question leads us to Marx's own assertion about ideology regarding how the dominant ideas of the ruling class become the ruling ideas of the time, and the role played in the creation of ideological notions by the intelligentsia (Marx and Engels 1976: 59). His own susceptibility to ideology lies in his growing up in a bourgeois family, and intellectually in the tradition of European Enlightenment, which made a distinction in gendered terms about nature and culture. This distinction was the axiom of philosophical thought as well as the commonsense of the time. Marx himself sought to go beyond this binary by positing through the idea of conscious labour a mediatory relationship between nature and culture. But this critical insight was not brought to bear in any clear way on the family and social reproduction, since he did not associate them with conscious labour or transformation of nature. Thus, nature and culture/development of productive forces, reproduction and production, remain separated through gender. While he saw a natural affinity between men, conscious labour and transformation of nature, he saw women as partially immanent in nature. Her activities of motherhood and nurturance were to be mediated through the family form. Women's identity with nature was further deepened by the type of labour they publicly performed outside of the industrial labour force. Domestic services, nursing and manual work in general were considered as natural functions rather than social and labour skills. The ideology of femininity, core of the bourgeois notions of the family and home, invested women with finer sensibilities. But these were attributes of middle-class women in the Romantic discourse of the time. They conferred upon idealized women, home and the family an aura of beauty, bounty and moral purity. In the context of this idealization working-class women were found wanting. This bourgeois ideology became a source of sublimation of physical and emotional labour, as well as of the violence constructing the patriarchal family.

In Marx's support for the family and the family wage we find a mixture of bourgeois gender ideology with pragmatism. Aware of the perennial poverty of working-class women and their families, he suggests a modified version of Romantic motherhood. In their case the reasoning becomes more economic, because working class women could spend less money by staying at home, than by going out to earn it. He says:

> Since certain family functions, such as nursing and suckling children, cannot be entirely suppressed, the mothers who have been confiscated by capital must try substitutes of some sort. Domestic work, such as sewing and mending, must be replaced by the purchase of ready-made articles.
>
> (Marx 1974: 518, n.39)

This is obviously not a solution for the massive life crisis of a society in the grip of 'primitive accumulation' brought about by the process of the transition to capitalism. Marx is also susceptible to the moral panic in Victorian society as it was detected that women's labour in early capitalism radically removed them from gender norms. He supportively quotes from an inspector's report on 'gangs' of women, married and unmarried, who

> will sometimes travel many miles from their own village: they are to be met morning and evening on the roads, dressed in short petticoats, with suitable coats and boots, and sometimes trousers, looking wonderfully strong and healthy, but tainted with customary immorality and heedless of the fatal consequences which their love of this busy and independent life is bringing on their unfortunate offspring who are pining at home.
>
> (Marx 1974: 522)

As examples of harm caused by women's work outside of the home, their withholding full commitment to social reproduction, Marx also mentions the high rate of child mortality among the working classes:

> As was shown by an official medical inquiry in the year 1861, the high death-rates are, apart from local causes, principally due to the employment of the mothers away from their homes, and to the neglect and maltreatment arising from their absence, which consists in such things as insufficient nourishment, unsuitable food, and dosing with opiates....
>
> (Marx 1974: 521)

Marx does not dispute with one Dr. Baker, that '... happy indeed will it be for the manufacturing districts of England, when every married woman having a family is prohibited from working in any textile works at all' (Marx 1974: 522). Marx's idea of alienation acquires a further dimension when considering women's work outside the home, because it caused a 'denaturalized' (Marx 1974: 521, n.46) behaviour leading to an 'unnatural estrangement between mother and child' (Marx 1974: 521). These notions do not challenge the ideology of naturalness of women's motherhood.

6 Uneven application of historical materialism and the intrusion of ideology

The lacuna in Marx's work regarding social reproduction and sexual division of labour derives from the fact that his theoretical energy is concentrated in deconstructing the commodity form and exchange value, which are the peculiarities of the capitalist mode of production. Thus, he sidesteps the issue of use value and how social reproduction brings exchange value and use value in an internal and dynamic relationship with each other. This vacuum leaves space for ideological intrusion, as we get only half of the story of capital. As capital is a constellation of social relations rather than the ownership of things, the focus on the commodity form conceals from us the full formative dimension of the capitalist mode of production. This further devalues women's labour, both in production of exchange value and in social reproduction. This situation is reminiscent of what Marx said about Aristotle's inability to see all human labour as labour of equal value. Marx explains Aristotle's blind spot by reminding us of the connection of theory with social conditions of the time. He notes:

> Greek society was founded on the labour of slaves, hence had as its natural basis the inequality of men and of their labour-powers. The secret of the expression of value, namely the equality and the equivalence of all kinds of labour because and insofar as they are human labour in general, could not be deciphered until the concept of human equality had already acquired the permanence of a fixed popular opinion.... Only the historical limitation inherent in the society in which he lived prevented him from finding out what 'in reality' this relation of equality consisted of.
>
> (Marx 1974:151–52)

Marx's own inability to see women's labour as conscious human labour, since he places it in the shadow of biological reproduction, was caused by the same problem that accounts for Aristotle's aporia. The conventional wisdom of his time was a part of the 'ruling ideas', and did not see women typically as producers of commodities. This illusion was further sustained by the fact of growing separation between productive and reproductive material and spatial practices: thus women's labour came to be conceived, like slave labour, as a form of natural life activity. Their labour was not seen as conscious and intentional exertion of labour power, but rather as an expression of their daily living. Such naturalization of labour of some within the society, Marx suggests, prevented Aristotle from conceptualizing labour *as such*. The same could be said about Marx's perception of women and their labour. Women's capacity for biological reproduction on a universal scale seems to have converted and expanded their biology into a normalization of sexual division of labour, that is, into an ideology. This view projects all of women's activities as natural as those of the slave in the perception of Aristotle. In the case of women, Marx applied his method of historical materialism in an uneven manner by not mentioning their innate capacity to transform nature.

Marx is trapped here in an ideological form of thinking. In his theorization the relationship between men and nature is not clear, except in their innate desire and capacity to transform or conquer it. This makes the notion of class become axiomatically male. In reverse, women's relation to nature is clear, but what is unclear is how they belong to class. Though living in two worlds of nature and society, women's sociality is seen as immanent in nature. Their attempts at transcendence and reflexivity amount to only a refinement of their affectivity and reproductive practices. In this gendered schema in which men are clearly identified with class, they can initiate a communist revolution, a possibility not accorded to women. Thus, men are endowed with a basis for unity in their potentialities for creating a future and women are accorded particularized lives precariously poised in their class belonging. Their future is personal or at most familial or communal, rather than oriented towards world historical social transformation. Though Marx never categorically denies women's social or historical belonging, the fact that he primarily identifies them with nature make them insider-outsiders of class and conscious class struggle, while men are seen as insider outsiders of nature and social relations of the family. Marx does not reflect on the serious implications of this type of ideological conceptualization. Any communist project based on these assumptions which bifurcate gender and class remains compromised and incomplete. So far, we lack the full physiognomy of the proletariat, the collective protagonist of revolution.

In addition to other reasons that I already mentioned, Marx's susceptibility to ideology needs to be explored in terms of his concept of 'practical consciousness' (Marx and Engels 1976: 43–44), which he understatedly advances during his critique of ideology. But considered as a part of his historical materialist method, this form of consciousness is an amalgam of experiential and habitual modes of communication, for example of language and types of knowledge that we inherit and produce in the course of socio-historical living. This mode of practical and ideational transmission is discussed along with Marx's inquiry into the production of ideology. Practical consciousness is intersubjective and continuous, and can convey ways of doing and thinking which are taken for granted as well. Though Marx identifies this type of consciousness as '… practical, real consciousness that exists for other men as well, and only therefore does it exist for me … [which] only arises from the need, the necessity, of intercourse with other men …' and further guarantees that it '… remains as long as men exist at all' (Marx and Engels 1976: 44), it is by no means an area that is sorted out or even can be so fully. Thus, its status as exclusively 'real consciousness' cannot be ascertained. It can as easily shade off into the realm of ideology, as ideology fractures and crumbles in all aspects of daily life. Thus, it can also be present as a substratum of consciousness constantly in need of scrutiny. In this the notion of practical consciousness resembles Gramsci's concepts of commonsense and hegemony (see Antonio Gramsci 1971: 55–59; also see Williams 1976) – a reservoir of multi-layered and unsorted ideas and beliefs, of perceptions and images that permeate social life. Depending on how it is politicized, practical consciousness, like commonsense, can provide substance for either revolution or reaction. While Gramsci explores at length the implications of these notions, Marx does not accord such attention to practical consciousness. Though the connection between practical consciousness and ideology is not formulated by Marx, we can attempt to do it ourselves. We are helped in this task by *The Eighteenth Brumaire of Louis Bonaparte*, where Marx critiques the role played by the past, both inherited and invented, and its impact on shaping the present ideologically, thus partially obscuring from the social actors the full historical and political import of their own activities (Marx 1979: 103–07; In this regard see also Hobsbawm and Ranger 2012). Understanding practical consciousness in this way explains to us how Marx himself could fall prey to ideology and become subject to the hegemony of bourgeois patriarchy. Articulating this concept once, Marx cryptically moves to the contra-ideological notion of 'positive science' (Marx and Engels 1976: 37). This is historical materialism by another name, that opens the gateway to communist revolution. But the hypothesis of a polymorphous consciousness offers us a conceptual key to the emergence of revolutionary or reactionary thought. This grey area can also show how Marx's own life within the bourgeois milieu of nineteenth century Europe is a contributing factor to his general acceptance of the bourgeois family and the form of gender and class organization this entails. It is not surprising that he finds the architecture and ethos of the family natural and substantive, and can partially share the aura of sentimentality regarding women and home. In many ways he was a romantic thinker. Even his portrayal of communist revolution in *The Manifesto of the Communist Party*, for example, touches on the sublime.

7 A methodological advancement: towards a comprehensive revolutionary agency

At this point we must perform a reflective gesture, by reintroducing Marx's critique of ideology to stretch Marx for articulating women's potential for social transformation. We must take full advantage of his method. His critique of ideology allows for pitting different forms of consciousness to the production of a revolutionary critique of their disjunctures and contradictions. Through this exercise the ideological, that is, historically occlusive consciousness comes into confrontation with socially oriented practical, empirical, experiential forms of consciousness. The thick historical description that Marx offers of lives and labour of women and men helps us to identify the ideological discourse of family, motherhood and sexual division of labour in the orbit of the mode of production as a whole. Reconnecting his critique of ideology to this larger context we can supply what is missing in him. In short, we can bring to the reificatory manner in which production and reproduction are separated in gendered and spatial terms his brilliant critique of the fetishism of commodities. Thus we can retain specific and empirical characteristics of social production and reproduction while establishing between them an internal generative relationship.

Now we need to recall another key aspect of historical materialism crucial to historical agency, by which we can relocate women in the task of history making. It is the assertion and demonstration in Marx's opus of the relationship of consciousness to society, and the critical and practical ability of people to discern historical determinations. To think otherwise and to accord a primacy to ideology (in Marx's sense) would be the ultimate ideological form of thinking. Understanding this allows us to fill the gap that Marx leaves regarding active political agencies and subjectivities of women. We can now bring to the fore how the experiences of labouring women described in *Capital,* Volume 1, both in production and reproduction, proletarianizes women in the political sense of the term. The reality of a formative connection between life experience and revolution which was boldly asserted by Marx in the *Manifesto of the Communist Party* as the motive force of a new history, in Chapters 10 and 15 of Volume 1 is expressed in occasional utterances. By his own account he could be sure about the development of a new consciousness arising in the new labour force for capital. Women and children, through many decades of intense proletarianizing experiences, could not but develop a new consciousness. Such dispossession and extraordinary changes in life could not but affect the entire society's conception of social, sexual and productive relations. This new consciousness is manifested in ways that outraged the propertied patriarchal reforming middle classes. Feminist social historians that I have earlier alluded to, and many more, suggest that employed and unemployed working class women and young persons did not share their sentiments. They were not caught up in the moral panic regarding the work they did to secure a living. They saw their labour as hard, but not unnatural. They appeared denatured only to those who invented the tradition of appropriate feminine and masculine conduct. Their exhortative jeremiads and what Marx himself learned about the new consciousness in the new times provided him with important insights regarding the creation of a new communist society. In keeping with his view that consciousness is socially grounded, he foresaw a different future for societies forged from the inferno of capitalism. His expectation regarding these new times went well beyond family relations to new political consciousness and politics. In the new working classes he saw the 'grave diggers' (Marx and Engels 1976b: 496) of capitalism, and the logic of historical materialism could extend that identity to both sexes. The following passage from Marx should exemplify my point.

> However terrible and disgusting the dissolution of the old family ties within the capitalist system may appear, large-scale industry, by assigning an important part in socially organized processes of production, outside the sphere of the domestic economy, to women, young persons and children of both sexes, does nevertheless create a new economic foundation for a higher form of family and of relations between the sexes. It is of course just as absurd to regard the Christian-Germanic form of the family as absolute and final as it would have been in the case of the ancient Roman, the ancient Greek, or the Oriental forms, which, moreover, form a series in historical development. It is also obvious, that the fact that the collective working group is composed of individuals of both sexes and all ages must under the appropriate conditions turn into a source of human development, although in its spontaneously developed, brutal, capitalist form, the system works in the opposite direction, and becomes a pestiferous source of corruption and slavery, since here the worker exists for the process of production, and not the process of production for the worker.
>
> (Marx 1974: 620–21)

For Marx, capitalism brought about not only a 'new economic foundation for a higher form of family', but also changed 'relations between the sexes', that is, in society at large. We need to note that his idea of revolutionary social transformation necessitated fundamental changes in gender relations. His dismissal of the 'Christian-Germanic form of the family' and earlier family forms points out that all family forms, and therefore gender relations or sexual division of labour, are transitional and dependant on the dominant mode of production. They arise in their peculiarities in given historical conditions and die with them. Marx does not lament this transition to new forms or advocate return to a past golden age, although in its 'spontaneously developed' capitalist form he finds the family 'brutal'. So, women in 'trousers' striding about in roads far away from 'home', without their 'pining' offspring (see Marx 1974: 521, n.46), seems to be not such a bad thing after all. Gender transgressive behaviour on the part of both men and women might awaken society to realize that there is nothing natural about gender, and that the process (and the fruits) of production exist for the producer, not vice versa. Is that not the goal of communist revolution? In this historical materialist framework Marxism/communism and feminism would not have to remain in an 'unhappy marriage', but rather step out of the discourse of marriage and family altogether.

Though Marx occasionally tried to develop this strand of critique (see Brown 2012), his revolutionary proposal lacks a comprehensive vision. It remained a critical/political path not taken, either by Marx or largely by the communist movements that came after him. In the history of communism Clara Zetkin, Alexandra Kollantai, Nadezhda Krupskaya and Rosa Luxembourg are shining stars, and there was massive participation of women in the organizations and labour movements leading to the Russian Revolution.[21] Communist or other forms of national liberation struggles closer to our time, such as in China, Cuba, Vietnam, Nicaragua and other countries, also mobilized enormous numbers of women. But the questions of relations between gender and class and of women's revolutionary potential and consciousness are still not at the centre of the communist projects. Feminist critique has indeed been influential among some communists, but a thorough anti-patriarchal analysis is still not integral to the understanding of class and class struggle. This would entail formulating social relations such as class and gender and social formations such as the family in constitutive terms. We are still working on that.

Notes

1 I would like to deeply thank my partner, Michael Kuttner, for helping me through the stages of writing this chapter. My thanks also go to Gökbörü Sarp Tanyıldız, PhD student, Sociology Department, York University, for his insightful comments.

2 Often interchangeable, the term communism will be used here to focus on the type of Marxism practiced by communist parties.

3 See Hartman (1979). She provides a basic problematic for examining relations between feminism and Marxism. The notion of an 'uneasy relationship' seems more to the point. Also see Himani Bannerji (1995), for a response. Here 'race' has been inserted into the mix.

4 Patriarchy adds a power dimension to the notion of gender. In my usage gender will imply patriarchy.

5 Among the early communists who saw gender as a central topic of communism are Engels (1820–95), August Bebel (1840–1913), Lenin (1870–1924), Alexandra Kollantai (1872–1952) and Clara Zetkin (1857–1933), who framed the so-called woman question.

6 The dualist frame persists, though feminist Marxists try to provide a non-dualist view. See Juliet Mitchell (1971, 1984), who wants to add capitalism as an economic system to patriarchy as an ideological one.

7 This concept is now pervasive among Marxists and non-Marxists in and out of academic fields. Encountered with the problem that patriarchy is only one of the contradictions facing us, while race and other social relations of power are left unchallenged, black and women of colour feminists (second wave) resorted to using this term. The term itself was coined in 1989 by Kimberlé Crenshaw, who spoke of structural, political, representational intersectionalities. See Crenshaw (1989, 1991). For a critique of this concept see Bannerji (2015).

8 Such ideas are not meant to be products of mental and manual division of labour, but rather what Marx calls 'practical consciousness'. See Marx and Engels (1976: 43–44).

9 In Marx's imagination this figure was associated with the figure of Prometheus, as shown in the allusion to the chains that the proletariat has to lose, similar to the Greek hero chained to a rock by Zeus's command for defying the gods.

10 Etymologically (Greek) the word 'proletariat' is not masculine. If anything, it is associated with only the capacity for childbearing, by extension the very poor and their basic labour power. From the nineteenth century, this concept has developed a masculine connotation, not so much by its direct meaning as by its usage in the literature of communism.

11 A similar approach is taken by Marx (1975) and numerous other texts.
12 For other important sources see also Engels 1975; Engels 1990.
13 Especially see Chapter 27, 'Expropriation of the Agricultural Population from the Land', and Chapter 28, 'Bloody Legislation Against the Expropriated since the End of the Fifteenth Century, The Forcing Down of Wages by Act of Parliament'. See also Thompson (1975).
14 For men and women in feudal production, see Perelman (2000).
15 Among many books on the bourgeois family see Eli Zaretsky (1976), Leonore Davidoff and Catherine Hall (1987), Wally Seccombe (1992), as well as Philippe Ariés and Georges Duby (1990) and P. Ariés (1962).
16 See also Hill (1961) and Eric Hobsbawm (1996) for a description of devastation and dislocation accompanying and following the Puritan Revolution which overturned land relations of Tudor and Stuart rule. They show the same vagabondage, travelling bands of desititutes, and horrific work life that Marx depicts in *Capital,* Volume I, see Chapters 27 (The Expropriation of the Agricultural Population from the Land) and 28 (Bloody Legislation against the Expropriated).
17 Thomas Robert Malthus's *An Essay on the Principle of Population* (1798), not surprisingly, was written at this period of transition. The notion of over-population in relation to food and waged work was the context of this book. Advanced as a law of nature, this notion functioned as a legitimizing ideology for concealing the predations of capital. See also, Amiya Kumar Bagchi (2005: xx–xxi, 77–87).
18 The family wage has a complicated history. It began in the employer's custom of paying one wage to the entire family, ensuring the labour of all in the unit at his disposal. This custom disappeared in the chaos of rising capitalism, where individual workers were payed separately, based on age and gender. In its next phase family wage was calculated on the basis of differential needs for the reproduction of different sectors of workers. The idea was to restrict women's labour at home and give the male head of the family a wage adequate for that. In practice neither this idealized family nor family wage materialized.
19 A fascinating novel was written on this topic and the lives of domestic workers by George Moore (1894).
20 Working class women themselves secured some representation through the Women's Protective and Provident League (WPPL) in the 1870s, which later became the Women's Trade Union League (WTUL). Though marginalized by the Trade Union Congress (TUC), labour militancy was strong among women. See Melanie Reynolds (2006) and Gerry Holloway (2007).
21 For a gripping recounting of the development towards the Russian Revolution by a woman member of the Bolshevik communist party, see Cecilia Bobrovskaya (2017).

References

Ariés, Philippe (1962) *Centuries of Childhood: A Social History of Family Life*, Translated by R. Baldick, London: Jonathan Cape.

Ariés, Philippe and Duby, Georges (eds.) (1990) *A History of Private Life*, vol. 4, Cambridge, MA: Harvard University Press.

Bagchi, Amiya Kumar (2005) *Perilous Passage: Mankind and the Global Ascendancy of Capital*, Lanham, MD: Roman & Littlefield.

Bannerji, Himani (1995) 'But Who Speaks for Us?', in *Thinking Through: Essays on Feminism, Marxism and Anti-Racism*, Toronto: Women's Press, pp. 55–95.

Bannerji, Himani (2011) 'Building from Marx: Reflections on "Race", Gender and Class', in S. Carpenter and S. Mojab (ed.), *Educating from Marx: Race, Gender and Learning*, New York: Palgrave Macmillan, pp. 41–60.

Bannerji, Himani (2015) 'Ideology', in in Shahrzad Mojab (ed.), *Marxism and Feminism*, London: Zed Books, pp. 163–80.

Benjamin, Walter (1968) 'The Work of Art in the Age of Mechanical Reproduction', in Hannah Arendt (ed.), *Illuminations: Essays and Reflections*, New York: Schocken, pp. 217–52.

Berman, Marshall (1988) *All That Is Solid Melts into Air: The Experience of Modernity*, New York: Penguin Books.

Bobrovskaya, Cecilia (2017) *Rank-and-File Bolshevik: A Memoir*, New Delhi: Leftword Books.

Brown, Heather (2012) *Marx on Gender and the Family: A Critical Study*, Leiden: Brill.

Crenshaw, Kimberlé (1989) 'Demarginalizing the Intersection of Race and Sex: A Black Feminist Critique of Anti-discrimination Doctrine, Feminist Theory and Antiracist Politics', in *University of Chicago Legal Forum, Special Issue, Feminism in the Law: Theory, Practice and Criticism*, Chicago: University of Chicago Law School, pp. 139–68.

Crenshaw, Kimberlé, (July 1991) 'Mapping the Margins: Intersectionality, Identity Politics and Violence against Women of Colour', In *Stanford Law Review* 43, no. 6: 1241–98.

Davidoff, Leonore and Hall, Catherine (1987) *Family Fortunes: Men and Women of the English Middle Class, 1780–1850*, London: Hutchinson.

Gramsci, Antonio (1971) *Selections from the Prison Notebooks*, New York: International Publishers.

Hartman, Heidi (July 1, 1979) 'The Unhappy Marriage of Marxism and Feminism: Towards a more Progressive Union', in *Capital & Class* 3, no. 2: 1–33.

Hill, Christopher (1961) *The Century of Revolution, 1603–1714*, New York: Norton.

Hill, Christopher (1972) *The World Turned Upside Down: Radical Ideas During the English Revolution*, London: Temple Smith.

Hobsbawm, Eric (1996) *The Age of Revolution, 1789–1848*, New York: Vintage.

Hobsbawm, Eric and Ranger, Terence (eds.) (2012) *The Invention of Tradition*, Cambridge: Cambridge University Press.

Holloway, Gerry (2007) *Women and Work in Britain Since 1840*, London: Routledge.

Linebaugh, Peter (1991) *The London Hanged: Crime and Civil Society in the Eighteenth Century*, London: Verso.

Linebaugh, Peter and Rediker, Marcus (2000) *The Many-headed Hydra: Sailors, Slaves and Commoners and the Hidden History of the Revolutionary Atlantic*, Boston: Beacon Press.

Malthus, Thomas Robert (1798) *An Essay on the Principle of Population*, London: J. Johnson.

Marx, Karl (1973) *Grundrisse: Foundations of the Critique of Political Economy*. Translated by Martin Nicolaus, New York: Vintage.

Marx, Karl (1974) *Capital Volume One*, New York: Vintage.

Marx, Karl (1975[1844]) 'Economic and Philosophic Manuscripts of 1844', *Marx Engels Collected Works*, vol. 3: *Marx and Engels, 1843–44*, Moscow: Progress Publishers, pp. 229–346.

Marx, Karl (1976 [1845–6]) 'Theses on Feuerbach', in *Marx Engels Collected Works*, Vol. 5: *Marx and Engels April 1845–April 1847*, Moscow: Progress Publishers, pp. 3–5.

Marx, Karl (1979) 'The Eighteenth Brumaire of Louis Bonaparte', in *Marx Engels Collected Works*, vol. 11: *Marx and Engels 1851–1853*, Moscow: Progress Publishers, pp. 99–197.

Marx, Karl and Engels, Friedrich (1975 [1844–1845]) 'The Holy Family: Or Critique of Critical Criticism', in *Marx and Engels Collected Works*, vol. 4: *Marx and Engels 1844–45*, Moscow: Progress Publishers, pp. 3–23.

Marx, Karl and Engels, Friedrich (1976 [1845–1846]) 'German Ideology', in Marx Engels Collected Works, Vol. 5: *Marx and Engels April 1845–April 1847*, Moscow: Progress Publishers, pp. 19–539.

Marx, Karl and Engels, Friedrich (1976b) 'Manifesto of the Communist Party', in *Marx Engels Collected Works*, vol. 6: *Marx and Engels 1845–48*, London: Lawrence and Wishart, pp. 477–519.

Mitchell, Juliet (1971) *Women's Estate*, Harmondsworth: Penguin.

Mitchell, Juliet (1984) *Women, the Longest Revolution*, New York: Pantheon.

Moore, George (1894) *Esther Waters*, London: Walter Scott.

Perelman, Michael (2000) *The Invention of Capitalism: Classical Political Economy and the Secret History of Primitive Accumulation*, Durham, NC: Duke University Press.

Reynolds, Melanie (2006) 'A Man Who Won't Back a Woman is No Man at All: The 1875 Heavy Woolen Dispute and the Narrative of Women's Trade Unionism', in *Labour History Review* 71, no. 2: 187–98.

Sauer, R. (March 1978) 'Infanticide and Abortion in Nineteenth Century Britain', in *Population Studies*, vol. 32, no. 1: 81–93.

Seccombe, Wally (1992) *A Millennium of Family Change: Feudalism to Capitalism in Northwestern Europe*, London: Verso.

Smith, Dorothy E. (1990) 'The Ideological Practices of Sociology', in *The Conceptual Practices of Power: A Feminist Sociology of Knowledge*, Toronto: University of Toronto Press, pp. 31–57.

Smith, Dorothy E. (2005) 'Knowing the Social: An Alternative Design', in *Institutional Ethnography: A Sociology for People*, Oxford: AltaMira Press, pp. 27–45.

Thompson, Edward Palmer (1975) *Whigs and Hunters: The Origins of the Black Act*, New York: Pantheon.

Walkowitz, Judith (1980) *Prostitution and Victorian Society*, Cambridge: Cambridge University Press.

Weber, Max (1958) *The Protestant Ethic and the Spirt of Capitalism*, New York: Scribner.

Williams, Raymond (1976) *Keywords: A Vocabulary of Culture and Society*, London: Fontana.

Williams, Raymond (1977) *Marxism and Literature*, Oxford: Oxford University Press.

Zaretsky, Eli (1976) *Capitalism, the Family and Personal Life*, London: Pluto Press.

9 Marx and Engels

The intellectual relationship revisited from an ecological perspective

Kohei Saito

1 Introduction

Famously enough, there have been numerous critiques against Marx due to his alleged 'Prometheanism', and even self-claimed Marxists concluded that his productivism was incompatible with environmentalism.[1] However, with the deepening of ecological crises under neoliberal globalization, 'Marx's ecology' recently attains more attention. Ecosocialists employ the concept of 'metabolic rift' originated from *Capital* and actively analyse the destructive side of capitalist production such as global warming, disruption of the nitrogen cycle, and extinction of species. Consequently, ecology has become one of the central fields for enriching the legacy of Marx's *Capital* after 150 years.

However, not every Marxist agrees with Marx's ecology. There remain persistent calls to reject it, because his sporadic remarks in *Capital* cannot provide a theoretical foundation for analysing today's ecological crisis. Especially, 'Western Marxists' are often dismissive of an ecosocialist project. For example, in an interview published in *Examined Life*, Slavoj Žižek ironically maintains that ecology is 'a new opium for the masses' (Žižek 2009: 158).

One of the reasons for this rejection can be traced back to an old problem pivoting around the 'intellectual relationship' between Marx and Engels. Western Marxism initiated by Georg Lukács regarded the natural science as Engels' domain of expertise. However, since Western Marxism neglected Marx's research on natural sciences, it faces a dilemma that they cannot develop a Marxist critique of ecology unless it admits its own earlier one-sided interpretation. Owing to this dilemma, some Marxists hysterically reject the idea of ecosocialism.

In contrast, John Bellamy Foster and Paul Burkett adopted a more fruitful approach. Arguing that there exists no difference of opinion between Marx and Engels in terms of ecology, they developed the concept of metabolic rift (Foster and Burkett 2016: 16). They effectively employ Marx's methodological framework and analyse the current environmental issues and demonstrate the relevance of Marx's ecology today (see Foster *et al.* 2011). They also show the importance of Marx's ecology as an integral part of his general project of critique of political economy and conduct dialogues with ecological economics (see Burkett 2006). Nevertheless, this also raises the question whether differences between Marx and Engels in terms of political economy, whose existence Foster and Burkett do not deny, lead to different views on ecology.

This chapter takes up a synthetic approach: by focusing on Marx's research in the field of natural sciences ignored by Western Marxism, it aims at revealing ecological differences between Marx and Engels. Presupposing their collaborations and common understandings to some extent, I will analyse *Capital* in its relation to new materials published in the *Marx-Engels-Gesamtausgabe*, which Foster and Burkett do not consider. By doing so, it will be possible to sketch the theoretical direction to develop Marx's unfinished project of *Capital* in the twenty-first century.

2 Intellectual division of labour?

Western Marxism regarded the natural science as Engels' domain of expertise and separated it from Marx's philosophy to save the latter from the mechanism and economic determinism of the Soviet 'dialectical materialism'. In fact, if Nikolai Bukharin were right about the independent existence of dialectics in nature, it would be possible to conceptualize a dialectical method through natural sciences and then to apply it to human society. Western Marxism problematized such a positivist consequence and tried to rescue Marx from a mechanistic worldview by strictly limiting dialectics to society. Western Marxism, highlighting the intellectual division of labour between Marx and Engels, scapegoated the latter, who should be responsible for the unjustifiable extension of dialectics to nature (Lukács 1971: 24). Ironically, it was Engels himself who emphasized this division of labour. According to his preface to the second edition of *Anti-Dühring* published after Marx's death, 'Marx was well versed in mathematics, but we could keep up with natural science only piecemeal, intermittently and sporadically'. However, Engels later, reflecting on this blind spot, 'went through as complete as possible a "moulting", as Liebig calls it, in mathematics and the natural sciences' (Engels 1987a: 11). In fact, *Anti-Dühring* and *Dialectics of Nature* document that Engels seriously studied physics, chemistry and biology. His works greatly influenced the formation of the worldview of traditional Marxism because Marx did not write a book on nature.

However, Engels in his preface to *Anti-Dühring* hid some important information from his readers. At the time, this editor of *Capital* was occupied with sorting out Marx's manuscripts and notebooks, so he knew that Marx also eagerly studied natural sciences. However, Engels did not mention this fact, and simply said that Marx 'only piecemeal, intermittently and sporadically' followed natural sciences.

Marx in his letter to Engels dated on 4 July 1864 conveyed that he was inspired by Engels to read Carpenter's *Phycology* as well as Spurzheim's *Anatomy of the Brain and the Nervous System*, and wrote: 'I invariably follow in your footsteps' (Marx and Engels 1985: 546). However, reading the seventh edition of Justus von Liebig's *Agricultural Chemistry* in 1865, Marx more intensively read natural sciences. His reading list after 1868 covers various fields such as chemistry, geology, mineralogy, physiology and botany. On 19 December 1882, Engels even acknowledged that Marx was more familiar with what can be considered as the problem of increasing entropy with the consumption of fossil fuel: The

> working individual is not only a stabiliser *of present* but also, and to a far greater extent, a squanderer *of past*, solar heat. As to what we have done in the way of squandering our reserves of energy, our coal, ore, forests, etc., *you are better informed than I am.*
>
> (Marx and Engels 1992: 411, emphasis added)

Nevertheless, Engels in the preface to *Anti-Dühring* did not mention this point and instead proclaimed that his dialectics of nature was an application of the dialectical method 'founded and developed' by Marx (Engels 1987a: 9).

This is strange. Engels emphasized that ideas developed in *Anti-Dühring* is fully compatible with Marx's vision, saying that he 'read the whole manuscript to him before it was printed', and Marx fully agreed with him (Engels 1987a: 9). However, such a 'proof' was highlighted *only after Marx's death* (Carver 1983: 123). On the other hand, Engels did not refer to Marx's serious engagement with natural sciences, although the existence of Marx's notebooks on natural sciences would be the strongest proof for the dialectics of nature as their collaborative project. One is thus tempted to symptomatically interpret this unnatural silence: *Engels tacitly admitted that Marx's interest in natural sciences possessed a different character from his own.*

3 The scope of the metabolic rift theory

Since it is well-known today that *both* Marx and Engels passionately studied the natural science, the one-sidedness of Western Marxism is apparent. Nevertheless, one cannot immediately argue that they shared the same interest in ecology. It is necessary to investigate the issue more carefully.

Of course, not all Western Marxists deserve the same degree of criticism. Although Lukács at first reproached the application of dialectic to nature, he later changed his view, admitting that Marx did not completely separate the relationship between 'society' and 'nature' but comprehended the both in their integrity. Lukács recognized that the concept of 'metabolism [*Stoffwechsel*]' expresses this unity, which has become the key term for the Marxist analysis of 'metabolic rift' (see Foster 2013).

The most important meaning of Marx's concept of metabolism in *Capital* is his characterization of labour as the mediating activity of metabolism between humans and nature: 'Labour is, first of all, a process between man and nature, a process by which man, through his own actions, mediates, regulates and controls the metabolism between himself and nature' (Marx 1976: 283). In any society, humans must work upon nature in a conscious and teleological manner and satisfy their needs in order to live on this planet. Marx expressed this transhistorical relationality between humans and nature with the concept of 'metabolism'. The concrete ways of the metabolism between humans and nature, however, largely differ, depending on how this mediating activity of labour is socially organized. In the *Grundrisse* Marx pointed to the particular relationship between humans and nature under capitalist production characterized by the '*separation*' of humans from nature (Marx 1973: 489). Marx's *Capital* precisely analyses human alienation and alienation from nature under capitalist production due to this alienated relationship.

As elucidated in *Capital,* Volume I, the transhistorical 'labour process' receives a new form as a 'valorization process' under capitalism, and the material process of metabolism between humans and nature is accordingly transformed. While pre-capitalist societies aimed at the production of concrete use-values, capitalist production primarily seeks the production of value. Whereas labour used to be conducted under social and natural limitations to satisfy concrete human needs, capitalist production pursues after endless valorization, so that labour and nature is thoroughly reorganized from a perspective of the maximal objectification of abstract labour.

Under the primacy of the logic of capital's valorization, not only functioning of nature but also the aspect of concrete labour in the labour process is abstracted and subordinated. Metabolism between humans and nature is mediated by value as the objectification of abstract labour, which is nothing but the expenditure of human labour power in general, and it is transformed in a most favourable way to capital's valorization. Marx's *Capital* repeatedly points to the robbery character of this transformation of the material world from the perspective of production of surplus value and to the danger of destructive consequences: 'The same blind desire for profit that in the one case exhausted the soil had in the other case seized hold of the vital force of the nation at its roots' (Marx 1976: 348). Marx problematized the capitalist squandering in relation to the two fundamental factors of production: the exhaustion of 'labour power' and 'natural forces'.

Famously, it was Liebig's *Agricultural Chemistry* that prompted Marx to integrate an analysis of the 'robbery' system of agriculture into *Capital* (see Foster 2000: 155). Liebig criticized the modern capitalist agriculture as robbery, which only aims at the maximization of short-term profit and lets plants absorb as many nutrients in the soil as possible without replenishing them. He even warned against the collapse of European civilization due to a loss of material foundation caused by soil exhaustion. Marx in *Capital* praised Liebig's 'immortal merits' for revealing 'the negative, i.e. destructive side of modern agriculture' and wrote:

> [Capitalist production] prevents the return to the soil of its constituent elements consumed by man in the form of food and clothing; hence it

> hinders the operation of the eternal natural condition for the lasting fertility of the soil. Thus it destroys at the same time the physical health of the urban worker, and the intellectual life of the rural worker.
>
> (Marx 1976: 637)

During the nineteenth century the exhaustion of the soil became a social issue. Food consumed by increasing populations in large cities flowed through water closets into rivers as sewage. Excrements gave out a foul smell in the city of London, and cholerae became prevalent. Here the antagonism between agriculture and industry is manifest. Marx, integrating Liebig's *Agricultural Chemistry*, formulated the problem of soil exhaustion as a contradiction that capitalist production created amidst the metabolism between humans and nature.

Marx highly valued Liebig because *Agricultural Chemistry* provided a scientific foundation for his critical analysis of the social division of labour, which he had already conceptualized as the 'contradiction between town and country' in *The German Ideology* (Engels 1987a: 64). Through the reception of Liebig, Marx clearly recognized the necessity to comment in more detail how capitalism transforms and undermines the relationship between humans and nature. In other words, one reason for his intensive research on natural sciences is to investigate into the causes and influences of an 'irreparable rift' in the universal metabolism of nature, as in *Capital,* Volume III (Marx 1981: 949).

Historically speaking, the problem of soil exhaustion due to a lack of inorganic substances was largely resolved thanks to the invention of the Haber-Bosch process enabling mass industrial production of ammonia. Yet the excessive dependence on chemical fertilizer causes other issues such as low water and nutrient holding capacity and more vulnerability to diseases and insects. Nitrogen remaining in the soil also flows into the environment, causing red tides, while nitrate nitrogen pollutes water and vegetables. In this sense, 'rifts' of the metabolism are not fixed, but at best are 'shifted' to other problems (see Clark and York 2008). Similar 'metabolic shifts' can be found in extractive industries such as mining oil and rare metals. Insofar as value cannot fully take the metabolism between humans and nature into account, the realization of sustainable production under capitalism always faces insurmountable barriers. Thus, Marx's unification of theory of value and metabolism in *Capital* provides a methodological foundation for critically analysing the robbery system of capitalism.

4 Engels and *Capital*

Despite his serious attempt to study natural sciences, Marx died before completing *Capital*, so Engels had to take up the task to edit *Capital,* Volumes I and III. When Engels neglected Marx's notebooks on natural sciences in *Anti-Dühring*, there existed a subtle difference between Marx and Engels concerning the concept of 'metabolism'. This problem is discernible in Engels' edition of *Capital.*

Certainly, Engels recognized the importance of Liebig's critique of robbery agriculture. For example, in *The Housing Question*, he referred to Liebig and pointed to the 'antithesis of town and country' and argued for the reconstruction of 'an intimate connection between industrial and agricultural production', as he demanded the 'combination of agriculture with manufacturing industries' in the *Manifesto of the Communist Party* (Engels 1988: 384; Marx and Engels 1976: 505). Also, in editing *Capital,* volume III, Engels supplemented Marx's description of robbery agriculture with concrete examples. He added the following passage, for example: 'In London, for example, they can do nothing better with the excrement produced by 4½ million people than pollute the Thames with it, at monstrous expense' (Marx 1981: 195). Here one can observe the intellectual collaboration between Marx and Engels.

However, things look differently when 'metabolism' at stake. Although Engels was aware that Marx discussed the problem of soil exhaustion with Liebig's concept of metabolism, he intentionally changed a particular sentence in *Capital*, Volume III. In his original manuscript, Marx wrote:

> [In] this way [large-scale landownership] produces conditions that provoke an irreparable rift in the interdependent process between social metabolism and natural metabolism prescribed by the natural laws of the soil. The result of this is a squandering of the vitality of the soil, and *trade carries this devastation far beyond the bounds of a single country* (Liebig).
>
> (Marx 1992: 752–3)

Referring to Liebig, Marx highlighted the danger of a serious global disruption in the interdependent process between 'social metabolism' (capitalist production, circulation and consumption) and 'natural metabolism'. He clearly formulated a tensed relationship between the capitalist economic form-determination and the natural properties in the material world.

Engels modified the first sentence as follows: 'in this way it produces conditions that provoke an irreparable rift in the interdependent process of social metabolism, a metabolism prescribed by the natural laws of life itself' (Marx 1981: 949). Now the word 'natural metabolism' is omitted and 'soil' is changed to 'life', so that the contrast between social and natural metabolism became obscure. Certainly, there are number of cases where Engels modified Marx's expressions whenever unclear, confusing, or mistaken. However, in this passage, Marx's intension is not only clear but also this is a key passage for his theory of metabolism. What does Engels' change imply?

Here it is helpful to consider Engels' 'dialectics of nature'. According to him, *Anti-Dühring* intended to grasp laws penetrating nature and history and especially to 'strip of this [Hegelian] mystic form and to bring clearly before the mind in their complete simplicity and universality'. His project claimed to be a materialist one, which avoided Hegel's misconception of 'building the law of dialectics into nature' and aimed at 'discovering them in it and evolving them from it' (Engels 1987a: 11–13). In other words, his project seeks to grasp the laws as they objectively exist in nature. Instead of epistemologically explaining natural phenomena with a dialectical method, it is, an ontological investigation in that it dialectically develops movements and evolution in nature (see Jordan 1967: 167).

Notably, Engels' dialectics of nature is tied to a practical demand for the realization of 'freedom' through the 'domination' and 'control' of external nature. In fact, the construction of socialism as a free society means for Engels to become the 'real, conscious lord of nature':

> The extraneous objective forces that have hitherto governed history pass under the control of man himself. Only from that time will man himself, with full consciousness, make his own history – only from that time will the social causes set in movement by him have, in the main and in a constantly growing measure, the results intended by him. It is the humanity's leap from the realm of necessity to the realm of freedom.
>
> (Engels 1987a: 270)

According to Engels, not only by abolishing the reified domination of capital independently of human consciousness and behaviour, but also by fully appropriating the law of nature, humans can leap to 'the realm of freedom'.

Of course, Engels did not think that the recognition of laws of nature would lead to an arbitrary manipulation of nature. In *Dialectics of Nature*, he warned against 'revenge' by nature: 'Let us not, however, flatter ourselves overmuch on account of our human victories over nature. For each such victory nature takes its revenge on us' (Engels 1987b: 460–1). Engels recognized the limits of nature and critically observed arbitrary human behaviour toward nature, especially capitalist production oriented toward short-term profit maximalization. If the law of nature is ignored, the domination over nature fails and labour will bring about unforeseen results: humans cease to be an active, labouring subject, but are obliged to behave passively at the mercy of nature's power.

Engels' ecology pivoted around nature's 'revenge' and criticized the short-sighted profit maximalization. The passage on metabolic rift in *Capital,* Volume III is also modified by Engels in accordance with this scheme of nature's revenge. Engels' edition of *Capital* came to emphasize that the violation of natural laws of life would lead to a fatal consequence for human civilization, while the methodological approach unique to Marx's metabolic theory, which investigates how the law of value dominant in the social metabolism modifies natural metabolism and causes an irreparable rift, has become rather unclear. Engels judged that Marx's original expression about the entanglement between economic form-determination and material world was hard to understand for readers and changed the sentence into a more 'accessible' scheme of revenge by nature.

What underlies this editorial change by Engels is the fact that he did not cherish Liebig's theory of metabolism. Indeed, Engels in *Dialectics of Nature* referred to Liebig's concept of metabolism *in the context of criticizing* him as a 'dilettante' in biology (Engels 1987b: 576). Concerning the origin of life, Liebig denied the possibility of the historical evolution of organic life and accepted the hypothesis of 'eternal life' which was 'imported' on to the planet from universal space. Engels argued that life is the process of metabolism that historically emerged and evolved from non-life, and 'protein' confirms this point: 'Life is the mode of existence of protein bodies, the essential element of which consists in *continual metabolic interchange with the natural environment outside them*' (Engels 1987b: 578). Engels saw the origin of life in the chemical process of assimilation and excretion of protein, and he pointed to the possibility of artificially creating a living organism by creating protein in a laboratory.

In the 1840s Liebig conceived the process of absorption, assimilation and excretion of nutrition as 'metabolism' and tried to explain the life activity as a chemical process, while he could not fully abandon vitalist ideas (see Wendling 2009: 81). Engels rejected Liebig's vitalism that separated biology from chemistry and recognized the inexplicable principles unique to living beings. According to Engels, there exists metabolism of inorganic bodies as a chemical interchange with their environment, and once 'protein' historically evolved, metabolism comes to exist as life.

Notably, while Engels' concept of metabolism emphasized the historical emergence of protein, he rejected Liebig's understanding of metabolism and thus did not apply it to environmental issues. Consequently, lost is the role of theory of metabolism to analyse the relationality of humans and nature from both transhistorical and historical perspective and to reveal the particularity and contradictions of this relationship under the capitalist mode of production has been lost. Rather, Engels limited the theoretical scope of metabolism to the process of origin and evolution of life that proceeded *independently of* human beings. For Engels' *Anti-Dühring* the motor of dialectics characterized by 'negation of negation' is 'a law which … holds good in the animal and plant kingdoms, in geology, in mathematics, in history and in philosophy' (Engels 1987a: 131). The main role of 'metabolism' is accordingly not an ecological one, but a demonstration that this law penetrates the whole of nature.

Though Engels partially took up Liebig's view, he did not adopt the concept of the disturbance of metabolism between humans and earth in *Capital* but kept holding the earlier scheme of the 'antithesis of town and country' in *The German Ideology*. He was not able to fully recognize that Marx's theoretical leap is documented in his analysis of the interdependent process between social and natural metabolism. In other words, Engels could not entirely grasp the foundation of Marx's critique of political economy after the 1850s, which deals with how the metabolism between humans and nature is modified and reorganized through the formal and real subsumption of labour under capital. This is the point where the difference of political economy between Marx and Engels led to that of ecology. Certainly, the 'antithesis of town and country' can be fruitfully reinterpreted as the antagonism between 'centre' and 'periphery' to analyse the modern ecological imperialism as an ecological critique of capitalism. However, this alone should not underestimate the significance of the fact that Marx started analysing the disturbance of metabolism between humans *and* the earth in *Capital*.

Marx's analysis started with the recognition that in every society humans must work upon nature. Then he analysed *why* and *how* alienation and the inversion of subject and object emerges by the particular form of labour under the capitalist mode of production. Thus, it is not enough to criticize the ecological crisis by denouncing the mass production for the sake of profit maximalization or by morally proclaiming the necessity of the coexistence of humans and nature. According to Marx, the ecological issues must be explained from the 'separation' of humans from nature as the fundamental objective condition of production, and it is necessary to show how the penetration of the reified logic of capital radically alters human consciousness and behaviour and even disrupts the universal metabolism of nature.

While the 'antithesis' and 'combination' of the town and country remained static and abstract in *The German Ideology* and *The Manifesto of the Communist Party*, the concept of metabolism in *Capital* can analyse the dynamic historical process of production process and capital accumulation. It also makes clear the necessity for the realization of sustainable production to radically change the form of labour, i.e. the abolition of 'private labour' and 'wage labour'. In contrast, Engels remained the general standpoint of the 1840s, and rejected Liebig's theory of metabolism. Since the metabolism between humans and nature as a link of critique of political economy and ecology is missing, his view remained static idea of nature's 'revenge'. This difference also leads to different visions of the future socialist society.

5 Dialectics of 'domination' and 'revenge'

Marx and Engels regarded the conscious and teleological control of laws of nature through labour as a unique human activity, and they often characterized it as 'control' over nature. For example, Engels wrote in *Anti-Dühring*: 'Freedom therefore consists in the control over ourselves and over external nature, a control founded on knowledge of natural necessity' (Engels 1987a: 106). Such remarks are taken as by critics as a proof of 'Prometheanism'. A counterproof is Engels' warning against a 'revenge' by nature because he believed the necessity of correctly recognizing the law of nature and applying it properly, which is the only way to reach the realm of freedom. However, there are new criticisms. For example, Jason W. Moore argues in *Capitalism in the Web of Life* that it is 'static' to think that if the law of nature continues to be ignored, nature will take a revenge on humans *one day*. In *Uneven Development*, Neil Smith also rejected this type of 'left apocalypticism' (see Moore 2015: 80; Smith 2008: 247).

In contrast, Marx did not treat the disruption of the universal metabolism of nature under capitalism as a revenge by nature. *Capital* analysed the problem from two more aspects. First, capital does not accept such limits imposed by nature. As discussed in *Capital,* Volume II, 'the scale on which this capital operates to form values and products is elastic and variable' (Marx 1978: 433). In the *Grundrisse*, Marx also pointed out that his elasticity of capital is a potent of capital, which confronted with difficulties of capital accumulation, progressively establishes 'a system of general utility' though further development of technologies and invention of new use-values. However, since capital cannot take into account material aspects except abstract labour, its attempt to overcome natural limits does not solve its own contradiction but rather deepens it on a larger scale. An investigation into this *dynamic* relationship between capital and nature was the main topic for the later Marx. While Engels formulated the transhistorical law of nature as 'science' of the universe, Marx's research shifted more and more to empirical topics in geology, agricultural chemistry and mineralogy. Namely, he aimed at comprehending capital's astonishing elasticity in the interdependent historical process in which humans modifies nature and vice versa.

Second, Marx's description of the disruption of the metabolism avoids an apocalyptic tone of nature's revenge and highlights the *active* factor of resistance. Boundless extension of working hours as well as the transformation of the production process seeking after the production of surplus value result in alienation of labour and physical and mental illness, which ultimately calls for the conscious regulation of reified power such as establishing the normal working day and schools for vocational teaching founded by the state. A similar path can be envisioned towards nature. The disruption of the universal metabolism of nature obliges one to establish a more conscious social management of productive activities, as Marx emphasized in *Capital*:

> But by destroying the circumstances surrounding that metabolism, which originated in a merely natural and spontaneous fashion, [the capitalist mode of production] compels its systematic restoration as a regulative law of social production, and in a form adequate to the full development of the human race.
>
> (Marx 1976: 637–8)

Since capitalist production cannot fully take into account complex dimensions of the social and natural metabolism, it destroys nature, annihilates the possibilities of coevolution of humans and nature and even threatens human civilization. All what capital cares about is whether accumulation can be somehow achieved, so it does not really matter even if the most parts of the planet becomes unsuitable space to live for humans and animals to live. Thus, instead of waiting for the collapse of capitalism thanks to nature's revenge, it is indispensable for the realization of future society that individuals confronting the global ecological crisis take measures for the conscious and active control over the metabolism with their environment.

In *Capital,* Volume III, Marx famously wrote:

> [S]ocialized man, the associated producers, govern the human metabolism with nature in a rational way, bringing it under their collective control instead of being dominated by it as a blind power; accomplishing it with the least expenditure of energy and in conditions most worthy and appropriate for their human nature. But this always remains a realm of necessity. The true realm of freedom, the development of human powers as an end in itself, begins beyond it, though it can only flourish with this realm of necessity as its basis.
>
> (Marx 1981: 959)

As seen above, Engels argued for the necessity to consciously apply the law of nature, and a 'realm of freedom' precisely consists of this control over nature. However, Marx emphasized another point. He thought of it as a necessary condition that producers confronted with the disruption of metabolism associate with each other and put a 'blind power' under their conscious control. Without such control human existence would be threatened. However, 'this always remains a realm of necessity'. The new society based on association should realize free development of individuality, but this takes place beyond freedom of labour. Labour is indispensable for human existence, but it is only one part of human activity. If freedom of labour can be realized with the aid of productive forces developed under capitalism, expanded free time beyond freedom of labour should realize the true realm of freedom (see Stanley 2002: 23).[2]

For Marx, freedom is not limited to the conscious regulation of the law of nature through natural science, but it includes creative activities of art, enrichment of love and friendship, and hobbies such as sport and reading books. In contrast, Engels, who was primarily concerned with dialectics of nature, put importance on human freedom based on the recognition of the transhistorical law of nature, and it is the control over nature that immediately realizes the realm of freedom. This view impoverishes the content of the realm of freedom, so that Engels did not highlight what Marx formulated as the full development of individuality in communism, but put forward the Hegelian view of freedom that can be realized by consciously following the necessity.

6 Notebooks and critique of political economy

Marx's theory of metabolism also helps understand the meaning of his notebooks on natural sciences after 1868. Hints for imagining the unwritten part of *Capital* exist in these little-known notebooks. In fact, Marx's interests in the natural science go beyond the theory of ground rent. His reception of Liebig cannot be contained in it but deals with the reorganization and contradiction of the relationship between humans and nature under capitalist production. Simply put, Marx aimed at comprehending how disharmonies in the material world would emerge from modifications of that metabolism by the reified power of capital.

In this context, Marx's excerpts from Karl Fraas, a German agronomist, are of great importance. Marx wrote in his letter to Engels dated on 25 March 1868 that he found an 'unconscious socialist tendency' after making detailed notes (Marx and Engels 1987: 559). Prompted by Marx's high evaluation, Engels later read Fraas' *Climate and Plant World over Time*, which deals with climate changes in ancient civilization such as Mesopotamia, Egypt and Greece, due to massive deforestation. There are excerpts from this book in Engels' notebook of 1879–1880. Although they are of short length because they were made from Fraas' book, *Dialectics of Nature*, Engels' paraphrasing precisely documents that his view on Fraas was clearly influenced by Marx's. In this sense, the intellectual relationship between Marx and Engels in the field of natural science had been reversed compared to 1864.

First, in the above letter, Marx highly valued Fraas' insight that 'cultivation – when it proceeds in natural growth and is not *consciously controlled* … – leaves deserts behind it' (Marx and Engels 1987: 559). Engels wrote down the same opinion in his notebook: '*The development of people's agriculture leaves behind an enormous desert*' (Engels 1999: 515). Engels also summarized the significance of Fraas' work as a 'main proof that civilization in its conventional forms is an antagonistic process which exhausts the soil, devastates the forest, renders the soil infertile for its original products, and worsens the climate'. As an example, Engels noted that in Germany and Italy the average temperature increased '5 to 6 degrees (°Re)' (Engels 1999: 512). This understanding that unconscious production results in 'deserts' is reflected in nature's revenge in *Dialectics of Nature*. In fact, Engels argued in the relevant passage based on Fraas:

> The people who, in Mesopotamia, Greece, Asia Minor and elsewhere, destroyed the forests to obtain cultivable land, never dreamed that by removing along with the forests the collecting centres and reservoirs of moisture they were laying the basis for the present forlorn state of those countries.
>
> (Engels 1987b: 461)

Second, Marx in the same letter characterized Fraas as a 'Darwinist before Darwin' (Marx and Engels 1987: 558), and Engels also quoted a passage from Fraas that reminds one of Darwin's 'natural selection':

> As said, oak is also quite sensitive to elements of natural climate (temperature and humidity), and when there is any subtle change in them, oak is left behind in the competition against more durable and less sensitive surrounding trees that strive together for natural growth and self-preservation.

Engels read Fraas to refute the 'belief in the stability of plant species' based on a Darwinian argument (Engels 1999: 515). He must have thought that his interest was identical with Marx's.

However, Marx's interest in Fraas was not limited to nature's revenge and a Darwinist argument. In the beginning of 1868, Marx in addition to Fraas' work carefully read Georg Ludwig von Maurer's *Einleitung zur Geschichte der Mark-, Hof-, Dorf-, und Stadtverfassung und der offentlichen Gewalt*, in which the German historian of law dealt with the Germanic system of landed property. In the same letter to Engels dated 25 March 1868, Marx found the same 'socialist tendency' in Maurer's work (Marx and Engels 1987: 557). Why did Marx simultaneously study the Germanic society which appears to have no connection with natural sciences?

A hint can be found in Fraas' work. In *Agrarian Crisis and its Healing Methods* of 1866, Fraas quoted from Maurer's book and evaluated the sustainability of Germanic communes:

> If the Mark village did not allow sales except among village members of wood, straw, dung, and even livestock (pigs!) and also ordered that all the crops harvested within the village, and even wine, should be consumed within the village (out of this practice various socage rights [*Bannrechte*] were to emerge), the means must have been retained for the maintenance of land power, and furthermore, the use of additional nutrients from forests and pastures, and even the use of meadows manured by rivers served to increase the [soil's] power everywhere.
>
> (Fraas 1866: 210)

Frass did not maintain that all pre-capitalist societies ignored the law of nature and left deserts behind them. Rather, in the Germanic society the soil productivity increased under the sustainable production. In contrast to Greek and Roman societies where commodity production existed to some extent and the communal tie was somewhat dissolved, the Germanic communes imposed a communal control over the land usage, which enabled sustainable cultivation. Reading Fraas' book, Marx was interested in Maurer's analysis to find the 'socialist tendency', so that he paid more attention to the metabolism between humans and nature in pre-capitalist societies.

In contrast to nature's revenge due to the ignorance of the law of nature in pre-capitalist societies, Marx recognized that the sustainable metabolism between humans and nature in the communal production functioned as the source of 'vitality'. In drafts of letter to Vera Zasulich, Marx, referring to Maurer again, argued for the possibility of Russia to pursuing a socialist path based on reminiscences of the vitality of archaic communes without following the Western capitalist development (Marx and Engels 1989: 350, 366). This vitality comes precisely from the power of sustainable agrarian communes. The metabolism there was mediated by a totally different way from in capitalism – even if this was rather unconsciously accomplished by tradition and customs, and not by the recognition of the law of nature – and its sustainability could provide a material foundation for resistance against capital's logic. As Fraas and Maurer focused on this vitality, Marx found a socialist tendency in their works. Here lies his practical interest in Fraas.

Furthermore, Marx's notebooks of 1878 that contain geological excerpts from John Yeats and Joseph Beete Jukes are noteworthy as an expansion of his theory of metabolism. These long excerpts deal with various topics, and their meaning cannot be reduced to ecology. Nevertheless, Marx studied geology for the sake of political economy. For example, Marx noted that an 'enormous sum of money is wasted in coal-mining alone due to ignorance' (Marx 2011b: 478), and documents Jukes' comment on 'great practical importance' of geology in the *Student Manual of Geology*, which is

> one of the chief points in the practical applications of geology in the British islands [both for the purpose of guarding against] a wasteful expenditure of money in rash enterprises, as well as [for] directing it where enterprise where [may have a] chance of being successful.
>
> (Marx 2011b: 642)

Furthermore, Marx paid attention to Jukes' description on how the progress in geology improves methods of discovery and mining of raw and auxiliary materials such as coal and iron and increases productivity and how improvements in transportation influence the relationship between industry and agriculture (as well as extractive industry).

Marx also paid attention to how geologic strata as a natural condition that humans cannot modify influences the social development: 'England is divided into two totally dissimilar parts, in which the form and aspect of the ground, and condition and employment of the people, [were] alike contrasted with each other'. Namely, the part to the north-west part of this life is 'chiefly Palaeozoic ground, often wild, barren and mountainous, but in many places full of mineral wealth.' The part to the south-east of it consists of 'Secondary and Tertiary ground, and generally soft and gentle in outline, with little or no wealth beneath the soil.' As a result, the 'mining and manufacturing populations' are to be found in the first district, and the 'working people of the latter' are mainly 'agricultural' (Marx 2011b: 641). In *Capital,* Volume I, Marx envisioned a 'new and higher synthesis, a union of agriculture and industry' beyond their anthesis (Marx 1976: 637). However, the unchangeable geologic characteristics that Jukes pointed out must be much more carefully treated in this project. In fact, Marx highlighted these passages in his notebooks.

In relation to Fraas and Darwin, Jukes also discussed how climate and precipitation effect the geological formation as well as flora and fauna. In the section titled 'Palaeontology', Jukes, directly referring to Darwin, pointed to great climate changes over time and argued that 'alternation of climates involves destruction of species' (Marx 2011b: 219). In this vein, Marx also noted Jukes' remark that '*extinction of species* is still going on (*man himself* is the most active exterminator)' (Marx 2011b: 233). Marx studied climate change from a long-term geological perspective and their impact upon the environment, paying particular attention to human impacts, as Fraas did. A similar remark on climate change in North America can be found in his excerpt from Yeats' *Natural History of the Raw Materials of Commerce*: '*The enormous clearings* have, on the other hand, *already sensibly modified the climate*' (Marx 2011a: 36). Here Marx's interest in Darwin and Fraas is not limited to Engels' encyclopaedic topics such as the origin of life, natural selection, and evolution, but more concrete ways of human metabolic interaction with nature.

7 Conclusion

Despite his efforts, Marx was not able to fully integrate his new findings into *Capital*. Nevertheless, it is possible to observe key differences between Marx and Engels. Engels' focus was the encyclopaedic recognition of the law of nature with the aid of natural sciences to realize the realm of freedom. While Marx's materialist method investigates the inevitability of the inversion of subject/object and essence/appearance under certain social relations, Engels' materialism, founded on the dualism of consciousness and matter, advocated the ontological primacy of the latter. It is characterized by a philosophical and transhistorical scheme, and so he ended up rejecting Liebig's concept of metabolism and basically remained satisfied with the 'antithesis of town and country' conceptualized in the 1840s.

In contrast, Marx after *The German Ideology* was not interested in such philosophical issues. By enriching the concept of metabolism, he aimed at comprehending physical and social transformation of the relationship between humans and nature from historical, economic and scientific perspectives. Especially, the development of technology under the modern industrial system reorganizes the entire metabolic interaction between society and nature on an unprecedented scale. In the 1860s Marx recognized the destructive potentiality of the modern technological application of natural sciences as 'productive forces of capital' and warned against capitalism's unsustainable production.

Unfortunately, due to the difference of theoretical concern, Marx's notebooks were totally neglected by Engels and other Marxists. After 150 years since the publication of *Capital*, Volume 1, it is necessary to examine these forgotten notebooks to rediscover an astonishing scope of Marx's critique of political economy.

Notes

1 This work was supported by JSPS Kakenhi Grant Number JP18K12188 as well as by the Ministry of Education of the Republic of Korea and the National Research Foundation of Korea (NRF-2018S1A3A2075204).

2 John Stanley argues for the identity of Marx's and Engels' socialist vision from this passage, but it is not convincing.

References

Burkett, Paul (2006) *Marxism and Ecological Economics: Toward a Red and Green Political Economy*, Leiden: Brill.
Carver, Terrell (1983) *Marx and Engels: The Intellectual Relationship*, Brighton: Wheatsheaf.
Clark, Brett, and Richard, York (2008) 'Rifts and Shifts', in *Monthly Review*, vol. 60, no. 6: 13–24.
Engels, Friedrich (1987a [1878]) *Anti-Dühring*, in *Marx Engels Collected Works*, vol. 25: *Friedrich Engels: Anti-Dühring, Dialectics of Nature*, Moscow: Progress Publishers, pp. 5–309.
Engels, Friedrich (1987b [1878]) *Dialectics of Nature*, in *Marx Engels Collected Works*, vol. 25: *Friedrich Engels: Anti-Dühring, Dialectics of Nature*, Moscow: Progress Publishers, pp. 313–587.
Engels, Friedrich (1988 [1872–73]) 'The Housing Question', in *Marx Engels Collected Works*, vol. 23: *Marx and Engels: 1871–74*, Moscow: Progress Publishers, pp. 317–91.
Engels, Friedrich (1999 [1879–80]) 'Exzerpte aus Carl Fraas: Klima und Pflanzenwelt in der Zeit', in *Marx-Engels-Gesamtausgabe* (MEGA^2), vol. IV/31, Berlin: Akademie Verlag, pp. 512–15.
Foster, John Bellamy (2000) *Marx's Ecology: Materialism and Nature*, New York: Monthly Review Press.
Foster, John Bellamy (2013) 'Marx and the Rift in the Universal Metabolism of Nature', in *Monthly Review*, vol. 65, no. 7: 1–19.
Foster, John Bellamy, and Burkett, Paul (2016) *Marx and the Earth: An Anti-Critique*, Leiden: Brill.
Foster, John Bellamy, York, Richard and Clark, Brett (2011) *The Ecological Rift: Capitalism's War on the Earth*, New York: Monthly Review Press.
Fraas, Carl (1866) *Ackerbaukrisen und ihre Heilmittel*, Leipzig: Brockhaus.
Jordan, Zbigniew A. (1967) *The Evolution of Dialectical Materialism*, London: Macmillan.
Lukács, Georg (1971) *History and Class Consciousness*, London: Merlin Press.
Marx, Karl (1973) *Grundrisse*, London: Penguin.
Marx, Karl (1976) *Capital*, vol. 1, London: Penguin Books.
Marx, Karl (1978) *Capital*, vol. 2, London: Penguin Books.
Marx, Karl (1981) *Capital*, vol. 3, London: Penguin Books.
Marx, Karl (1992 [1863–1865]) *Das Kapital (Ökonomische Manuskript 1863–1865). Drittes Buch*, in *Marx-Engels-Gesamtausgabe* (MEGA^2), vol. II/4.2, Berlin: Dietz.
Marx, Karl (2011a [1878]) 'Exzerpte aus John Yeats: The Natural history of the Raw Materials of Commerce', in *Marx-Engels-Gesamtausgabe* (MEGA^2), vol. IV/26, Berlin: Akademie Verlag, pp. 3–41.
Marx, Karl (2011b [1878]) 'Exzerpte aus Joseph Beete Jukes: The Student's Manual of Geology', in *Marx-Engels-Gesamtausgabe* (MEGA^2), vol. IV/26, Berlin: Akademie Verlag, pp. 139–679.
Marx, Karl and Engels, Friedrich (1976a) 'The German Ideology', in *Marx Engels Collected Works, vol. 5: Marx and Engels: 1845–47*, London: Lawrence & Wishart, pp. 477–539.
Marx, Karl and Engels, Frederick (1976b) *The Manifesto of the Communist Party*, in *Marx Engels Collected Works*, vol. 6: *Marx and Engels: 1845–48*, London: Lawrence & Wishart, pp. 477–519.
Marx, Karl and Engels, Frederick (1989) 'Preface to the Second Russian Edition of

the Manifesto of the Communist Party,' in *Marx Engels Collected Works*, vol. 24: *Marx and Engels: 1874–83*, New York: International Publishers, pp. 425–6.

Marx, Karl and Engels, Friedrich (1985) *Marx Engels Collected Works*, vol. 41, *Letters 1860–64*, Moscow: Progress Publishers.

Marx, Karl and Engels, Friedrich (1987) *Marx Engels Collected Works*, vol. 42, *Letters 1864–68*, Moscow: Progress Publishers.

Marx, Karl and Engels, Friedrich (1992) *Marx Engels Collected Works*, vol. 46, *Letters 1880–83*, London: Lawrence & Wishart.

Moore, Jason W. (2015) *Capitalism in the Web of Life*, London: Verso.

Smith, Neil (2008) *Uneven Development*, Athens: The University of Georgia Press.

Stanley, John L. (2002) *Mainlining Marx*, Piscataway, NJ: Transaction.

Wendling, Amy E. (2009) *Karl Marx on Technology and Alienation*, New York: Palgrave.

Žižek, Slavoj (2009) 'Ecology', in Astra Taylor (ed.), *Examined Life: Excursions with Contemporary Thinkers*, New York: The New Press, pp. 155–83.

10 Marx's *Capital* and the earth

An ecological critique of political economy

John Bellamy Foster

1 Introduction

Marx's *Capital* is known almost as much for its subtitle, *A Critique of Political Economy*, as it is for its title. In this chapter I shall advance the view that Marx's *Capital*, in its widest conception, constituted an *ecological* critique of political economy. Such an ecological critique can be discerned in all of Marx's work. The roots of this can be found in his earliest writings, influenced by his study of Epicurus's materialism, Feuerbach's humanism, and Hegel's dialectics. It is present in his treatment of the alienation of both labor and of nature in his *Economic and Philosophic Manuscripts of 1844*.

However, I would like to focus here on how Marx's *Capital* itself (including the various incomplete drafts and his later researches into the political economy of natural conditions) marks the culmination of his specifically ecological critique of capitalism. Moreover, I want to ask a disturbing question: Why is it that contemporary Marxian thinkers, while now commonly acknowledging the ecological dimension of Marx's thought, nonetheless marginalize this aspect of Marx's critique, as if were a minor and exotic issue—or even attempt to argue that Marx, for of all his ecological sensitivity, fell prey to certain fundamental flaws in this area? (See, for example, Daniel Tanuro 1973: 136–43; Joel Kovel 2002: 209–12). Furthermore, how is this related to the rejection of any relation of Marxism to natural science, which came to characterize Western Marxism beginning in the 1960s, and which has only been reinforced subsequently by the culturalist turn, postmodernism, and now post-humanism?

These of course are not merely academic queries. If Marx's critique of *Capital* is to be taken seriously a century and a half later, in the Anthropocene epoch, it has to be able to address the Earth System crisis of our time. A critique that remains within the domain of political economy in the narrow sense is therefore no longer sufficient. Rather the ecological critique of political economy embedded in Marx's dialectical method is crucial to the revolutionary praxis in the Anthropocene.

Here it is useful to quote Rosa Luxemburg, who observed that Marx's great "scientific achievement" in *Capital* transcended the immediate needs of the movement, with the result that much of what he provided with its "immeasurable field of application" was not utilized or even fully discerned by the socialist movement that followed faced as it was with certain practical challenges of the time. "Only in proportion as our movement progresses and demands the solution to new practical problems," she declared, "do we dip once more into the treasure of Marx's thought, in order to extract therefrom and to utilize new fragments of his doctrine" (Luxemburg 1970: 111).

2 The universal metabolism of nature

Marx's *Capital* is unlike any other work in classical political economy in that it is connected throughout to developments in natural science, and is predicated on the existence of natural conditions and natural limits. This is because, for Marx, the materialist conception of history was seen as dialectically interwoven with the material conception of nature. Although he was principally concerned with developing the materialist conception of history, this required constant attention to new discoveries in the materialist conception of nature, that is, the natural science of his day. The labor and production process was after all a material-physical process involving the transformation of nature and of human relations to nature—and dependent on certain unalterable natural conditions. Humanity, Marx argued, could affect the outward forms of nature and life, nevertheless it remained itself inescapably a part of nature on which it was ultimately dependent.

Marx's materialist-dialectical view meant the labor and production process had to be conceived in dual terms, as related to *use value*, i.e., connected to material conditions and production in general, and *exchange value*, i.e., associated with valorization based on abstract labor and specifically capitalist production. All flows in the capitalist economy had this contradictory, dual aspect: material-physical (related to use value) and more narrowly economic (related to valorization). It was the contradiction between use value and exchange value in these terms that Marx considered the single most important methodological premise governing his entire critique of political economy (Marx and Engels 1975: 180).[1] The larger environmental implications associated with the contradiction between use value and exchange value are what ecosocialists have in mind when they refer to Marx's ecological value-form analysis.[2] This is also connected to the notion of unequal ecological exchange, whereby a given individual, class, or country receives less natural use-values in exchange for more.

Indispensable to an understanding of these contradictions within production, for Marx, was a dialectical world view. Dialectics in what Georg Lukács called its most "merely objective" form, as represented by Hegel's "Doctrine of Essence," is about the recognition of the relation between part and whole in a process of ever-present movement, repulsion, reciprocal interaction, negation, and qualitative transformation (Lukács 1971: 207).[3] Dialectical inquiry thus focuses on the concrete mediations that constitute a given historically-specific reality. Such concrete (or second-order) mediations invariably lead to new contradictions and crises, creating the need for further transformations. If capitalism was, for Marx, an integrative system, and hence needed to be analyzed dialectically, it was also true that it existed materially within another, more universal system of nature, with which it necessarily interacted. Nature was both internal to and external to society, simply because humanity-society was a part of nature and a manifestation of its being. To attempt to analyze society apart from nature and material existence was pure idealism, because to do so was to deny the realm of sensuous existence. Conversely, any attempt to reduce society to nature led to crude mechanism.

The core concept that Marx employed beginning in the 1850s to explore the complex, dialectical interconnections of nature and society was metabolism. This was not introduced as a metaphor, but rather as a critical-scientific category to explain the systemic material interconnections and flows basic to the organization of the material world and of life itself. Marx wrote of the "metabolic processes of human labor," and saw the labor process as "the universal condition for the metabolic interaction [*Stoffwechsel*] between man and nature" (Marx 1976: 207, 290). With this concept, he was able to address the dialectics of nature and history in a meaningful way, conceiving their interrelation, and building it into his critique of political economy.

In doing so, Marx drew on natural science, including *Mikrokosmos* written by his close friend the physician-scientist-Communist Roland Daniels, a "work of genius" that extended the concept of metabolism to a rudimentary ecological system analysis. Equally important were the German chemist Justus von Liebig's writings on agricultural chemistry, which delved into the nutritive cycles and the disruption of the soil metabolism due to capitalism industrial agriculture (see Foster and Clark 2016: 5–6; Foster 2000: 147–63; Daniels 1988: 49).[4] The concept of metabolism was initially more important for the development of an ecological-systems perspective than the category ecology itself, coined by Ernst Haeckel in 1866 (the year before the publication of Marx's *Capital*) to stand for Darwin's "economy of nature" (Golley 1993: 2, 207).

Influenced by Daniels and Liebig, and others, and seeking to understand the ecological contradictions of capitalism, Marx introduced the separate notions of "the universal metabolism of nature," for nature's processes as a whole, "social metabolism" for human production, and the "irreparable rift in the interdependent process of social metabolism" (or metabolic rift), for the alienated metabolism characteristic of the capitalist commodity economy (Marx 1988: 54–66, 1976: 198, 1981: 949). The broad methodological approach adopted by Daniels, Liebig and Marx in its emphasis on metabolism and metabolic flows (or nutrient flows)—though in Marx the issue was the social metabolism—was to give rise, as other thinkers took up this frame of analysis, to what was later to be called ecosystem theory, which constitutes the core of how we now see ecology. In fact, Marx's close friend E. Ray Lankester, England's leading zoologist in the late nineteenth century, was a major ecological critic of capitalism, while it was Lankester's student, the botanist Arthur Tansley, founder of the British Ecological Society, and like Lankester a strong materialist and Fabian-style socialist, who in the 1930s was to introduce the concept of ecosystem analysis (Ayres 2012: 41–3).

Marx was led by his dialectical conception of the universal metabolism of nature to form the most radical definition of ecological sustainability ever developed. No one, not even all the countries and all the peoples of the world, Marx argued, own the earth, they merely hold it in trust as "*boni patres familias*" [good heads of the household] and are responsible for maintaining it and even improving it for future generations. Socialism was itself defined by Marx in these terms: as the rational regulation by the associated producers of the human metabolism with nature, in such a way as to conserve human-social energy while fulfilling the need for free human development (Marx 1981: 754, 911, 959).

Commenting on the ecological contradictions in his time—disturbance in the soil metabolism, natural-resource scarcities, deforestation, regional climate change, desertification, extinction of species, the growing division between town and country—Marx conceived of these methodologically in terms of various rifts in the earth's universal metabolism emanating from the one-sided process of capital accumulation. A central aspect of his critique, arising from his ecological value-form analysis, was the recognition that the capitalist valorization process taken as a whole was inherently destructive of natural-material use values, generating ever greater ecological contradictions and social costs (Kapp 1950: 33–6).

In his final years, Marx entered into deep natural scientific studies meant to extend his critique of political economy in ecological directions exploring the relation between geological and historical time. He studied the role of coal deposits on urban development in Britain through the writings of Canadian naturalist Grant Allen, and took detailed extracts in his notebooks from the work of British geologist Joseph Beete Jukes on the way in which shifts in isotherms, or in the earth's temperature regions, generated species extinction through climate change over geological time—long before today's climate-change crisis made this a contemporary historical concern in the late twentieth and early twenty-first centuries. Marx took careful note of Jukes's statement, that: "The extinction of species is still going on, man himself being now the most active exterminator" (Allen 1880; Jukes 1872: 504; Hundt 2012).

These various investigations were long seen as a product of an eclecticism that was supposed to have entered into Marx's work in his last decade, giving rise a series of digressions that prevented him from completing *Capital*.[5] However, they are now viewed as fundamental elements in his critique of political economy that increasingly took an ecological turn.

3 The expropriation of nature

A crucial aspect of Marx's method points to the theory of unequal ecological exchange, i.e., to questions of the expropriation or robbery of ecological resources. Recently, some left ecological thinkers have tried to generalize his analysis by pointing to the concept of appropriation, and particularly the "appropriation of the unpaid work" of nature (and society) as the key to a left ecological critique.[6] This, however, constitutes a fundamental error. It is important to recognize that for Marx, in his own words, "all production is appropriation of nature on the part of an individual within and thorough a specific form of society" (Marx1973a: 87). Nor is the appropriation of nature in this sense to be decried. Production and property of any sort, including communal property, are impossible without the appropriation of nature. It is a requirement of society and even of human life itself. The free appropriation of nature by societies throughout history is therefore not to be condemned in and of itself, according to Marx's analysis—nor is it to be confused with exploitation.

But private property in general, and particularly capitalist commodity production, necessarily requires as its logical and historical precondition, the *expropriation*, i.e., the robbery of individuals, classes, and nature's metabolism itself—in order to lay the grounds of commodity production. Where expropriation is concerned, there is no quid pro quo or equal exchange, and the conditions of natural, human, and social reproduction are not maintained. If the exploitation of labor power is designed to reproduce the value of labor power, Marx also notes capitalist society systematically "squanders" actual human labor power (the human body) on which it is based, leading many workers to an early grave (Marx 1981: 182).

From his *Economic and Philosophical Manuscripts* of 1844 to *Capital* in 1867 Marx was thus clear that the precondition of capitalist private property was the expropriation of the worker from the land (and of the land from the worker). Marx's most famous discussion of this was in *Capital* itself in the section on "So-called Primary Accumulation" (Marx 1976: 871, 1970: 309–22). Here Marx was commenting critically on the concept of original or primary accumulation (mistakenly translated into English as "primitive accumulation") as that had been developed previously by classical-liberal political economists. In referring to "so-called primary accumulation," Marx signaled his rejection of this notion. Instead, he employed the concept of expropriation, meaning systematic robbery, to describe the relation of capitalist private property to peasants who were expropriated, and to the land (nature). Such expropriation, including the expropriation of the commons, was the precondition on which capitalism was built, and a continuing reality underlying its world domination. Moreover, expropriation, extending globally in Marx's day through colonialism and slavery, was a constantly recurring part of capital's overall logic. The revolutionary movement against capital, he famously concluded, required the expropriation of the expropriators (Marx 1976: 930).

Expropriation, for Marx, is to be distinguished not only from appropriation, but also from exploitation. The exploitation of labor under capitalism, which was the source of surplus value for Marx, occurred within a context of equal exchange—a basic presumption of all schools of economics down to the present day. But behind the quid pro quo relations, which defined the realm of the exploitation of labor power and the generation of surplus value, was a deeper, wider, and more pervasive phenomenon of expropriation. This could be seen in the expropriation of the land, the squandering of nature itself (transgressing the necessary conditions of its reproduction), and the robbery of domestic labor (reflecting the fact that women were, as Marx and Engels (1976: 46) put it, slaves in the household). In certain conditions, capital also instituted superexploitation, where the value of labor power was not reproduced.

All of these were to be regarded as forms of non-economic (or supra-economic) expropriation within Marx's broader historical vision of capitalist dynamics. Like Liebig Marx saw capitalism in many respects as characterized by earth robbery (*Raubbau*) or what was to be called the robbery economy (*Raubwirtschaft*) (Brock 1997: 177–8; Marx 1976: 638).[7] Concealed behind the capitalist law of value, and left out of its accounting, was a wider vampire-like system that sucked the blood from the world. It was in this sense that Marx decried the system's failure to recognize earth contribution to development, seeing this simply as "a free gift of Nature to capital" (Marx 1998: 732).[8]

Marx not only argued that capitalism "robbed" the soil, he insisted that England had "indirectly exported the soil of Ireland" and that Ireland's "manure was … exported" to England with Ireland gaining little or nothing in return—an early form of unequal ecological exchange. England was forced to import guano from Peru in what amounted to a neocolonial relationship to restore its own exhausted soil. "One part of the globe," Marx stated, is converted "into a chiefly agriculture [and raw material] field of production for supplying the other part, which remains a pre-eminently industrial field" (Marx and Engels 1971: 290–2; Marx 1973: 90; Marx 1976: 579–80, 860), Marx 1981: 753, 949). What was involved here was not just the transport of values but the pillage of the ecological conditions in the periphery: a system of unequal ecological exchange based on a worldwide expropriation of natural resources falling outside the circuit of value, treated by the system as a free gift to capital (Foster and Holleman 2014).

4 Hesitations before Marx's ecology

Marx's theory of metabolic rift, his ecological value-form analysis, and his theory of expropriation and unequal ecological exchange have enabled ecosocialists to integrate more fully the political-economic and ecological critiques of capitalism as a system. These discoveries with respect to the dialectical interpenetration of the economic and ecological contradictions of the system, in Marx's analysis, have had an extraordinary impact on environmental sociology and in some cases environmental science, as well as affecting environmental movements. Explorations of capitalism's ecological rift over the last two decades have helped in the analysis of a myriad of contradictions in such areas as climate change, ocean systems, soil and fertilizers, deforestation, coal mining, desertification, and the industrialization and mechanization of so-called animal husbandry (see Wishart, Jonna, and Besek 2016). Marx was the first to raise of the issue of what he called agricultural and food regimes, now a perspective widely used in world-system theory (see Foster 2016). Through the efforts of Paul Burkett in particular a new Marxian ecological economics was introduced, transcending many of the reifications of economical economics (Burkett 2006). Ian Angus has applied Marx's concept of the metabolic rift to the understanding of the Anthropocene Epoch (Angus 2016).

The revelations and rediscoveries, which are still ongoing, with regard to Marx's ecology and its application, represent a revolution in the understanding of Marx's thought not seen since the retrieval of his early writings on alienation. Yet, most standard, general treatments of Marx's thought today relegate his ecological ideas to a footnote or two, and display certain hesitations, even in some cases excluding it altogether from their analysis.[9] Here we run especially into deep prejudices with respect that seem to persist in face of a mountain of research to the contrary. The general abandonment of materialism on the left from the 1960s onward led to a myopic view of Marx's work and even of dialectical thought, which systematically excluded all physical science and hence what we now call ecological considerations from his analysis—so that all of these issues were marginalized. Even a thinker as erudite as David Harvey recently wrote that "Marx could not abide social theories that depended on so-called natural conditions or forces to explain anything about capitalism" (Harvey 2017: 162).[10]

In some instances, there have been attempts on the left, particularly by first-stage ecosocialists, to argue that Marx's own ecological analysis was fundamentally flawed, though such attempts—for example, the idea that Marx and Engels downplayed or even rejected the second law of thermodynamics or that they completely ignored the role of coal in the development of capitalism—have been shown to be false.[11] More recently, in the face of this failure to find any anti-ecological analysis in Marx and Engels, critics have resorted to utilizing four broad polemical devices, allowing them to challenge the ecological-materialist underpinnings of Marx and Engels's thought in ways that are designed to largely supersede all questions evidence.

First, it is frequently said that those thinkers, including myself, who have retrieved Marx's ecological critique and have dispelled earlier myths in this respect, are simply out to suggest that Marx and Engels were politically correct Greens from the standpoint of the early twenty-first century, and that Marx and Engels were right in everything they said—even that their analysis is "sufficient" in the present.[12] This polemic is misguided, however, since today's ecological Marxists are chiefly concerned, not with some abstract notion of ecological correctness, but rather with the question of whether classical historical materialism, as exemplified by Marx's *Capital*, provides us with critical-methodological tools and the broad ecological critique of political economy that can help guide today's revolutionary praxis. The issue is not whether Marx and Engels anticipated today's Green theory, but whether they can help us transcend it, creating a more revolutionary ecological movement. As Lukács famously said, orthodoxy in Marxism "refers exclusively to *method*" (Lukács 1971: 1). What is being sought in ecological Marxism is a more unified materialist-dialectical method aimed at a transformative praxis.

Second, we are frequently told by first-generation ecosocialists—those who seek to demonstrate that there are fundamental ecological flaws in Marx and Engels's analysis as a basis for separating themselves from classical Marxism—that Marx and Engels were Promethean hyper-industrialists and that their ideas pointed to some of the worst aspects of the Soviet emphasis on heavy industry (Löwy 1997: 33–34; Benton 1996).[13] However, no evidence that Marx and Engels presented such views has ever been discovered—at most what we are offered is a few phrases taken out of context such as the famous panegyric to the bourgeoisie and its promotion of industry in the first part of *The Communist Manifesto*.[14] Given that that Marx and Engels's complete works take up over 100 volumes the inability to come up with a single paragraph convincingly demonstrating that they held to such Promethean-hyper-industrialist views is itself significant. As Eric Hobsbawm definitively pronounced in his *The Age of Extremes*, "No discussion ... of rapid industrialization with priority for the heavy industries was to be found in the writings of Marx and Engels" (Hobsbawm 1994: 277). Marx was in many ways as concerned with agriculture as he was with manufacturing. In fact, his later writings and researches are primarily directed at agriculture and natural resources questions, reflecting his growing interest in the ecological problem (Saito 2016).

Third, Marx's theory of metabolic rift has been criticized by ecosocialists as a form of "dualistic" rather than dialectical thinking, since it points to the existence of both humanity and nature and the development of rifts or ruptures between the two. In *Capital* Marx wrote that capitalist production "disturbs the metabolic interaction between man and the earth." World-ecology theorist Jason Moore has recently criticized this as a "dual systems approach" characterized by "Nature/Society" divide. Outlooks such as those of Marx and Engels in the nineteenth century, according to Moore, are to be rejected as reflecting a "Cartesian binary" that posits "two metabolisms, one Social and one Natural" (Marx 1976: 637; Moore 2015: 13, 80).[15]

Yet, logically Marx's ecological argument in *Capital* is no more dualistic in this respect than it is to refer to the heart as distinguished from the entire body—in an attempt to examine their interactions. In any dialectical-systems analysis, it is essential to abstract the part from the whole in order to learn about their interaction, and the various mediations that lie in between. It is precisely because the concept of metabolism is directed at analyzing the complex, systemic mediations between humanity and the earth that it is plays such an indispensable part in guiding ecological analysis. If there is a conflict between capitalism and the earth depicted in Marx's analysis, this is not due to some contradiction in his logic; rather the contradiction is that of the alienated system of commodity production itself.

A fourth device has been to argue that while Marx delved into the ecological contradictions of capitalism, he failed to place any intrinsic value on nature, adopting a purely instrumentalist approach (Kovel 2002: 197–8, 210–11). Nevertheless, we can see Marx's concern with the intrinsic value of nature in his criticisms of the systematic animal abuse in capitalist industry and to his worries regarding the extinction of species (see Saito 2016: 62).

More significantly, Marx's recognition of intrinsic value is evident in his aesthetics. For Marx, the entire realm of aesthetics, including the concept of beauty emanates from human sensuousness. Human beings are conceived of as both *human* and *natural* beings—insofar as they are not alienated social beings. In sharp contrast to Hegel, Marx declares, "That abstract thought is nothing in itself; that the absolute idea is nothing for itself; that only *nature* is something." Intrinsic value in Marx's aesthetics is not therefore something abstract, but a sensuous-material relation of human beings to the world. Because of this, he writes, human beings also form "objects in accordance with the laws of beauty" (Marx and Engels, 1975: 277, 300–4, 343–4; Foster and Burkett 2017: 54).

All four of the broad polemical responses to Marx's ecology, referred to above, are idealist in character. To privilege the question of whether Marx was right in terms of today's Green ideology is to take an essentially idealist and abstract ethical-foundationalist stance.[16] Likewise, to downplay his ecological contributions by claiming that he was Promethean, dualist, or instrumentalist (rejecting intrinsic value) is to raise issues that are idealist in character and related to Green ethics. None of these criticisms, as we have seen hold water, precisely because they fail to perceive the deep materialism of Marx's ecology.

Marx's lasting contributions to ecology are most evident when they are understood in terms of the development of ecological science itself. This is threatening to many left thinkers since probably the greater part of Western Marxism has long rejected science and any meaningful materialist-realist philosophy. As Sebastiano Timpanaro wrote in the opening sentence of his *On Materialism*, "Perhaps the sole characteristic common to virtually all contemporary varieties of Western Marxism is their concern to defend themselves against accusations of materialism" (Timpanaro 1975: 29). The subsequent cultural turn and the growth of postmodernism and now post-humanism have, for the most part, only deepened this default. Rather than looking for dialectical, coevolutionary relations between human society and nature (of which humanity is a part), post-humanists treat them as bundles, webs, networks, and hybrids, in a kind of abstracted empiricism, that excludes dialectical development.[17]

It should be immediately evident in a period of planetary emergency that a critical-materialist outlook engaged with natural science is called for, demanding the return to classical historical materialism in this respect. Moreover, much work in the Marxian tradition that has been rejected to the point of being forgotten—as too materialist or positivist—needs to be retrieved as well. Marx's *Capital* needs to be read in new ways, generating a tradition and a knowledge *that we can use* in building the present.[18] Any analysis of Marx's work that excludes his ecological understanding is as weak and as useless in the present as an analysis that excludes his concept of alienation. As Luxemburg said, the development of the socialist movement itself in the face of changing material conditions compels us to "dip once more into the treasure of Marx's thought, in order to extract therefrom and to utilize new fragments of his doctrine." A whole new Marxian ecological materialism and a new conception of socialism as a society of substantive equality and ecological sustainability is developing in the twenty-first century. A century and a half after the publication of Marx's *Capital* we are learning new things from his *ecological critique of political economy*, including the need to start again in our revolutionary struggles on a fuller, deeper basis, rooted in the earth itself. "Well grubbed, old Mole!" (Marx 1963: 121).

Notes

1 For Marx, as he indicates here, even the distinction between concrete and abstract labor, was merely an aspect of the distinction between use value and exchange value.

2 Marx's ecological value-form analysis is explored in great detail in Paul Burkett (2014).

3 Lukács refers here to "the merely objective dialectics of nature." This was to be distinguished in his conception from the subjective dialectics of identical subject-object, which was to be the focus of his *History and Class Consciousness* and which became the main preoccupation of Western Marxism. Nevertheless, Lukács in his later work was to return to the issue of the objective dialectics of nature.

4 The characterization of *Mikrokosmos* as "a work of genius" comes from Martin Hundt (2012). Daniels's work was not published due to his early death (it was only brought out in the 1980s) but he did have one reader who commented on his book manuscript and whom he influenced: Karl Marx.

5 On the importance of Marx's last decade and the errors in seeing this as a non-productive period See Teodor Shanin (1983).

6 See, for example, Jason W. Moore (2015: 17, 70, 102). Moore's use of the concept of the appropriation of nature generates a double confusion from a classical historical-materialist perspective: (1) Moore says Marx employed the notion of the appropriation of nature as the equivalent of exploitation—an entirely different concept; (2) in his own extended usage of the concept of appropriation Moore equates it with expropriation—also a different concept.

7 Liebig also wrote of *Raubwirtschaft* or robbery economy (also called plunder economy).

8 On Marx's use of the vampire metaphor, see Mark Neocleous (2003).

9 For example, Marx's ecological critique is almost completely absent, receiving at most bare mention, in such important works as David Harvey (2014), Michael Lebowitz (2010), and Terry Eagleton (2012).

10 Harvey appears to contradict himself later on the same page, referring to "the dialectical metabolic relation to nature." It is important to note, that the rejection of the relation of Marx's analysis to natural conditions and natural science (and a dialectics of nature) on the part of Marian thinkers would have been incomprehensible to earlier left generations. See, for example, Bernal (1952).

11 For the distinction between first-stage and second-stage ecosocialism and for an anti-critique that demonstrates the fallacy of arguing that Marx and Engels downplayed thermodynamics and fossil fuels see John Bellamy Foster and Paul Burkett (2017).

12 See, for example, Daniel Tanuro (2012), where the criticism is launched (in opposition to Paul Burkett and me) that Marx and Engels were not, despite all of their ecological insights," "ecologically correct" by today's standards—as if this, and not their *method of analysis* (which of course requires understanding what it was that they said about ecology) is the real issue. See also Kovel (2002: 210–11); Maarten de Kadt and Salvatore Engel Di-Mauro (2001: 50–6).

13 Alf Hornborg argues against what he calls "selective exegesis" of Marx's texts, in which evidence from the texts is introduced in the context of interpretations of his system as whole. This serves to justify Hornborg's declaration in the very next sentence that Marx and Engels had a "Promethean trust in technological progress"—an assertion for which he believes evidence ("selective exegesis") would be entirely superfluous—as he himself has simply pronounced it to be so (Alf Hornborg 2014: 11–18). The persistence of the Promethean myth with respect to Marx and Engels, and the reluctance of some ecosocialist theorists to drop it, can be seen in the evolution of the overall impressive work of Löwy, who has presented this criticism of Marx in the past, but who has more recently moved towards a nuanced view, conceding now that there is no evidence whatsoever for the Promethean criticism. And yet he nevertheless tries to retain it in part, seeking to find some concrete basis for contending that Marx and Engels had an "uncritical stance towards the productive forces created by capital." See Löwy (2017: 13).

14 The theoretical significance of the fact that Marx and Engels in the first part of *The Communist Manifesto* "launched out on a panegyric upon bourgeois achievement that has no equal in economic literature" was first emphasized by Joseph Schumpeter in his famous 1949 essay "The Communist Manifesto in Sociology and Economics" (Schumpeter 1949: 209.) Quotations that rely directly on this panegyric to bourgeois industrialism as a way of compromising Marx and Engels's commitment to ecology still appear—as in Löwy (2017: 11)—but fundamentally misunderstand the way in which the critique in the *Manifesto* was constructed. On this whole issue see John Bellamy Foster (2009: 213–32).

15 It should be noted that Moore does not criticize Marx directly but rather attributes Marx's views on metabolic rift incorrectly to me, and criticizes me for these supposedly "dualistic" conceptions. The real target, however, is Marx.

16 On the radical historical rather than foundationalist approach to ethics that characterizes Marx's thought see Cornel West (1991).

17 On post-humanism, see Hornborg (2016).

18 See Eric Foner's related comments on a history *we can use* in Foner (2017).

References

Allen, Grant (1880) 'Geology and History', in *Popular Science Monthly*, vol. 17: 495–507.

Angus, Ian (2016) *Facing the Anthropocene*, New York: Monthly Review Press.

Ayres, Peter (2012) *Shaping Ecology*, Oxford: John Wiley and Sons.

Benton, Ted (ed.) (1996) *The Greening of Marxism*, New York: Guilford.

Bernal, John D. (1952) *Marx and Science*, London: Lawrence and Wishart.

Brock, William H. (1997) *Justus von Liebig*, Cambridge: Cambridge University Press.

Burkett, Paul (2006) *Marxism and Ecological Economics*, Boston: Brill.

Burkett, Paul (2014) *Marx and Nature*, Chicago: Haymarket Books.

Daniels, Roland (1988 [1851]) *Mikrokosmos*, Frankfurt am Main: Verlag Peter Lang.

de Kadt, Maarten and Engel Di-Mauro, Salvatore (2001) 'Failed Promise', in *Capitalism Nature Socialism*, London: Routledge, vol. 12, no. 2: 50–6.

Eagleton, Terry (2012) *Why Marx Was Right*, New Haven, CT: Yale University Press.

Foner, Eric (2017) 'Trump Is Just Tearing Off the Mask: An Interview with Eric Foner', in MR Online. https://mronline.org/2017/05/14/trump-is-just-tearing-off-the-mask/.

Foster, John Bellamy, (2000) *Marx's Ecology*, New York: Monthly Review Press.

Foster, John Bellamy (2009) *The Ecological Revolution*, New York: Monthly Review Press.

Foster, John Bellamy and Holleman, Hannah (2014) 'The Theory of Unequal Ecological Exchange', in *Journal of Peasant Studies*, London: Routledge vol. 41, no. 1–2: 199–233.

Foster, John Bellamy (2016) 'Marx as a Food Theorist', in *Monthly Review*, vol. 68, no. 7: 1–22.

Foster, John Bellamy and Clark, Brett (2016) 'Marxism and Ecology', in *Monthly Review*, vol. 68, no. 5: 5–6.

Foster, John Bellamy and Burkett, Paul (2017) *Marx and the Earth*, Chicago: Haymarket.

Golley, Frank Benjamin (1993) *A History of the Ecosystem Concept in Ecology*, New Haven, CT: Yale University Press.

Harvey, David (2014) *Seventeen Contradictions and the End of Capitalism*, Oxford: Oxford University Press.

Harvey, David (2017) 'A Commentary on A Theory of Imperialism', in *Utsa Patnaik and Prabhat Patnaik, A Theory of Imperialism*, New York: Columbia University Press, pp. 155–72.

Hobsbawm, Eric (1994) *The Age of Extremes*, London: Penguin Book.

Hornborg, Alf (2014) 'Ecological Economics, Marxism, and Technological Progress' in *Ecological Economics*, vol. 105: 11 18.

Hornborg, Alf (2016) 'Post-Capitalist Ecologies', in *Capitalism Nature Socialism*, London: Routledge, vol. 27, no. 4: 61–76.

Hundt, Martin (2012) 'The Connection of Mind and Nature: Marx's 1878 Notebooks on Geology', in *International Marxist-Humanist*, www.internationalmarxisthumanist.org/articles/connection-mind-nature-marxs-1878-notebooks-geology-martin-hundt.

Jukes, Joseph Beete (1872) *The Student's Manual of Geology*, Edinburgh: Adam and Charles Black.

Kapp, K. William (1950) *The Social Costs of Private Enterprise*, Cambridge, MA: Harvard University Press.

Kovel, Joel (2002) *The Enemy of Nature*, London: Zed.

Lebowitz, Michael (2010) *The Socialist Alternative*, New York: Monthly Review Press.

Löwy, Michael (1997) 'For a Critical Marxism', in *Against the Current*, vol. 12, no. 5: 33–4.

Löwy, Michael (2017) 'Marx, Engels, and Ecology', in *Capitalism Nature Socialism*, London: Routledge, vol. 28, no. 2: 13.

Lukács, Georg (1971) *History and Class Consciousness*, London: Merlin Press.

Luxemburg, Rosa (1970) *Rosa Luxemburg Speaks*, New York: Pathfinder.

Marx, Karl (1963) *The Eighteenth Brumaire of Louis Bonaparte*, New York: International Publishers.

Marx, Karl (1970) *Early Writings*, London: Penguin.

Marx, Karl (1973) *On the First International*, New York: McGraw Hill.

Marx, Karl (1975 [1844]) *Economic and Philosophic Manuscripts of 1844*, in *Marx Engels Collected Works*, vol. 3, New York: International Publishers.

Marx, Karl (1976) *Capital*, vol. 1, London: Penguin.

Marx, Karl (1981) *Capital*, vol. 3, London: Penguin.

Marx, Karl (1988 [1861–1863]) *Economic Manuscript of 1861–63*. in *Marx Engels Collected Works*, vol. 30, New York: International Publishers.

Marx, Karl (1998) *Capital*, vol. 3, in *Marx Engels Collected Works*, vol. 37: *Karl Marx, Capital, Vol. III*, New York: International Publishers.

Marx, Karl and Engels, Frederick (1971) *Ireland and the Irish Question*, Moscow: Progress Publisher.

Marx, Karl and Engels, Frederick (1975) *Selected Correspondence*, Moscow: Progress Publisher.

Marx, Karl and Engels, Frederick (1976 [1845–1846]) *The German Ideology*. in *Marx Engels Collected Works*, vol. 5, New York: International Publishers.

Moore, Jason W. (2015) *Capitalism in the Web of Life*, London: Verso.

Neocleous, Mark (Winter 2003) 'The Political Economy of the Dead: Marx's Vampires', in *History of Political Thought*, vol. 24, no. 4: 668–84.

Saito, Kohei (2016) 'Marx's Ecological Notebooks', in *Monthly Review*, vol. 67, no. 9: 25–42.

Saito, Kohei (2016) 'Why Ecosocialism Needs Marx', in *Monthly Review*, vol. 68, no. 6.

Shanin, Teodor (1983) (ed.) *Late Marx and the Russian Road*, New York: Monthly Review Press.

Schumpeter, Joseph A. (1949) 'The Communist Manifesto in Sociology and Economics', in *Journal of Political Economy* 57, no. 3: 199–212.

Tanuro, Daniel (1973) *Green Capitalism: Why It Can't Work*, London: Merlin Press.

Tanuro, Daniel (2012) 'A Plea for the Ecological Reconstruction of Marxism' International Viewpoint 3, www.europe-solidaire.org/spip.php?article27100.

Timpanaro, Sebastiano (1975) *On Materialism*, London: Verso.

West, Cornel (1991) *The Ethical Dimensions of Marxist Thought*, New York: Monthly Review Press.

Wishart, Ryan, Jonna, R. Jamil and Besek, Jordan (2016) 'The Metabolic Rift: A Selected Bibliography', in *Monthly Review*, https://monthlyreview.org/commentary/metabolic-rift/.

11 Five explicit and implicit notions of revolution in *Capital*, Volume I, as seen from a multilinear, peripheral angle

Kevin B. Anderson

1 Introduction

It has been sometimes said of *Capital* that, as against the *Communist Manifesto*, it is a scholarly theoretical work that does not call for or even sketch the notion of revolution. From this standpoint, the main theme of the book is the enfoldment of the capital form, with many dialectical twists and turns. This is certainly not a false picture. And as is well known, the censors allowed the 1872 Russian edition of *Capital* to appear because they considered it a purely scholarly work. However, such a picture is incomplete, as it severs Marx the revolutionist from Marx the social theorist, as Joseph Schumpeter tried to do some 75 years ago in his *Capitalism, Socialism, and Democracy* (1942).

A different view has been put forward by several schools of Marxist thought, from Raya Dunayevskaya's Marxist-Humanism in the 1950s, up through some of the autonomist Marxists of the 1970s, which have seen *Capital* as a work imbued with class struggle and even revolution (see Dunayevskaya 1958; Cleaver 1979). I will follow these lines of argument in order to specify some of the multiple ways that Marx writes of, or hints at, a variety of notions of revolution in *Capital*, vol. 1. One of my inspirations here is Susan Buck-Morss's *Hegel, Haiti, and Universal History*, a study of the influence of the Haitian Revolution on the *Phenomenology of Spirit*. But where her book is almost purely speculative in the sense that no mentions of the Haitian revolution can be found in Hegel's *Phenomenology* or his other writings, my chapter will base itself upon textual evidence, although sometimes little more than hints, which I will link to other Marx writings during or after *Capital*, Volume 1. The 1872–1875 French edition of *Capital*, Volume I is a crucial part of this textual evidence (Marx 1989). This lesser-known version, the last one Marx personally prepared for publication, features numerous passages not taken up by Engels in what became the most widely translated and circulated version of the book, based on his fourth German edition of 1890.[1]

2 A working class revolution posed at a high level of abstraction

Although not discussed that much today, the penultimate chapter of *Capital*, Volume I, often thought to be its real conclusion, and possibly placed differently in the book to avoid the censors (Marx 1963),[2] is 'The Historical Tendency of Capitalist Accumulation'. It ends with a brief sketch of working-class revolution in an industrially developed capitalist society. Marx outlines the process of revolution as follows:

> Along with the constant decrease in the number of capitalist magnates, who usurp and monopolize all the advantages of this process of transformation, the mass of misery, oppression, slavery, degradation and exploitation grows; but with this there also grows the revolt of the working class, a class constantly increasing in numbers and trained, united and organized by the very mechanism of the capitalist process of production.
>
> (Marx 1976: 929)

Over time, all these developments of (1) productive forces and (2) a united working class become 'incompatible with their capitalist integument' (Marx 1976: 929). Next comes the death knell of 'capitalist [private] property' where the 'expropriators are expropriated' (Marx 1976: 929).[3] In a nod to the Hegelian dialectic, Marx adds: 'Capitalist production begets, with the inexorability of a natural process, its own negation. This is the negation of the negation' (Marx 1976: 929). In this way, *Capital*, Volume I ends with a dialectical thunderclap of revolution.

These pages have been endlessly debated over whether Marx's supposed 'prediction' of imminent revolution has been proved wrong by history. Leaving that debate aside, what is also notable about this chapter is its quite high level of abstraction.[4] The preceding chapters, as well as the succeeding and technically final one on settler colonization, are filled with a wealth of social and economic detail, most of it drawn from the British experience. But the 'Historical Tendency of Capitalist Accumulation' chapter is written at a much higher level of abstraction, without reference to any specific country.

All of this leads to the conclusion that this concluding chapter on anticapitalist revolution is meant neither as a prediction of immediate events, nor even as a concrete description of revolution. The state is not mentioned; nor are ethnic divisions among the workers; nor are other classes of working people like the peasantry; nor are subjective factors like the development of the labour or socialist movements. In short, I think that Marx presents here a chemically pure class-based revolution against capital that is not intended as a description of any specific capitalist society or any specific revolution that might occur. Those would be messier and more variegated.

3 Ireland and the specificity of ethnicity, colonialism, and class

When *Capital*, Volume I first appeared in 1867, Ireland was not merely an oppressed nation ruled by a foreign power, Britain. As outlined in the last section of the long chapter on the 'General Law of Capitalist Accumulation', Ireland was also the victim of a particularly capitalist form of colonialism. It radically overturned the entire economic system, dispossessing a subsistence-farming peasantry in favour of value-creating production like sheep farming, and turning the island into an impoverished agricultural dependency of Britain, all in the service of capital accumulation.

The chapter on the accumulation of capital seems to end with the prospect that the British Isles, divided as they are by class and ethnic bitterness, will decline in the face of an ascendant U.S. capitalism across the ocean, itself strengthened by massive Irish emigration. In terms of Britain, Marx concludes:

> Like all good things in the world, this profitable mode of proceeding has its drawbacks. The accumulation of the Irish in America keeps pace with the accumulation of rents in Ireland. The Irishman, banished by the sheep and the ox, reappears on the other side of the ocean as a Fenian. There a young but gigantic republic rises, more and more threateningly, to face the old queen of the waves. 'A cruel fate haunts the Romans, the crime of fratricide'
>
> (Marx 1976: 870)[5]

But is this passage concerned only with British decline, U.S. ascendancy, and intercapitalist rivalry? The brief, almost cryptic, reference to the large number of Fenians among the Irish Americans hints at something else as well.

In 1867–1870, after the first edition of *Capital*, Volume I, came off the press, Marx came out strongly in support of the Fenian movement, a progressive form of Irish nationalism based among the peasantry rather than the upper or middle classes, and which kept its distance from the Church. At some crucial junctures, he managed to get the General Council of the International Working Men's Association to do so as well. Marx also theorized in 1870 about revolution and barriers to revolution in Britain and Ireland in the 'Confidential Communication',[6] a statement of the International he penned in French. Here, he described how the Irish working people, both in in their home country under the death grip of British colonial rule, or inside Britain as immigrant labour in the brutal capitalist factories, were victimized by stereotyping and what would today be termed racism. The condescending attitude of British workers toward their Irish counterparts, who had emigrated to join the lowest levels of the British working classes, created a division within the class, to the benefit of capital. In this sense, Marx's discussion concerned a form of what later came to be called false consciousness.

Ever the dialectician, however, Marx also held that such false consciousness could be turned upon its head, with revolutionary impulses from the most severely oppressed working people serving as the spark for a wider conflagration that would engulf workers from the dominant ethnic group as well. In the Confidential Communication, he first noted that England was the real 'lever' of a potential European revolution:

> Although revolutionary *initiative* will probably come from France, England alone can serve as the *lever* for a serious *economic* Revolution. It is the only country where there are no more peasants and where landed property is concentrated in a few hands. It is the only country where *the capitalist form*, that is to say, combined labour on a large scale under the authority of capitalists [*des maîtres capitalistes*], has seized hold of almost the whole of production. It is the only country where the *vast majority of the population consists of wage laborers....*[7]
>
> (Marx 1966: 356–7)

So far, this was not so different from the model of revolution at the end of the chapter on 'Historical Tendency of Capitalist Accumulation'.

Marx added a twist to his argument, however, to the effect that some roadblocks held back such a working-class uprising. Among these were certain cultural and historical features of the English labour movement, which the International could help to ameliorate:

> The English have all the *material* conditions [*matière nécessaire*] for social revolution. What they lack is *a sense of generalization and revolutionary passion.* It is only the General Council [of the International] that can provide them with this, that can thus accelerate the truly revolutionary movement in this country, and consequently *everywhere.*
>
> (Marx 1966: 357; see also Marx 1985: 87)

But another set of issues concerned England and Ireland, not only the poisonous attitudes of English workers toward their Irish counterparts, but also the possibility that an agrarian uprising inside Ireland could weaken the English dominant classes, open a pathway for an English revolution.

Stressing that the English ruling class was composed of landlords as well as capitalists, and that the landlords had estates in both Britain and Ireland, he added:

> ... Ireland is the *bulwark* of English landlordism. If it fell in Ireland, it would fall in England. In Ireland this is a hundred times easier because *the economic struggle there is concentrated exclusively on landed property*, because this struggle is at the same time national, and because the people there are more revolutionary and angry than in England.
>
> (Marx 1966: 358–9; see also Marx (1985: 87–8)

He concluded: 'To this end the great blow must be struck in Ireland' (Institute of Marxism-Leninism of the C.C., C.P.S.U. 1966: 358–9; see also Marx 1985: 89). Thus, if the English workers were to overthrow the rule of capital, they needed to contend not only with the owners of industry, but also with the more conservative landowning aristocracy, deeply rooted in the military forces that would be used to suppress any uprising. But those landlords had a major weak spot, their holdings in Ireland, where the Fenian nationalist movement constituted a potential ally of the British working classes against both capital and landed property.

Thus, Marx's reference to the 'Fenian' in *Capital* hints at revolutionary possibilities not only in Ireland, but also in Britain, and to their intertwining, especially if one links that reference to his longer discussion in the Confidential Communication. These texts taken together are an example of Marx's mature theory of revolution and capital accumulation at a specific juncture, Britain and Ireland in 1867–1870. It is not an abstract model so much as a very concrete description of the intertwining of class with race/ethnicity/nationalism in terms of both capitalist hegemony and the threat of revolution by an ethnically diverse but potentially united labouring people, both industrial worker and peasant.

4 Race, class, and revolution in the U.S., from above and below

Another type of revolution mentioned in *Capital* centres on the Civil War in the U.S. of 1861–1865 and the period of Reconstruction that followed, with Northern troops occupying the South until 1877. In the preface to the 1867 edition, Marx refers to radical transformations in the offing in both Britain and Reconstruction America as proof of the generalization that 'society is no solid crystal' (Marx 1976: 93). In terms of the U.S., he writes that 'after the abolition of slavery, a radical transformation in the existing relations of capital and landed property is on the agenda', referring to what is today termed 'forty acres and a mule', the land grants that Radical Reconstructionists attempted to cede to the former slaves (Marx 1976: 93; see also Marx and Engels (2016); for discussions, see Nimtz 2003 and Anderson 2010). This initiative was blocked by a single vote when the effort to impeach the virulently racist and obstructionist President Andrew Johnson failed in the Senate in 1868, one year after Marx published those lines. The attempt to impeach Johnson occurred at the high tide of Reconstruction as a revolutionary event. But even without that radical land reform measure, which would have gained for the emancipated slaves not only political freedom, but also economic sustenance, the Civil War and Reconstruction carried with them many revolutionary effects and potentials.

In a certain sense, the Civil War was a revolution from above, enacted by the Federal Government during the war itself and then afterwards in the occupied South, as seen in the attempt at radical land reform by the Congress.

But it was not only that. The revolutionary process also involved extensive participation from below by the African American masses, both free and slave, and before, during, and after the war. For example, as the Marxist historian Bruce Levine notes, even something as seemingly top-down as Lincoln's Emancipation Proclamation of 1863 was used as an agitational document by the Union Army. It distributed thousands of copies, which were passed hand-to-hand. These soon reached enslaved Blacks way behind the Confederate lines, prompting mass escapes from the plantations that weakened and demoralized the Southern forces (Levine 2013).

In *Capital*, Volume I, Marx wrote of the revolutionary possibilities that awaited the U.S. now that slavery was abolished: 'In the United States of America, every independent workers' movement was paralyzed as long as slavery disfigured a part of the republic. Labour in a white skin cannot emancipate itself where it is branded in a black skin' (Marx 1976: 414). As evidence of this, he noted that a National Labor Union was formed for the first time in the U.S. in the aftermath of the war, in 1866, and that it called for the eight-hour day as an antidote to 'capitalistic slavery', thus explicitly criticizing capitalism (Marx 1976: 414).

The Civil War in the U.S. also had international dimensions, as Marx also wrote the 1867 preface to *Capital*: 'Just as in the eighteenth century the American war of independence sounded the tocsin for the European middle class, so in the nineteenth century the Civil War did the same for the European working class' (Marx 1976:91). At that time, he of course could not have known of the Paris Commune of 1871, but he was certainly aware of stirrings of European labour during the Civil War. British workers had mobilized in support of the North even as their own government, which was threatening intervention on behalf of the South, was trying to gain their support for war by blaming the mass layoffs in the cotton mills on the Northern blockade of Confederate ports. Those who organized the mass workers' meetings across Britain in opposition to the government's war cries counted among their number many of the labour activists who, in 1864, founded the First International in London.

5 Communal villages as loci of revolution, in Russia and beyond

The chapters on 'Primitive Accumulation of Capital'[8] centre on the earliest days of capitalism, with special attention to the dispossession or expropriation of the British peasantry from the land and to the African slave trade as part of that early capitalist accumulation. This forms the basis of a new economy based upon slave labour and wage labour, with the latter driven into the towns to become the proletariat. It is at the end of this trajectory, as discussed above, that the by now large and powerful working class rises up and expropriates its expropriators, the capitalist class, in what he calls the negation of the negation. The trajectory seems at first glance unilinear and determinist, at least with regard to the dispossession of the peasantry, for as Marx writes at one point: 'Only in England, which we therefore take as our example, has it the classic form' (Marx 1976: 876).

A lot of ink was spilled in Russia over this sentence, which formed part of the 1867 edition that was translated into Russian in 1872. Many radical Populists in Russia yearned for a rural communism, based upon the *mir* or traditional village commune, hoping that it could be radicalized and modernized without going through the terrific suffering of capitalist dispossession and uprooting. Others, sometimes beginning to consider themselves Marxists, held that the uprooting of the village commune was inevitable and necessary, albeit painful, as the demise of feudalism had been in the West.

In the 1872–1875 French edition of *Capital*, Marx widens the dialectic of primitive accumulation, capital, and labour. As discussed above, the process of primitive accumulation of capital in the 1867 edition ends with a revolutionary working-class expropriation of capitalist property, after those workers have gone through all the horrors of uprooting and industrial wage labour.

But here in the French edition, he opens up his dialectical presentation to account for particularity and difference by decisively altering a key sentence from 1867 about British history as the 'classic form' of primitive accumulation. In the French edition, this sentence, probably reworked in 1874 or 1875, reads. 'So far, it has been carried out in a radical manner only in England: therefore, this country will necessarily play the leading role in our sketch. But all the countries of Western Europe are going through the same development' (Marx 1991: 778). Here, the dialectic of primitive accumulation and subsequent proletarian revolution amid capitalist modernity is not pushed aside, but its scope is limited to Western Europe, and, presumably, other areas of the world that were already embarking upon a capitalist form of modernization. As for Russia and other areas of the world far from the centre of the capitalist mode of production, a more open road existed. It seems that this was far from an obscure passage in Marx's mind, as he proceeded to quote it in several letters to Russian revolutionaries, including the well-known one of 1881 to Vera Zasulich.

To be sure, *Capital*, Volume I says nothing directly about the theory he developed in his last years concerning the revolutionary possibilities of the Russian village commune, let alone his research on indigenous and non-Western forms of communism in his 1879–1882 notebooks that covered village social structures and gender relations in India, Algeria, Latin America, and Native American societies, among others. But the altered passage in the French edition of *Capital* about the concept of primitive accumulation being applicable only to Western Europe left the road open for a new kind of conceptualization of international revolution. In his and Engels's 1882 preface to a new Russian edition of the *Communist Manifesto*, and in a manner parallel to the way in which he had discussed Ireland and Britain, Marx now saw Russia as a possible starting point for a wide-ranging working class upheaval in Western Europe: 'If the Russian revolution becomes the signal for a proletarian revolution in the

West, so that the two complement each other, the present Russian common ownership of land may serve as the starting point for communist development' (Marx and Engels 1989: 426). Fittingly, this subtle conceptualization of the interplay of forces of revolution across vast geographic and sociological distances occurred in Marx's last published writing.

6 Free and associated labour after the abolition of the state

This point bears not only on Marx's conceptualization of revolution, but also upon his visionary theoretical alternative to capitalism. We can, he writes in the fetishism section of the first chapter of *Capital*, Volume I, transcend the ideological stranglehold of capitalism theoretically by looking at non-capitalist modes of production. In this light, Marx examines briefly European feudalism, but while this helped to grasp the uniqueness of capitalist social relations better, feudalism was certainly not a positive alternative to capitalism.[9]

Such a positive form of a non-capitalist society comes instead out of Marx's dialectical imagination, where he takes revolutionary aspirations and trends inside the present order and moves them much further, into a revolutionary communist future: 'Let us finally imagine, for a change', he writes, 'an association of free men [*Menschen*, human beings],[10] working with the means of production held in common' (Marx 1976: 171). In contrast to capitalism's distorting fetishism, 'social relations … are here transparent in their simplicity' (Marx 1976: 172) He also writes that the distorting and obscuring lens of capitalism 'is not removed' until the production process changes, 'until it becomes production by freely associated men, and stands under their conscious and planned control' (Marx 1976: 173). That is communism in the positive sense.

But how to get there? One way is revolution, and as we have seen above, Marx had a number of conceptualizations of revolution. One element not discussed here so far, however, is the need to abolish the state, a theme that comes to the fore in his writings during the same period, 1867–75, when he continued to work on *Capital*, Volume I, through the second German edition of 1872 and the French edition of 1872–1875. Marx wrote on numerous occasions of the free association or freely associated labour as fundamental to his concept of communism, as he did here in *Capital*.[11] But in the 'Civil War in France,' his analysis of the Paris Commune of 1871, he connects freely associated labour to the abolition of the state as a prerequisite for the abolition of capitalism itself.

Using almost the same wording as in the fetishism section of *Capital*, Volume I, Marx writes of the Paris Commune in terms of freely associated labour:

> It wanted to make individual property a truth by transforming the means of production, land, and capital, now chiefly the means of enslaving and

> exploiting labor, into mere instruments of free and associated labor. But this is Communism, 'impossible' Communism!
>
> (Marx 1986: 335)

He also writes of the abolition of the state, that the Paris Commune had moved toward 'the destruction of the State power which claimed to be the embodiment of that unity independent of, and superior to, the nation itself, from which it was but a parasitic excrescence' (Marx 1986: 332). Finally, Marx notes that the Commune, which continued to maintain wage labour and other capitalist forms, was not itself communism, but it did constitute 'the political form at last discovered under which to work out the economical emancipation of Labour' (Marx 1986: 334).

Two things stand out here in terms of the relation of his concept of an anti-statist, anticapitalist revolution in these two texts, 'Civil War in France' and *Capital*, Volume I. First, as mentioned above, the language about freely associated labour as an embodiment of modern, democratic communism is virtually the same in the two texts.

Second, there is the possible influence of the events of Paris Commune on the structure of *Capital*, Volume I. For while the language cited above about freely associated labour had already appeared in the first German edition of 1867, it was not highlighted very much, but buried in the middle of a long chapter on 'Commodities and Money.' By the second German edition of *Capital* that appeared in June 1873, and in the slightly earlier – at least for the first chapter – French edition, which began to appear in September 1872, Marx gave the language about freely associated labour far greater prominence by creating for the first time a named section of Chapter 1 entitled, 'The Fetishism of the Commodity and Its Secret', which formed that chapter's conclusion and which included additional material not found in the 1867 edition (MEGA II/7, pp. 52–63; Marx 1987: 102–13). Moreover, in his letter to French editor Maurice La Châtre that appeared as a preface to the first instalment of the serialized French edition, he called attention to the 'rather arduous' theoretical character of the 'first chapters,' but asked readers to bear with him (Marx 1976: 104). In so doing, he was very likely calling attention to the material at the end of the first chapter, in the fetishism section, that spoke of freely associated labour, which was a major theme of 'Civil War in France' as well. These connections between *Capital*, Volume I, and the Paris Commune seem plausible enough today, once they are unpacked.[12] But they would not have been clear to French and German censors at a time when the Paris Commune, suppressed in spring 1871, was still causing hysteria within political establishments across Europe.

Thus, I am suggesting that the language of the 'Civil War in France' and of *Capital*, Volume I on freely associated labour is interconnected, and that the post-Commune editions of *Capital* bring that language to greater prominence. In this sense, *Capital*, Volume I contains, at least at an implicit level, a link to the anti-statist, communist spirit of the Commune.

7 Conclusion

In this chapter, I have argued that *Capital*, Volume I can be connected to five different notions of revolution: (1) a working class uprising that wells up as a revolutionary negation of the centralized productive apparatus of modern industrial capitalism, as in Britain at the time, but posed at a high level of abstraction; (2) the much more specific and concrete notion of a British workers' revolution being sparked by an agrarian revolution in Ireland, which would shake up the ethnicized false consciousness of British workers and unite them in an anticapitalist revolution with their immigrant Irish coworkers; (3) revolution from above and below, and in connection to the racialized capitalism of the U.S. during and after the Civil War; (4) revolution out of joint with the main thrust of *Capital*, Volume I, beginning in non-capitalist agrarian societies with communal village systems that, in resisting capitalist encroachments, could also emit sparks might ignite the revolutionary labour movement of Western Europe; (5) revolution that abolishes the modern centralized state as in the Paris Commune, during which freely associated labour was briefly established before its bloody defeat.

In short, we can discern, in *Capital*, Volume I and related writings, a Marx who thinks of revolution in terms of capital and labour, but not in a reductionist manner that excludes factors like race, ethnicity, colonialism, the state, and the relationship of non-capitalist social structures to modern capitalist ones.

Notes

1 The fourth German edition is reproduced, with a 60-page appendix containing the passages not included by Engels (Marx 1991). Engels's 1890 edition has been the basis for the standard English version (Marx 1976).

2 Editor Maximilien Rubel regards this chapter as the book's true ending, despite its placement as the second-to-last chapter. He makes the plausible suggestion that Marx did so to hide 'the revolutionary conclusions of his theory' from the German censors (Marx 1963: 1706).

3 In the French edition, Marx writes 'capitalist property,' leaving off the word 'private,' (Karl Marx 1989: 679). I owe this point to Paresh Chattopadhyay.

4 Bertell Ollman (1993) has emphasized Marx's differing levels of abstraction.

5 The quote is from the Roman poet Horace.

6 The statement has become known as the 'Confidential Communication,' but was recorded as 'Le Conseil générale au conseil fédéral de la Suisse romande'. See Marx (1966 and 1985).

7 See also Marx (1985: 86). Here and below, emphasis in original.

8 Marx separates the discussion of 'primitive accumulation' into eight discrete chapters in the 1872–75 French edition, also dropping the modifier 'so-called.' English editions have adopted the former change, but not the latter.

9 Luca Basso (2015) has underlined this point.

10 Marx usually uses the German word *Menschen* in these kinds of general statements, a term that could more accurately be translated as 'human beings' rather than 'men.' See, for example, this passage in the 1867 first German edition of *Capital* as reproduced in MEGA II/5, p. 48.

11 Paresh Chattopadhyay (2016) has focused on this theme for decades, as seen in the recently issued collection of his writings; see also Hudis (2012).
12 The earliest such analysis was carried out by Raya Dunayevskaya (1958).

References

Anderson, Kevin B. (2010) *Marx at the Margins: On Nationalism, Ethnicity, and Non-Western Societies*, Chicago: University of Chicago Press.

Basso, Luca (2015) *Marx and the Common: From Capital to the Late Writings*, Chicago: Haymarket.

Buck-Morss, Susan (2009) *Hegel, Haiti, and Universal History*, Pittsburgh: University of Pittsburgh Press.

Dunayevskaya, Raya (1958) *Marxism and Freedom: From 1776 until Today*, New York: Bookman Associates.

Chattopadhyay, Paresh (2016) *Marx's Associated Mode of Production: A Critique of Marxism*, New York: Palgrave.

Cleaver, Harry (1979) *Reading Capital Politically*, Austin: University of Texas Press.

Hudis, Peter (2012) *Marx's Concept of the Alternative to Capitalism*, Leiden: Brill.

Levine, Bruce (2013) *The Fall of the House of Dixie: The Civil War & the Social Revolution that Transformed the South*, New York: Random House.

Marx, Karl (1963) *Oeuvres. Économie I*, Paris: Éditions de la Pléiade.

Marx, Karl (1966) 'Le Conseil générale au conseil fédéral de la Suisse romande,' *General Council of the First International. 1868–70. Minutes*, Moscow: Progress Publishers, pp. 84–91.

Marx, Karl (1976) *Capital: A Critique of Political Economy*, vol. 1, New York, Penguin Books.

Marx, Karl (1985) 'The General Council to the Federal Council of Romance Switzerland,' in *Karl Marx and Friedrich Engels Collected Works*, vol. 21, New York: International Publishers, pp. 84–91.

Marx, Karl (1986) '*The Civil War in France*. Address of the General Council of the International Working Men's Association', in *Karl Marx and Friedrich Engels Collected Works*, vol. 22, New York: International Publishers, pp. 307–59.

Marx, Karl (1987) *Das Kapital. Kritik der pölitischen Ökonomie. Erster Band. Hamburg 1872*, in *Marx-Engels Gesamtausgabe* (MEGA2), vol. II/6, Berlin: Dietz Verlag

Marx, Karl (1989) *Le Capital Paris 1872–75*, in *Marx-Engels Gesamtausgabe* (MEGA2), vol. II/7, Berlin: Dietz Verlag.

Marx, Karl (1991) *Das Kapital. Kritik der pölitischen Ökonomie. Erster Band. Hamburg 1890*, in *Marx-Engels Gesamtausgabe* (MEGA2), vol. II/10, Berlin: Dietz Verlag.

Marx, Karl and Engels, Frederick (1989) 'Preface to the Second Russian Edition of the *Manifesto of the Communist Party*', in *Marx Engels Collected Works*, vol. 24: *Marx and Engels: 1874–83*, New York: International Publishers, pp. 425–26.

Marx, Karl and Engels, Frederick (2016) *The Civil War in the United States*, New York: International Publishers.

Nimtz, August (2003) *Marx, Tocqueville, and Race in America: The 'Absolute Democracy' or 'Defiled Republic,'* Lanham, MD: Lexington Books.

Ollman, Bertell (1993) *Dialectical Investigations*, New York: Routledge.

Schumpeter, Joseph (1942) *Capitalism, Socialism, and Democracy*, New York: Harper & Row.

12 Had *Capital* been written today

Pietro Basso

1 Why such a schema of exposition of *Capital*?

Any great work of the human mind inevitably suffers from its time. This is true also of *Capital*, a monument of the human mind that loses neither power nor topicality – indeed essentially gains in both – with the passage of time. For anyone approaching it today cannot but hear, especially in its form of exposition, the echo of scientific and cultural disputes from the mid-nineteenth century. I am not mainly referring to the writing style, which such an astute student of Marx as Rosa Luxemburg well and truly slated in a letter of March 1917: 'The famous first volume of Marx's *Capital*, with its profuse rococo ornamentation in the Hegelian style, now seems an abomination to me' (Bronner 1978: 185). What I have in mind, rather, is the structure or sequence in which the material is presented – or, to be more specific, the way in which it is organized and presented in Volume One. Let me be as clear as I can. Why does Marx begin with the immense array of commodities – that is, with the already formed capitalist mode of production, with commodity capital as the *result* of the development of capitalist social relations – and not with so-called primitive accumulation as the historical *starting point* of the capitalist mode of production? What *obliged* him to make this choice?

Marx, we know, took over the schema of exposition he had used eight years earlier in the *Contribution to the Critique of Political Economy*, the book that anticipated the beginning of his work on *Capital*. And that schema corresponded to his aim of developing a new scientific conception of capitalist social relations, of the place that labour, wage labour, the labour that produces exchange-value, exchange-value itself and money occupy within those relations. Marx saw this as an attempt to develop the science of political economy by means of an *internal* critique (as Engels put it). This was the theoretical victory on which Marx was relying for his party. It was not an easy victory to carry off – essentially for two reasons. First, political economy until Ricardo, despite its uncertainties, confusions and errors (which science does not have them?), had drawn much closer to understanding the mysteries of the new mode of production. And second, during these years, the new social-economic formation was experiencing its triumph; those who focused on its 'bad side' had so far been at best theorists of a future they imagined in the name of abstract ideals of justice completely removed from the actual results of capitalism, or people suffering from some nostalgia for precapitalist forms of production, exchange and existence.

Marx's dialogue – and struggle – with bourgeois economists operated on completely different, historical-materialist foundations, devoid of abstract ideals of justice or nostalgia for the past. His idea of how to overcome the capitalist mode of production involved a critique from within of capitalism and the economic theory corresponding to it. Not for nothing does *Capital* retain the subtitle he used eight years earlier: it is a *Critique of Political Economy*, not simply of the relations of production and reproduction peculiar to capital. Being a man used to great challenges, however, he does not rest content with that. He is also anxious to launch a challenge to those who seek to bury Hegel and the revolutionary implications of his dialectical logic, or who, whatever their intentions, empty it of content and subject it to ridicule. It is a theoretical challenge at once philosophical and political, issued on behalf of historical materialism and the workers' movement, the 'class that holds the future in its hands' (Marx and Engels 1976: 494). For the author of *Capital* does not agree to work only in economic science, to mould a *new economics* that will resolve the contradictions in which classical political economy has become entangled – an economics valid in itself, by virtue of its rigour and its capacity to explain how things stand and how they are developing in the most complex, mystified and self-mystifying form of society that has ever existed. He also wants to show how the explosive force of capitalism, evident in its raising of labour productivity and its pressure to create a fully-fledged world market, sets up antagonisms that open the way to a 'higher economic organization of society', to communism.

Many documents show that Marx was fully aware of the difficulties in the early chapters of *Capital*, and so concerned about it that he rewrote some passages several times. Yet, as far as we know, he never thought of changing the order of exposition set out in the schema of 1859. This remained the same even when he decided to modify the method: no longer 'rising from the abstract to the concrete', as in the *Introduction* of 1857, but 'rising from the particular to the general',[1] from the commodity as the 'elementary form' of the capitalist social drama to the 'economic law of motion of modern society' and its internal contradictions. What explains this stubborn infliction of a beginning so much like a seventh-grade mountain face, with no warming-up in advance? Marx, the founder of critical political economy, wants to settle accounts once and for all both with previous economic theories and with the last great production of philosophy, the rational kernel of Hegel's logic, by incorporating their highest achievements in a dialectical exposition of the material of economics.

2 A compulsion that came from the past

He is intent on doing this because in his view these two sources of knowledge are still alive. And he feels he must claim their legacy in overcoming it, against their vulgar epigones who merely fritter it away. The *Economic and Philosophical Manuscripts of 1844* and the *Grundrisse* (*Foundations of the Critique of Political Economy*) remained unpublished, while the *Contribution to the Critique of Political Economy* had been largely ignored. So, in 1867 it was as if Marx was making his first public appearance as a materialist, critical-dialectical, theorist of capitalism and its economic doctrines. This is why his struggle started with an examination and acute re-elaboration of the categories of classical political economy, centred on the most elementary 'things' in its presentation of capitalist society. In reality, he shows, these are not things but relations between people and ultimately between classes: the commodity, value, labour and money. With his magnificent 'unscrambling' of each of these categories in turn and of their underlying social-historical relations, he takes us step by step to the secret laboratory of production, where the enigma of surplus-value will be unravelled. This is the central aim that will make it possible to grasp the internal linkages within capitalist production and its further evolution. In this approach, the *logical* element in Marx's method prevails over the *historical* element, and when he enlists historical facts he does so mainly to confirm the theoretical assumptions. It does not seem exaggerated to say that in Volume I history, with all its sound and fury, bursts onto the stage only in Chapter Ten, 'The Working Day', which depicts the creeping civil war between the capitalist class and the working class over the length of the working day. History is allowed to appear only *after* the lenses required to bring it into focus – the categories (themselves historical, of course) – have been adequately sharpened.

This is how Marx chose to proceed in 1867 – or rather, a decade earlier. And all we can do today is understand why the decision, with its attendant contradictions, was in some respects *forced* on him. This compulsion derived above all from his studies of philosophy and economic doctrines in the 1840s and 1850s. It was a compulsion that came to him from the past. To be sure, the notebooks containing the material of *Theories of Surplus-Value* were compiled in the years between 1861 and 1863, but Marx's theory of value, surplus-value and money was already complete by 1859. And the years after 1863 were devoted more to the definition of a new exposition of the material he had already gathered, and to the tireless drafting and polishing of the book of his life, than to further completely new investigations of economic theory.[2] Of course, his studies of economic theory did not stop; he continued them especially with regard to the expanded reproduction of capital and land rent, but I think we can say that, from the mid-1860s, partly because of his involvement in the International Working Men's Association, *the centre of gravity of Marx's research moved from economic theories to historical studies*. His settling of accounts with philosophy and political economy, following that with law happened in his youth, was now essentially over, as he concentrated more and more on the history of forms of society prior to the capitalist mode of production, the dynamic of its formation in antagonism with those forms, and the transition from capitalism to socialism. The shift is discernible in his work on the French edition of *Capital* (1872), which contained additions more or less exclusively to Part Eight, 'The so-called Primitive Accumulation'.[3] Thanks to Kevin Anderson's important *Marx at the Margins* (Anderson 2010) and the work of other researchers,[4] we can now see perfectly clearly Marx's growing commitment to the historical-ethnological study of precapitalist social formations and countries under European colonial rule. Also clear is the impact of these studies on his general conception of historical processes, on the location of capitalism within a complex, non-linear succession of modes of production, and also, of course, on his political positions regarding anti-colonial struggles (Lenin 1968: 653–80 and 573ff.).

3 Today, beginning from the 'primitive accumulation' ...

This said, we must consider whether it makes sense today, in critically examining the nature of capital, to begin as in 1867 with analysis of the commodity and that whole type of phenomenology. My own answer is: *definitely not* – for the simple reason that the dual struggle with political economy and the squanderers or liquidators of Hegel's thought belongs entirely to the past. It is a closed chapter. Marx is alive, whereas his theoretical adversaries of 1867 were laid to rest quite a while ago, and there is no chance that they will come back to life. It is not only today that official political economy has lost any claim to scientific status. That happened when it ditched the theory of surplus-value and turned in the direction of utility value and later marginal utility, effecting a subjectivist reversal while paradoxically postulating a system in total equilibrium with a static productive structure. In this way, *it moved ever further from the actual reality of capitalism*, which is riven with growth dynamics and increasingly violent and uncontrolled crisis tendencies, with such an obsessive quest for profit that its swollen fictitious capital is saddling generations to come with the burden of superexploited labour. Classical political economy did not fear to look the contradictions of capital in the face. Neoclassical economics avoids and conceals them. And that line of march has become more pronounced with the advent of neoliberalism. As I. Mészáros noted, the neoliberal guru Friedrich von Hayek is a perfect example of pseudo-scientific, ahistorical and irrational theory, so extreme that he rejects the feasibility of any cause-effect analysis and, in an inversion of a basic fact about the real world, conceives of labour as a product of capital. When he asserts that 'the curious task of economics is to demonstrate to men how little they really know about what they imagine they can design', when he feels no shame in claiming that any macroeconomics is rationally impossible, we are obviously outside any possibility of rational debate. We are facing the most cynical and tautological apologia for capital (Mészáros 1995: 118ff.). Nor is it an accident that the most significant twentieth-century work in the field of economics, Keynes's *General Theory of Employment, Interest and Money* (Keynes 1973), which its author disgracefully claimed to be revolutionary, has been influential more in economic policy than economic theory. Its understanding of capitalism takes us not an inch further than what classical political economics and Marxist criticisms thereof already said long ago. Lord Keynes's superior wisdom was not required to discover the anti-scientific character of equilibrium theory.

Similarly, in the twentieth and twenty-first century philosophy has certainly not emerged from the deep coma into which it fell when it tumbled disastrously from the heights of Spinoza, Kant and Hegel. The extraordinary prestige enjoyed by Heidegger, at least in Italy, is sufficient evidence of this. The theoretical energy of his philosophy goes entirely into the coining of an infinite series of inextricable tautologies, which may mean an infinite number of things without telling us anything precise; he also shows a seemingly infinite capacity to transfigure, adulterate and erase every single problem he 'analyses', to turn around and around in preliminary exercises that never deliver any truth content, that is, any reality content, using categories as if they were so many wisps of smoke. His is a real labyrinth from which you exit weary and dazed, with not a shred more knowledge than you entered it with;[5] all you get is the intended effect of alienation from real social existence at that point in time, due to the anodyne attempt to dull critical capacities. It would be pointless to do battle with these dark shades that lack vitality or meaning, still less to 'flirt' with their language or – worst of all – their method. This is also why Althusser's proposed philosophical reading of *Capital* (Althusser 1965) in the mid-1960s proved to be so sterile, leaving behind only an inconsistent opposition between the 'first' and the 'second' Marx. What we do need is a *historical-social* reading of *Capital*, designed to show how and why its background is a vision of the historical advent of capitalism as a totality, as a world economy, and how much Marx could anticipate in its essentials the contradictions of late capitalism.

In 2017, I would argue, *the exposition of Volume I should start with Part Eight, 'The so-called Primitive Accumulation'*. This would put the emphasis on *historical* rather than logical method, since the main struggle to wage *today* concerns the limited historical character and obsoleteness of the capitalist mode of production, and the disastrous spiralling of its antagonism with social labour and non-human nature. For in the last few decades, the formidable, and united, ideological efforts of the mandarins of global capital have hammered in the message that there is no alternative to capitalism, that, whatever its defects, it remains by far the best mode of organization and reproduction of social existence. The chief argument for this is that it ultimately corresponds to *human nature* (some have even discovered a *natural* rate of unemployment …); and that the most *natural* of its dimensions is precisely the *market* – so long as it is allowed to operate freely, with no impediments from the unions or the state. The collapse of 'actually existing socialism' and its theoretical self-justifications created the ideal conditions for this huge chain of lies to impose itself to the maximum, not only in the field of theory but as self-evident truths that stand in no need of proof.

4 … would be more appropriate

To begin a study of capital with its historical genesis would be very useful today for a number of reasons. First, it would allow us to see how for Marx the formative terrain of the capitalist mode of production was *global* from the very outset, embracing not only England but Ireland, the Indies and China. At the same time, though not in the same way, a 'centre' and a 'periphery' took shape right at the beginning, linked by an uneven and combined mechanism of capital accumulation. And contrary to the classical economic vision of a harmonious formation of the world market, Marx showed that in reality colonialism, the 'colonial system', was a fundamental element in primitive accumulation; it remains such today, in the only partly new forms of financial and thermonuclear neocolonialism. Second, Marx's fascinating historical account of the genesis of capitalism also brings out its *modus operandi* that is again clearly visible today: that is, 'the separation of the workers from ownership of the means for the realization of their labour', and 'the dissolution of private property based on the labour of its owner'. This is taking place before our (often inattentive) eyes in the countryside all over the world, where small producers are each year driven from the land in their tens of millions and forced to internal and international migration. Marx's great historical and theoretical canvas also shows the decisive role that the state has played in support of newly emergent capital, through state and private violence against direct producers, black slaves and colonized peoples, and exposes for what it is any mythical-idyllic representation of the birth of capitalism. Besides we can see how methods characteristic of so-called primitive accumulation are again with us today, as global capital plunders nature in 'peripheral' continents and appropriates the labour-power of peasants and labourers, snatching them from the land by economic and extra-economic coercion without having to pay the costs of their training and reproduction. Nor is that all. An opening account of the complex global-historical process helps us to keep the formation of capitalism *in perspective*, that is, to place it between a precapitalist past and a future that is not only postcapitalist but anticapitalist, in which capitalist property is transformed into 'social property' based on 'co-operation and the possession in common of the land and of the means of production' (Marx 1996: 751). In this section too we come across Hegel's dialectical logic, but the negation of the negation here refers strictly to the social system *as a whole*. From my point of view, therefore, there is no opposition at all between historical method and logic method; only a question of a different 'priority' today, due to a changed framework.

In my view, the topical effect of Volume I would be further reinforced if – before embarking on the necessary analysis of the commodity – Marx presented us with the 'general absolute [an unusual word for him!] law of capitalist accumulation', as he does in Chapter 25. The mass of the proletarian reserve army always tends to increase: this law, with its macroscopic practical implications in these early decades of the twenty-first century, imposes itself even on those who obstinately deny out of a sense of *parti pris* the inherent contradictions of this form of society. Finally, the last chapters of Volume One anticipate in some degree the key question of expanded reproduction and the total social capital, helping us to look ahead to the present day with its capital concentration and its now hypertrophied system of government and private debt.

In addition to the books on capital, the complete and definitive schema outlined by Marx in 1859 foresaw three other books, on the state, foreign trade, and the world market. These were not planned as mere appendages, as we can tell from Chapter 31 of Volume One, which contains a memorable page foreshadowing the three missing books. I would like to take the liberty of recalling it here:

> The discovery of gold and silver in America, the extirpation, enslavement and entombment in mines of the aboriginal population, the beginning of the conquest and looting of the East Indies, the turning of Africa into a warren for the commercial hunting of blackskins, signalized the rosy dawn of the era of capitalist production. These idyllic proceedings are the chief momenta of primitive accumulation. On their heels treads the commercial war of the European nations, with the globe for a theatre. It begins with the revolt of the Netherlands from Spain, assumes giant dimension in England's Anti-Jacobin War, and is still going on in the opium wars against China, &c.
>
> The different momenta of primitive accumulation distribute themselves now, more or less in chronological order, particularly over Spain, Portugal, Holland, France, and England. In England at the end of the 17th century, they arrive at a systematical combination, embracing the colonies, the national debt, the modern mode of taxation, and the protectionist system. These methods depend in part on brute force, e.g., the colonial system. But they all employ the power of the State, the concentrated and organized force of society, to hasten, hothouse fashion, the process of transformation of the feudal mode of production into the capitalist mode, and to shorten the transition.
>
> (Marx1996:739)

In this Michelangelesque depiction of the dawn of the capitalist age in world history, the key figure of the state stands out clearly and demolishes, as if in advance, the brazen neoliberal apologia for free individual initiative. Without the state, without its concentrated, organized violence against European small producers and workers, and – more brutally still – against toilers in the colonies, as well as against capitalist rivals, *there would have been no capital*! Yesterday as today. For in that rosy dawn we can see the outlines of the long gloomy sunset of actually existing capitalism, which over the centuries has been governed by the same laws of motion that Marx so masterfully identified.

If the beginning of the exposition is rejigged in this way, it would indeed be right to say: a century and a half old, but does not look it at all.

Notes

1 Marcello Musto (2008) highlights this passage and the complexity of Marx's method of exposition in *Capital*. For Roman Rosdolsky, Marx himself presents his procedure as a path from the surface of economic relations 'to their inner, basic but hidden essential structure, and the conception corresponding to it' (see Rosdolsky 1977: 51).
2 If we leave aside the reworking of material for *Capital*, Marx wrote only two new texts of 'pure' theory in the years after the publication of Volume One: 'The Relation of the Rate of Profit to the Rate of Surplus-Value' (1875) (Marx 1998); and 'Marginal Notes on Adolph Wagner's Lehrbuch der politischen Oekonomie' (1881) (Marx 1989).
3 See Anderson (1983: 4). It should be noted that for Marx this edition had a 'scientific value independent of the original'.
4 I am thinking, for instance, of Krader, (1972; 1975); Pradella (2015); Musto (2016).
5 I am here borrowing from some of the pungent criticism in Alfonso Berardinelli (1988: 49ff.). Yet Giovanni La Guardia (2003) is right to underline that *Being and Time* has an 'expressly antimaterialist inspiration', that Marxism is its 'strategic objective' of attack.

References

Althusser, Louis, Balibar, Étienne and Establet, Roger, Macherey, Pierre and Rancière, Jacques (1965) *Lire le Capital*, 2 vols, Paris: Maspero.

Anderson, Kevin B. (1983–4) 'The 'Unknown' Marx's *Capital*, Vol. I: The French Edition of 1872–75, 100 Years Later', in *Review of Radical Political Economics*, vol. 15, no. 4: 71–80.

Anderson, Kevin B. (2010) *Marx at the Margins. On Nationalism, Ethnicity and Non-Western Societes*, Chicago and London: University of Chicago Press.

Berardinelli, Alfonso (1988) 'I rumori dell'Essere. Heidegger, Derrida, Severino', in *Diario*, vol. 4, no. 6: 49–71.

Bronner, Stephen (eds). (1978) *The Letters of Rosa Luxemburg*. Boulder, CO: Westview Press.

Keynes, John M. (1973) *The General Theory of Employment, Interest and Money*, London: Macmillan.

Krader, Lawrence (1972) 'Introduction', in Karl Marx, *The Ethnological Notebooks of Karl Marx*. Assen: Van Gorcum, pp. 1–93.

Krader, Lawrence (1975) *The Asiatic Mode of Production: Sources, Development and Critique in the Writings of Karl Marx*, Assen: Van Gorcum.

La Guardia, Giovanni (2003) 'Le Dieu caché. Sociologia del dio nascosto', in Jean Ferrari (eds.), *Le Baroque*, Dijon: Figures Libres, pp. 53–73.

Lenin, Vladimir Il'ich (1968) *Notebooks on Imperialism*, in *Collected Works*, vol. 39 London: Lawrence & Wishart.

Marx, Karl (1989) 'Marginal Notes on Adolph Wagner's *Lehrbuch der politischen Oekonomie*', in *Marx Engels Collected Works*, vol. 24: *Marx and Engels: 1874–83*, London: Lawrence & Wishart, pp. 531–59.

Marx, Karl (1996) *Capital, Volume One*, in *Marx Engels Collected Works*, vol. 35: *Capital, Vol. I*, London: Lawrence & Wishart.

Marx, Karl (1998) *Capital, Volume Three*, in: *Marx Engels Collected Works*, vol. 37, *Capital, Vol. III*, London: Lawrence & Wishart.

Marx, Karl, Engels Frederick (1976) 'Manifesto of the Communist Party', in *Marx Engels Collected Works*, vol. 6: *Marx and Engels: 1874–83*, London: Lawrence & Wishart, pp. 425–6.

Mészáros, István (1995) *Beyond Capital. Towards a Theory of Transition*, London: Merlin Press.

Musto, Marcello (2008) 'History, Production and Method in the "1857 Introduction"', in Marcello Musto (Ed.) *Karl Marx's Grundrisse. Foundations of the Critique of Political Economy 150 Years Later*, London: Routledge, 2008, pp. 3–32.

Musto, Marcello (2016) *L'ultimo Marx, 1881–1883*, Rome: Donzelli.

Pradella, Lucia (2015) *Globalisation and the Critique of Political Economy. New insights from Marx's Writings*, London: Routledge.

Rosdolsky, Roman (1977) *The Making of Marx's Capital*, London: Pluto Press.

Part III

The politics of *Capital*

13 Reading *Capital* as political theory

On the political theory of the value-form

William Clare Roberts

1 Introduction

As most people know, the subtitle of *Capital* declares Marx's work to be 'a critique of political economy'. Marx undertakes this critique in three different registers. First of all, *Capital* contains a thoroughly internal critique of political economy. This is a self-critique of political economy in the name of a better political economy, a correction of the political economy of the classical liberal school. Second, the book also contains a historical or historicizing critique of political economy. At this level, *Capital* criticizes political economy for naturalizing or eternalizing categories and concepts that are proper only to the modern world of capitalist production. This is a critique of political economy in the name of a 'historical materialism'. Finally, *Capital* also contains a political critique of political economy. According to this critique, political economy is an ideology of domination, which attempts to justify the capitalists' class domination.

This third critique rarely gets the attention it deserves; it often gets folded into or reduced to or identified with the historicizing critique. Nonetheless, Marx's political critique is not identical or reducible to his historical critique. It is one thing to say that political economy *naturalizes* socio-historical relations, or makes them seem eternal when in fact they are historically local. It is another thing to say that political economy *justifies* relations of domination by making them out to be relations of freedom. To naturalize is not to justify; what is unchangeable is neither right nor wrong, and so transcends the need for justification. Likewise, to justify is not to naturalize; what is good or just *should* not be changed, which presupposes that it can be changed. The claim that political economy justifies relations of domination is the core of Marx's political critique of political economy, and it is the task of this chapter to bring this political critique to the fore.[1]

Political economy justifies relations of domination as relations of freedom, Marx argues, by reflecting upon and developing *part of* the common sense of participants in the sphere of market exchange. In modern commercial society, in the market, a form of unfreedom appears to be freedom because the wills of others appear in the guise of the prices or commodities. This appearance of the wills of others as the price of commodities is not a false appearance. In market prices, our relations with one another 'appear as what they are': they really are relations amongst commodities. But, these market relations also appear to be free relations because, first of all, the people that we meet in the market do not seem to have any discretion regarding the costs they impose on us in terms of the goods that they offer. We are all price takers, not price makers, as the economists say. Second, exchanging commodities excludes, normatively, threats and uses of force. Therefore, it seems as if no one is impinging upon our freedom when we buy and sell in the market. However, this sense is not exhaustive of our experience of the market. Those who are dependent upon the market for their survival and their well-being experience something besides their one-to-one interactions with shopkeepers and employers. The prices of goods and the level of wages are susceptible to unpredictable movements irrespective of the needs and desires of those individuals who are ruined or put out of work thereby. Attention to this experience of the market as something that imposes itself upon us in an unpredictable and mysterious way was very much alive in the discourse of nineteenth-century socialists before Marx. Marx seeks, in *Capital*, to develop this other aspect of market experience, and to show that it is more revelatory of the dynamics of the market than is the experience of freedom developed by political economy.

Of particular importance for those who want to understand Marx, Owenites in Britain and Proudhon in France had articulated a more or less coherent language of protest against market dependence. Both sought to explain the experience of powerlessness before the market or domination by the market by tracing this experience back to what they called the 'money mystery', or 'the fetishism of gold'. The extent to which Marx borrowed his phrasing in *Capital* from these pre-existing critical discourses is not widely appreciated. As a result, the precise differences between Marx's account of the market in Chapters 1 through 3 of *Capital* and the Owenite-Proudhonian account are invisible. When Marx's theory of exchange and money is compared to the Owenite-Proudhonian theory, the political stakes of Marx's theory become palpable. To this end, this chapter will summarize the Owenite-Proudhonian account of the 'mystery' and 'fetishism' at work in the market, emphasize Marx's two theoretical innovations, and draw out the political consequences of Marx's own theory by way of a comparison with the recent accounts of Michael Heinrich and Moishe Postone.

2 The money-mystery before Marx

The notion that a 'mystery' lay behind the operations of the monetary economy was quite old by the time Marx would have first encountered it. It goes back at least to 1818, when William Cobbett, in *Cobbett's Political Register*, called the Bank of England the 'great tool of tyrants' and a 'partner with them in cruelty and plunder', and argued that the 'paper-money mystery' was 'a *mystery* as complete and almost as sacred, as any other of those mysteries, by the means of which artful and impudent knaves have contrived to rob the labouring part of mankind' (Cobbett 1818: 285). According to Cobbett, the Bank and its paper-money were a thicket in which it was nearly impossible to determine what was really going on, a hiding place for conspiracy. As such, the Bank ran counter to the republican concern 'that citizens be able to determine where the responsibility for a bad outcome actually lies' (see MacGilvray 2011: 41–2).

Worries about currency manipulation and financial conspiracy were as prevalent among early socialists as they had been among older radicals. William Thompson, for example, argued in *Labour Rewarded* that

> there is not one of the old expedients of force and fraud practiced on the Industrious Classes, not even the iniquities of human wholesale butchery under the name of wars, that has produced, and is at every moment liable to produce, more extensive misery to those classes, than arbitrary alterations in the currency by the portion of the Idle who form the governing classes.
>
> (Thompson 1969: 62)

But socialists no longer hunted the mystery of money only or primarily in central bank machinations. They also tried, as John Francis Bray did in *Labour's Wrongs and Labour's Remedy*, to identify the 'occult operations' of money itself, as it circulates in society (Bray 1968: 139). Similarly, John Gray claimed in *The Social System* that commercial London presented itself as 'a puzzle', and that he wanted 'to penetrate the unfathomable mystery with which everything seemed to be invested' (Gray 1973: 339). This puzzle and mystery was identified by Thompson's disciple William Pare in his 1850 preface to Thompson's *Inquiry into the Principles of the Distribution of Wealth*; 'How comes it that the fruits of labour of the industrious, after years of incessant and successful exertion, are mysteriously – and without imputation of fault to them, without any convulsion of nature – swept away?' (Thompson 1850: xxviii) This 'strange anomaly of human affairs' obsessed the Owenites, and many other early socialists. After all, they represented workers' perspectives in a rapidly industrializing world in which all-around dependence upon the market was a novel phenomenon.

The explanation of this strange anomaly offered by the Owenites was straightforward. First, there is a class of people who, by their know-how and hard work, make all of the good things enjoyed as wealth. Alongside them, there is another class of people who, by their possession of money, the medium of exchange, are empowered to buy up and enjoy the vast majority of those good things. Unfortunately, the producers do not themselves possess the medium of exchange, and neither can they buy what they need directly with their own products. They are therefore dependent upon selling their products to the money-owners. The money-owners, for their part, make nothing, but still possess the means of obtaining whatever they want. How come? As John Francis Bray put it in *Labour's Wrongs and Labour's Remedy*:

> The present circulating medium, … as the economists confess, is made by a class of capitalists called bankers … and for this medium of exchange, or money, it is acknowledged that the bankers receive commodities of certain parties. These *second* parties, in turn, exchange the money for other commodities from some *third* party; and upon the same principle, of giving value for value, the exchange goes on among all succeeding parties. Thus *real value* is rendered in exchange for real value in every case except the *first transaction* – that between the banker and the person who receives his medium – and in this first negotiation, according to the showing even of the economists, there is a vile and cunning robbery committed upon the productive classes; … Thus the productive classes give to the banking and trading capitalists their labour – their very sweat and blood – and the latter give to them in exchange – what? They give them a shadow – a rag – a 'bank-note!'
>
> (Bray 1968: 147–8)

Thus, Bray concluded that money is 'the secret of the almost omnipotent might of the capitalist' (Bray 1968: 136). Thus, also, Thompson was fond of calling commercial society an 'empire of force and fraud' (see Thompson 1850, passim.). The near monopoly of the wealthy over the means of exchange was a self-perpetuating engine of unequal exchanges. The bargaining power it gave to the wealthy ensured that the poor producers were never able to exact a fair price for their products, leaving them in the same penury and need of purchasers as before.

All of the patent remedies entertained by the Owenites and likeminded socialists – easy fiat money, free credit, labour-exchanges, combinations, cooperative communities – were aimed at getting the workers free of this need for money, either temporarily or permanently. Except in the case of easy money, they were supposed to empower the industrious classes to produce their own means of exchanging their commodities directly among themselves. The point was to withdraw what Locke had called in his *Second Treatise of Government* 'the tacit and voluntary consent' that has made gold and silver and their paper representatives, 'which may be hoarded up without injury to any one', into wealth itself (Locke 1988: 302). The money-mystery rests on the consent of the producers. Therefore, what Owen said of religion in his 'Second Lecture on the New Religion' he could just as easily have said of money;

> when [it] is stripped of the mysteries with which the priests of all times and countries have invested it, and when such is explained in terms sufficiently simple that the common mind can fully comprehend it, without fear or alarm from the misguided imagination, all its divinity vanishes; its

> errors become palpable; and it stands before the astonished world in all its naked deformity of vice, hypocrisy, and imbecility.
>
> (Owen 1991: 310)

The entire misfortune of the producing classes is explained by their ignorance of the secret of the money-mystery. Once this mystery is disclosed, their subjugation and their poverty will vanish like a bad dream. Only a false consciousness of their situation keeps the labouring classes from refusing any longer to sacrifice their efforts and products for the exclusive advantage of their masters.

On 31 July 1848, this conception of the problem facing working people was articulated publicly in Paris, addressed to the most august representatives of the upper classes. Standing before the Constituent National Assembly, the only supporter of his own motion to establish a free credit bank financed by a one-third tax on rents and interest,[2] Proudhon argued that the only way to guarantee the right to work, established in Articles 2, 7, and 132 of the Constitution, was to guarantee demand for the workers' products. According to Proudhon, this demand was present *in potentia*; 'the power to consume, in society and in the individual alike, is infinite'. What prevents us from actuating our 'love of comfort and effective enjoyment', and thereby guaranteeing to the producers of the means of that comfort and enjoyment a rich reward for their efforts, is the fact that goods can only be circulated between producers and consumers by the intercession of 'gold and silver as instruments of exchange'. This creates a bottleneck in the circulation of goods. The monopoly power of the holders of gold and silver allows them to charge interest and to buy up large holdings of capital and land, for which they can charge rent. The poor producers, meanwhile, are stranded on the shores of their own products, which they can neither enjoy directly nor exchange directly for what they need. Free credit would deliver them from their enforced hermitage, and allow them to bring home the good things that other have created. By this means, 'consumption will be relieved of all burdens, as will the faculty of enjoyment', and the labours of all will be guaranteed to be fruitful. All that is needed, Proudhon proclaimed, between bouts of '*laughter and sundry exclamations*' from the Assembly, was to allow 'the fetishism of gold [*le fétichisme de l'or*]' to give way to 'the realism of existence' (Proudhon 1938: 366).[3]

3 Marx's theoretical intervention

Marx sought, in *Capital*, to decisively and definitively displace this sort of explanation of workers' troubles. The problem, according to Marx, is that neither Proudhon nor the Owenites have a good grasp of how markets actually work. They made three errors in Marx's eyes. First of all, they treated money, or gold, as an alien intrusion into the exchange of products. They thought of it as a medium of circulation without any value of its own, created by bankers and governments and sustained by superstition. Therefore, second, they wanted, in one way or another – either by free credit, as in Proudhon, or by labour notes, or by other means – to make workers' products directly exchangeable for other goods without having to meet up with this rare and artificial medium of exchange. Finally, they assumed that the money-owners' stranglehold on gold and cash compels producers to sell their goods below their real value, determined by the labour bestowed upon them in their creation. Proudhon and the Owenites were very alive to the fact that market dependence feels a lot like enslavement to a capricious master, on whose unpredictable whims one hangs. However, according to Marx, they had no good explanation of why this is the case. As a result, they over-personalized the relations of domination experienced in the modern market, and they treated these relations as the consequences of the moral qualities of the people thereby related. Thus, they reduced the workers' difficulties to the 'fact' that people want the wrong things, or that people are superstitious, or that a few people are, behind the scenes, in control of the monetary economy.

Understanding and appreciating this background is crucial for appreciating what Marx is attempting in Part One of *Capital*. In these opening chapters, Marx intervenes into this existing socialist discourse and articulates a different understanding of the market, one that better grounds the workers' experience of its capricious nature. In order to do so, Marx makes four interrelated arguments in Part One of *Capital*. First, he argues that commodities are already money in 'germ' (Marx 1976: 163). That is, the evils that Proudhon and the Owenites want to pin on money are already there in the commodity itself. Second, Marx argues that value can only be expressed in exchange. We can't find out what the value of something is, except by confronting it with other commodities and finding out what it is worth in exchange. As he puts it, exchange value is the necessary form of appearance, or the necessary form of expression of value. Third, Marx argues that the labour that is the substance of value cannot be measured anywhere except in exchange. The labour that forms value is abstract labour. It is not the concrete, actual labour that one can observe, experience, and measure with a stopwatch. Moreover, the labour that forms value is socially necessary labour, and for Marx that means it has to satisfy a social need, i.e. prove itself to be required in the exchange of its produce. It is only when your goods sell that you find out whether or not the labour you expended was socially necessary or not. Fourth – and bringing the previous arguments together – the fetishism and mystery that attend commerce, the obscurity of one's fate in the market, the unpredictable and uncontrollable movements of prices, and the orientation of one's own action by the anticipation of these movements of prices: these are baked into the commodity-form itself. They are part and parcel of the circulation of commodities via exchange, and of production for exchange, which are themselves the necessary concomitants of the capitalist mode of production using wage-labour. They would not be touched at all by easy credit or labour-money, or by any of the other schemes that nineteenth-century socialists proposed. To bring Marx's critical point up to date, they would also not be touched by Keynesian helicopter drops of money, or by basic income plans, or things like this.

Let's examine these four arguments in a bit more detail. First, Marx displaces the explanatory appeal to the money mystery. The difficulties that bedevil the producer stem from generalized exchange as such, of which money is a necessary and automatic concomitant; as Marx writes in *Capital*, 'money necessarily crystallizes out of the process of exchange', and so commercial society 'sweats money from every pore' (Marx 1976: 181, 208). The source of the problems identified by the Owenites and Proudhon lies in the fact that producers are related to one another by exchange itself. It is, therefore, the purpose of Sections Three and Four of Chapter One of *Capital* to reduce 'the enigma of money' to the 'enigmatic character of the product of labour, as soon as it takes the form of a commodity' (Marx 1976: 139).[4]

Second, Marx denies that the divergence between price and value hides any systematic shifting of value away from the rewards of labour and towards money-owners. Rather, this divergence is the mechanism by which price comes to reflect value dynamically and on average (see Marx 1981: 292).[5] In a competitive commercial economy, overpriced goods lose market share until they are no longer overpriced. Marx's analysis of the value-form is meant to prove that the commodity in the equivalent form always functions as a proto-money. Only the equivalent instantiates socially average abstract labour, the determinant of value. It is only by being actually exchanged for the equivalent that the first commodity proves to be of value. Hence, the labour embodied in the original commodity only counts as value-forming labour once it has been equated with – by being exchanged with – the labour embodied in the equivalent.

Third, therefore, Marx is critical of the role played by the labour theory of value in Owenism and Proudhon. According to the pre-Marxian account of the money-mystery, labour is the normative truth of value, the truth obscured and falsified by the mysterious formation of monetary prices in exchange. Marx argues, as we have seen, that this mystery attends any and all generalized exchange relations, and is not specific to money. He also argues, however, that the labour the Owenites and Proudhon want to find *behind* the mystery is, in fact, the mystery itself. Value just is the form taken by social labour in capitalism (Elson 1979). The labour theory of value does not, therefore, support the claim that the producers are getting bilked, or getting anything less than their due. They are dominated by the market, and exposed to its whims and caprices, but that does not mean they are being cheated when they do not get the price they expect for their wares. Rather, it means that the information according to which they form their expectations is drawn from their experience of past exchanges and useful labour, neither of which are relevant for the establishment of value.

The value of commodities is not determined by the labour *actually* spent on them, but by the labour necessary to produce them in a socially average way. Moreover, as Marx pints out in *Capital*, 'if a thing is useless, so is the labour contained in it; the labour does not count as labour, and therefore creates no value' (Marx 1976: 131). Socially necessary labour must fulfil a social need, not just a technical requirement. But, if I am producing for exchange, I cannot know beforehand whether or not my labour will be useful to others, or whether my product will fulfil someone's need. As Marx puts it, 'only the act of exchange can prove whether that labour is useful to others, and its product consequently capable of satisfying the needs of others' (Marx 1976: 180).[6] Therefore, there can be no way of observing and measuring the labour-time exhibited by the value of a commodity. It is impossible to know what place one's labour has in the social division of labour, and how it compares to the labours of others, until one enters the market and sells – or fails to sell – one's produce (see Heinrich 2012: 50–1). This is precisely the phenomenon the Owenites and Proudhon are concerned about, but their attempt to explain it actually renders it senseless.

Thus, finally, the Owenites and Proudhon are mistaken in thinking that the uncertainties and calamities of commercial exchange can be avoided by getting rid of the means of circulation, money, or by declaring all commodities directly exchangeable with one another. As soon as one commodity is equated with another in exchange (even if only prospectively), the peculiar forms of relativity and equivalence come into play, and with them the uncertainty of each producer as to what expression the value of their commodity will find. The producer always needs what another has, and what another has always appears, therefore, as the medium through which exchange becomes possible. A system of exchange without money, if it were possible, would present all of the same difficulties as a system of monetary exchange.

4 Market domination: neither personal nor objective

Up to this point, I have set off Marx's political critique of political economy against pre-Marxian critiques, which were alive to the experience of unfreedom in the market, but only because they over-personalized to operations of the market, seeing in money a conspiracy and a form of personal power. Descendants of these critiques are still with us, and Marx's rejoinder is still a powerful alternative for being able to incorporate political economy's insights about the decentralized operations of markets without losing hold of the experience of being dominated by the market.

However, there is today also another interpretation of Marx's critique of political economy, one which appeals precisely to the impersonality of modern social domination, but which thereby, I think, forfeits Marx's political edge. Marx's understanding of the dynamics of competitive exchange destroys the basis of the Owenite and Proudhonian plans for getting producers out from under the thumb of the market. However, Marx did not break with their underlying republican diagnosis of market anarchy as a manifestation of mass domination. On the contrary, Marx grounds this diagnosis.

If, as Marx writes in *Capital*, 'the exchange of commodities implies no other relations of dependence than those which result from its own nature', this presupposes that understanding these new relations of dependence, proper to commercial society, requires understanding the nature of exchange (Marx 1976: 120–1). Exchange has given birth to new forms of power, which are no longer 'based on personal relations of domination and servitude', but are, rather, 'impersonal' (Marx 1976: 247, n.1). These powers, of money and of commodities, despite their impersonality, are still 'exercise[d] over' people whenever they enter the market (Marx 1976: 262).

The impersonality of this modern form of domination manifests itself in the fetish character of commodities, the way in which they function as the conduits of social power and of the information for practical deliberation. Fetishism was developed by German critical theory into a suggestive account of *social domination*, defined by Moishe Postone's *Time, Labor, and Social Domination* as 'the domination of people by abstract social structures that people themselves constitute' (Postone 1993: 30; see O'Kane 2013). In this development, Marx's criticism of other socialists is correctly seen to imply the need for a correct understanding of the dynamics of capitalist society, and of the political economy that expresses these dynamics theoretically. However, the erasure of the political problematic undergirding Marx's theory has had distorting effects. The critical theory of social domination has never clarified how abstractions can dominate people, or why we should care about an abstract domination. My analysis of Part One of *Capital* makes possible a recovery of the political issue at the bottom of abstract domination.

For Marx, the circulation of commodities has two distinct but interrelated effects upon the practical life of those dependent on the market for survival. First, it quantifies their deliberations by imposing the price form on them. You have to think not only about the particular characteristics of goods with which one is concerned, or what you want; you also have to think about the quantitative relations of equivalence in which those goods stand in relation to all other goods. Second, it also compels deliberations to take account of a new sort of uncertainty – the uncertainty of the *movements* of these relations of equivalence.

The first effect is the abstract rationality analysed by Lukács. For Lukács, what mattered was, as Vandenberghe writes in *A Philosophical History of German Sociology*, that the 'coordination of action … is imposed from outside by the autonomous movement of things on the market (*cash nexus*)'. This provokes agents to 'adopt the objectifying attitude of instrumental-strategic action towards themselves and others' and for 'thingness' to become the determining modality of thought' (Vandenberghe 2009: 148 quoted in O'Kane 2013: 28; see, also Postone 2003). The emphasis in Lukács's work is on the objects exchanged, and on the quantitative relations of equivalence among them. In Adorno's writings, much more explicitly than in Lukács, one finds a theory of fetishism as social domination, keyed to exchange as a practice.[7] As in Lukács, however, this domination is portrayed as a process of subject formation, whereby individuals become integrated into capitalist society by internalizing, or, better, by *becoming* ideology (O'Kane 2013, ch. 4). This process of subject formation is understood, crucially, as the creation and maintenance of a certain relationship between people and things.

This understanding of social domination generates real confusion, both theoretically and regarding Marx's argument. This theoretical confusion is apparent in two of the most sophisticated followers of Lukács and Adorno, Moishe Postone and Michael Heinrich. Both insist that capitalism must be grasped as 'a system of abstract, impersonal domination' (Postone 1993: 125), or of 'impersonal, objective domination' (Heinrich 2012: 75). But both are quite vague about where this domination comes from and why it counts as domination. Heinrich claims, in the same breath, that modern domination takes the form of 'an overwhelming social interaction that cannot be controlled by individuals', and that 'people (all of them!) are under the control of things'. Moreover, he traces this objective domination back to the fact that, in modern society, 'people relate to things in a particular way – as commodities' (Heinrich 2012: 75). But why do people relate to things as commodities, and how does this constitute such a problematic situation that it merits being called *domination*? Because Heinrich understands objective domination as a relationship between people and things, he does not indicate that the things in question only mediate relations with other people, and that it is the relationship to other people, the dependency upon their arbitrary and incontestable actions and desires, that makes this into an instance of domination.

Postone runs into a similar problem. His argument is that 'social domination in capitalism does not, on its most fundamental level, consist in domination of people by other people, but in the domination of people by abstract social structures that people themselves constitute' (Postone 1993: 30). This might have led to a real breakthrough if he had noted that domination, in order to be a political problem, must be domination by other people, and that, therefore, the constitution of a social structure by people must be understood as a *mediated* relationship among people. As Marx put it in his *Economic and Philosophic Manuscripts of 1844*,

> If the product of labour does not belong to the worker, if it confronts him as an alien power, then this can only be because it belongs to some other man than the worker.... Not the gods, not nature, but only man himself can be this alien power over man.
>
> (Marx 1975: 278)

Domination mediated in this way is indirect or impersonal, but it is still the domination of people by people. Instead, however, Postone goes in the opposite direction, claiming that capitalist domination 'subjects people to impersonal, increasingly rationalized structural imperatives and constraints. It is, in his phrase from "Lukács and the Dialectical Critique of Capitalism", the domination of people by time' (Postone 2003: 18).[8] Domination here loses all reference to an alien, incontestable will, and becomes nothing more than a metaphor.

Marx, despite his proclivity for arresting turns of phrase, was much more precise and careful than Lukács and his followers. Although Marx does refer to 'objective' or 'external' dependency or domination, he also clarifies, as in the *Grundrisse*, that objective domination is not domination *by objects*, but domination by 'social production', or by the 'mutual social relationship of individuals' (Marx 1986: 101, 132).[9] The key texts from *Capital*, in this regard, are tolerably straightforward. Of the members of commercial society Marx says that 'their own social movement has for them the form of a movement of things, and instead of controlling it, they are under its control' (Marx 1976: 167–8).[10] That is, individuals fall under the control of the social movement, the changing relations of interdependency upon other people. Thus,

> there develops a whole circle of social-natural interrelations, uncontrollable by the people involved. The weaver can only sell his linen because the farmer has already sold his wheat, the hothead can only sell his Bible because the weaver has already sold his linen, the distiller can only sell his firewater because the other has already sold the water of everlasting life, and so forth.
>
> (Marx 1976: 207–8)[11]

Because the domination of market society is impersonal, the specific individuals on whom one is dependent are of no import; what remains the same, no matter who one's customers and competitors are, is the relationship of all-around dependence on one another's production and consumption. Thus, in the *Grundrisse*, Marx calls this modern social domination, this 'objective dependence', the 'domination of relationships'. Because 'relationships can naturally be expressed only in ideas', Marx thought it unsurprising that 'philosophers have seen the peculiarity of modern times in the individuals' being dominated by ideas', or 'abstractions' (Marx 1986: 101). It would be tendentious to claim that Heinrich and Postone have fallen back into this 'German ideology', but we can say that, in the absence of an analysis of the market as a system for aggregating wills, the diagnosis of social domination becomes little more than a vague and unpersuasive complaint, cut off from any articulable interest or political constituency. The freedom of the market is the domination of the mass of producers. This is the political theoretical core of Marx's theory of the value-form.

Notes

1 This chapter draws from Chapter Three of my book (Roberts 2017).

2 The revenue from the tax was to be divided between the free credit bank, rent and interest rebates, and reductions on other taxes. Proudhon's bill, together with Adolphe Theirs's negative report for the Finance Committee, and Proudhon's floor speech can be found in Pierre-Joseph Proudhon (1938: 343–406).

3 Marx published an unsigned report on Proudhon's speech in the *Neue Rheinische Zeitung* on 5 August 1848 (Marx 1977: 321–4). In the German report, Proudhon decries '*der Fetischismus des Geldes*' (Marx and Engels 1971: 306).
4 I have modified the translation to follow the French, which uniformly renders the German *Rätsel* as *énigme*; the Fowkes translation uses *mystery* and *enigma* indifferently, but *mystery* should translate *Geheimnis*.
5 Compare Marx 1986: 340–1.
6 From this one can see how ridiculous is the notion that Marx fatally ignores utility in his discussion of value, as, for instance, in Jon Elster (1985: 139–40).
7 This may indicate the influence of Alfred Sohn-Rethel (1978).
8 Postone's reading of Marx is determined in this regard by his opposition to what he calls traditional Marxism, which he understands to have conflated the impersonal, abstract domination of capitalism with class domination veiled by market interactions. I agree that, for Marx, modern, impersonal domination is not itself a form of class domination (even though it grounds a new form of class domination), but Postone is wrong to think that the market's relevance is exhausted by the question of whether it transmits class domination.
9 Postone stresses these very passages, but he denies, without any evidence or argument, that the dominating social relationships can be understood as market relationships; see Postone, (1993: 125–6).
10 Fowkes, like Moore and Aveling before him, mistranslates this passage, turning it into an affirmation of Lukács's position, that 'things, far from being under [the exchangers'] control, in fact control them'. The German is ambiguous: '*Ihre eigne gesellschaftliche Bewegung besitzt für sie die Form einer Bewegung von Sachen, unter deren Kontrolle sie stehen, statt sie zu kontrollieren*'. Does *deren* refer to *Form* or *Bewegung* or *Sachen*? The French, however, clears up this grammatical ambiguity: '*leur propre mouvement social prend ainsi la forme d'un mouvement des choses, mouvement qui les mène, bien loin qu'ils puissant le diriger*'. See Marx 1987: 105, 1989: 56.
11 These interrelations are social because they are among people; they are natural because, as he put it in the *Grundrisse*,

> the mutual social relationship of individuals as an independent power standing over them, whether it is conceived of as a force of nature, an accident, or in any other form, is a necessary result of the fact that the starting point is not the free social individual.
>
> (Marx 1986: 132)

References

Bray, John Francis (1968) *Labour's Wrongs and Labour's Remedy; or, The Age of Might and the Age of Right*, New York: A.M. Kelley.

Cobbett, William (1818) *Cobbett's Political Register* 34 (28 November 1818).

Elson, Diane (1979) ed. *Value: The Representation of Labour in Capitalism*, London: CSE Books.

Elster, Jon (1985) *Making Sense of Marx*, Cambridge: Cambridge University Press.

Gray, John (1973) *The Social System: A Treatise on the Principle of Exchange*, Clifton, NJ: A.M. Kelley.

Heinrich, Michael (2012) *An Introduction to the Three Volumes of Karl Marx's Capital*, New York: Monthly Review Press.

Locke, John (1988) *Two Treatises of Government*, Cambridge: Cambridge University Press.

MacGilvray, Eric (2011) *The Invention of Market Freedom*, New York: Cambridge University Press.

Marx, Karl (1975), *Economic and Philosophic Manuscripts of 1844*, in *Marx Engels Collected Works*, vol. 3: *Marx and Engels, 1843–44*, New York: International Publishers.

Marx, Karl (1976) *Capital: A Critique of Political Economy*, vol. 1, London: Penguin.

Marx, Karl (1977) 'Proudhon's Speech Against Thiers', in *Marx Engels Collected Works*, vol. 7, New York: International Publishers, pp. 321–4.

Marx, Karl (1981) *Capital: A Critique of Political Economy*, vol. 3, New York: Vintage Books.

Marx, Karl (1986) *Economic Manuscripts of 1857–1858*, in *Marx Engels Collected Works*, vol. 28, New York: International Publishers.

Marx, Karl (1987 [1872]) 'Das Kapital Kritik der politischen Ökonomie Erster Band Hamburg 1872', in *Marx Engels Gesamtausgabe* (MEGA2), vol. II/6, Berlin: Dietz.

Marx, Karl (1989 [1872–5]) 'Das Kapital', in *Marx Engels Gesamtausgabe* (MEGA2), vol. II/7, Berlin: Dietz.

Marx, Karl and Friedrich Engels (1971) *Karl Marx – Friedrich Engels – Werke*. Vol. 5, Berlin: Dietz Verlag.

O'Kane, Chris (2013) *Fetishism and Social Domination in Marx, Lukács, Adorno, and Lefebvre*, Doctoral thesis, University of Sussex.

Owen, Robert (1991) *A New View of Society and Other Writings*, Edited by Gregory Claeys, London: Penguin, 1991.

Postone, Moishe (1993) *Time, Labor, and Social Domination: A Reinterpretation of Marx's Critical Theory*, Cambridge: Cambridge University Press.

Postone, Moishe (2003) 'Lukács and the Dialectical Critique of Capitalism.' in Robert Albritton and John Simoulidis (eds.), *New Dialectics and Political Economy*, New York: Palgrave Macmillan, pp. 78–100.

Proudhon, Pierre-Joseph (1938) *Deuxième Mémoire Sur La Propriété. Avertissement Aux Propriétaires. Programme Révolutionaire. Impôt Sur Le Revenu. Le Droit Au Travail et Le Droit a Propriété*, Edited by C. Bouglé and H. Moysset. Ouvres Complètes de P.-J. Proudhon, Nouvelle Édition, vol. 10, Paris: Marcel Rivière.

Roberts, William Clare (2017) *Marx's Inferno: The Political Theory of Capital*, Princeton, N.J: Princeton University Press.

Sohn-Rethel, Alfred (1978) *Intellectual and Manual Labour: A Critique of Epistemology*, London: Macmillan.

Thompson, William (1850) *An Inquiry into the Principles of the Distribution of Wealth Most Conducive to Human Happiness Applied to the Newly Proposed System of Voluntary Equality of Wealth*, 2nd edn. London: Longman.

Thompson, William (1969) *Labour Rewarded: The Claims of Labour and Capital Conciliated; or, How to Secure to Labour the Whole Product of Its Exertion*, New York: A.M. Kelley.

Vandenberghe, Frédéric (2009) *A Philosophical History of German Sociology*, London: Routledge.

14 The neglected chapters on wages in *Capital*

Gary Teeple

1 Introduction

The three volumes of *Capital* comprise the core of Marx's analysis of capitalist production as relations between embodiments of value.[1] The substance of value, he argues, is 'congealed labour-time' (Marx 1977a: 130), and all the components of the capitalist labour process, namely, constant capital (raw materials and instruments of production) and variable capital (labour-power) are analysed as quantities of value. But it is labour that produces all new value – the value of wages and surplus-value (v + s). The arguments in every chapter of *Capital*, from Part Two on, imply the necessary relations of v and s – their production, realization, division, distribution, and contradictions. *Capital* is not merely about surplus-value, as if that could be understood apart from variable capital, but about the dynamic and contradictory relation between these two value-forms.

The struggle over wages goes well back into antiquity, dating from the moment that wages constituted a form of remuneration for work performed (Ste. Croix 1981; Ward 1900). But the phenomena of wages did not become a central object of study until the late eighteenth and early nineteenth centuries when it became one side of the contradiction between labour and capital that stood at the heart of the reproduction of the capitalist mode of production. And when the majority of productive work was done by hired workers and not by serfs, slaves, petty-commodity producers, artisans, or through the guilds – relations in which wages comprised only a small part, if any, of labour's share of the product. Once the working class had become the main producer of value, which was divided with capital through class struggle, then, wages became a significant issue for study (see, for instance, Smith 1937, book 1, ch. VII).

In the face of increasing strikes and the growth of workers' organizations and their embrace of the labour theory of value in the early nineteenth century, political economy could not treat wages in the relatively impartial manner that was found in some of the early works of the discipline (Marx 1977a: 174–5, n.34). Because the conflict between labour and capital was usually over wages, mainstream classical economics soon framed their analysis with dogmatic assertions about wages. And so arose the many attempts to argue that wages were an inflexible and fixed form of capital, making the demands for more appear to be pointless.

2 Wages as fixed

The concept of the wage or labour 'fund' was promoted in the early nineteenth century for just this reason. In *Capital*, Marx took issue with the idea that wages comprised a fixed amount of the total product at any given time, and that any improvement in wages could only come with fewer workers, through emigration, or lower birth rates. Demands for wage increases, it was argued, would dampen the rate of accumulation and counter the rights of capital over 'the division of social wealth'. An increase in the 'wage fund', the argument went, could only come at 'favourable and exceptional' times. Such an idea was simply dogma, Marx contended, unsupported by evidence of the movement of wages or commonplace logic. Capital, he argued, 'is elastic, and constantly fluctuates ...' (Marx 1977a: 760; Lapides 1998: ch. 5; Abalos 1997-8).

Marx also took issue with the position put forward by the economist Senior, who in the face of demands for a shortened working day, argued that 'the whole net profit is derived from the last hour' of the work day, implying that to shorten working hours would 'destroy' profits (Marx 1977a: 333). Marx's retort was to point to the varying ratio of wages to profits: every moment of the working day produced both v and s; the issue was 'the relative magnitude' of each, over which the two sides struggled (Marx 1977a: 339).

There were also arguments from the left, namely, Lasalle's notion of the 'Iron Law of Wages'. Borrowing from Malthus and Ricardo, Lasalle asserted that the 'law' dictated that wages always tended towards the minimum necessary. Malthus' theory of population, cast as a natural law, stated that population growth outstripped the ability to provide means of subsistence; competition therefore always drove wages to minimal levels. In this light, Lasalle suggested that the establishment of workers' cooperatives with the aid of the state, achieved through the electoral process, was the only way to circumvent this fate. His 'Iron Law' consigned workers' struggles to mainstream politics and made the role of trade unions more or less redundant; there was no point to fight for improved conditions or wages because a natural 'law' could not be changed. The idea obscured the fact that wages are elastic like profits and that the impetus for struggle over wages rests on this elasticity. The assertion of an Iron Law denied the very premise of the conflict over wages. If workers' salvation lay only in aid from the state, moreover, that would preclude their struggle for socialism (Baumol 1983).

Marx opposed Malthusian based theories of subsistence wages (Marx 1977a: 639, n.41), like the Iron Law, because they implied that poverty wages and 'redundant' or 'surplus' populations were not the product of the capitalist mode of production, but rather of natural factors unrelated to the social system. Population size was not the independent variable that Malthus asserted, argued Marx;

it was a dependent variable. A 'surplus' population was part of a 'reserve army of labour', a product of the cycles of capital accumulation (Marx 1977a: 781); population size was always dependent on the mode of production. Malthusian theories implied, moreover, that no matter what the system – capitalist or socialist – the same population dynamic would assert itself, and so obscure the real reasons for the condition of the working class (Meek 1953).

Marx challenged arguments that sought to limit the demands of workers for a greater share of the value they created not only because the struggle over wages was necessary for their well-being and a key indicator of the status of the conflict between labour and capital, but also because these arguments portrayed the shares of the total product as fixed or necessary and not flexible, implying the size of the share a matter of natural laws or economic stability, not class conflict. Despite the importance of the struggle over the share of the pie, however, Marx stressed that an improved share was not the ultimate goal of the working class (Marx 1977b).

The class bias in these attempts to justify the restrictions to wages with assertions about natural limits and negative consequences can be grasped without understanding what wages actually are. But to fathom the source of the value of the total social product and the conflict underlying its division into wages and profits, *the very form of wages has to be understood.* The wage-form itself, argued Marx, obscures the nature of all these relations, making workers' struggles over wages easier to counter or dismiss. Central to the argument of *Capital* is the question of the relative share of the total social product that goes to wages and profits.

3 The analysis of wages in *Capital*

The suggestion that *Capital* is about the political economy of capital alone as if separate from a consideration of labour, as if there were a 'missing book on wage-labour' (Lebowitz: 1992: X, 152),[2] is difficult to fathom. A cursory review of Marx's argument preceding the chapters on wages (which we have omitted here) suffices to make the point that the whole of *Capital*, with except the first chapter, is about the conflict between labour and capital.

Chapter 1 might be taken as an exception for here Marx maps out the premises of his argument. He defines the value of a commodity as 'congealed labour-time', its magnitude calculated as units of socially necessary labour-time or abstract labour, and its appearance as exchange-value (price) (Marx 1977a: 129–135). The whole of Part One traces the development of value, this 'congealed labour-time', from its emergent form in accidental or isolated exchanges of commodities to its money form, in which value finds its own form and begins its own history as a commodity. In this history, money first facilitates the exchange of equivalent for equivalent (C-M-C), but once money becomes capital (M-C-M + ^M), the circuit reveals an output that is greater than the value of the inputs. Even so, value, now in the form of capital, remains 'congealed labour'.

Part Two is largely intended to counter the notion that this surplus-value arises in the sphere of circulation (C-M-C). In Chapter 6, 'The sale and purchase of labour-power', Marx analyses this sale and purchase in 'the sphere of circulation or commodity exchange' (Marx 1977a: 280). Labour-power is a commodity, he says, with 'the peculiar property of being a source of value', i.e. its use-value, labour, creates value in the sphere of production, but its exchange value is determined in the marketplace, the sphere of exchange (Marx 1977a: 270). In the marketplace, in theory at least, equivalent is exchanged for equivalent. 'The value of labour-power', Marx writes, 'is the value of the means of subsistence necessary for the maintenance of its owner' (Marx 1977a: 274). Here, posed in value terms is Marx's determination of the value of wages later discussed in Chapter 19.

Although all the intervening chapters deal with the relation between labour and capital, the immediately preceding chapters are a preamble to Part Five on 'Wages'. In Chapter 17, Marx explores the relation between the price of labour-power and surplus-labour. The concepts of wages and profits are not used here because the concept of wages involves a different level of analysis, as we shall see in Chapter 19, and the concept of profit is much narrower than the concept of surplus-value, which embraces all the value produced beyond the value of labour-power. He itemizes the factors that determine the relative magnitude of surplus-value and of the price of labour-power (s and v). These are (1) 'the length of the working day', (2) 'the normal intensity of labour', (3) and the 'productivity of labour'. How these three factors vary in relation to one another determines the relative share of total new value that is divided into the value of labour-power or surplus-value. This relative share is ultimately determined by class struggle over each of these factors (Marx 1977a: 659).

Chapter 18 also sets the stage for the chapters on wages. In this chapter, Marx uses his analysis of the *rate of surplus-value* in a critique of mainstream views. In part, it is about what wages represent – the value of labour-power (v), not the value of what is produced by labour (v + s). To measure *surplus* as a ratio of the *value of the product* (c + v) is to obscure the actual relations between labour and capital because it presents s and v as mere 'fractions of the value-product', which 'conceals' the fact that workers are paid out of variable capital for creating all new value (v + s) and suggests that workers have no claim over the product of their labour because they appear to be paid for all of it (Marx 1977a: 670–1).

Similarly, to represent s/v as *unpaid labour/paid labour* is to misrepresent the fact that the capitalist pays for labour-power not labour. If capital paid for labour, then, the value produced during the whole working-day would equal the value of wages, a mistaken notion found in the phrase: 'a fair day's pay for a fair day's work'. Capital, says Marx, pays for the value of labour-power, which means the value of the means of subsistence necessary to reproduce labour-power and so not equal to the value of the whole day's product (Marx 1977a: 671–2).

4 The chapters on wages

Marx has pointed to the importance of distinguishing labour from labour-power, and necessary labour-time and surplus labour-time, and how mainstream political economy obscures these differences. The commodity that is remunerated is labour-power; its use is labour. Chapter 19 is about the *form* that the value of labour-power takes, namely, wages, and how this form, parading as the price of labour, disguises the nature of the price and value of labour-power. Here Marx examines the wage form as ideology, as obfuscation of the value of labour-power.

The chapter begins with:

> On the surface of bourgeois society the worker's wage appears as the price of labour, as a certain quantity of money that is paid for a certain quantity of labour.
>
> (Marx 1977a: 675)

There are several key words here. The phrase, 'on the surface', is a reference to the appearance of things as opposed to their essence; the verb 'appears' suggests wages are not what they are claimed to be; and 'labour', as Marx has argued, is the expenditure of energy, to be contrasted with labour-power, i.e. the skills and knowledge that are embodied in a worker and employed while working (i.e. expending energy). The point is that wages are seen as 'the price of labour', that is, the price of the energy put out for the length of the working day; whereas, they are, as Marx argued, the price of labour-power, which theoretically should equal the value of the means of subsistence necessary to reproduce that labour-power (Marx 1977a: 675–7).

The argument is succinctly put:

> It is not labour which directly confronts the possessor of money on the commodity-market, but rather the worker. What the worker is selling is his labour-power. As soon as his labour actually begins, it has already ceased to belong to him; it can therefore no longer be sold by him. Labour is the substance, and the immanent measure of value, but it has no value itself.
>
> (Marx 1977a: 677)

Where does this notion of wages as 'the value of labour' come from?

> It is an expression as imaginary as the value of the earth. These imaginary expressions arise, nevertheless, from the relations of production themselves. They are categories for the forms of appearance of essential relations.
>
> (Marx 1977a: 677)

Marx then examines the usual explanation of mainstream political economy on how this price is determined – through the pressures of supply and demand. They can explain the fluctuation of the price above and below 'a certain mean', he says, but once the supply and demand 'balance, the oscillation of prices ceases …'. At this point, the explanation of the price ceases as well because supply and demand cannot explain the mean. He then shows that political economy in fact resorts to the notion of the cost of production of 'labour', which amounts to the value of the means of subsistence underlying the value of labour-power. 'Therefore, what they called the "value of labour" is in fact the value of labour-power …' (Marx 1977a: 678).

Following this conclusion, he points to the obscurantist nature of wage labour and compares wage labour with the nature of labour under the corvee and slavery, in which paid and unpaid labour are clearly demarked.

> The wage form thus extinguishes every trace of the division of the working day into necessary and surplus labour, into paid and unpaid labour. All labour appears as paid labour.
>
> (Marx 1977a: 680)

Marx then spells out the signal ideological importance of the use of the concept of 'wages' for the status quo.

> We may … understand the decisive importance of the transformation of the value and price of labour-power into the form of wages, or into the value and price of labour itself. All the notions of justice held by both the worker and the capitalist, all the mystifications of the capitalist mode of production, all capitalism's illusions about freedom, all the apologetic tricks of vulgar economics, have as their basis the form of appearance discussed above, which makes the actual relations invisible, and the indeed presents to the eye the precise opposite of that relation.
>
> (Marx 1977a: 680)

The 'notions of justice' we assume to refer to the implication that wages represent equal value for equal value, whereas they are the value of v in exchange for producing the value of v + s. The 'mystifications' could refer to the concept of wages obscuring the source of surplus-value, allowing profit to be seen as an addition at the point of sale. The 'illusions about freedom' point to the contract as if it were between equals, with no advantage for either side. But one must work, while the other chooses who works; yet, the contract is necessary to both sides. It is not a matter of choice – it is necessary for one side to live, and for the other to produce surplus-value. As for 'apologetic tricks', profit appears to arise in circulation and not production, obscuring the exploitation of workers; and because the entire time worked appears to be paid for, 'the category of surplus labour-time does not exist at all for [the capitalist or economist]' (Marx 1977a: 690) and so capitalist appropriation of the surplus seems justified. And because capitalists own all the components of value (c + v + s) they appear to 'work' too and should be rewarded with a revenue stream for their contribution. The 'actual relation [is] invisible', says Marx, wages disguise necessary and surplus labour-time, the time for producing v and s.

Marx sees the wage form as central to the obfuscation of all the relations of production, for employers and workers alike. But since the confusion works in favour of the employer, it is the workers who suffer the negative implications of the perception that wages are the price of labour, which prevents an understanding of their exploitation.

He explains how this inversion, this ideological view, comes about. In short, it rests on the confusion of the exchange-value and use-value of the commodity of labour-power. The exchange-value is the monetary expression of the value of labour-power, while the use-value is the labour – two entirely different things. But since the workers are paid after they have performed labour, the use-value, it appears that it was the actual work that was paid for. Yet, as he says, labour has no value, although it creates value; it is simply the expenditure of energy (Marx 1977a: 681).

The final paragraph of the chapter contains a concise statement of Marx's notion of ideology, which rests on the difference between essence and appearance.

> what is true of all forms of appearance and their hidden background is also true of the form of appearance 'value and price of labour', or 'wages', as contrasted with the essential relation manifested in it, namely the value and price of labour-power. The forms of appearance are reproduced directly and spontaneously, as current and usual modes of thought; the essential relation must first be discovered by science. Classical political economy stumbles approximately onto the true state of affairs, but without consciously formulating it. It is unable to do this as long as it stays within its bourgeois skin.
>
> (Marx 1977a: 682)

Wages, in short, are an ideological form of the value of labour-power. They are the form of appearance of the value of labour-power taken as if the essence, and in this way the ideological form serves to obscure the essential relations, undermining an understanding by the working class of the nature of its exploitation.

5 Chapter 20: time-wages

Marx begins this chapter with the sentence: 'Wages themselves again take many forms' (Marx 1977a: 683). We are all familiar with some of them, namely, tips, grants, lump-sum contracts, salaries, hourly and piece rates, 'in kind' (Christmas turkey), work-related competitions, etc. Marx says that he will consider only two forms, the most common to this day: *time-wages* and *piece-wages*.

Because wages represent remuneration for the value of labour-power, parading as the value of labour, Marx's first task is to show how to calculate time-wages (an hourly, daily, weekly, etc. rate) on the basis of the value of labour-power, to give the 'price of labour,' i.e. the time that for whatever period v + s is produced. 'The average price of labour is the average daily value of labour-power divided by the average number of hours in the working day' (Marx 1977a: 684). The 'price of labour' may be read as the hourly wage rate; and Marx says that this will be used 'as the unit measure for the price of labour' (Marx 1977a: 684).

He then refers the reader to Chapter 17 where he says that the laws he mapped out there (variations 'in relative magnitude of price of labour-power and surplus-value') can be read as applying to the wage-form. And the difference between *nominal and real wages* may be read as the difference between 'the exchange value of labour-power and the sum of the means of subsistence' (Marx 1977a: 684). *Nominal wages*, then, are the 'form of appearance' of the exchange-value of labour-power, while *real wages* are the value of labour-power.

A good part of the rest of the chapter deals with how the difference between nominal and real wages can be manipulated to increase the relative share of surplus-value in the valorization process. Time-wages obscure the fact that the rate is calculated on the basis of a number of hours per week/month/year to provide the means to reproduce the worker, but if there is no guarantee of this requisite number of hours, despite high time-wages, they can be below the value of labour-power (Marx 1977a: 684). Time-wages also disguise exploitation by making it appear that the worker is paid for the whole time worked. And they open the door to constant attempts by capital to expand surplus labour-time at the expense of necessary labour-time by the use of 'overtime,' 'bonuses,' and shortened holidays, sick days, parental leave, etc.

Marx also mentions the variety of ways in which wages are kept low through the use of foreign labour, immigration policies, women and children, in short, the expansion of labour supply – not to mention in our day, the use of state subsidies for handicapped and underage labour, illegal labour, and so on. He also maps out the implications of chronic low wages or 'underemployment', namely, the 'desire' for more work time, or more jobs to make ends meet, in a word, overwork (Marx 1977a: 685), and a permanent stratum of working poor (Marx 1977a: 688–9). Here is one rationale for keeping the minimum wage low: to force workers to press for longer hours so that the cumulative wage can approach a living wage, whereas the demand of an indexed 'living' wage would be necessary to address the issue of low wages.

6 Chapter 21: piece-wages

Piece-wages comprise the other main form of wages along with time-wages, but they appear to be different; 'at first sight', says Marx, they seem to be remuneration for the product of labour. Like time-wages, however, they have to be converted into units of the value of labour-power in order to discover the hourly or daily rate they represent and the degree to which they equal the value of labour-power expended (Marx 1977a: 693).

Like time-wages, the form of piece-wages carries a number of implications, all of which aid in the expansion of the extraction of surplus from the worker, or the reduction in remuneration, in disguised ways. The mere setting of the piece rate is a matter of contention given that what the rate represents is not directly visible; it has to be calculated in relation to the value of labour-power, also a contested measure. Given that much piece-work is done by workers in isolation, it is more difficult to contest the rate than if the work were done in a factory. Once established, the piece-rate puts part of the issue of 'quality control' in the hands of the worker, but this in turn becomes a basis of employer assessment and a significant way of reducing the price of a 'piece' (Marx 1977a: 694). The need for supervision, a question of *faux frais* for capital, is greatly reduced given that piece-work shifts much of the role of supervision into self-supervision by the worker. Because 'only the labour-time embedded in the product counts as socially necessary and is paid as such', it is in the 'interests of the workers' to intensify the labour, find ways to improve productivity, and to lengthen the working day to produce as many 'pieces' as possible (Marx 1977a: 695).

Piece-wages not only increase the extraction of surplus from the worker, but also provide illusions of self-employment (Marx 1977a: 697), mitigating solidarity and potentially promoting competition amongst workers. This form of wages, moreover, says Marx, lends itself to wage theft given the number of ways in which the piece and its production can be assessed by the employer.

All the characteristics of this form lead Marx to say that 'the piece-wage is the form of wage most appropriate to the capitalist mode of production' (Marx 1977a: 698); in other words, the form that provides capital with the greatest possibilities of extracting the maximum of surplus from the worker and that best disguises the robbery. But it is also the form that makes international comparisons easiest because embedded in it as its value is the national measure of productivity and intensity of labour (Marx 1977a: 701), not to mention the other factors that make up the national average value of labour-power.

7 Chapter 22: national differences in wages

This chapter makes the point that comparisons of national wage rates must take into 'account all the factors that determine changes in the amount of the value of labour-power' (Marx 1977a: 701). The most important of these would include, according to Marx, the length of the working day, rates of productivity and intensity of labour, and the moral, cultural, and historical expectations for a certain standard of living.

While differences in national wage rates still exist across the world, they are no longer based on the dramatic differences in levels of industrialization that existed in the nineteenth century. Although Marx made many references to the 'world market', it was a market of competing national corporations, which generally saw the largest share of their profits generated within national boundaries and, beyond these, for the most part within colonial boundaries. This is not the case today; a world market is not a global economy, with colonial barriers gone, trade blocs encompassing all the industrial nations and many regional economic blocs embracing the so-called developing nations, a global quasi-state or institutionalized enabling framework for capital, military alliances across the world, production or 'value' chains spanning the globe, ubiquitous computer-based technology in production and distribution, information and communication technology connecting the world 24/7/365, and transnational corporations sitting on top of it all and whose profits flow from every quarter. The international is not the global, and this difference has implications for wage rates.

Because production chains stretch over many countries over every region of the world, and because they employ for the most part advanced technologies, there is a global averaging tendency to the length of the working day, productivity and intensity of labour, and standard of living. All the world's main capital and consumer goods are produced in such 'chains' – cars, trucks, trains, planes, ships, computer-based technology, foodstuffs, textiles, clothes, construction equipment and materials, minerals/metals, etc. They produce a tendency towards a broad convergence of wages and conditions of work. The jurisdictional divide, however, between national labour markets defining labour unions and workers' rights and the global labour market open to capital make the struggle over wages increasingly difficult for the working classes.

8 Concluding remarks

The chapters on wages are largely about two things. One is the ideological nature of the wage-form and how this form obscures the real relations of production (labour mistaken for labour-power: appearance for essence). The other is the use of these various forms to defraud workers of the value of their labour-power. But underlying both of these points, and Marx's reason for examining the peculiarities of wages, is a third point: the question of *relative wages*. This is about the share of the total product that goes to labour and how capital strives to maximize the surplus extracted at the expense of wages, the main thread of the argument of *Capital*.

The whole system rests on the pumping of surplus-value out of the working classes in increasing amounts (Marx 1977a: 1038, 1049). As 'the driving force behind capitalist production' (Marx 1977a: 1951), as Marx puts it, the necessity to extract ever more surplus generates chronic struggle over the share of wages and the conditions of work. This struggle, then, goes to the heart of the system in a way that none of the other struggles in a capitalist society do. It embodies the contradiction between the well-being of the working classes and the growing accumulation of capital. For this reason, both sides use the powers and leverage available to extract what each requires for its own reproduction, always at the expense of the other.

This struggle takes place within a legal/political framework that is far from neutral. It is a system defined by corporate private property, a framework of systemic inequalities. The advantage almost always goes to capital because the state as the representative of prevailing property relations defends by definition the interests of corporations as the main embodiments of private property, and because corporate capital is the active agent – the driving force of development and the *raison d'être* of the system. Competition between capitals and between capital and labour and the consequent technological changes provide the momentum to the system. By contrast, the working classes are generally reactive, countering as best they can the constant encroachments on wages and working conditions, resisting increases in the extraction of surplus-value at their expense. Unless spurred by ideas about alternative systems and strategic analysis, however, the working classes remain largely defensive in disposition.

For many decades in the industrial nations, the distribution of the national income between wages and profits remained relatively stable. Certainly, between World War II and the late 1970s, a constellation of forces made for a comparatively steady income and wealth distribution in the industrial nations (Kaldor 1968: 350). By the end of the 1970s, however, growing disparities of wealth and income distribution began to appear throughout much of the world, continuing to the present. This shift in distribution was hastened by the adoption of neo-liberal policies everywhere in the 1980s, which mirrored rapid changes in technology and the gradual shift of political and economic power to the global level.

Measuring wealth and income distribution across nations is notoriously difficult. Different living costs, cultural expectations, levels of development and taxation, state redistribution, among other factors, not to mention the use of different measures, make comparisons open to question. Nevertheless, growing disparities in the share of national income are reported to be rising almost everywhere (Diwan 2006; Guscina 2006). In the USA in 2006, 'the share of national income captured by corporate profits ... was at its highest level on record' (CBPP 2007a). 'Total employee compensation,' including wages, benefits, and state redistribution, was falling in relation to the share of profits. The disparities in income also grew rapidly; the top 1 per cent of households took almost 20 per cent of total national pre-tax income, while the 'bottom' 99 per cent garnered about 80 per cent in 2005 – about a 2 per cent rise and fall respectively from the previous year (CBPP 2007b). In Europe, particularly in Germany, France, and Britain, labour's share has fallen over the last 25 years (Glyn 2006). Japan, according to the OECD, 'witnessed a sharp decline in its national wage share – from 75 per cent in 1980 to 61 per cent in 2005' (OECD 2007). In China, the World Bank revealed that, despite the continuous rapid growth of its economy, 'the wage share [of GDP] declined from 53 percent in 1998 to 41.4 percent in 2005' (World Bank 2007). Similar findings have been reported in Australia and Canada, among other nations (Russell and Dufour 2007).

This decline of the wage share does not necessarily translate into an absolute or relative decline of *real wages*; it refers only the relative decline of wages' share of the net national income. In other words, it is possible to have a declining share, and even a declining absolute value of wages, and still maintain a given standard of living or even improve it with a greater mass of consumer goods and services – if the value of these means of subsistence is falling faster than the value of wages (Marx 1977a: 769). It is also possible to have rising nominal wages and falling real wages if the value of the means of subsistence rises faster than the growth of purchasing power. There can also be economic growth without growth in the share to the working classes, all the while maintaining or increasing the standard of living. The different strata and sectors of capital and labour share the benefits of economic growth and productivity unevenly and according to many factors. The possibility of these paradoxes, however, does not mean that they are the actual trends; declining real wages and living standards since the 1980s have been recorded across most of the industrial nations (Standing 2017).

The secular declining wage share of national income, however, is not an insignificant trend. In general, the struggle over shares is central to the reproduction of the whole system; it is a struggle over what amounts to the distribution of the social product and the ability of its classes to survive contradictory demands. The distribution points to the relative benefits of economic activity divided between classes and strata.

For capital, this trend signifies a relative increase in the mass of profits. This, in turn, increases the power of capital over the state (buying political influence, threats of capital strikes, ownership of public debt, competitive leverage over states, etc.) and over labour ('run-away' plants, 'outsourcing', 'off-shoring', robotization of production and distribution, wage cut demands, strike and/or union 'free' contracts, 'right to work' laws, retrenchment of employment standards and workers' compensation, etc.). The increase in profits also facilitates accumulation and investment in new technology (raising the organic composition of capital), leading to higher productivity and less effective demand for labour.

The significance of this trend is not lost on the working classes. Of the total social product, their labour produces more in the form of profits and less as wages. Even if this is not experienced as a decline in living standards, it is understood as 'unfair', as distributional 'injustice', as 'working harder for the boss'. If the decline in fact translates into decreasing or stagnant real wages and standards of living or increasing un- and underemployment, it produces social unrest of varying sorts. At the very least, it leads to apathy and cynicism and produces a distrust of the system as illegitimate, as not representative of 'citizens' and their needs.

The falling share of wages is not likely to change directions in the near future. Capital has all the advantages given the two-tiered labour markets, the subservience of the state, and the permanent revolution in computer-based technology. The rise of the global labour market, a composite of national markets, accessible only by capital, has undermined the strength of the nationally restricted union movements; the struggle for a larger share at the national level without leverage at the global level is a lost cause. Capital, by contrast, can roam at will across the global labour market, which provides it with much of the leverage it has over states and nationally bound labour.

The 'industrial reserve army' as part of this labour market now grows across the world beyond the power of individual states to control. Marx attributed this 'army' as having enormous influence over wages rates: 'Taking them as a whole, the general movements of wages are exclusively regulated by the expansion and contraction of the industrial reserve army, and this in turn corresponds to the periodic alterations in the industrial cycle' (Marx 1977a: 790). If we include in this category, the unemployed, the under-employed, the minimally self-employed or those in the 'informal economy,' and uncounted populations in vast slums, then, although good figures are not available, even the estimates give us numbers in the many hundreds of millions (Foster, McChesney and Jonna 2011). To these we can add increasing use of prison labour, and the growth of child labour, 'guest' workers, temporary foreign workers, illegal immigrants, and slave-like treatment and trafficking of millions.

The state plays an important role on the supply side of the labour market. Whereas in the postwar era it was forced to ameliorate the impact of the labour market and business cycles on the condition of the working class with the Keynesian welfare policies, after decades of of neo-liberal and now austerity policies have retrenched much of the protection and de-commodification provided by welfare policies and labour legislation.

The demand side of the labour market is provided by capital, and here we meet the other part of the contemporary predicament for the working classes and wages as the source of their livelihood. The current projections of demand are grim, but they are more or less the realization of Marx's well-known analysis of the effects of growing organic composition of capital in the *Grundrisse.*

The continuous introduction and application of machinery reduces the side of living labour, variable capital, to an ever-decreasing amount, while machinery, like a force of nature, produces more wealth than ever before, progressively eroding the production of value. Here is Marx:

> ... to the degree that large industry develops, the creation of real wealth comes to depend less on labour time and on the amount of labour employed than on the power of the agencies set in motion during labour time, whose 'powerful effectiveness' is itself ... out of all proportion to the direct labour time spent on their production. 'Real wealth' is created 'in the monstrous disproportion between the labour time applied, and its product, as well as in the qualitative imbalance between labour ... and the power of the production process it superintends. *Labour no longer appears so much to be included within the production process....*
>
> (Marx 1987: 90–91; see also Marx 1973: 704–5). [Emphasis added]

Labour becomes less and less necessary, and the production of commodities as exchange-values approaches an end. As Marx puts it:

> The theft of alien labour time, on which the present wealth is based, appears as a miserable foundation in the face of this new one, created by large-scale industry itself.
>
> (Marx 1987: 91)

Once wealth is created by machinery more or less on its own, it no longer takes the form of commodities because it has no value.

> labour time ceases and must cease to be its measure, and hence exchange value [must cease to be the measure] of use value.... With that, production based on exchange value breaks down....
>
> (Marx 1987: 91)

But now the contradiction of the capitalist mode of production lies exposed.

> Capital itself is the moving contradiction, [in] that it presses to reduce labour time to a minimum, while it posits labour time, on the other side, as sole measure and source of wealth.
>
> (Marx 1987: 91)

In short, the 'forces of production' have reduced value to inconsequential quantities, while the 'relations of production' remain predicated on the realization of exchange value (Marx 1987: 91). Once wealth no longer has value, there is no production of variable capital and surplus-value, there is no productive class and no wages, and no longer the possibility of realizing the product of machine production within the persisting relations of production based on the production of value and its private appropriation.

It could be argued that we are on the cusp of this contradiction. Why else would the World Economic Forum be discussing the question of a 'basic income', and why the numerous current state experiments with such programs? Stop-gap and feeble measures to be sure, but they provide some insight into how capital views the future.

Notes

1 With special thanks to Mohammad Ferdosi and Paula Rauhala for their critical comments and suggestions.

2 This question of the 'missing book' was convincingly addressed some time ago by Rosdolsky (1968) and later by Lapides (1998). *Capital*, we argue, in its entirety is about the contradiction between labour and capital; there can be no political economy of capital separate from that of labour. In the final chapter of *Capital*, often the object of neglect or confusion by commentators, Marx points to how the problem of labour supply in the colonies revealed the 'secret' of capitalism, namely, that there can be no capital accumulation without labour and no labour without capital; the two cannot be analysed separately from each other.

References

Abalos, José M. G. (1997–1998) 'Marx's Theory of Wages', in *International Journal of Political Economy*, vol. 27, no. 4: 96–114.

Baumol, William J. (1983) 'Marx and the Iron Law of Wages', in *The American Economic Review*, vol. 73, no. 2: 303–8.

CBPP (2007a) Center on Budget and Policy Priorities, Report, 29 March 2007.

CBPP (2007b) Center on Budget and Policy Priorities, Report, 24 October 2007.

Diwan, Ishac (2006) *Debt as Sweat: Labor, financial crises, and the globalization of capital*, Washington, DC: World Bank.

Foster, John B., McChesney Robert W., and Jonna R. Jamil (2011) 'The Global Reserve Army of Labor and the New Imperialism', in *Monthly Review*, vol. 63, no. 6.

Glyn, Andrew (2006) *Capitalism Unleashed*, Oxford: Oxford University Press.

Guscina, Anastasia (2006) *Effects of Globalization on Labor's Share of National Income. IMF Working paper*, 06/294, Washington, DC: International Monetary Fund.

ILO (9 August 2007) 'Asian Employment Forum': interview with S. Yamamoto, ILO Regional Director for Asia and the Pacific.

Kaldor, Nicholas (1968) 'Alternative Theories of Distribution', in Brian J. McCormick and Eric O. Smith (eds.), *The Labour Market*, Harmondsworth: Penguin Books, pp. 349–79.

Lapides, Kenneth (1998) *Marx's Wage Theory in Historical Perspective*, Westport, Connecticut: Praeger.

Lebowitz, Michael (1992) *Beyond Capital: Marx's Political Economy of the Working Class*, New York: St. Martins Press.

Levin-Waldman, Oren M. (2011) *The Case of the Minimum Wage*, New York: State University of New York Press.

Marx, Karl (1973) *Grundrisse*, Harmondsworth: Penguin, 1973.

Marx, Karl (1977a) *Capital, Volume One*, New York: Vintage Books.

Marx, Karl (1977b) 'Wage Labour and Capital.' in *Marx Engels Collected Works*, vol. 9: *Marx and Engels 1849*, London: Lawrence and Wishart, pp. 197–228.

Marx, Karl (1987) *Economic Manuscripts of 1857–58*, in *Marx Engels Collected Works*, vol. 29: *Marx 1857–61*, Moscow: Progress Publishers.

Meek, Ronald L. (ed.) (1953) *Marx and Engels on Malthus*, London: Lawrence and Wishart.

OECD (2007) Employment Outlook, 'How Does Japan Compare?'

Rosdolsky, Roman (1968) *The Making of Marx's 'Capital'*, London: Pluto Press.

Russell, Ellen and Dufour, Mathieu (2007) *Rising Profit Shares, Falling Wage Shares*, Toronto: Canadian Centre for Policy Alternatives.

Smith, Adam (1937) *Wealth of Nations*, New York: Random House.

Standing, Guy (2017) *The Corruption of Capitalism*, London: Biteback Publishing.

Ste. Croix, Geoffrey E.M. (1981) *The Class Struggle in Ancient Greek World*, Ithaca, New York: Cornell University Press.

Ward, Cyrenus O. (1900) *The Ancient Lowly* Chicago: Charles H. Kerr & Co.

World Bank (2007) China Research Paper No. 7, (Rebalancing China's Economy—Modeling A Policy Package, Jianwu He & Louis Kuijs).

15 The persistence of Marx's humanism, from the doctoral dissertation on Epicurus to *Capital*

Mauro Buccheri

1 The plague

In the ubiquitous swamp of Neoliberal capitalism, a time of pestilence and plagues, of zombies, vampires and other monsters of the market, of fuzziness and uncertainty, of religious fundamentalisms and solitary atheism, of violence and repressive tolerance, of *Empire* and *Multitude*, of globalization and right-wing populism, of culture wars, and abject poverty, failed and failing states, of nuclear war anxieties, of despots, oligarchs and fading democracies, of simulacra and spectacles, of favelas and World Cup soccer, Arab Springs and the Banana Republics of consumer society – and of academic controversies about what is or is not modernity, post-modernity, the nature of political economy, the nature of *human nature*, Late Capitalism, the aesthetic, the ethic, the truth, the dialectic, genes, memes, real, virtual, self, the Other, Dasein, and so on – we know with certainty only that the survival of our species is at risk. It is even probable that we will destroy, along with ourselves, most of, if not the entire, biosphere.

This apocalyptic scenario is historically visible, envisioned by philosophers, writers and artists, not to mention Hollywood cinema, by Marxists, conservatives and nihilists, Gaia as well as Medea theorists (Buccheri 2005: 73–108). There are also those who believe that Salvation may come from a renewed mythological and symbolic order,[1] or revolutionary insurgent multitudes which somehow will come to the rescue of a world fallen into the *Void of the Exchange Value*, of universal saleability, of technological autism and idolatry, and of mindless consumerism, all shrouded in the fog of postmodern schizoid euphoria.

The multitudes – whose symbolic forms and mythologies have been hollowed out by the hegemony of the *exchange value* – would by a mystical Event begin a new history of humanity. Between absolute myth and the absolutism of the *exchange value*, there is, however, a third way, the path travelled on by Marx himself with a sustained, passionate inquiry into what humanity had become in the inferno of nineteenth-century capitalism, from *The First Writings* and *The Economic and Philosophical Manuscripts of 1844* to *Capital* and '*L'ultimo Marx*' (Musto 2016: 3–48), charting for us a course between an improbable return to pre-modern symbolic forms and the self-annihilation of humanity, or, perhaps what is even worse, its transformation into the post-human cyborg.

In the pestilential swamp of Neoliberal capitalism the 'End of the Human' – the human as understood by Marx and humanism – is taking place almost unnoticed. We were beginning to understand who we have been and to think about who we might wish to be, when the event was suddenly upon us: human life itself reduced to surplus value. The beginning of the 'end of the human' has been preceded and accompanied by if not the demise certainly the eclipse of humanism and the emergence of misguided post-humanist ideologies, even where – in the left hemisphere[2] – it should have been housed, defended and, when historically necessary, renewed; a radical renewal is now imperative not only in the light of the tragic history of the twentieth century (Miliband 1995: 58–62), but also of the vertiginous scientific and technological advances of the last 30 years, in particular in the fields of biotechnology, eugenics and biopolitics with catastrophic dehumanizing effects already visible (Harari 2014: 266–74, 397–416). In short, a new humanism is indeed needed in this time of domination of the *exchange value*, when all can be bought and sold.

How does one get out of the dehumanizing neoliberal swamp in which the contemporary world has fallen? Perhaps the question that we must ask – to rethink the human against the background of humanism's historical ebb and flow and misguided transhumanist cyborg manifestos – is the question with which Camus's *Myth of Sisyphus* begins after the dismissal of metaphysics:[3]

> There is but one truly serious philosophical problem and that is suicide. Judging whether life is or is not worth living amounts to answering the fundamental question of philosophy. All the rest … comes afterwards. These are games; one must first answer. And if it is true, as Nietzsche claims, that a philosopher to deserve our respect must preach by example, you can appreciate the importance of that reply, for it will precede the definitive act. These are facts the heart can feel; yet they call for careful study before they become clear to the intellect.
>
> (Camus 2005:1–2)

The fundamental philosophical and existential problem therefore is asking if life is worth living; and if it is, how then are we to live? Camus's answer comes in the conclusion of the *Myth of Sisyphus*:

> I leave Sisyphus at the foot of the mountain! One always finds one's burden again. But Sisyphus teaches the higher fidelity that negates the gods and raises rocks. He, too, concludes that all is well. This universe henceforth without a master seems to him neither sterile nor futile.…

> The struggle itself towards the heights is enough to fill a man's heart. One must imagine Sisyphus happy.
>
> (Camus 2005: 119)

The 'eternal' return of capitalism from every crisis is such 'rock', but socialist humanism also 'eternally' returns to regenerate the hope that Promethean Sisyphus may become Orphic Cadmus (Buccheri 2017: 88–9), that human creativity and wise science may interrupt the Sisyphean eternal return of the same and open up as yet unforeseen, unimagined utopian spaces of being, so that the Pleasure Principle may prevail over the Gospel of Labour.

Jacques Monod's *Chance and Necessity* (1971), a significant contribution to a secular and humanist ethic of knowledge,[4] begins with the quoted conclusion of Camus's interpretation of the myth of Sisyphus. Todorov's liberal humanism, as theorized in *The Imperfect Garden*, also finds in the Myth of Sisyphus its symbolic order (Buccheri 2017: 78–85). If, as Camus, Monod and Todorov believe, life is indeed worth living, even though and perhaps because 'One always finds one's burden again' – but in a universe 'without a master' that is neither 'sterile' nor 'futile' – is the symbolic order embodied by Sisyphus good enough for our time? Is there an alternative, politically, historically and ethically credible, to Liberal humanism which is on its deathbed?

Let's look for an alternative in the history of humanism and of Marxist humanism in particular. My own fidelity to humanism lies in the belief that – if we can at least 'imagine Sisyphus happy' – we must begin by resisting:

> … resistance – Tony Judt writes, quoting Camus – was not about heroism at all – or, if it was, then it was the heroism of goodness. It may seem a ridiculous idea, but the only way to fight the plague is with decency….
>
> (Judt 2001: XIII)

Rieux remarks at one point, 'you have to be mad, blind or a coward to resign yourself to the plague' (Camus 2001: 96). But what is the plague? It is 'dogma, conformity, compliance and cowardice' (Judt 2001: XIV) which now allows neoliberal capitalism to dehumanize us as once did Fascism, of which Camus's *Plague* is an allegory. Neoliberal capitalism's forms of 'evil' are more dangerous than Fascism because they are so pervasive to have become 'invisible', to seem 'natural' and hence believed to be inevitable.

The last sentence of Camus's great novel, Tony Judt writes, 'rings truer than ever, a fireball in the night of complacency and forgetting'; Rieux, the protagonist of *The Plague*, knew 'that the plague bacillus never dies or vanishes entirely … and that perhaps the day will come when, for the instruction or misfortune' of humanity, the plague 'will rouse its rats and send them to die in some well-contented city' (Camus 2001: 237–8).

Camus's 'prophecy' has come to pass, the new plague is upon us, but its ubiquitous presence remains 'invisible', even to those who should know better: the 'night of complacency and forgetting', of 'dogma, conformity, compliance and cowardice' is upon us, the new plague bacillus, neoliberalism, is no longer dormant, and the day of reckoning is coming for 'the misfortune' of humanity, but perhaps also for its 'instruction': the plague has 'roused its rats' and sent them to die in 'the well-contented' cities of the globalized and commodified world of Late capitalism, where human life itself has become surplus value (see Cooper 2008).

Nevertheless, there is a 'way out', the promise of a remedy that lies in the history of humanism and, in particular, of Marx's, or Marxist humanism.

2 The promise of Marx's humanism from the doctoral dissertation on Epicurus to *Capital*

If, as William Roberts persuasively argues in *Marx's Inferno*, *Capital* should be read as a text of political theory and intervention but also, I would argue, as an existential descent into the hell of nineteenth century industrial capitalism – structured according to Dante's moral ontology of the three *capital* sins of *Hell*,[5] – then Marx's humanist struggle for the emancipation of humanity according to its potential as *species-being*[6] begins with his doctoral dissertation on Epicurus whose Garden is a powerful counterpoint to the industrial hell on earth of nineteenth century England, announced in 1859 as such by Marx in the *Preface to A Contribution to the Critique of Political Economy* (Marx 1974: 424–8).

As a student of Greek philosophy, particularly of third century BCE atomism, stoicism and skepticism, working on his dissertation – on the difference between Democritus' and Epicurus' atomism – Marx must have known of the 'unprecedented' level of wonder reached by 'everyday consciousness' in Athens (Epicurus 2012: VIII), however put at risk by the political turmoil of the Hellenistic period and by the fragmented nature of the philosophical discourses taking place among Athenian citizens at the time, thus undermining humanism's quest for what was then the central theme of philosophical inquiry: how to live. Marx also saw the similarities between the intellectual and political crisis of third-century Athens and nineteenth-century Germany reeling from the recent death of Hegel in 1831.

This awareness, as one reads Marx's dissertation, becomes more and more evident and manifests itself initially as the 'instinctive' humanism of him who hates 'the pack of gods' and would 'Better be the servant of this rock/Than to be faithful boy to Father Zeus' (Marx 1974: 90) embodied in the mythical figure of Prometheus, as Marx writes in the foreword to his doctoral dissertation:

> Philosophy, as long as a drop of blood shall pulse in its world-subduing and absolutely free heart, will never grow tired of answering its adversaries with the cry of Epicurus: *Not the man who denies the gods worshipped by the multitude, but he who affirms of the gods what the multitude believes about them, is truly impious.*
>
> (Marx 1974: 89–90)

Marx's humanism is grounded in and legitimized by, on the one hand, 'a-theism' – whose etymology may be interpreted rather than *without a God*, as *abandoned* or *neglected* by the gods who simply do not care about human existence, as Epicurus' philosophy emphasized – and on the other by the acknowledgement that 'human self-consciousness' is 'the highest divinity' (Marx 1974: 90) and the foundation of free will; Prometheus, as a rebel against the gods and humanity's mentor, is indeed 'the most eminent saint and martyr in the philosophical calendar' (Marx 1974: 90). Marx's humanism as a profound commitment to make human existence as meaningful and happy as the constraints of nature permit – confirmed by his lifelong engagement with and love for world literature as a source and a repository of our humanity (see Prawer 1978)[7] – evolves from the original philosophical 'intuition' to the historical humanism of the *Economic and Philosophical Manuscripts of 1844* – where it acquires the dimension of economic alienation as the denial of our *species-being*'s potential – to revolutionary praxis in the *Manifesto of the Communist Party* and, finally, to political economy and political theory in *Capital*, rooted in the ethical imperative to understand 'scientifically' the nature of capital's laws of accumulation and circulation.[8]

It is my contention that – to leave behind the dualistic opposition between the Early and the Late Marx, between utopian and 'scientific' Marxism, socialist humanism and structuralist Marxism, with its anti-humanist inclinations – Marx's humanism constitutes the connecting tissue of his life and works, of his political theory and 'scientific' analysis of capital, an Ariadne's thread never severed, always guiding and inspiring him to continue his search for political, economic and anthropological truths that would lead humanity out of the hell of industrial capitalism and into 'Purgatory', or to use Calvino's expression, at least a *Non-inferno*,[9] from which, as autonomous subjects, humans can pursue the Epicurean art of living happily here on earth.

The contrast between the epigraph at the entrance of Epicurus' garden and Dante's warning at the entrance of Hell is quite telling and worth emphasizing for what it reveals about Marx's humanism. Marx understands – as he gets ready to undertake the dangerous quest to lay bare the laws of capital – the intellectual and existential challenges facing him; he knows that the search for truth requires the renewal of the *Self*, that the end pursued is a radical metamorphosis similar to Dante's *trasumanar*.[10] It is worth noting that Marx's identification with Dante's journey implies – as for example the references to Cacciaguida indicate[11] – that he is well aware his own journey has a double dimension: individual and collective, as it is implicit in his notion of *species-being;* he also knows, as Dante knew, that descent *ad inferi* is unavoidable, that the way down and the way up are one and the same, that emancipation cannot come without the full knowledge of and rebellion against the hell of industrial capitalism, and thus the reference to Dante's *Inferno*:

> Ed elli a me, come persona accorta:
> 'Qui si convien lasciare ogni sospetto
> Ogni viltà convien che qui sia morta.'
> And he to me, as one who understands:
> 'Here must all fear be left behind;
> Here let all cowardice be dead.']
>
> (Dante, *Inf.* III, vv. 13–15) (Marx 1974: 428)

On the other hand, Marx also knew of the Garden of Epicurus, devoted to the theory and practice of the art of living meaningful and happy lives, at the entrance of which one would read:

> Stranger, here you will do well to tarry; here our highest good is pleasure. The caretaker of that abode, a kindly host, will be ready for you; he will welcome you with bread, and serve you water in abundance, with these words: 'Have you not been well entertained? This garden does not whet your appetite, but quenches it.'
>
> (Epicurus 2012: VII–VIII)

We can indeed 'return' to Epicurus' garden, to the true materialist nature of reality and to the ethics of joy rather than being slaves of the biblical intimation to 'Accumulate', but we must first face the heart of darkness of capital.

From the perspective of an eagle's eye view, Marx's complex and vast *oeuvre* – ranging from philosophy and political theory to historiography and political economy, from journalism to cultural and political polemics and controversies – yields a clear sense of the consistency of its totality, kept together by the centripetal force of his commitment to the emancipation of humanity, whose potential for meaningful existence, now alienated by capitalism, is rooted in the nature of its *species-being*. Marx's notion of *species-being* – crucial, I believe, for the understanding of his worldview and defined by the capacity for agency – has its origin not only in the philosophy of Feuerbach and Aristotle, not to mention the little theorized and barely noticed affinity with evolutionary theory, but also in his doctoral dissertation where he opts for and defends the atomism of Epicurus because of the concept of *swerve* which introduces, in the deterministic world of Democritus, free will as the defining trait of being human.

Without *swerves* no political theory, no philosophy, no science or ethics can make a difference: if we indeed live in a Democritean universe there is no hope! The only possible myth to live by is the myth of Sisyphus, the eternal return of the same. But, as Marx argues in his doctoral dissertation, our mythologies begin with Prometheus' theft of fire and gift to humanity, with an act of rebellion and a technological *swerve* away from, on the one hand, the will of the gods and, on the other, the constraints of nature; it is, to use a literary example, a transition similar to that from the *laws of necessity* or *ananke* that dominate in the *Iliad* to the independence of thought and action of Ulysses in the *Odyssey*.

Prometheus is indeed a proto-humanist who rebels against the gods and the rigid constraints of nature. In this view, Marx's idea of human agency has its origin in the Epicurean notion of the *swerve* from which it grows into *the Economic and Philosophic Manuscripts of 1844's* economic and philosophical analysis of alienation, the *Not-Yet* of the *Manifesto of the Communist Party*, and the theorizing of ideology as false consciousness in the *German Ideology*, which implies by contrast the existence of a universal, non-doctrinaire truth and, finally, to the courageous Dantean descent into the infernal logic of capital. Marx's contribution to the critique of ideology plays a significant historical role in the unmasking of what later will be identified by Nietzsche as the dominant trait of human psychology: self-deception.[12]

From this *katabasis* into hell Marx returns – much as Dante does in Canto 1 of *Purgatory*[13] – 'a riveder le stelle', covered with soot, but armed with the 'scientific' truth of capital and the *Not-Yet* of revolutionary humanism. From this perspective, there is no dualistic opposition or epistemological break between the first writings of Marx and, as Marcello Musto writes in *l'ultimo Marx*.[14]

Ernest Bloch, in *The Principle of Hope*, proposed 'a penetrating distinction between the 'cold currents' and 'warm currents' in Marxism'. The former – writes Razmig Keucheyan in *The Left Hemisphere* – 'conceived Marxism as a positive, "demystifying" science', whose task is to dispassionately 'reveal the "objective" functioning of the social world' of capitalist modernity. Kautsky and Althusser, among others – goes on Keucheyan – 'belong to this group By contrast, the warm currents confide in Utopia and hope and admit the share of subjectivity and even 'belief' involved in Marxism. Benjamin, Marcuse and Goldman belong to this tradition'. Bloch himself represents the warm currents and believes that 'their existence was legitimate', but also that the cold currents 'should place themselves in the service of the warm' (Keucheyan 2014: 217).

Both currents, of course, not only are present in Marx, but indeed their coexistence and equipollence constitute the originality and the enduring quality of Marx's life and works, a coexistence that, for the time being, must be maintained but by emphasizing the need, in the long run, for the warm current to leave behind the cold and turn Marxism into 'absolute' humanism.[15]

3 Coda: forms of rebellion*

> What is a rebel? A man who says no,
> but whose refusal does not imply renunciation.
> He is also a man that says yes, from the
> Moment he makes his first gesture of
> rebellion. A slave who has taken orders all his
> life suddenly decides that he cannot obey some
> new command. What does he mean by saying no?
>
> (Camus 1991: 13)

Thus, begins Camus' *The Rebel* in the search for an understanding of metaphysical and historical forms of rebellion. Metaphysical rebellion – which must precede historical rebellion, as Marx's materialism also requires – ranges from 'the sons of Cain' and 'absolute negation' to the 'absolute affirmation' of Stirner's 'Unique' and Nietzsche's nihilism. The *No* to metaphysics (recall Marx's *No* to the gods embodied in the rebellious figure of Prometheus) leads to historical rebellion and to historical nihilism; however, if properly learned, the lessons of rebellion should lead to 'Thought at the meridian'[16] and beyond nihilism.

Resistance and rebellion are indeed in the nature of our *species-being* and this – even if often tragically so – bodes well for the future of humanity. But, if the long silence of Prometheus must come to an end, what is to be done? The new plague, neoliberal capitalism, is elusive, often hidden, 'invisible' to the eyes of the many, but no less real and 'evil' than the plague of fascism. How must then the silence of Prometheus come to an end? What articulation should the new *No* take? What voices need to speak out? If when Prometheus acts, when people revolt and revolts turn into failed revolutions – and they have always failed to overcome universal alienation in the specific sense of Marxian humanism[17] – must we not then practice Camus' moderation and the patience (or 'slow impatience'[18]) of Magri's (2011) *Tailor of Ulm*? And, as Étienne Balibar suggests, imagine a possible encounter between Lenin and Gandhi (Keucheyan 2014: 252)? Put another way, if revolts and revolutions to emancipate humanity from the universal alienation of capitalism have failed, must we not learn patiently why they have failed, try again and fail better until we get it right?

If in Camus' words 'real generosity towards the future lies in giving all to the present' (Camus 1991: 304), then 'all of us, among the ruins, are preparing a renaissance beyond the limits of nihilism …' (Camus 1991: 305); this *meridian of thought*, he goes on, in the light of the earth 'remains our first and our last love' (Camus 1991: 306), a love and a joy that 'excludes nothing': neither that 'phantom Nietzsche, … continually invoked … as the blasted image of … nihilism' nor 'the prophet of justice without mercy who lies, by mistake, in the unbelievers' plot at Highgate Cemetery; nor the deified mummy of the man of action in his glass coffin;' (Camus 1991: 306). All, concludes Camus, 'may indeed live again, side by side … but on condition that it is understood that they correct one another, and that a limit, under the sun, shall curb them all …' (p. 306). To avoid the fate of Icarus, it must be understood that 'they correct one another' because 'the only definitive crime' is excess (Camus 1991: 28). Nietzsche's nihilism of self-deception must turn into self-overcoming, Marx's justice must have mercy and Lenin must 'return' as a man of action neither deified nor in a glass coffin. The need to end the silence of Prometheus must be tempered by the patience of the *Tailor of Ulm* and the dialectical imagination which reminds us of Cervantes' intimation:

> Too much sanity may be madness –
> and the maddest of all – to see life as it is,
> and not as it ought to be.

Notes

1 See for absolute literature and absolute myth, Calasso (2001).
2 For anti-humanism see Keucheyan (2014: 45–6, 192–3); see also Wolin (1995: 175–209).
3 'No metaphysics, no belief is involved in it for a moment. These are the limits and the only bias of this book' (Camus 2005: 1).
4 Such a rigorous ethic of knowledge, as expressed in *Chance and Necessity*, in particular pages 164–168, is also what distinguishes Marx's commitment to the scientific analysis of the laws of capital, but also to embrace the revolutionary *swerve* of his radical humanism as, for example, theorized in the *Manifesto of the Communist Party*. On the one hand, there is the chance for change introduced by the *swerve*, on the other, the laws of capital.
5 Roberts writes that his argument is twofold:

> First, I contend that, in *Capital*, Marx had a grand aspiration, to write the definitive analysis of what is wrong with the rule of capital, and that he hung this aspiration on a suitably grand literary framework: rewriting Dante's *Inferno* as a descent into the modern 'social Hell' of the capitalist mode of production. Dante, of course, staged his own, individual, salvation story, telling us how his encounter with the evil of the world prepared his soul for its journey to blessedness. But his pilgrim was also supposed to be an Everyman, whose descent into damnation and resurrection into grace might be reiterated by all of the faithful. Marx, on the other hand, cast himself as Virgil for the proletariat, guiding his readers through the lower recesses of the capitalist economic order in order that they might learn not only how this 'infernal machine' works, but also what traps to avoid in their efforts to construct a new world. Second, I argue that in order to understand Marx's attempt to realize this grand aspiration, *Capital* is best read as a critical reconstruction of and rejoinder to the other versions of socialism and popular radicalism that predominated in France and England in the 1860s and 1870s, when Marx was composing his magnum opus....
>
> (Roberts 2017: 1–2)

6 On Marx's use and origin of the concept of *species-being* and alienation, see Marx (1974: 431–2, 347–51, 386–91); see also Leopold (2007: 184–6).
7 Marx's works contain numerous literary and philosophical references, as one would expect from a 'theoretical' humanist. Marx paid a great deal of attention to the stylistic and aesthetic dimension of his writing. See also Hobsbawm (1998: 15) on Marx's aesthetic and literary powers.
8 For a comprehensive summary of *Capital* and its role in Marx's oeuvre as a whole, see Bottomore (1991: 66–8). 'The place of *Capital* – Lawrence Harris writes – in Marx's work as a whole is contested'; nonetheless, from the perspective of humanism, it makes sense to emphasize 'its roots in his earlier work and the continuous development of essentially Hegelian concerns such as Hegel's dialectic and Marx's early concept of alienation' (Bottomore 1991: 67). See also on alienation and capitalism, and the emphasis on continuity from Marx's early works to *Capital*, Marx's account in in the *Grundrisse* and *Capital*, Volumes I and III: Marx (1973: 461–2) and Marx (1996: 1005–6, 1007, 1054, 1056, 164–5); Marx (1981: 959).
9 According to Italo Calvino, to avoid falling into nihilism, we need to 'recognize who and what, in the midst of *inferno*, are not *inferno*, then make them endure, give them space' (Calvino 1974: 165).
10 Marx's equivalent to Dante's *trasumanar* is, I would argue, 'to overcome' and overcoming can only occur through the radical humanism of the *Manifesto of the Communist Party* and the 'scientific' knowledge of the laws of capital. Here are the

verses from *Paradiso Canto I*, vv. 70–72 on *trasumanar:* Trasumanar significar *per verba*/non si poria; però l'essemplo basti/a cui esperienza grazia serba (Words may not tell of that trans-human change;/And therefore let the example serve, though weak,/For those whom grace hath better proof in store).

11 On Marx and Dante, see Prawer (1978: 238–9,420–1).

12 See on this, Nietzsche (2006: XVII-XVIII):

> We are unknown, we knowers, ourselves to ourselves … we have never searched for ourselves – how should it then come to pass, that we should ever find ourselves? … Of necessity we remain strangers to ourselves … in ourselves we are bound to be mistaken….;

according to Robert B. Pippin (2010: XVII), there are 'two issues of central concern for Nietzsche: self-deceit and "self-overcoming", topics that themselves almost require images and metaphors to be stated properly: that one can "hide" from oneself and that one can "overcome" oneself'.

13 Marx (1996) for example, refers also to Purgatory and Paradise (see Roberts 2017 and Prawer 1978).

14 Marx is still interested in and curious about, mathematics and philosophical anthropology. Marx always follows the humanist ethics of knowledge wherever it may take him.

15 An 'absolute' humanism where both science and utopia dialectically coexist.

16 This is a reference to Nietzsche's philosophy.

17 That is to create the necessary economic conditions for realizing the potential of our *species-being.*

18 See Keucheyan (2014: 62) for notion of 'slow impatience'.

References

Bottomore, Tom (ed.) (1991) *A Dictionary of Marxist Thought, Second Edition*, Cambridge: Blackwell.

Buccheri, Mauro (2005) 'The Return of Orpheus or the Persistence of Literature and Myth', in Mauro Buccheri, Elio Costa and Donald Holoch (eds), *The Power of Words: Literature and Society in Late Modernity*, Ravenna: Longo Editore.

Buccheri, Mauro Fahimul, Quadir and Scardellato, Gabriele (eds) (2017) *Towards a Democratic Cosmopolis: Recognition, Citizenship and Diaspora*, Welland: Editions Soleil.

Calasso, Roberto (2001) *Literature and the Gods*, New York: Alfred A. Knopf.

Calvino, Italo (1974) *Invisible Cities*, San Diego, Ca: Harcourt Brace.

Camus, Albert (1991) *The Rebel: An Essay on Man and Revolt*, New York: Vintage Books.

Camus, Albert (2001) *The Plague*, Harmondsworth: Penguiun Books.

Camus, Albert (2005) *The Myth of Sisyphus*, London: Penguin Books.

Cooper, Melinda (2008) *Life as Surplus: Biotechnology and Capitalism in the Neoliberal Era*, Seattle: University of Washington Press.

Epicurus (2012) *The Art of Happiness*, New York: Penguin Books.

Harari, Yuval Noah (2014) *Sapiens: A Brief History of Humankind*, Toronto: McClelland and Stewart.

Harvey, David (2014) *Seventeen Contradictions and the End of Capitalism*, New York: Oxford University Press.

Hobsbawm Eric J. (1998) 'Introduction' in Karl Marx, Friedrich Engels, *The Communist Manifesto. A Modern Edition*, London: Verso, pp. 3–29.

Judt, Tony (2001) 'Introduction', in Albert Camus, *The Plague*, Harmondsworth: Penguiun Books.

Keucheyan, Razmig (2014) *The Left Hemisphere: Mapping Critical Theory Today*, London: Verso.

Leopold, David (2007) *The Young Karl Marx: German Philosophy, Modern Politics, and Human Flourishing*, Cambridge: Cambridge University Press.

Magri, Lucio (2011) *The Tailor of Ulm: Communism in the Twentieth Century*, London: Verso.

Marx, Karl (1973) *Grundrisse: Foundations of the Critique of Political Economy (Rough Draft)*, Harmondsworth: Penguin.

Marx, Karl (1974) *Karl Marx. Early Writings*, London: Penguin Books.

Marx, Karl (1981) *Capital*, Vol. III, London: Penguin.

Marx, Karl (1996) *Capital*, Vol. 1, *in Marx Engels Collected Works*, vol. 35: *Capital, Vol. I*, New York: International Publishers.

Marx, Karl (2006) *First Writings*, Brooklyn, New York: IG Publishing.

Marx, Karl and Engels, Frederich (1998) *The Communist Manifesto, A Modern Edition*, London: Verso.

Miliband, Ralph (1995) *Socialism for a Skeptical Age*, London: Verso.

Monod, Jacques (1971) *Chance and Necessity: An Essay on the Natural Philosophy of Modern Biology*, New York: Alfred A, Knopf.

Musto, Marcello (2016) *L'ultimo Marx: 1881–1883 saggio di biografia intelletuale*, Roma: Donzelli.

Nietzsche, Friedrich (2006) *On the Genealogy of Morals*, New York: Barnes and Noble.

Pippin, Robert B. (2010) *Nietzsche, Psychology, and First Philosophy*, Chicago: University of Chicago Press.

Prawer, S. S. (1978) *Karl Marx and World Literature*, Oxford: Oxford University Press.

Roberts, William Claire (2017) *Marx's Inferno: The Political Theory of Capital*, Princeton, NJ: Princeton University Press.

Wolin, Richard (1995) *Labyrinths: Explorations in the Critical History of Ideas*, Amherst: University of Massachusetts Press.

16 The ambivalence of cooperation

Alfonso M. Iacono

1 The rediscovery of man as a *social animal*

The last decades have witnessed a high praise of individualism – right at the centre of globalization processes – and the rather crude reappearance of the much abused metaphor of the *invisible hand*. Now something seems to have changed. After the euphoria of the 1980s, some of the attention has shifted from a naive (but extremely advantageous for some people) philosophy of the individual, towards the collaborative and cooperative faculties of human beings. In a sense, what has reassumed, if not a central, then at least a peripheral position, is the Aristotelian image of man as *zòon politikón*: that is to say of man as a *social animal*, as Seneca and Thomas Aquinas translated it. Once again, the social element started to be viewed as a constitutive part of the individual's formation from an ethical, political and cognitive perspective. The sociologist Richard Sennett has recently published a research on the cooperative faculties of human beings, which is explicitly influenced by the theories of Amartya Sen and Martha Nussbaum and is significantly entitled *Together*. 'Sen and Nussbaum's views' he writes, 'have been an inspiration for me, and provide the orienting theme for this book: people's capacities for cooperation are far greater and more complex than institutions allow them to be' (Sennett 2012: 29). Basically, what happens in the social system we live in, is that the cooperative capacity of human beings is unable to express itself fully; in particular, it does not ensure the complete realization of the individual's cognitive and emotional abilities. The scenario that emerges from this thesis is, on the one hand, that society does not enhance the cooperative faculties of human beings and, on the other, that these faculties realize themselves through emotional and cognitive capacities and vice versa (in the sense that the latter realize themselves, in their turn, in collaboration and cooperation).

According the psychologist Michael Tomasello and his team, the cooperative faculty is the element which characterizes and distinguishes young children from baby chimpanzees:

> And so, whereas the 'cultures' of other animal species are based almost exclusively on imitation and other exploitive processes, the cultures of

> human beings are based not only on exploitation, but on fundamentally cooperative processes as well. To an unprecedented degree, *homo sapiens* are adapted for acting and thinking cooperatively in cultural groups, and indeed all of humans' most impressive cognitive achievements – from complex technologies to linguistic and mathematical symbols to intricate social institutions – are the products not of individuals acting alone, but of individuals interacting.
>
> (Tomasello 2009: xv–xvi)[1]

A curious but significant aspect of this revival of interest in social and cooperative man is that Senn and Sennett, together with Tomasello and the others, regard Adam Smith as the theoretician of sympathetic feelings and refer to his *Theory of Moral Sentiments*, rather than to the theory of the *invisible hand* (a metaphor which – unintentionally and unbeknown to Smith – was turned into the moral paradise of possessive individualism).

The renewed openness towards social man was also stimulated by the important theory of mirror neurons (I refer, in particular, to the work of Vittorio Gallese)[2] and by Antonio Damasio's theory of conscience and the self (Damasio 2010).

However, the story of man as a *social animal* has some bizarre features: it has been almost two centuries since we started announcing the decline of *homo oeconomicus*; and yet, it has been almost two centuries since this figure kept reappearing in a variety of transformations, overshadowing the image of man as a *social animal. Homo oeconomicus* is much the same as a political party in power: nobody admits to having voted for it, or to having the intention to vote for it, but, in spite of that, it gains a massive majority.

Aristotle's *zòon politikón*[3] – translated by Seneca[4] and Thomas Aquinas[5] as '*sociale animal*' – has recently been reformulated into 'political animal'.[6] Quite a few authors have placed the concept of *zòon politikón* in opposition to modern man: not in the terms of a nostalgic reference to the Greek world, of course, but rather in the sense of a critical comparison pertaining to the current period of time (under this aspect it does not seem inappropriate to see the role of this process as somewhat utopian). But still, notwithstanding Hannah Arendt's observations on the meaning of politics and on the notion of *zòon politikón* in the Greek polis – which are irreducible both to Christian and to modern culture (Arendt 1958: 27–8) – there remains the fact that the modern propensity to separate politics from the other social spheres tends to restrict (in factual, rather than theoretical terms) the domain of politics. This area is restricted to such an extent that it renders ambiguous the translation of *zòon politikón* as 'political animal'; at least as far as the modern utopian role of this image is concerned. This utopian role has found an expression in the criticism which has been directed against economy and politics: two spheres kept (par excellence) separate by our modern Western society. From this point of view, *zòon politikón* can be translated as 'social animal', but only if the meaning assigned to this term implies, on the one hand, a relationship with economy, seen as something more than a simple 'commerce with things', and, on the other hand, a relationship with politics, seen as collective action, and not just as an elitist management of power. As far as the critique of modern economy is concerned, both Karl Marx and Karl Polanyi placed the image of man as 'social animal' in opposition to *homo oeconomicus*; whereas, in regard to the critique of politics, Moses Finley evoked this image as a way of contrasting the reduction of modern democracy to an oligarchic instrument (Finley 1985).[7]

During the 1950s, Karl Polanyi, Conrad M. Arensberg and Harry W. Pearson affirmed that by then the image of the so-called *primitive economic man* was used by just a few scholars. The discoveries made by Comte, Quetelet, Marx, Maine, Weber, Malinowski, Durkheim and Freud 'figure predominantly in the accretion of our current knowledge that the social process is a tissue of relationships between man as biological entity and the unique structure of symbols and techniques that results in maintaining his existence' (Polanyi *et al.* 1957: 239). And yet, almost a century after Marx's condemnation of the Robinsonades of classical political economy and more than 30 years after the publication of Mauss' *The Gift*, that affirmation seemed nevertheless too optimistic. In all probability, the authors themselves were aware of this, since they found it necessary to specify that the traditional conception of economic man – isolated, individualistic, dedicated to the traffic of goods, characterized by a calculating and utilitarian reasoning – was far from being surmounted:

> At important junctures we fall back on the earlier rationalizations of man as a utilitarian atom. And nowhere is this lapse more apparent than in our ideas concerning the economy. Approaching the economy in any of its widely varied aspects, the social scientist is still hampered by an intellectual heritage of man as an entity with an innate propensity to truck, barter and exchange one thing for another. This remains so in spite of all the protestations against 'economic man' and the intermittent attempts to provide a social framework for the economy.
>
> (Polanyi *et al.* 1957: 239)

In 1972 the anthropologist Marshall Sahlins argued that:

> Endemic to the science of Economics for over a century, the formalist-substantivist debate seems nevertheless lacking in history, for nothing much seems to have changed since Karl Marx defined the fundamental issues in contraposition to Adam Smith (cf. Althusser *et al.*, 1966, Vol. 2). Still, the latest incarnation in the form of anthropology has shifted the emphasis of discussion. If the problem in the beginning was the *naive anthropology* of Economics, today it is the *naive economics* of Anthropology.
>
> (Sahlins 1972: xi)

Sahlins shows the limits of the naive economics of anthropology and shifts the focus of theoretical assessment from the study of the need-serving activities of individuals to the vital, material and symbolic processes of society. From this point of view, *economy* ceases to be a category of behaviour and becomes, instead, a category of culture, 'in a class with politics or religion rather than rationality or prudence' (Sahlins 1972: xii).

In 1986 the anthropologist Mary Douglas felt the need to criticize the image of the egoistical, utilitarian and calculating individual:

> Yet, when it comes to the detailed analysis, the theory of individual rational choice finds nothing but difficulties in the notion of collective behavior. It is axiomatic for the theory that rational behavior is based on self-regarding motives. The individual calculates what is in his best interest and acts accordingly. This is the basis of the theory on which economic analysis and political theory are based, and yet we get the contrary impression. Our intuition is that individuals do contribute to the public good generously, even unhesitatingly, without obvious self-serving. Whittling down the meaning of self-serving behavior until every possible disinterested motive is included merely makes the theory vacuous.
>
> (Douglas 1986: 9)

But, notwithstanding the criticism levelled against the isolated, atomized, utilitarian and calculating individual, this image has continued to reflect the common prevailing sense of what is usually considered to be man's abstractly typical behaviour in society. And indeed, the recurrent need to criticize that image is a clear sign of its persistence.

What's more, the theories of anthropologists such as Marshall Sahlins and Mary Douglas enjoyed – at least during the 1980s – a circulation which went beyond the sphere of anthropological competences and studies. But this is no longer so today. In all probability, the spread and reinforcement of the so-called globalization can be said to have marked the end of an era which began in 1955 with the publication of Lévi-Strauss's *Tristes Tropiques*. Now we have moved into a new one, which attempts to deal with global homologation and local diversification: the last two consequences of a historical process which was already adumbrated in the masterpiece of Lévi-Strauss.

The origins of the image of the isolated, atomized, utilitarian and egoistic individual – an image which enjoyed a great success in the past and continues to be quite popular today, even though in a slightly disguised form – can be traced back to the well known Robinson Crusoe. But it was Adam Smith's particular version of this character that marked the distinctive traits of the 'naive economics of anthropology' analysed by Sahlins. Unlike Daniel Defoe's Robinson, the individual delineated by Adam Smith is not isolated on a desert island. He lives his life among other people and depends on them:

> In civilized society he stands at all times in need of the cooperation and assistance of great multitudes, while his whole life is scarce sufficient to gain the friendship of a few persons. In almost every other race of animals

> each individual, when it is grown up to maturity, is intirely independent, and in its natural state has occasion for the assistance of no other living creature. But man has almost constant occasion for the help of his brethren, and it is in vain for him to expect it from their benevolence only. He will be more likely to prevail if he can interest their self-love in his favour, and shew them that it is for their own advantage to do for him what he requires of them.
>
> (Smith 1976: 26)

This human being, who lives his life in isolation among other people, who needs their cooperation but cannot expect any solidarity from them, seems the anthropological and social result of the tendency to truck, barter and exchange:

> But without the disposition to truck, barter, and exchange, every man must have procured to himself every necessary and conveniency of life which he wanted. All must have had the same duties to perform, and the same work to do, and there could have been no such difference of employment as could alone give occasion to any great difference of talents.
>
> (Smith 1976: 29)

Cooperation, as Adam Smith saw it in his *Wealth of Nations*, is a system of reciprocal dependence between people, rationalized by the division of labour and, above all, completely independent from what Michael Tomasello called *shared intentionality* (Tomasello and Carpenter 2007).

Isolation, egoism, cooperation without solidarity, strategies used for gaining advantages from the egoism and the interests of others, utilitarian rationality: these are the characteristics which emerge from the image of Adam Smith's *economic man* (and which are quite different from the picture built up in his *Theory of Moral Sentiments*).

2 Karl Marx and Karl Polanyi

Both Karl Marx and Karl Polanyi juxtaposed this image with the Aristotelian idea of man as a 'social animal'. In the context of the critique of a utilitarian social vision, the sense of this contraposition can be analysed from two perspectives. The first one concerns the link between historical construction and universality. The second regards the relationships that human beings forge with one another within the cooperative and social systems.

Marx refers to the Aristotelian concept of man as a 'social animal' in at least three occasions: in the 1857 *Introduction* (Marx 1993: 84), in his *Forms which precede capitalist production* (Marx 1993: 496) and in Volume I of *Capital* (Marx 1993: 444). In the first of these writings, the Aristotelian image of man as a 'social animal' is directly placed in opposition to Adam Smith's 'individual and isolated hunter and fisherman'. Marx affirms that the point of departure of his analysis is provided by individuals producing in society. On the basis of this methodological assumption he criticizes Adam Smith and David Ricardo for using the image of a single individual (the *primitive economic man*) as the starting point from which to develop their deductions about society's structure, interconnections and internal divisions. According to Marx, Adam Smith's and David Ricardo's reasoning constitutes a form of anticipation: they project into the past the image of a 'primitive economic man', who has all the characteristics of the modern middle-class individual.

The idea according to which the modern middle-class individual turns into a *primitive economic man* depends on the fact that his history begins to unfold from a unilateral characteristic: that is, his supposed propensity to barter and trade. This permanent and ahistorical characteristic presents itself as his natural condition and, consequently, as a universal anthropological condition regarding all human beings in every epoch, ever since the beginning of history. Once this characteristic is taken as natural and assumed to be universal, the *primitive economic man* starts representing the first step of a socio-historical development, which teleologically leads us to the modern middle-class individual. There is, then, a kind of circular movement by which the *primitive economic man* is secretly deduced from the modern middle-class individual. This underdeveloped modern economic man is the starting point of a linear and progressive history which, however, leads us to the effective point of departure: that is, once again, modern economic man.

Marx contrasts this view (which is endorsed by Adam Smith and David Ricardo) with the Aristotelian image of man as a 'social animal':

> The more deeply we go back into history, the more does the individual, and hence also the producing individual, appear as dependent, as belonging to a greater whole: in a still quite natural way in the family and in the family expanded into the clan [*Stamm*]; then later in the various forms of communal society arising out of the antitheses and fusions of the clans. Only in the eighteenth century, in 'civil society', do the various forms of social connectedness confront the individual as a mere means towards his private purposes, as external necessity. But the epoch which produces this standpoint, that of the isolated individual, is also precisely that of the hitherto most developed social (from this standpoint, general) relations. The human being is in the most literal sense a *Zòon politikon* not merely a gregarious animal, but an animal which can individuate itself only in the midst of society.
>
> (Marx 1993: 84)

Yet, in addition to Marx's critique of the historical, teleological and universalistic elements concealed in Adam Smith's *primitive economic man*, a further question has to be taken into consideration: namely, the role played by individuals within social and cooperative systems. The historical scheme proposed by Marx in opposition to Adam Smith's shows the same antagonism that, at a later time, will inform Ferdinand Tönnies's concepts of *community* and *society* (Tönnies 1957).In the picture presented by Marx, modern society appears as an instrument for reaching the individual's personal ends and, as such, clashes with them. His reference to Aristotle serves to underline the fact that – notwithstanding the clash between society and individuals, and in spite of the individual's tendency to see society as an 'external necessity' – human beings never cease to be social animals in the Aristotelian sense (although they might forget this). Consequently, they are cooperative beings, but in a different sense from that employed by Adam Smith. Using contemporary terns, we might say that Marx is favourably disposed towards a system of *shared intentionality*, rather than towards unintentional cooperation, a system where everybody does his best for the others and depends on them in an unconscious and egoistical way. Behind a market system *whose invisible hand* settles things up, so to say, in an automatic way by using a cybernetic approach based on *feedback* (this, for example, is the idea put forward by von Hayek), Marx (and Polanyi with him) recognizes the despotic traits of a cooperatively organized factory: a system characterized by an intentionality which is neither shared nor voluntary, but imposed.

Marx directs his attention mainly to those particular social relations which he calls relations of production and which, as is well-known, play a general role in his theory. In this context, his description of the opposition between society and individuals contains, as in a dark mirror, the opposition between community and labourers. He emphasizes this point precisely in the passage (contained in *Forms which precede capitalist production*) where he refers to the Aristotelian *zòon politikón* and where he affirms that man isolates himself only through the process of history:

> Exchange itself is a chief means of this individuation [*Vereinzelung*]. It makes the herd-like existence superfluous and dissolves it. Soon the matter [has] turned in such a way that as an individual he relates himself only to himself, while the means with which he posits himself as individual have become the making of his generality and commonness. In this community, the objective being of the individual as proprietor, say proprietor of land, is presupposed, and presupposed moreover; under certain conditions which chain him to the community, or rather form a link in his chain. In bourgeois society, the worker e.g. stands there purely without objectivity, subjectively; but the thing which *stands opposite* him has now become the *true community* [*Gemeinwesen*], which he tries to make a meal of, and which makes a meal of him.
>
> (Marx 1973: 433–4)

In a situation where society is conceived as a tool for the achievement of private ends, community becomes something that transforms workers into instruments. In the process of production the relationship is overturned. This aspect is particularly emphasized in a further passage where Marx refers once again to the notion of *zòon politikón*: that is to say, in his discussion of cooperation in Volume I of *Capital*. What is foregrounded here is the effect produced by the fusion of many individual forces into a single overall force: cooperation seems to work according to the modalities of a system where the whole is more than the sum of the parts, because it ensures that a certain number of people, who work together, are able to produce much more than the same number of people working in isolation. 'This originates from the fact that man, if not as Aristotle thought a political animal,[8] is at all eveynts a social animal' (Marx 1990: 444). Here, Marx introduces a theoretical change in the image created by Aristotle: the sociability, which man possesses by nature, is not determined by the city but, rather, by a cooperative faculty developed earlier, before the creation of a city system. However, in Marx's interpretation, the relationships people establish with one another within cooperative and social systems are reduced to labour relations of production. As a consequence, the aspects connected with – as Marx would put it – the *superstructure*, are underestimated. Besides being determined, the superstructure determines – through its collective forms – the motivations and the productive actions of the individual. Mimetic abilities, symbolic activities, forms of communication, emotions: all these elements contribute to the composite meaning of human cooperation.

Polanyi, too, juxtaposes the Aristotelian image of man as a 'social animal' to Adam Smith's idea of the *primitive economic man*. In the essay entitled 'Our Obsolete Market Mentality' he highlights the fact that the birth of laissez faire administered a shock to 'civilized' man's views of himself and argues – implicitly echoing Marx – that liberal economy was a violent break with the conditions that preceded it. He then affirms that:

> This new world of 'economic motives' was based on a fallacy. Intrinsically, hunger and gain are no more 'economic' than love or hate, pride or prejudice. No human motive is per se economic. There is no such thing as a *sui generis* economic experience in the sense in which man may have a religious, aesthetic, or sexual experience. These latter give rise to motives that broadly aim at evoking similar experiences. In regard to material production these terms lack self-evident meaning.
>
> (Polanyi 1947: 111)

By underlining the fact that it is not possible to undergo an economic experience in the same way that we undergo a religious, aesthetic or sexual one, Polanyi addresses a problem which Durkheim, among others, had already approached and examined, but in a more complex way. The relationship with production and economy depends always on social forms of solidarity, reciprocity and cooperation. In their turn, these forms are by no means generated by immediate productive or economic needs. Polanyi makes good use of a series of reflections and researches, which tended to see the sociability of the human being as a determining characteristic of its biological nature:

> The economic factor, which underlies all social life, no more gives rise to definite incentives than the equally universal law of gravitation. Assuredly, if we do not eat, we must perish, as much as if we were crushed under the weight of a falling rock. But the pangs of hunger are not automatically translated into an incentive to produce. Production is not an individual, but a collective affair. If an individual is hungry, there is nothing definite for him to do. Made desperate, he might rob or steal, but such an action can hardly be called productive. With man, the political animal, everything is given not by natural, but by social circumstance.
>
> (Polanyi 1947: 111)

Analogously to Marx, Polanyi underlines the fact that production is not an individual, but a collective act. Nevertheless, their viewpoints diverge on some issues. In all likelihood, Marx would have endorsed Polanyi's idea that with man everything is given by social (and not by natural) circumstances. Yet, in his view, social circumstances tend to translate themselves into historical ones, where communities tend to organize their work in a cooperative and antagonistic way. For Polanyi, however, things are somewhat different. On the one hand, he lays emphasis on the non-economic, psychological, traits of social activities; on the other, he stresses the breach brought about by market society. In this way he gives prominence to a feature which was already latent in Marx: the exceptionality of this system as compared with previous ones. This exceptionality is explained in the following terms: 'Instead of the economic system being embedded in social relationships, these relationships were now embedded in the economic system'(Polanyi 1947: 114). Nevertheless, the change in the relationship between economy and society is not so radical as to induce people to act only when motivated by economic or productive incentives. This is the reason why Polanyi evokes the Aristotelian concept of man as a 'social animal' and joins Malinowski, Thurnwald and Mauss in their critique of the fallacious eighteenth-century image of the *primitive economic man*.

> The semblance is compelling that hunger and gain are *the* incentives on which any economic system must rest. This assumption is baseless. Ranging over human societies, we find hunger and gain not appealed to as incentives to production, and where so appealed to, they are fused with other powerful motives. Aristotle was right: man is not an economic, but a social being. He does not aim at safeguarding his individual interest in the acquisition of material possessions, but rather at ensuring social good-will, social status, social assets. He values possessions primarily as a means to that end. His incentives are of that 'mixed' character which we associate with the endeavor to gain social approval – productive efforts are no more that incidental to this.
>
> (Polanyi 1947: 112)

As a rule, says Polanyi, man's economy is submerged in his social relations. But the capitalist system breaks this rule. This leads to a far-reaching consequence: when, on the contrary, society is submerged in the economic system, human beings feel the need to produce – institutionally and culturally – organized and symbolic forms of collective identity (Polanyi 1947: 112).[9] This need is dictated by the destructive power of market laws.

> To separate labor from other activities of life and to subject it to the laws of the market was to annihilate all organic forms of existence and to replace them by a different type of organization, an atomistic and individualistic one. Such a scheme of destruction was best served by the application of the principle of freedom of contract. In practice this meant that the non contractual organizations of kinship, neighborhood, profession, and creed were to be liquidated since they claimed the allegiance of the individual and thus restrained his freedom.
>
> (Polanyi 1957: 171)

Therefore, the market has to destroy the communal systems of the individuals in order to obtain labour. As the historian E.P. Thomspon showed in his classic paper *Time, Work-Discipline, and Industrial Capitalism*, the relationship between these elements is based on the destruction of the labourers' culture of origin (Thompson 1967). Yet, the process that leads to the destruction of modern man's sociability, in favor of his economic traits, cannot be absolute: there will always remain – or will always be created anew by the individuals – some communal forms of collective, often antagonistic, identities. What emerges, according to Polanyi, in market societies, is a condition of separateness between the community and the individual: it affects the economic field and, as a consequence, the labourer becomes available on the marketplace.

> It is the absence of the threat of individual starvation which makes primitive society, in a sense, more humane than market economy, and at the same time less economic. Ironically, the white man's initial contribution to the black man's world mainly consisted in introducing him to the uses of the scourge of hunger. Thus, the colonists may decide to cut the breadfruit trees down in order to create an artificial food scarcity or may impose a hut tax on the native to force him to barter away his labour.
>
> (Thompson 1967: 172)

This is precisely where the paradox of the marketplace arises: the market imposes its freedom by destroying the economic and social life forms of non-market societies.

The Aristotelian image of man as a 'social animal' is used by Polanyi with the aim of highlighting – by way of contrast – the exceptionality of the modern market society's condition and of its *primitive economic* (invented in the eighteenth century) *man*.

It is a society in which social relationships tend to be embedded into economic ones. If we think about the construction of the historical order in which human beings build up their relationships, we will see that this condition of exceptionality entails, on the one hand, the assertion of historical discontinuity, at least between the capitalist system and the social forms which preceded it. On the other hand, it negates the historical universality (on whose shoulders stands the image the eighteenth-century individual) of cooperative and social relations based fundamentally on egoistic and utilitarian interests. This negation is connected to the general idea of the irreducibility of social individuals to their economic and instrumental behavior and motives.

3 Mary Douglas, cooperation and collectivity

In her study *How Institutions Think* the anthropologist Mary Douglas affirms that 'when it comes to the detailed analysis, the theory of individual rational choice finds nothing but difficulties in the notion of collective behavior' (Douglas 1986: 9). She delves into the question of collective behaviour and argues that it is not possible to speak of society as a whole if people do not share any thoughts or feelings or, more specifically, if their categories of thinking are utterly different from one another. This is the point where the theory of the rational choice shows its limits:

> Not just any busload or haphazard crowd of people deserves the name of society: there has to be some thinking and feeling alike among members. But this is not to say that a corporate group possesses attitudes of its own. If it possesses anything, it is because of the legal theory that endows it with fictive personality. Yet, legal existence is not enough. Legal presumptions do not attribute emotional bias to corporations. Just because it is legally constituted, a group cannot be said to 'behave' – still less to think or feel. If this is literally true, it is implicitly denied by much of social thought. Marxist theory assumes that a social class can perceive, choose, and act upon its own group interests. Democratic theory is based on the idea of the collective will. Yet, when it comes to the detailed analysis, the theory of individual rational choice finds nothing but difficulties in the notion of collective behavior. It is axiomatic for the theory that rational behavior is based on self-regarding motives. The individual calculates what is in his best interest and acts accordingly. This is the basis of the theory on which economic analysis and political theory are based, and yet we get the contrary impression. Our intuition is that individuals do contribute to the public good generously, even unhesitatingly, without obvious self-serving. Whittling down the meaning of self-serving behavior until every possible disinterested motive is included merely makes the theory vacuous.
>
> (Douglas 1986: 9)

The idea that collective behaviour cannot easily be framed within a utilitarian conception of society as composed of adult, calculating and egoistical individuals (whose rationality makes them act according to these qualities) has been explored, through different angles of approach, by Tocqueville, Marx, Durkheim and Polanyi, to quote just a few.

> After the birth of a human being his early years are obscurely spent in the toils or pleasures of childhood. As he grows up the world receives him, when his manhood begins, and he enters into contact with his fellows. He is then studied for the first time, and it is imagined that the germ of the vices and the virtues of his maturer years is then formed. This, if I am not mistaken, is a great error. We must begin higher up; we must watch the infant in its mother's arms; we must see the first images which the external world casts upon the dark mirror of his mind; the first occurrences which he witnesses; we must hear the first words which awaken the sleeping powers of thought, and stand by his earliest efforts, if we would understand the prejudices, the habits, and the passions which will rule his life. The entire man is, so to speak, to be seen in the cradle of the child.
>
> (Tocqueville 1839, vol. I, ch. 2: 23–4)

What lurks behind these deterministic considerations is the fundamental idea that the individual is formed through the interaction with his/her family: family ties contribute to shape the communion of thought categories, habits and passions which, right from the start, place the individual within society. Approaching the question from another perspective, Marx strongly criticized classical economic theory and its focus on isolated individuals. In fact, the Aristotelian concept of *zòon politikón* substantiates his view that social relationships presuppose the formation of the individual, and that the idea of an isolated individual is closely intertwined with the development of social relationships: the more these relationships are developed, the more the idea of an isolated individual emerges with ever increasing clarity.

However, the modern revival of Aristotle's *zòon politikón* poses a significant question: what is the place of passion, of habits, of shared thought-categories, of collective representations and of symbolic exchange in a world characterized by the separation and the autonomization of the economic and the political spheres; a world ruled by a rationality which allows the relationship between man and things to prevail over the relationship between man and society? In short, what is the place of all those elements which transform a social system into a whole with an identity of its own?

If we take as our starting point the issue of the social origin of cognitive processes and use it as a basis for understanding the concepts of cooperation and solidarity, we will be able to foreground the following considerations:

a The theories which support the thesis of the individual's rational choice take into account only adult, abstract individuals, who act intentionally and whose action is driven by interest and calculation. However, notwithstanding the separateness of the spheres of human action, concrete individuals inhabit many different emotional and cognitive dimensions;

b The analysis of organized groups has necessarily to take into account the emotional orientation and the social processes, which preside over the formation and building of knowledge;

c The individuals act and acquire knowledge within contexts where communication has a specific significance. This presupposes systems of interaction;

d The social origin of knowledge is also grounded in affective experiences. So, cooperation presides over the construction of perception and knowledge from the very first interaction phases between adults and children.

4 The ambivalence of cooperation

Cooperation, as a faculty of the human species, is therefore quite ambiguous: it oscillates between two poles: on the one hand, living together in an organized way sets the individual capacities free; on the other hand, these capacities are oppressed by the despotic dominance of the people who are in charge of the cooperative organization. The power that bears within itself the seeds of cooperation and enables human beings to develop their humanity, is the very same power that can become a curse. The ambivalence of cooperation can easily be observed in three different human activities: music, war and work. An orchestra, an army and a workforce represent three kinds of cooperation. Musicians playing together in an orchestra, working together in an organized way – that is to say, by dividing their tasks and displaying different abilities – aim at preserving the musical unity of an artistic composition. A more or less analogous organization can be found in the army, where soldiers aim at exercising their strength and inflicting an arguably legitimate violence. What factory workers aim to achieve by working together is the production of goods. These examples show three different forms of planned cooperation: the individual ability of human beings to stay together is interlaced with a planned organization of this staying together. Therefore, the person who manages the organization and the planning is the one who holds overall power.

As we have already seen, Karl Polanyi and Mary Douglas foregrounded the fact that the utilitarian conception of society – focused on adult, calculating and egoistical individuals, whose rationality makes them act according to these qualities – is unable to account for collective behaviour. Collective behaviour – and collaboration is certainly part if it – eludes this conception. 'This power arises from co-operation in a planned way with others, he strips off the fetters of his individuality, and develops the capabilities of his species' (Marx 1990: 447). And yet, when considering the capitalist mode of production, this very same cooperative capability on the contrary becomes a systematic means of exploitation; it tends to remove individual faculties and to transfer them to the instruments of labour. Mechanicalism – the most complex aspect of capitalist cooperation – is a perfect example of this.

Quoting Destutt de Tracy, Marx defines cooperation as a '*concours de forces*' (Marx 1990: 443) and, referring to military discipline and organization, sees it as a collective power, which is far greater than the sum of the individual forces taken separately.[10] Here, he refers to Gian Rinaldo Carli, who argues that

> the strength of the individual man is very small, but the union of a number of very small forces produces a collective force which is greater than the sum of all the partial forces, so that merely by being joined together these forces can reduce the time required, and extend the field of their action.
>
> (Carli 1804 in Verri 1804: 196)

The ambivalence of cooperation is clearly stated in this passage: on the one hand, it is a faculty which enhances individual abilities, while on the other – as Michel Foucault will show – it can serve as a tool of discipline, surveillance and power:

> Modern industry never views or treats the existing form of a production process as the definitive one. Its technical basis is there- fore revolutionary, whereas all earlier modes of production were essentially conservative.29 By means of machinery, chemical pro- cesses and other methods, it is continually transforming not only the technical basis of production but also the functions of the worker and the social combinations of the labour process. At the same time, it thereby also revolutionizes the division of labour within society, and incessantly throws masses of capital and of workers from one branch of production to another. Thus large- scale industry, by its very nature, necessitates variation of labour, fluidity of functions, and mobility of the worker in all directions. But on the other hand, in its capitalist form it reproduces the old division of labour with its ossified particularities. We have seen how this absolute contradiction* does away with all repose, all fixity and all security as far as the worker's life-situation is concerned; how it constantly threatens, by taking away the instruments of labour, to snatch from his hands the means of subsistence, 3 0 and, by suppressing his specialized function, to make him superfluous. We have seen, too, how this contradiction bursts forth without restraint in the ceaseless human sacrifices required from the working class, in the reckless squandering of labour-powers, and in the devastating effects of social anarchy.
>
> (Marx 1990: 617–18)

In their evolution towards automation and towards the new information and communication technologies, the machines influence human activities and relations and perform a continuous and revolutionary process of substitution: on the one hand, this process provides human beings with a glimpse of the possibility of having more free time and being able to avoid boring and physically exhausting work; on the other hand, this process dramatically results in the expulsion of labourers and in unemployment. In fact, the disastrous levels of unemployment that we have in the world today rank among the highest ever recorded. The price we pay for our social system is a disarmed and, consequently, dangerous permeability to the demands of the marketplace: a marketplace where things become substitutes for human beings and human beings are slowly turned into things.

What Marx sees as a specific ability of the human species – that is to say, cooperation as a capacity which favours the development of the individual's social character – constitutes, at the same time, the fundamental form of the capitalist mode of production, which removes individual faculties and exploits labour-power. So, our life is made up of the contradiction between our social and cooperative abilities and various forms of control and exploitation of these very same abilities.

5 The flexible human being becomes temporary

What we are witnessing today is a growing clash between 'a new cosmopolitan elite of 'symbolic analysts' who control the technologies and the forces of production, and the growing numbers of permanently displaced workers who have little hope and even fewer prospects for meaningful employment in the new high-tech global economy' (Rifkin 1995: xvii)

In the 1980s, when globalization discourse first emerged, people started to witness the dissemination of a specific worldview, which was later to become the dominant one. In this worldview, there was room for the lowering of wages, for the reappearance of disguised forms of slavery, for the dislocation of production sites to far-away corners of the earth, for wars fought in the name of humanity, for the omnipotence and idolization of the so-called managers, for bank speculations, for the weakening of moral values in the name of efficiency and realism, for the savage privatization of public spaces, for the end of social responsibilities.

There was also room for the concept of temporary employment: what once was just an unpleasant transitional phase of our existence, silently turned into a permanent condition. The idea of temporariness – seen as a permanent feature of work assignments – was, de facto, pushed forward by aggressive right-wing policies. Wan looking and by now ineffectual left-wing parties – ashamed of themselves and looking for servile entrepreneurial acknowledgements – de facto accepted this idea and called it *flexibility*. But what does flexibility really mean? Theoretically, it is a wonderful thing: you can change your job; you do not feel imprisoned in the repetitiveness of everyday routine and behaviour; you are unhampered by a permanent full-time employment, which conditions your whole life; you are completely free to choose. Is this not a marvellous world? After all, Adam Smith – as the father of political economy – had argued as early as in the eighteenth century that the repetitiveness of factory work killed the intelligence of the labourers.

In practical terms, the tale of flexibility reminds us of the adventures of Pinocchio and Lucignolo in the Land of No School (also translated in English as 'The Land of Toys'). The famous puppet thought he was going to have fun and turned into a donkey instead. The donkeyish side of *flexibility* is *temporariness*. You have to change your work according to the market fluctuations; your whole life is conditioned by the lack of a permanent job; you have no freedom of choice. Temporariness not only creates and fuels the sense of uncertainty about the future and about work assignments, but it also tends, on the long run, to hurt and bend people's dignity and self-respect: people are so exposed to blackmail that they see their independence vanish and lose their will to fight. The real problem lies in the fact that temporariness is not just a momentary condition anymore: it has become, as I have already said, a permanent condition of life in a world where there is neither room for collective values, nor for hope in the future, or for the anger stirred up by a present which offends our dignity and our pride. Our critical sense stays hidden in the privacy of our thoughts, but eventually it slowly dissolves in a mediatically induced self-deception: we oscillate between a feeling of false euphoria – produced by the advertisements of a non-existent world – and the show of corruption, immorality and egoism that we witness every day on TV. We watch this show in silence, as through a keyhole, staying sheltered from the hazards of the outside world. The growth of inequalities and the successful rhetoric of temporariness represent the other side of cooperation: on this side, the defining faculty of the human species, the faculty that distinguishes humans from chimpanzees – our close relatives in the evolutionary ladder – becomes the most efficient tool through which human beings can exploit other human beings.

This process has spread to every part of the world and continues to have profound consequences: it has stirred up an intense hatred towards power and politics; it has led to the loss of independence and self-esteem, because people are forced, despite themselves, to crawl and beg in the hope of gaining favours. Subjection is a strange antipolitical blend of acquiescence, conniving consent and hatred. This situation is aggravated by temporariness. Let us call things by their correct names, without hypocrisies. Temporariness is a slavery condition which has been shamefully confused with flexibility: a typical privilege of people who have a permanent job. It can be alleviated only if we are able to see in it future work possibilities, only if we are able to envisage a solid future of stability. But the fact is that nobody seems to care about this nowadays. There is so much arrogance in the idea that a permanent job is monotonous! And yet, only people who have a permanent job can display this arrogance. For some years I worked as a temporary employee, but ever since I took a permanent teaching position I have enjoyed the boring monotony of my job. Sometimes I look for changes and introduce variations, but this search is a luxury I can afford. Change is attractive only if it is freely chosen. Being forced to undergo change, out of necessity, is, to say the least, discouraging. Flexibility implies a choice; temporariness entails compulsion. Moreover, temporariness hinders and slows down the process of emancipation from the family: although the family remains the only rescue, the only emotional and economic shelter available, it can easily turn into a prison where time seems to have stopped. But time passes inexorably. To stay young in old age was seen, in the past, as an illusory privilege of rich and well-to-do people. Now, this privilege is democratically spreading to the masses (the Western ones, I mean). To be a temporary worker and have grey hair is like serving a sentence.

Translated from the Italian by Victoria Tchernikova and Sylvia Greenup

Notes

1 See also Tomasello (2014), Rilling *et al.* (2002), Tomasello and Vaish (2013).

2 See Gallese (2001, 2013, 2014), Wojciehowski and Gallese (2011).

3 Aristotle, *Politics*, I.2, 1253a 2–3; *Nicomachean Ethics*, 9.9. 1169b 20.

4 Seneca, *De Beneficiis*, 7.1.

5 Thomas Aquinas, *Summa Theologica*, Prima Pars, q. 96, a. 4.

6 On the misunderstanding inherent in the translation of 'politikon' as 'socialis see Arendt (1958: 23).

7 Polanyi's and Finley's reading of Aristotle is at the centre of the essay by Veca (2011).

8 See Jean-Pierre Vernant on the difference between Greek and modern reason: according to Vernant, the former was the product of 'relations of human beings with one another', whereas the latter 'the product of human commerce with things' (Vernant 1982: 132). The primacy of the relationship between 'man and object' over the relationship between 'man and society' is analysed in Dumont (1976).

9 On the question of collective identity see Hobsbawm and Ranger (1983), Balibar and Wallerstein (1991), Anderson (1983), Bhabha (1990), Testi (2010).

10

> Just as the offensive power of a squadron of cavalry, or the defensive power of an infantry regiment, is essentially different from the sum of the offensive or defensive powers of the individual soldiers taken separately, so the sum total of the mechanical forces exerted by isolated workers differs from the social force that is developed, when many hands co-operate in the same undivided operation, such as raising a heavy weight, turning a winch, or removing an obstacle.
> (Marx 1990: 443)

References

Anderson, Benedict (1983) *Imagined Communities*, London: Verso.

Arendt, Hannah (1958) *The Human Condition*, Chicago: The University of Chicago Press.

Balibar, Etienne and Wallerstein, Immanuel M. (1991 [1988]) *Race, Nation, Class: Ambiguous Identities*, London: Verso.

Bhabha, Homi K. (ed.) (1990) *Nation and Narration*, London and New York: Routledge.

Damasio, Antonio (2010) *The Self Comes to Mind*, New York: Pantheon Books.

Douglas, Mary (1986) *How Institutions Think*, Syracuse, NY: Syracuse University Press, 1986.

Dumont, Louis (1976) *Homo Aequalis*, Paris: Gallimard.

Finley, Moses (1985 [1973]) *Democracy Ancient and Modern*, New Brunswick, NJ: Rutgers University Press, 1985.

Gallese, Vittorio (2001) 'The 'Shared Manifold' Hypothesis. From Mirror Neurons To Empathy', in *Journal of Consciousness Studies*, vol. 8, no. 5–7: 33–50.

Gallese, Vittorio (2013) 'Corpo non mente. Le neuroscienze cognitive e la genesi di soggettività ed intersoggettività', in *Educazione Sentimentale*, no. 20: 8–24.

Gallese, Vittorio (2014) 'Bodily Selves in Relation: Embodied Simulation as Second-person Perspective on Intersubjectivity', in *Philosophical Transition of Royal Society*, vol. 369, no. 1644: 42–5.

Wojciehowski, H. and Gallese, V. (2011) 'How Stories Make Us Feel: Toward an Embodied Narratology', in *California Italian Studies*, vol. 2, no. 2.

Hobsbawm, Eric and Ranger, Terence (1983) *The Invention of Tradition*, New York: Cambridge University Press.

Marx Karl, (1993) *Grundrisse Foundations of the Critique of Political Economy* (Rough Draft) , Penguin Books, London..

Marx Karl, (1990) A Critique of Political Economy Volume One, Penguin Books, London.

Polanyi, Karl (1947) 'Our Obsolete Market Economy: 'Civilization Must Find a New Thought Pattern'', in *Commentary*, vol. 3, pp. 109–17.

Polanyi, Karl (1957 [1944]) *The Great Transformation*, Boston: Beacon Press.

Polanyi, Karl, Arensberg, Conrad M., and Pearson, Harry W. (1957) 'The Place of Economics in Societies', in *Trade and Market in the Early Empires, Economies in History and Theory*, Glencoe, IL: The Free Press, pp. 239–42.

Rifkin, Jeremy (1995) *The End of Work: the Decline of the Global Labor Force and the Dawn of the Post-market Era*, New York: Jeremy P. Tarcher and Putnam.

Rilling James K., Gutman, David A, Zeh, Thorsten R., Pagnoni, Giuseppe and Berns, Gregory S. (2002) 'A Neural Basis for Social Cooperation', *Neuron*, vol. 35: 395–405.

Sahlins, Marshall (1972) *Stone Age Economics*, Chicago: Aldine-Atherton.

Sennett, Richard (2012) *Together. The Rituals Pleasures and Politics of Cooperation*, New Haven, CT and London: Yale University Press.

Smith, Adam (1976 [1776]) *An Inquiry into the Nature and Causes of the Wealth of Nations*, ed. by R.H. Campbell and A.S. Skinner, vol. 1, Indianapolis: Liberty Classics, Oxford University Press.

Testi, Arnaldo (2010) *Capture the Flag. The Stars and Stripes in American History,* New York, New York University Press.

Thompson, E.P. (1967) 'Time, Work-Discipline, and Industrial Capitalism', in *Past & Present*, no. 38: 56–97.

Tocqueville, Alexis de (1839) *Democracy in America*, New York: George Adlard.

Tomasello, Michael (2009) *Why We Cooperate*, Cambridge, MA: The MIT Press.

Tomasello, Michael (2014) *Natural History of Human Thinking*, Cambridge, MA: Harvard University Press.

Tomasello, Michael and Carpenter, Malinda (2007) 'Shared Intentionality', in *Developmental Science*, vol. 10, no. 1: 121–5.

Tomasello, Michael and Vaish, Amrisha (2013) 'Cooperation and Morality', in *Annual Review of Psychology*, no. 64: 231–55.

Tönnies, Ferdinand (1957 [1887]) *Community and Society*, East Lansing: Michigan State University Press.

Veca, Ignazio (2011) 'Polanyi e Finley leggono Aristotele: reciprocità e householding tra economia e morale', in *Annali della Scuola Normale Superiore di Pisa*, vol 3, no. 1: 205–34.

Vernant, Jean-Pierre (1982 [1962]) *The Origins of Greek Thought*, Ithaca, NY: Cornell University Press.

Verri Pietro (1804) *Meditazioni sulla economia politica con annotazioni di Gian-Rinaldo Carli*, t. XV, *Scrittori classici di economia politica*, Collezione Custodi, Milan, Destefanis.

17 Toward a Marxist revision of Marx's revision of Marxism in *Capital*

Bertell Ollman

1 Introduction

Every serious student of Marxism is aware of the distinction Marx makes in the Preface to *Capital*, Volume 1 between Inquiry and Presentation, but on at least two other occasions he also mentions the important role that self-clarification plays in his work (Marx 1904: 14). If we add this equally essential step to the first two, its place is after Inquiry, which supplies him with most of the material that requires clarification, and before Presentation, which combines most of what he has just analysed with a number of adjustments based on what he thought his main audience could understand ... and appreciate.

Is it possible that the *Economic and Philosophic Manuscripts of 1844* and the *Grundrisse* (1857–1858), which were his main works directed to Self-Clarification and were never intended for publication, offer a more accurate view of Marx's actual thinking about capitalism and much else than *Capital* (1867), which has received most of the attention? Is there, in short, an important distinction to be made between what Marx came to believe about our subject and how much of it he chose – for largely tactical reasons – to present to the public? Maybe Marx never dropped or even reduced his commitment to dialectics and alienation, for example, which play major roles in these unpublished writings, but a relatively small one – and then usually disguised – in *Capital*. If so, this may have satisfied most of his readers, but it also made it much easier for all of them ... and us to misinterpret a good deal of what he had to say.

An alternative to the approach I have suggested here is that Marx simply changed his mind about the importance of dialectics and alienation in the workings of capitalism. That is, of course, possible, for Marx changed his mind about a number of things in the course of his long career, as when he replaced 'labour' (an activity) with 'labour power' (the potential for engaging in such an activity) (Engels 1951: 67–72). But when that happens, he and/or Engels soon correct it and explain why they made the change, as in Engel's correction in the second edition of the *Manifesto of the Communist Party* of their opening remark in the first edition that all human history, and not just the history of class societies, contain class struggles (Marx and Engels 1998: 12, n.). There is never anything like this from either Marx or Engels about the diminished role that dialectics and alienation play in *Capital* as compared to their importance in the *1844 Manuscripts* and the *Grundrisse*. It is also worth noting that in an 1858 letter to Engels, Marx said that if time permits he would like to write something to clarify his rational reconstruction of Hegel's dialectical method, which suggests that he still held firmly to a version of Hegel's dialectic at this time and believed that many of his readers still needed special help at arriving at what that was (Marx and Engels 1941: 102).

2 The two Marxisms of Louis Althusser

Perhaps the most popular interpretation of Marxism, when I came of age to be concerned with such matters, could be found in Louis Althusser's book, *Pour Marx* (1965), in which he argued that a major change in Marx's thinking about dialectics and alienation took place well before he wrote the *Manifesto of the Communist Party* (1848), and that this is why these two theories play little if any role in *Capital* (1867) (Althusser 1966). I never accepted this interpretation, but over the years I've felt the need to qualify my earlier disagreement with Althusser for he had seen something that is 'there'. Except, he misunderstood it as an early/late difference in Marx's thinking rather than a difference in the main audiences Marx was trying to reach and what he came to believe was required to reach them.

This misunderstanding also led Althusser to exaggerate the changes that do appear in Marx's later writings and to treat them as coming much earlier than they did. In order to decide when these changes actually occurred, however, we need only look at the difference between Marx's all-out dialectical first Introduction to the *Contribution to a Critique of Political Economy* (1859) – a long Introduction that he never finished or published – and the very brief undialectical Preface with which he replaced it, which has served as the main source of most of the criticism of Marx as an 'economic determinist'. One of the more regrettable side-effects of the new Preface can be seen in G.A. Cohen's influential book, *Karl Marx's Theory of History: A Defence*, which relies heavily on this Preface, and the school of 'Analytical Marxism' that rose out of it (Cohen: 1978). But a Marxism without any dialectics is too deterministic, as Marx's hostile critics have never ceased to point out, and could only serve as a swan song for some of our best Marxist scholars, including Cohen – a close friend of the author's, to abandon Marxism altogether.

Marx was very disappointed when the book for which he had already sacrificed his dialectical Introduction attracted only a handful of readers, and it was shortly after that that he decided to present the scientific analysis he had been preparing for over a couple of decades without most of the dialectical framework and categories that had brought him this far. Marx's intended audience for *Capital*, after all, were workers who could read, different kinds of socialists, and the more curious and less biased economists who were attracted to books that promised something new, and – for this group – that did not stray too far from accepted standards of 'scientific method'. So if he began by believing that the language of dialectics would not put off too many of these readers, the commercial failure of his 1859 book and the frequent requests he received from Engels and other friends to simplify the larger work to come eventually won him over. This did not keep Marx in his Afterword to the second German edition of *Capital* from quoting at length from a reviewer of the Russian edition, that had just appeared, who showed a relatively good grasp of his dialectical method. Marx even followed this with the best brief summary of dialectics that I have seen anywhere (Marx 1958: 17–20). Unfortunately, the book that came right after these remarks stuck with all the compromises he made in the first German edition and continued to make in the French edition of *Capital* that came a little later in order, once again, to attract the largest possible audience.

There is no doubt that playing down (not omitting, but seriously playing down) dialectics in *Capital* brought him many more readers than he would have gotten otherwise, and, as someone who shares Marx's politics as well as his ideas, I recognize the importance of such numbers. But he paid a price for this, and we need to be aware of what that was, both in Marx's time and for today – the two are not the same – and whether there is still something we can do about it.

3 Marx's dialectical method

A brief summary of Marx's dialectical method is in order here if we are to learn what exactly he played down in *Capital* and what that cost him … and us. The place to begin is with the philosophy of internal relations that was largely inherited from Hegel, which holds that everything in reality is internally related, directly or indirectly, to everything else, and all of this is also evolving – though not always together – in one way or another, at one speed or another, and in one direction or another. On this view, everything becomes both a 'relation', a very complex one, and a 'process', a very long one, and there is no easy way of determining where either of them starts or ends. The more popular alternative is the philosophy of external relations, where everything in reality is conceived of as a separate part, or 'thing' (or 'factor' in the social sciences), that is logically distinct and static until something or someone comes along to establish a relationship or cause it to move. Both of these changes are usually limited and relatively easy to observe.

Faced with such a choice, most people, including this writer, would probably opt for the philosophy of external relations, for – from the above – it appears that working with this approach is easy, if not natural, while any attempt to study anything using the philosophy of internal relations could go on forever. And so it would, if Marx had not mastered the process of abstraction, or of focusing on, or highlighting, or singling out certain aspects of what lay before him for special attention. In an 1858 letter to Engels, Marx gives voice to the frustration that often accompanies having to decide how much of an internally related whole to convey in using a particular concept, but says, 'this is the only possible way to avoid having to deal with everything under each particular relation' (Marx 1941: 106). In a world where every relation extends directly or indirectly into everything else, much (most?) of Marx's time is spent focusing on what is of special interest to him on that occasion (or for that problem) without missing what else deserves to be included or getting overwhelmed by all the possibilities. (To complicate matters further, the term 'abstraction' is used in three other senses in Marx's writings – which helps explain why it has proved so difficult for most people to understand – but our immediate purpose does not require that we go over them here.)[1]

What is of special interest to us is that the distinctions that ensue from Marx's main use of the process of abstraction take place on three different terrains, which I have dubbed 'abstraction of extension' (or how much space and how long a time period are brought into the same focus); 'abstraction of vantage point' (or which feature or group of interrelated features is singled out to serve as the starting point from which to view and establish the order and emphasis that comes from being first); and 'abstraction of level of generality' (or which periods of history are viewed as separate wholes from which to abstract the 'extensions' and 'vantage points' best suited to analyse their distinctive 'laws of motion').

The five levels of generality that Marx treats in this way – moving from the more general to the most specific – are 5) the human condition (or what all human beings throughout the history of our species have in common), 4) class history (or what all societies divided into classes have in common), 3) capitalism (or what sets capitalism apart from the first two from the time it became the dominant mode of production in a society to whenever that ceases to be the case), 2) modern capitalism (or the most recent stage in capitalist society in which a number of new developments have evolved and begun to interact with each other to the point of developing its own law of motion within the larger and more general capitalist law of motion that continues to exist), and 1) the Here and Now (or all that happens to conditions, events and people that makes use of their proper names). Though Marx devotes most of his attention to capitalism in general (level 3), all of these levels of generality can be found in the present where their different laws of motion overlap and interact, and continue to exert at least some influence on one another.

It is also worth noting that working out of a philosophy of internal relations, with no absolute boundaries to force his hand, Marx has a great deal of flexibility in abstracting (and, when he considers it helpful, re-abstracting) the extension, vantage point and level of generality he favors for a particular study as well as in presenting the results of it to his readers. While taking full account of what our five senses can inform us about reality, it is his dialectic that enables Marx to find his way through the internally related and rapidly evolving system he has chosen to lay bare. This same flexibility, however, is also responsible for the elasticity in the meanings of all of Marx's major concepts, extending from slight to considerably more, and, with that, for the frustration felt by most of his readers who do not understand where this practice comes from. When the Italian sociologist and critic of Marx, Vilfredo Pareto, declared that 'Marx's words are like bats. You can see in them both birds and mice', he was only expressing something that many of Marx's own followers have experienced but were less inclined to express in such a colorful way (Pareto 1902: 332).

Engels addresses this problem briefly in his Introduction to volume III of Marx's *Capital*, but it has never been satisfactorily resolved. Engels points out, for example, that Marx's critics are wrong to

> expect fixed, cut-to-measure, once and for all applicable definitions in Marx's works. It is self-evident that where things and their interrelations are conceived, not as fixed, but as changing, their mental images, the ideas, are likewise subject to change and transformation; and they are not encapsulated in rigid definitions, but are developed in their historical or logical process of formation.
>
> (Engels 1959: 13–14)

Omitted here, however, is the role that the process of abstraction plays, alongside the 'historical and logical' context that Engels refers to, in establishing the often shifting boundary of what Marx wants to convey with one of his categories on any given occasion. It is only by knowing where this practice comes from and becoming comfortable with Marx's use of it that we can acquire enough of the same flexibility that Marx shows to put the 'Pareto problem' to rest.

With the process of abstraction in place, one of its first major services is to help Marx focus on a set of dialectical patterns found on all the levels of generality mentioned above as well as in the natural world. The most important of the categories he uses to refer to these patterns are 'quantity/quality change', 'identity/difference', 'appearance/essence', 'the interpenetration of polar opposite', 'negation of the negation' and, of course, 'contradiction'. Marx calls the Hegelian contradiction 'the source of all dialectics', and he uses this category much more often than any of the others (Marx 1958: 596, n.). They all share, however, the common function of allowing us to focus on a complex relation or change (or both), which makes them dialectical, that is not easy either to see or to comprehend without them. It is also possible – and often very helpful – to combine some of them, so that 'quantity/quality change', for example, enables us to follow the evolution that takes place in a contradiction as it evolves toward its resolution. The three major steps in Marx's dialectical method, then, are the philosophy of internal relations, the process of abstraction and the dialectical categories, and they need to be studied and used in just this order, because, after internal relations, the other two build on the one(s) that came before.

4 Marx's theory of alienation

Until now, I have emphasized the continuing importance of Marx's dialectical method in how he understood capitalism, an importance that goes well beyond what one might take out of his explicit use of dialectics in *Capital.* I also said earlier that the same thing applies to his theory of alienation, which played an equally important role in the writings Marx directed to his own self-clarification but received even less attention than dialectics in his published works. As regards alienation, the difference that I would like to lay bare here is apparent from the first pages of *Capital.* After presenting the 'commodity' – goods produced for sale rather than for use – as the distinctive form of wealth found wherever there is a capitalist mode of production, Marx goes on to describe the main properties of all commodities as being both useful and exchangeable, or having both 'use-value' and 'exchange-value'. A third form of value, 'surplus-value', which also brings the nature of exploitation under capitalism into focus, is introduced later on, but the problem I am raising does not require that we go there yet. My chief concern here is with Marx's incomplete inquiry into the nature of 'value', or 'value in general' as he sometimes refers to it – of which 'use-value', 'exchange-value', and surplus-value are but its main aspects – despite all the pages he devotes to it.

While the relation between the amount of value produced and the amount of labour time that went into its production is a frequent theme in Marx's published writings, and the identity of value and labour is mentioned a few times, *Capital* stops short of giving us a full account of the kind of labour involved in the production of value. Thus, in distinguishing between the 'quantity' and 'quality' of the labour involved in the production of value, Marx's best known description of the latter is that a commodity assumes the form of exchange-value 'when placed in a value or exchange relationship with another commodity of a different kind', that is, when there is nothing to hinder it from becoming available for exchange with other commodities (Marx 1958: 60). Elsewhere, we learn something about the workers involved in this process when Marx says that 'before entering the labour process, the worker's own labour has already been alienated from himself by the sale of his labour power [to the capitalist] … and realized in a product that does not belong to him'(Marx 1958: 570–1). While the term 'alienation' is used here, as it is a number of times in *Capital,* its sense is usually limited to 'separation in general' and doesn't include most of what is involved in such a separation or all that follows from it. The quote just above is something of an exception, then, in noting that one of the results of alienated labour is that the 'product does not belong to the worker', but this can also be taken as an indication that Marx never really changed his mind about his theory of alienation, which gets its only full description in the *Economic and Philosophic Manuscripts of 1944.*

It is only there that we learn that alienated labour consists of four interconnected relations: 1) workers' are separated from their productive activity (someone else tells them what to do, how to do it, and when to start and to stop doing it); 2) they are separated from the products of their work (whatever their needs, they have no right to use them or to have any say or even to know what happens to them); 3) they are separated from the class of people, the capitalists, who control both their productive activity and the products that result from it (one cannot have human relations with people who have so much power over you and are only concerned with maximizing their profits); and 4) arising out of all this, workers are separated from a great deal of their potential as human being, or what they could and would become under other conditions (one cannot undergo such separations for a long period without losing many of the mental and physical attributes that set us apart as a species) (Marx 1959: 69–80).

I do not consider this description more than a good start for what is needed to bring out the role of Marx's theory of alienation in his analysis of capitalism, but its emphasis on the different kinds of separation involved in alienation should be enough to prepare readers for what is to follow. I would only ask you to keep in mind that Marx never rejected his theory of alienation and that he always viewed his entire subject matter as internally related. This sentence is worth reading again.

So, what happens to a commodity that enables it to have, in Marx's words, 'a value or exchange relationship with another commodity of a different kind'? The answer is, 'Alienation Happens!' The human beings who made, grew, hunted, fished, or just found something in the early history of our species are usually viewed as having had a personal and/or group connection with 'it' that enabled them to use it as they wished. There was no separation, of the kind described above, between the people of that time and their productive activity, or its products, or the use of them by anyone in their community. This changed with the beginning of class society where a ruling class was able to separate a growing amount of the wealth produced in their society from the people who produced it. Rulers never lacked in colourful ways to rationalize their actions, but I can't believe there were many serfs or slaves who did not know who produced the wealth in their society and who reaped the benefits, except for what was needed to feed and house those who did the work. To the extent that the manner in which they were exploited may have contributed to some confusion about their conditions, however, we can see the beginning of the kind of alienation that Marx was later to describe: an alienation that combines unchecked exploitation with a complete misunderstanding of how it works.

Capitalism, which took a few centuries to evolve out of its feudal past, came up with a clever way of disguising the separation of wealth from the workers who produce it by paying them a 'wage' to do the same amount of work that their forbearers had been forced to do. This gave, and still gives, workers in our society the impression that they are 'free' to work or not, even though the wage on offer is generally little more than what workers in the earlier period needed to live and to continue working. Being paid for their work also enables workers under capitalism to buy some of what they need in the market, which is often taken as another sign of their 'freedom' … until one realizes that the standard of living that this makes possible – especially in Marx's day – showed only a slight difference, if that, from the way of life of those who received hand-outs from their owners or lords to keep them fit enough to work. Yet, in treating their wage as the only legitimate way to acquire what they need to live, workers in capitalism have conceded that producing all the wealth of society gives them no special right to use any of it. And with this, the capitalist system has finally achieved what the rulers of earlier times could only hope for: workers who are exploited to the maximum, most of whom continue to believe that they are being treated 'fairly' as long as they are paid what they were promised and on time. It is the separation between such workers and their productive activity, products and employers that Marx brings into sharp focus in his theory of alienation.

Once alienation gets underway, it begins to spread beyond the people who are directly affected by the rest of capitalist society through a process Marx calls the 'metamorphosis of value', or the movement of value's most distinctive qualities throughout the economy. This organic movement takes advantage of the process of exchange by which everything that is produced in capitalist conditions is expedited to the four corners of the system bringing their alienated relations with them. Both the form (how it appears to others) and its function (or how it interacts with the new conditions in which it finds itself) are affected. This is easiest to see in the kind of distortions associated with the 'fetishism' of commodities, where complex social relations are mistaken for things. Except it is not easy to recognize this as a mistake, because the greater part of what most of the people living in capitalism see and hear is already broken up for them by the philosophy of external relations with which they think about anything (which can be viewed as but another form of separation rooted in their/our common alienation).

If the metamorphosis of value first appears like a unidirectional organic movement within a relatively stable whole, it soon reveals itself as being, at the same time, a circular movement that ends up by reproducing the same conditions that brought about the need as well as the possibility for metamorphosis in the first place. Do not the workers still have to sell their labour power and hand over all they produce to the capitalists? Except now, this essentially organic movement has also begun to acquire more and more influence in the larger historical movement (the evolution that occurs in the capitalist whole over time, largely as a result of quantity/quality changes) of which it has always been an integral part. It isn't long before the growing interaction between the organic movement of metamorphosis of value and the historical movement of the whole converge into a single movement that Marx calls the 'law of motion' of the entire system. It is to 'lay bare', or reveal, the 'a law of motion' of capitalism – where every law is a 'tendency' – that Marx says is his 'ultimate aim' in writing *Capital* (Marx 1958: 10).

The monumental change all this represents from what went before can be observed in the lives of both the workers and their products. Besides the physical price every worker pays from being overworked and underpaid, most of them, including the better 'educated' ones, are far more confused about the nature of our current society and where and how they fit into it than workers in any society have ever been. As for the products, which have been 'freed' from any claims on them by those who made them, they assume the form of 'someone else's private property', who turn out to be the capitalists, who can, if they wish, use some part of it to hire workers to produce more such products.

But where does 'value' or 'value in general' come into all this? And the answer is – everywhere. Except, whereas Marx begins his account of capitalist production in *Capital* with 'value', I have gone back to the relations of alienated labour found in the *Economic and Philosophic Manuscripts of 1844* that help explain the origins of 'value' as well as the largely missing half of its 'qualitative' dimension once capitalism gets underway. It is through its alienation, through workers being separated from their productive activity, products and the people who control both, that labour becomes 'abstract and general', that is capable of producing commodities without any apparent ties to the people who made them that would interfere with their being easily exchanged for other commodities. 'Value', as used by Marx, could not have emerged or functioned as it does in capitalism if this complex relation – and, recall, everything in Marxism is a relation – did not also include the whole of Marx's theory of alienation.

5 Conclusion

Alienation and dialectics, our two main subjects, offer ideal vantage points from which to view the functioning of the other, but they can also be treated as one of the most important, if among the least recognized, contradictions in capitalist society. With its history of separating what cannot be separated without distortion, and its contribution to the creation and subsequent metamorphosis of value, including the latter's main by-product of fetishism, with all this, alienation bears a large part of the responsibility for capitalism's worst problems ... and mysteries. Just as dialectics, with its emphasis on internal relations and the 'Bigger Picture', along with the flexibility displayed by its accompanying process of abstraction, plays an equally important role in the clarification of these mysteries and, at least, a partial resolution of these problems (the rest awaits a successful workers' revolution). As for priorities, Marx specifies that it is not the 'unities' that characterize the natural world but the 'separations' which began to appear in class societies and only culminated once capitalism got underway that requires an 'explanation'. It is to this explanation that Marx's theories of alienation and dialectics made major contributions, but ones that could only work as well as they do together.

If alienation and dialectics are best treated together, therefore, it is not only because each theory provides the other with its sharpest contrast and most consistent foil, but that each one seems to need the other to display what it can do. As if this were not enough, highlighting the interaction between these two theories should also advance our understanding of the workings of the entire capitalist system in which they continue to play such important, albeit adversarial, roles. Given their place at the centre of Marx's analysis – the analysis he made to clarify his thinking about capitalism but chose not to emphasize in *Capital* – and all that they accomplish there, is it really too much to believe that the theory of alienation and the theory of dialectics may be the most important of all of Marx's theories? What about Marx's better-known economic theories? But if alienation occupies a full half of what is conveyed by 'value', and dialectics is what binds all of Marx's economic theories together and enables him to manipulate them as he does, then Marx's unpublished writings – where most of his work on alienation and dialectics is found – deserves as much of our attention as his published work.

With the social sciences dominated as never before by the capitalist-inspired 'folly' of separating out our internally related world into smaller and smaller quantifiable portions that hide all our bigger problems, we can no longer allow Marx's theories of alienation and dialectics to remain the least studied and least understood of his theories. Which they are. And we have not even begun to discuss the major implications of the interaction between alienation and dialectics for the class struggle. For whose class interests are best served by keeping everything separated from, well, from just about everything else? And how could a more dialectical approach that insists on re-establishing these broken connections turn that around?

All this needs to change!

Note

1 For still other senses of 'abstraction' used by Marx, see Ollman (2003: 60–2).

References

Althusser, Louis (1966) *Pour Marx*, Paris: Francois Maspero.

Cohen, G.A. (1978) *Karl Marx's Theory of History: A Defense*, Princeton, NJ: Princeton University Press.

Engels, Frederick (1951) *Marx and Engels Selected Works*, vol. I, Moscow: Foreign Language Publishing House.

Engels, Frederick (1959) 'Preface' to Karl Marx, *Capital* vol. III, Moscow: Foreign Language Publishing House, pp. 13–14.

Marx, Karl (1904) *A Contribution to a Critique of Political Economy*, N.I., Chicago: Stone.

Marx, Karl and Engels, Frederick (1941) *Marx and Engels: Selected Correspondence*, London: Dona Torr.

Marx, Karl (1958) *Capital* vol. 1, Moscow: Foreign Languages Publishing House.

Marx, Karl (1959) *Economic and Philosophical Manuscripts of 1844*, Moscow: Foreign Language Publishing House.

Marx, Karl and Engels, Frederick (1998) *The Communist Manifesto*, Chicago: Charles H. Kerr Publishing Co.

Ollman, Bertell (2003) *Dance of the Dialetic: Steps in Marx's Method*, Champaign: Universtity of Illinois Press.

Pareto, Vilfredo (1902) *Les systeme socialiste* vol. 2, Paris: Giard et Brière.

Index

Page numbers in **bold** denote tables.